Strategic Human Resource Management

A Balanced Approach

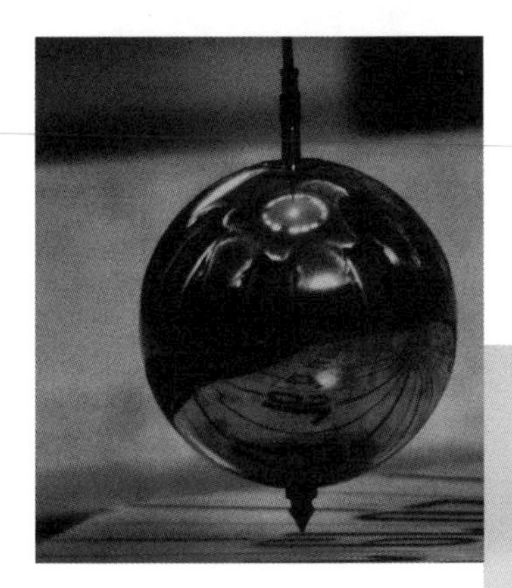

Strategic Human Resource Management

A Balanced Approach

Paul Boselie

The McGraw-Hill Companies

London Boston Burr Ridge, IL Dubuque, IA Madison, WI New York San Francisco
St. Louis Bangkok Bogotá Caracas Kuala Lumpur Lisbon Madrid Mexico City
Milan Montreal New Delhi Santiago Seoul Singapore Sydney Taipei Toronto

Strategic Human Resource Management: A Balanced Approach
Paul Boselie
ISBN-13 9780077119980
ISBN-10 0077119983

McGraw-Hill Higher Education

Published by McGraw-Hill Education
Shoppenhangers Road
Maidenhead
Berkshire
SL6 2QL
Telephone: 44 (0) 1628 502 500
Fax: 44 (0) 1628 770 224
Website: www.mcgraw-hill.co.uk

British Library Cataloguing in Publication Data
A catalogue record for this book is available from the British Library

Library of Congress Cataloging in Publication Data
The Library of Congress data for this book has been applied for from the Library of Congress

Acquisitions Editor: Rachel Gear
Development Editor: Jennifer Rotherham
Marketing Manager: Alice Duijser
Production Editor: Louise Caswell

Text design by Ken Vail Design
Cover design by Fielding Design
Printed and bound in the UK by Bell and Bain Ltd, Glasgow

ISBN-13 9780077119980
ISBN-10 0077119983

Mixed Sources
Product group from well-managed forests and other controlled sources
www.fsc.org Cert no. TT-COC-002769
© 1996 Forest Stewardship Council

Brief Table of Contents

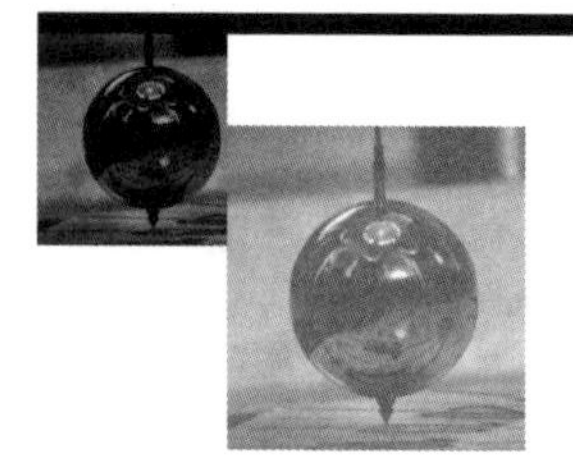

Detailed Table of Contents

Figures

Tables

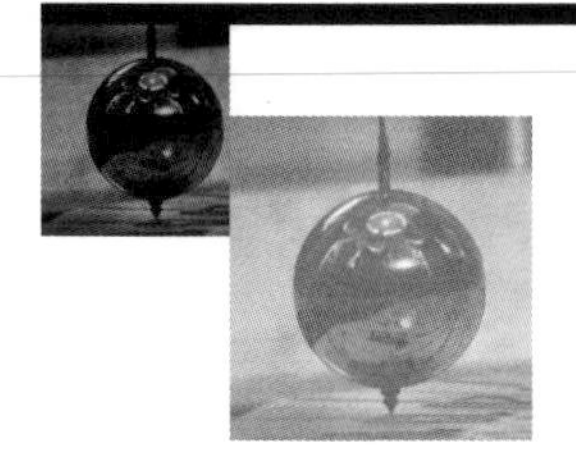

About the Author

Paul Boselie (PhD, MSc) is Professor in strategic human resource management (SHRM) in the Utrecht University School of Governance at Utrecht University (the Netherlands) and an Associate Professor in SHRM in the Department of HR Studies at Tilburg University (the Netherlands). His research traverses human resource management (HRM), institutionalism, strategic management and industrial relations. Paul Boselie's current research is mainly focused on the following themes:

- The added value of HRM in organizations (HRM and performance);
- HRM, compliance and risk management;
- HRM in international governmental organizations (IGOs) and non-governmental organizations (NGOs);
- New roles and competences for the HR function and HR managers/specialists in organizations (professionalization of the HR function);
- HRM and private equity;
- HRM and health care;
- HRM and child day care centres.

Paul's research has been published in the *Journal of Management Studies, Human Relations, Applied Psychology, Human Resource Management Journal, International Journal of Human Resource Management, International Journal of Manpower, Managing Service Quality, Management Revue* and *Personnel Review.* Paul's teaching involves executive training in strategic HRM for HR and non-HR professionals, an MA course on HR studies and a BA course on HRM. He is the European Editor of *Personnel Review* and a member of the Editorial Board of the *Journal of Management Studies*.

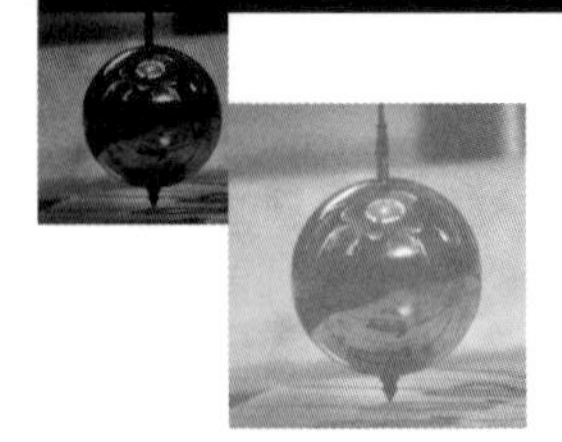

Preface

Writing this book on strategic human resource management (SHRM) has been a wonderful and exciting journey. It all started during the process of searching for a new book for my BA course on SHRM at Tilburg University (the Netherlands). The book we were using at that time was of high quality; however, the authors of that specific human resource (HR) book did not pay sufficient attention to the European institutional context, for example reflected in the role of trade unions and works councils, and there were no European case studies or illustrations. I was hoping to find a new SHRM book paying more explicit attention to the institutional context and people management issues, preferably with European illustrations from practice. The latter is important for the reading audience who are often confronted with a selection of US cases such as Coca-Cola, General Electric, General Motors, IBM, Microsoft and South West Airlines. It would be interesting to also highlight important lessons from European organizations such as BMW, easyJet, IKEA, Nokia and Shell. Unfortunately, there was no such book available on the market. Discussing this issue with representatives of McGraw-Hill was the starting point for writing this book. I hope you enjoy reading and studying it as much as I enjoyed writing it!

The target audience of this book is upper level students with some prior knowledge of HRM through, for example, a basic human resource (HR) course on the functional areas of HRM (e.g. selection, training, appraisal and pay) or through work experience (e.g. selecting a new colleague). This book can be used on BA 2, BA 3 and MA level, including MBA courses for practitioners. For students who lack basic knowledge of HRM, I suggest reading the chapters on HR practices in W. Bloisi (2007) *An Introduction to Human Resource Management*. London: McGraw-Hill (Chapter 2 on human resource planning and resourcing; Chapter 4 on recruiting the right people; Chapter 5 on selecting the right people; Chapter 6 on remuneration and reward; and Chapter 7 on learning, training and development); or the chapters on HR practices in R.A. Noe, J.R. Hollenbeck, B. Gerhart and P.M. Wright (2008) *Human Resource Management: Gaining Competitive Advantage*, 2nd edn. London: McGraw-Hill (Chapter 5 on planning and recruitment; Chapter 6 on selection and placement; Chapter 7 on training; Chapter 8 on performance management; and Chapter 11 on pay).

This book is positioned between the basic HR textbooks focused on the functional HR areas (e.g. Noe et al., 2006), and the advanced academic SHRM texts (e.g. Paauwe, 2004;[1] Boxall and Purcell, 2008[2]). The central theme in my book is HRM in the organizational context. The underlying philosophy is the assumption that HRM is much more than individual practices. SHRM is about the alignment between HR practices and the alignment of HR practices with the internal and external organizational context. The internal organizational context is, for example, determined by the history of the organization, the organizational culture and the technology in place. The external organizational context consists of market mechanisms (e.g. globalization and increased competition) and institutional mechanisms (e.g. labour legislation and the role of external stakeholders such as trade unions). The institutional mechanisms are often neglected or undervalued in other texts, while the institutional environment is highly relevant and important

[1] Paauwe, J. (2004) *HRM and Performance: Achieving Long-term Viability*. Oxford: Oxford University Press.

[2] Boxall, P. and Purcell, J. (2008) *Strategy and Human Resource Management*, 2nd edn. New York: Palgrave Macmillan.

for HRM in Europe simply because of the highly institutionalized European context in which organizations have to operate. These institutional notions are an essential part of this book in which multiple stakeholders such as trade unions and works councils are explicitly acknowledged in the shaping of the employment relationship through HRM. My overall aim in this book is to create context awareness in HRM or what I like to call 'HR sensitivity'.

Key characteristics of HRM are dualities (e.g. economic value and moral values related to managing people, or business goals versus societal goals), tensions (e.g. between trade unions and top management), contrasting interests (e.g. employees' interests versus employers' interests) and contradictions (e.g. highly motivated workers and increased risks of job stress and burnout). To fully understand these features this book takes a critical perspective with little or no best-practice solutions in HRM. In other words, the reader should not expect best practices lists and concrete tool-boxes. Instead, this book hopefully offers yardsticks for structuring and solving real-life HR issues in organizations. Some of the chapters (e.g. Chapter 5 'Achieving the right balance' and Chapter 14 'Human resource transformation') may require some time for full digestion.

Most of the chapters and topics discussed in this book are related to my prior research on HRM in the institutional context, HRM and performance, HR roles, performance management and high-performance work systems (HPWSs). Over the last decade there have been three major sources of inspiration that have influenced my writing. First, the book was affected by working with colleagues from different backgrounds, including psychology, critical management studies and occupational health psychology. Joint projects with psychologists such as Deanne Den Hartog, Paul Jansen and colleagues at Tilburg University have led to the individual employee awareness and the role of the front-line manager in HRM. My literature study with Anne Keegan, published in the *Journal of Management Studies*, took me on a valuable journey to critical approaches. And working with Marc Van Veldhoven, who has a background in occupational health psychology, brought in notions on 'blood, sweat and tears' (e.g. job stress, burnout and general employee well-being) related to HRM and HR interventions. Second, seminars and global conferences with SHRM colleagues from all over the world have been a big inspiration. Jaap Paauwe's approach on HRM and institutional context, but also on balancing economic and moral values, is still a valuable source of inspiration in my own work. Other academics who have affected me are Peter Boxall and John Purcell on SHRM and Pat Wright, David Guest and Riccardo Peccei on HRM and the individual employee. There are, of course, many others who have been a rich source of inspiration. Third, teaching a BA course on HRM at Tilburg University for multiple years has probably had the biggest impact on this book. Through this course I gained a lot of insights into what students like about the course, how they look at HR issues and how important HR lessons can be transferred to the hearts and minds of students. Some of the lessons I learned are hopefully integrated in my book, including concrete European cases and illustrations of organizations that are known to students, linking HR issues to contemporary key issues in organizations (e.g. a global and financial crisis), learning features in the text, individual and team assignments to help bridge theory and practice, and concrete learning goals at the beginning and end of each chapter.

The 14 chapters in this book could be covered in eight sessions during a regular course on SHRM. In my experience teaching the BA SHRM course at Tilburg University, I found that the following topics can be combined as part of one session:

Session 1 Chapter 1 Introduction and Chapter 2 Context
Session 2 Chapter 3 HRM/performance and Chapter 4 HR Metrics
Session 3 Chapter 5 Balance
Session 4 Chapter 6 HPWSs and Chapter 7 Selection and recruitment

Guided Tour

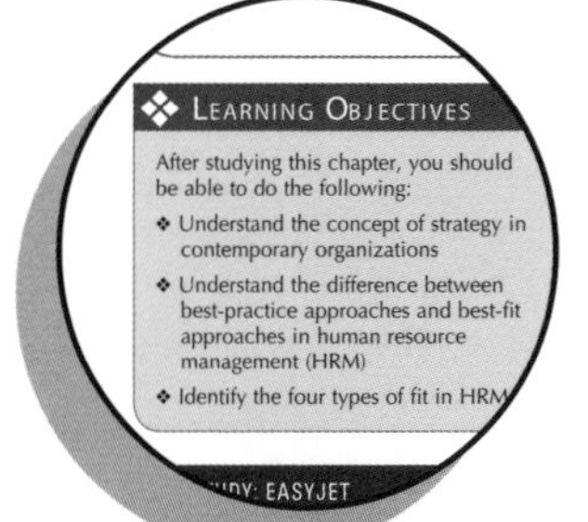

Learning Objectives

As an introductory overview, learning objectives help students quickly grasp the essentials they are expected to learn from each chapter.

Cases and Discussion Questions

Real-world scenarios or issues are used to illustrate contemporary HR issues in practice.

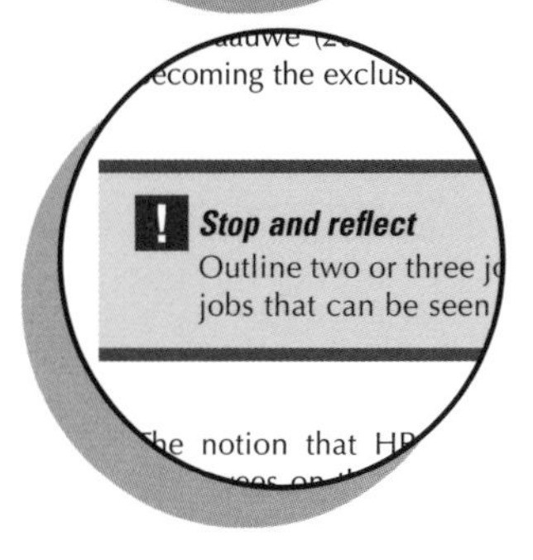

Stop and Reflect Boxes

Throughout each chapter these self-reflective exercises have been designed to encourage students to critically evaluate the topics and issues raised in the chapters and how they can be applied to real-life situations.

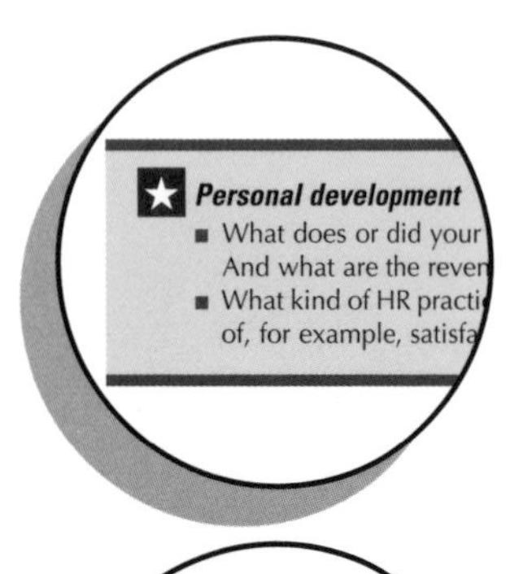

Personal Development Boxes

This feature has been incorporated into each chapter to help students think about how to bridge theoretical concepts with the development of personal skills appropriate to effective HRM.

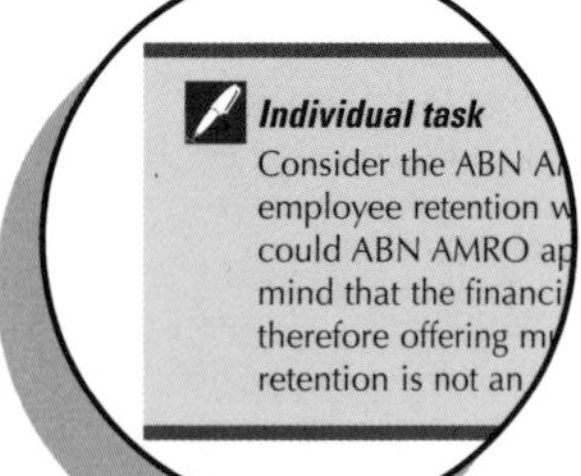

Experiential Exercises

'Individual' and 'Team' tasks at the end of each chapter that can be used as in-class exercises encouraging students to learn from direct experiences.

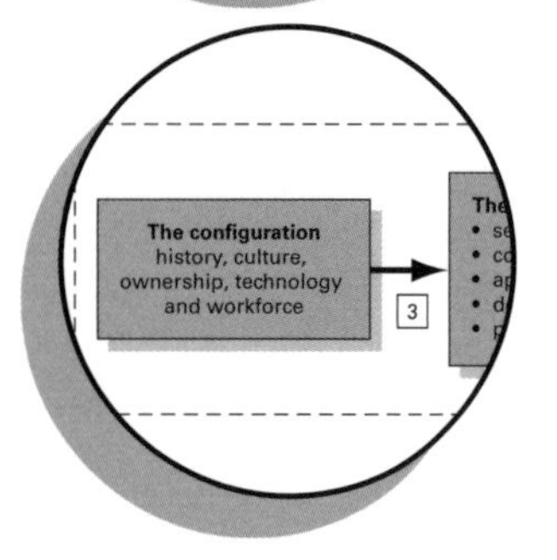

Figures and Tables

Each chapter provides a number of figures, photos and tables to help students to visualize key theories and studies.

Summary

The chapter summaries provide links to the learning objectives to help students remember key facts, concepts and issues. They also serve as an excellent study or revision guide.

Glossary of key terms

At the end of each chapter is a glossary of the most important concepts and theories. These definitions provide a quick and easy reference.

References and Further Reading

The References section lists all of the literature that the chapter refers to. At the end of each chapter Further reading sections highlight several sources that will help students to research and read around the topic in more depth.

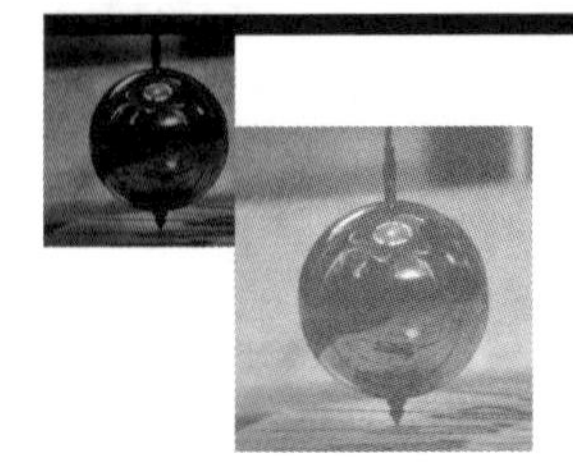

Technology to enhance learning and teaching

*Visit **www.mcgraw-hill.co.uk/textbooks/boselie** today*

Online Learning Centre (OLC)

Resources for lecturers include:

- Additional case studies
- Additional discussion questions
- PowerPoint slides

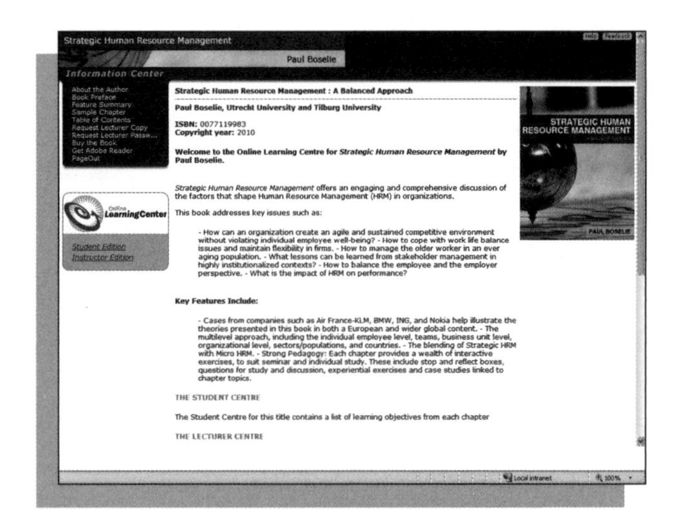

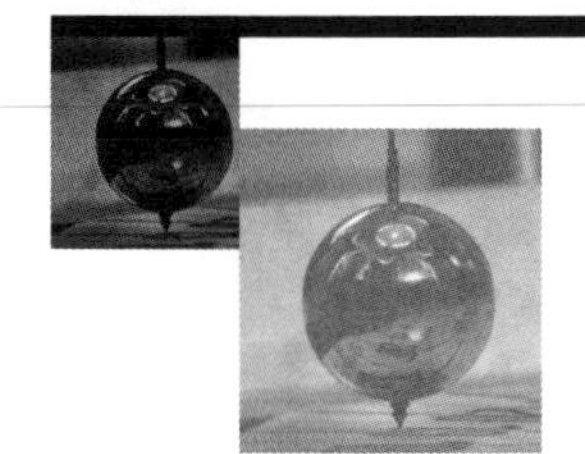

Custom Publishing Solutions: let us help make our content your solution

At McGraw-Hill Education our aim is to help lecturers to find the most suitable content for their needs delivered to their students in the most appropriate way. Our **custom publishing solutions** offer the ideal combination of content delivered in the way which best suits lecturer and students.

Our custom publishing programme offers lecturers the opportunity to select just the chapters or sections of material they wish to deliver to their students from a database called CREATE™ at **www.mcgrawhillcreate.com**

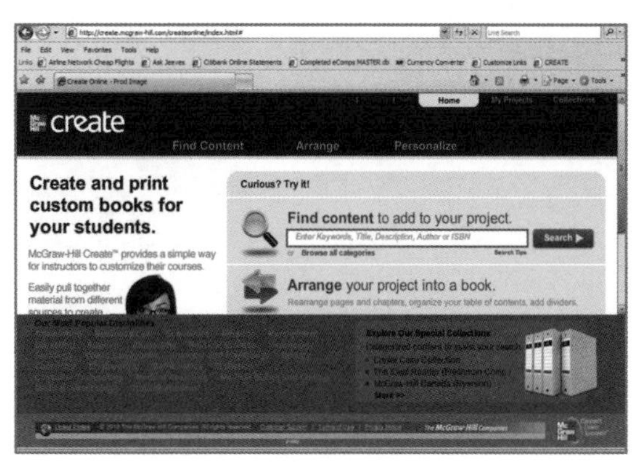

CREATE™ contains over two million pages of content from:

- textbooks
- professional books
- case books – Harvard Articles, Insead, Ivey, Darden, Thunderbird and BusinessWeek
- Taking Sides – debate materials

across the following imprints:

- McGraw-Hill Education
- Open University Press
- Harvard Business Publishing
- US and European material

There is also the option to include additional material authored by lecturers in the custom product - this does not necessarily have to be in English.

We will take care of everything from start to finish in the process of developing and delivering a custom product to ensure that lecturers and students receive exactly the material needed in the most suitable way.

With a **Custom Publishing Solution**, students enjoy the best selection of material deemed to be the most suitable for learning everything they need for their courses – something of real value to support their learning. Teachers are able to use exactly the material they want, in the way they want, to support their teaching on the course.

Please contact your **local McGraw-Hill representative** with any questions or alternatively contact Warren Eels e: **warren_eels@mcgraw-hill.com**.

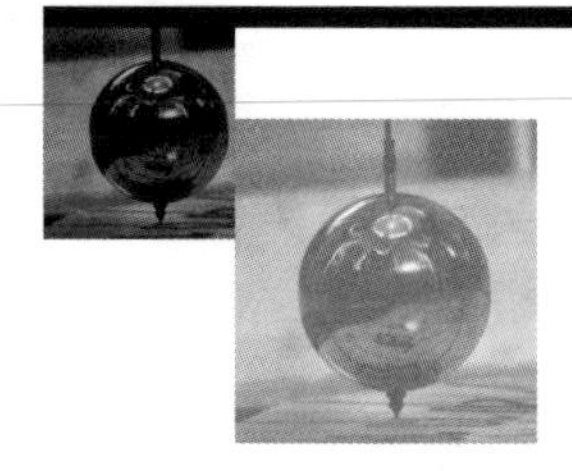

Author's Acknowledgements

The author would like to thank the Department of Human Resource Studies and the Faculty of Social and Behavioural Sciences at Tilburg University for facilitating this research project, in particular with regard to facilitating his sabbatical leave at Cornell University for working on this book.

The author would also like to thank Rachel Gear, Jennifer Rotherham and the rest of the McGraw-Hill publishing team for their excellent support during the writing process. Also special thanks to the anonymous reviewers who gave valuable and constructive feedback on the text at several stages of the process. Most of their comments are incorporated in this book.

The author would also like to thank Marinus Verhagen for his suggestions on and support with the book proposal and Chapter 4 (HR metrics), Marc Van Veldhoven for his suggestions on Chapter 5 (balanced approaches), Riccardo Peccei for his suggestions on Chapter 6 (high-performance work systems), Brigitte Kroon for her suggestions on Chapter 7 (recruitment and selection) and Norman Schreiner for his career insights on Chapter 10 (training). Special thanks to Jaap Paauwe for cooperation on earlier projects that contributed to Chapter 3 on HRM and performance, Chapter 8 on performance management and Chapter 12 on HR roles.

Also special thanks to Elaine Farndale and Deanne Den Hartog for cooperation on earlier projects that contributed to Chapter 8 on performance management.

The author would like to thank Floortje Lansbergen and Judith van den Broek for their support and comments on the textbook in the BA SHRM course. The author would also like to thank Pat Wright for sponsoring the author's sabbatical leave at Cornell University and the ILR School of Cornell University for hosting him. The author would like to thank the Utrecht University School of Governance of Utrecht University, in particular Peter Leisink, for the appointment as Full Professor in SHRM. A very special thanks to all the students of the BA SHRM course at Tilburg University and the students who wrote BA theses on topics and cases used in this textbook.

Finally, special thanks to Annemiek and Sam for their patience and unconditional support.

Paul Boselie

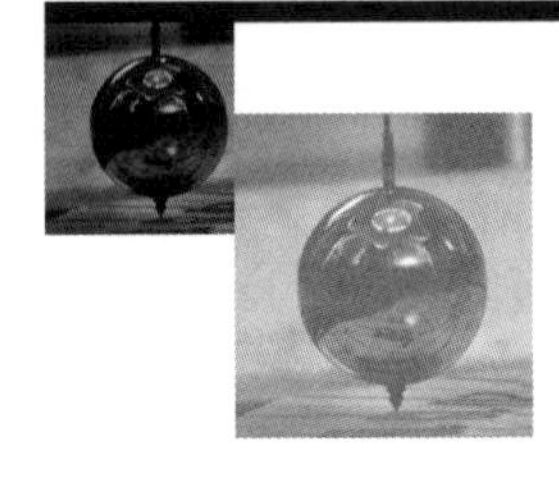

Publisher's Acknowledgements

Every effort has been made to trace and acknowledge ownership of copyright and to clear permission for material reproduced in this book. The publishers will be pleased to make suitable arrangements to clear permission with any copyright holders whom it has not been possible to contact.

Our thanks go to the following reviewers for their comments at various stages in the text's development:

Professor Chris Brewster, Henley Business School, University of Reading
Dr. Sylvia van de Bunt-Kokhuis, Vrije University Amsterdam
Professor Willem De Nijs, Nijmegen School of Management
Radboud University
Job Hoogendoorn, Rotterdam School of Management, Erasmus University
Dr. Roy Horn, Buckinghamshire New University
Vinke Joop, Arnhem Business School
John MacDonald, Doncaster Business School
John Neugebauer, University of the West of England
Dr. Werner Nienhueser, University of Duisburg-Essen
Professor Stephen Proctor, Newcastle University Business School
Dr. Peter Samuel, Nottingham University Business School
Henrik Sørensen, Aarhus University
Aileen Watson, University of Strathclyde
Donie Wiley, School of Business, National College of Ireland
Dr. Zeynep Yalabik, University of Bath, School of Management

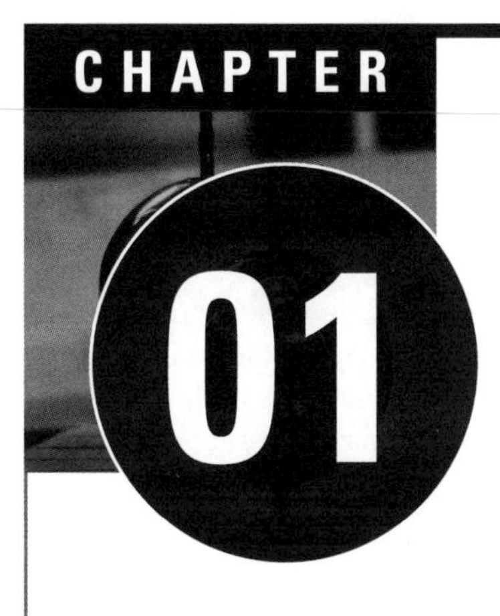

Introduction: Strategic Human Resource Management in the Twenty-first Century

Learning Objectives

After studying this chapter, you should be able to do the following:

- Understand the impact of organizational change on the employment relationship
- Outline micro human resource management (MHRM), strategic HRM (SHRM) and international HRM (IHRM)
- Discuss the concept of competitiveness
- Understand the difference between Anglo-American and Rhineland models in managing employees
- Identify the multiple stakeholders of an organization
- Understand the balanced approach to HRM

CASE STUDY: THE DUTCH MINISTRY OF DEFENCE

The fall of the Berlin Wall and the strategic reorientation of Dutch defences

On 9 November 1989 the barrier between West Germany and East Germany was removed and a new era in Europe began. The wall divided Berlin for 28 years and had become the symbol of separation between the East, with its communist countries including the Soviet Union, and the West, with its democratic, socialist and capitalist countries. The European continent itself and the world were about to transform with major political, economic, social and cultural implications. The cold war ended and the military threat from both sides was about to vaporize. Over three decades of potential threats from the East had resulted in a defensive strategy of the Dutch Ministry of Defence (n = 70000 employees) with a key role for the land forces. The 'old' enemies were about to become new allies and the military was forced to radically change its strategy. New challenges were soon found in United Nations (UN) and North Atlantic Treaty Organisation (NATO) peace-keeping missions all over the world, including missions to Lebanon, Srebrenica, Bosnia and, later on, Uruzgan. However, the transition from the old military model focused on a rather static and identifiable enemy in the East to the new model of global peace-keeping missions had a big impact on the people (soldiers and supportive staff) within the Dutch Ministry of Defence. Peace-keeping missions demand flexibility and adaptability from both the organization and its employees.

Organizational change towards the new model could only be achieved through the implementation of new managerial practices, including HRM (recruitment and selection, socialization, training and development, performance management (PM), etc.). This change included a shift from a traditional reactive and defensive approach to a proactive approach crossing borders. Peace-keeping missions include projects for specific time periods (e.g. one- or two-year assignments under the UN flag), international cooperation at all levels (soldiers in the field and staff on coordination level), sometimes serious constraints with respect to the soldiers' leeway to use military forces, and operating in different countries involving cultural diversity challenges and language barriers.

? Discussion questions

- Find out more about your country's involvement in peace-keeping missions.
- What kind of selection criteria do you think are relevant and important for future soldiers in peace-keeping missions?
- What is good organizational performance in the military?

Introduction

Employees are generally considered 'the organization's most valuable assets'. You can create higher productivity levels, improve service quality towards customers, expand sales and make more profits when you manage your workers according to HRM principles (Delery and Doty, 1996). This is at least what the theory on HRM suggests. Whether these claims are true in practice is another issue (Legge, 2005). Nowadays the majority of chief executive officers (CEOs) of leading companies underline the strategic importance of their human resources. However, as soon as an organizational crisis emerges, the employee emphasis is often downgraded through downsizing and mass layoffs. It is in times of major change that the management of employees is essential not only to achieve organizational goals but also to pay attention to the individual employee's well-being as well.

Overall, it is concluded in both theory and practice that employees matter and that the management of employees – HRM – is a potential source for achieving organizational goals (Boxall and Purcell, 2003). Later on in this chapter, and in this book generally, different goals are discussed, including individual employee goals, organizational goals and societal goals.

> 'employees matter and [...] the management of employees – HRM – is a potential source for achieving organizational goals.'

Strategic human resource management (SHRM) is a relatively young discipline – approximately 25 years old (see the classic publications of Beer et al., 1984 and Fombrun et al., 1984 – with a growing importance for organizations operating in a dynamic and continuous changing environment. Organizational change is inevitable for most contemporary organizations. Mergers, acquisitions and reorganizations have become common practices for most organizations, not just multinational companies (MNCs) but small and medium enterprises (SMEs) (Hayton, 2004; Sels et al., 2006) and not-for-profit organizations (e.g. hospitals) as well. Organizational change almost automatically affects one of the organization's most valuable assets: employees. Successful change highly depends on changing people in their attitudes, behaviour and cognition. The shift in the Dutch military after the fall of the Berlin Wall illustrates the fundamental change in the organization's environment affecting the nature of the business and the employee requirements. Instead of a strategy focused on defending the home country, the new strategy focuses on projects (peace-keeping missions), sometimes far away from the home country with a diversity of context specific challenges. The situations in Iraq and Afghanistan, for example, are completely different with respect to the peace-keeping forces and the local issues. This asks for flexibility and good people management.[1]

The new economy

The 1990s introduced a new concept mainly focused on the shift from a manufacturing and production economy into a service sector asset-based economy: the new economy (Porter, 1998). The old economy goes back to traditional industries, such as the steel, construction and motor industries. Work in the old economy was characterized by physical tasks, job design and work design based on mass production (assembly line), many relatively low-skilled workers and high degrees of unionization. The new economy is dominated by emerging branches of industry, including the information technology (IT) sector, the telecommunications sector and the financial institutions. Technological developments in the early 1990s led to the computer age and the World Wide Web (the Internet); and these developments acted as a facilitator for the rise of the services industry in the new economy. In the new economy assets are less tangible and are embedded in reputation, brands and knowledge of employees. Work in the new economy can be characterized by high knowledge intensity, web-based organizing, contacts through intranet or Internet connections (in contrast to face-to-face contacts in the past), centres on the other side of the world (e.g. the use of call centres) and the integration of work design, technology and services delivered. The old economy still exists in developing countries and countries with relatively cheap labour conditions (e.g. China). In fact, outsourcing and offshoring business activities to developing countries are another characteristic of the new economy. Organizational change has become a common practice in the new economy with major implications for employees. In Chapter 6 the emergence of HRM in the early 1980s is linked to rising industries that characterize the new economy based on Legge's (1995) analysis. In 2000/2001 the Internet bubble or hype, also known as the dot-com bubble, burst. In 2008/2009 the financial institution bubble burst causing a global crisis. The world will never be the same again and, although several new economy bubbles have burst, work in modern organizations, in particular in Western countries, has changed. And change itself has become a daily practice in organizations.

Organizational change and competitive advantage

The relevance of optimal coping with change is embedded in the concept of **competitive advantage**. Chapter 3 deals with this concept in more detail. For now, it is important to understand that competitive advantage is important for organizational survival and is at least partly manageable by HRM.

To put it very simply, competitive advantage represents an organization's position in comparison to its direct competitors. In other words, competitive advantage tells us something about

[1] The definition of 'good' and 'bad' people management is highly normative and heavily depends on the chosen viewpoint; for example, a viewpoint dominated by Anglo-American aspects versus a viewpoint dominated by Rhineland aspects. This issue is discussed in more detail later in the chapter and also in the other chapters of this book, mainly because it is one of the essential elements for HR decision making.

how well the organization is doing in comparison to others in the same branch of industry or in the same region. Competitive advantage might be reflected in better financial performance (e.g. bigger sales, higher profits and increased growth) and non-financial performance, including the organization's reputation in relation to customers and potential employees. The concept of competitive advantage represents a relative outcome:

> An organization with competitive advantage is doing better than its competitors irrespective of the actual firm performance (negative or positive). In the case of losses, the organization is still doing better than its competitors. And in the case of profits, the organization makes more profits than the others.

See Chapter 3 for a focus on notions of competitive advantage using the resource-based view (RBV).

Stop and reflect

Can you think of any factors that contribute to the competitive advantage of the military services with respect to attracting and retaining good employees (soldiers)?

The changing role of work in modern organizations

The rise of the new economy in the 1990s created a shift from (traditional) production to services in most Western societies. This shift has had a major impact on the nature of jobs in these societies. The computer has become an essential tool and medium for many workers, requiring different knowledge, skills and competences from individuals. Technology (home computers and Internet access) has also created opportunities for alternative work design; for example, enabling employees to work at home and still have access to organizational resources and networks. Opportunities to work at home can be a source for a better work–life balance and/or family-friendly employment (Felstead et al., 2002). Flexible working arrangements are becoming more important for dual-career couples with children (Dex and Scheibl, 2001). Taking the children to school and picking them up in the afternoon become major issues for parents that both work. Some hospitals have started to operate surgery hours after 10 a.m. to allow nurses to take their children to school. These new flexible work arrangements characterize modern organizations with benefits for both the employer (e.g. improved personnel planning in the case of the nurses in surgery) and the employee (e.g. a better work–life balance).

The ageing population in many Western countries is also affecting work in modern organizations (DeLong, 2004). The baby-boomers, born just after the Second World War, are about to retire creating all kinds of employment issues; for example, with regard to the potential loss of valuable knowledge, skills and abilities (DeLong, 2004). In some organizations the average employee age has gone up substantially because of a lack of inflow of young employees, causing personnel planning issues in the future and the risk of ever-increasing labour costs related to older workers in terms of higher salaries.

MHRM, IHRM and SHRM

Strategic human resource management can be a key to success in the process of organizational change; for example, through selecting top talent, rewarding excellent performance, employee development and culture management. This book uses a very broad and pragmatic definition of HRM: HRM involves management decisions related to policies and practices that together shape the employment relationship and are aimed at achieving individual, organizational and societal goals (Boselie, 2002). This definition acknowledges the relevance of different stakeholders and the goals linked to them. SHRM builds on this definition and in addition pays extra attention to the organizational context, reflected in special attention to potential alignment of the business strategy and HRM, the alignment of the institutional context and HRM, the linkage between business systems and HRM and the fit between HR practices.

Boxall et al. (2007: 1) state that HRM is 'the management of work and people towards desired ends' and they argue that this is a fundamental activity in any organization with human beings as employees. The authors identify three major sub-fields:

1 **MHRM** (micro human resource management) covers the sub-functions of HR policy and practice, including recruitment and selection, induction and socialization, and training and development. MHRM is closely related to the studies in organizational behaviour and occupational psychology that focus on the impact of single HR practices on employee attitudes and behaviours (Wright and Boswell, 2002).
2 **IHRM** (international human resource management) is concerned with HRM in MNCs and HRM across borders (Brewster, 2004). It focuses on issues such as the transferability of HR practices across business units in different countries, the optimal management of expatriates and the impact of different institutional country contexts on HRM.
3 **SHRM** (strategic human resource management) focuses on issues of linking HRM to the business strategy, designing high-performance work systems (HPWSs) and adding value through good people management in an attempt to gain sustained competitive advantage (Delery and Doty, 1996). The concept of 'fit' plays a central role within SHRM.

Stop and reflect

Outline the differences between MHRM, IHRM and SHRM. Can you think of similarities between them?

This book mainly uses the perspective of SHRM, although Chapter 5 pays specific attention to MHRM issues and Chapter 13 is devoted to IHRM. It focuses on SHRM in institutionalized contexts using European business cases and a South African business case illustrating that HRM is embedded in different institutional contexts, that effective people management includes managing multiple stakeholders such as trade unions, and that unique HR approaches can be developed by means of a balanced perspective.

Chapter 2 elaborates on the notion of different institutional contexts. But for here it is enough to understand that there are major differences between countries, for example, as a result of differences in legislation. In some countries it is quite easy to fire an employee (e.g. in the USA and the UK), while in other countries layoffs are constrained by law. In the Netherlands, for example, employees on a permanent contract get a month's salary for every year they have worked if they are dismissed. Legislation potentially affects people management and HRM; for example, through laws on labour flexibility, working conditions (safety), collective bargaining agreements (CBAs) and unemployment regulations.

Stakeholders of an organization represent all groups inside and outside an organization that can affect its strategy and goals. Internal stakeholders include employees, line managers, top management and employee representatives (e.g. in a works council). External stakeholders include shareholders, financiers, trade unions, national government, local government and other interest groups, for example Greenpeace.

Stop and reflect

Find out more about the trade union associations in your country (e.g. the main trade union associations, trade union membership and contemporary labour relations issues).

Three perspectives

The multidimensional strategic HR model in this book includes the following key characteristics:

1 *a multi-actor perspective* (multiple stakeholders including employees, managers, HR professionals, works councils, trade unions, top management, shareholders, financiers and government);
2 *a broad societal view* with an emphasis on different institutional contexts, for example on the level of branches of industry, regions and countries;
3 *a multi-level perspective* including the individual employee perspective and the strategic organizational perspective.

The multidimensional strategic HRM model is inspired by the European approaches to HRM and industrial relations (IR). This approach is reflected in Paauwe's (2004: 3) view on HRM. He argues that:

- human resources are something more than just 'resources';
- human resource management is not concerned solely with financial performance;
- human resource management focuses on the exchange relationship between employee and organization;
- the shaping of the employment relationship takes place in an era of continuous tension between the added value and moral values.

Human resources are people with feelings, emotions, interests, norms and values. Their behaviour inside and outside the organization is not solely determined by economic rationality (Paauwe, 2004). Other factors can affect and influence employee attitudes and behaviour, including sympathy towards others (e.g. newcomers), willingness to put extra effort into the job because of professional norms or feelings of moral obligation, and personal norms and values for action (e.g. refusing to work on Fridays, Saturdays or Sundays because of religious beliefs). Therefore employees are more than just resources for creating organizational success.

HRM can contribute to the organization's success in terms of increased financial performance (e.g. reflected in higher sales, profits, market share and market value), but the HR function has a much broader responsibility, including stakeholder management (managing works councils and trade unions) and relating (labour) legislation to the employment relationship within the organization. In other words, HRM also involves the administration related to legislation and the relationship management with crucial social partners including works councils and trade unions. Therefore the approach in this book explicitly incorporates notions on institutional mechanisms and acknowledges multiple stakeholders relevant to the shaping of HRM in organizations.

HRM focuses on the exchange relationship between the employee and the organization. This employment relationship contains different contract types. First, the relationship concerns legal aspects mostly written down in a contract. The legal contract of the employment relationship determines the rights and obligations of both the employee and the organization. Legal elements relate to, for example, the number of vacation days, the term of notice and issues with respect to confidentiality. Second, the employment relationship involves economic aspects. In other words, the employee and the employer determine how much effort the employee puts into the job reflected in the number of working days, and how much the employer will pay for the employee's efforts, for example in terms of salary. Third, the employment relationship involves the so-called psychological contract concerning all things that are not written down but are expected from both actors (employee and organization). For example, employees are willing to invest extra time in a project because they trust their direct supervisor that a successful project will contribute to an internal promotion in the next year. Finally, the employment relationship also incorporates social aspects related to the relationships and networks employees have within an organization; for example, the bond with colleagues in a team. In summary, the employment relationship is the focus of HRM and can be characterized by the following four contract elements:

1. legal contract;
2. economic or transactional contract;
3. psychological contract;
4. sociological contract.

Tensions

HRM operates in an area of continuous tension between added value and moral values (Paauwe, 2004). The added value represents the economic side of organizing work and mainly represents the role of HRM in creating economic value and increasing financial performance of an organization. The moral values reflect the notion of employees as human beings with feelings, emotions, opinions, norms and values. Legge (1995) discusses the distinction between 'hard' HRM that mainly focuses on the economics and 'soft' HRM that mainly focuses on the human side of organizing. She observes a dominance of attention to 'hard' HRM in both theory and practice. Legge calls this the dominance of human *resource management* in contrast to the softer perspective that puts people first: *human* resource management. Rebalancing the approaches towards economic and moral aspects in theory and practice is one of the major challenges in the field of HRM and therefore a main issue in this book.

Boxall and Purcell's (2003) comments on SHRM characteristics are also noteworthy. They argue that:

- HRM covers all workforce groups, including core employees, peripheral employees and contingent workers;
- HRM involves line and specialist managers, and is not solely aimed at employees;
- HRM is all about managing work and people, collectively and individually;
- HRM is embedded in industries and societies.

There is a general HRM tendency to exclusively focus on valuable employees (core employees) and minimize HR attention to peripheral workers (Keegan and Boselie, 2006). The distinction between different employee groups within an organization seems relevant and logical (Lepak and Snell, 2002). However, a growing number of scholars, including Boxall and Purcell (2003) and Paauwe (2004), argue that HRM should pay attention to the total workforce instead of becoming the exclusive terrain for talent management and leadership development (LD).

Stop and reflect

Outline two or three jobs that potentially can be considered peripheral and two or three jobs that can be seen as core in an organization.

The notion that HRM also includes line managers and HR professionals, and not just employees on the shopfloor, was also made by Guest (1987) in his analysis of the distinction between the traditional personnel management model and the emerging HRM model. HRM is explicitly focused on all employee categories within an organization. For example, line managers need to be trained to carry out their yearly appraisal of their subordinates (see Chapter 10 focusing on management development (MD)). HR professionals also need training and development to become a business partner; for example, through training in presentation, negotiation and networking (see Chapter 12 focusing on HR roles and competences).

Boxall and Purcell (2003) also emphasize that HRM is not just focused on the typical HR practices such as recruitment and selection, training and development, appraisal, rewards, promotion and participation. HRM also includes work design reflected in choices with regard to job autonomy, whether or not using teams to do the job, the degree of job rotation and the job design with regard to the number of tasks for individual employees (job enlargement) and their responsibilities (job enrichment). Boxall and Purcell (2003) conclude that HRM is involved in managing issues on multiple levels, including HRM at the individual employee level and HRM at a collective level; for example, with regard to negotiations with works councils and trade unions on a new organization CBA.

Finally, Boxall and Purcell (2003) argue that HRM is embedded in industries (branches of industry) and societies (countries and continents). The financial services sector has different legislation and procedures than the traditional manufacturing industries (e.g. chemicals). Countries may differ fundamentally on labour legislation affecting the HRM of an organization in that specific region, country or continent (e.g. the European Union (EU)).

Traditionally, a distinction is made between the **Anglo-Saxon or Anglo-American models** and **the Rhineland models**. The Anglo-American approaches in IR and HRM, for example in the USA, mainly focus on creating shareholder value in terms of profits and market value with little or no attention to other **stakeholders** including trade unions and works councils. In contrast, the Rhineland models, labelled 'Rhine' because of the Rhine river in Western Europe and the countries through which it flows, acknowledge multiple stakeholders and their interests explicitly taking into account employee interests in terms of well-being and societal interests. Gospel and Pendleton (2003) argue that there are major differences between the so-called Rhineland countries (including the Netherlands and Germany) and therefore we should be careful using this dichotomy. Still, the overall notion of whether to take into account mainly one stakeholder (the shareholder) or multiple stakeholders is important for a further understanding of the shaping of the employment relationship through HRM in organizations.

The balanced approach

In times of globalization and increased competition, there is a growing awareness that sustained competitive advantage depends on balancing market demands (e.g. lower costs, increase the organization's flexibility, shorten the production cycles) and institutional pressures (e.g. offer employment security, demonstrate corporate social responsibility towards the environment). In the strategic balance model, organizational success can only be achieved when financial performance *and* societal performance of an organization are above average in the particular population in which the organization is operating (Deephouse, 1999). In this view exclusive high scores on either financial *or* societal performance are bad for the long-term survival of an organization. Pure high financial outcomes might lead to serious social legitimacy issues, for example if these high scores go hand in hand with environmental pollution and labour intensification of those employed (Legge, 2005). Social legitimacy without good performance on efficiency and effectiveness, as is the case in some public sectors such as the National Health Service (NHS) in the UK (Bach, 2000), is also not good enough to survive in the long run.

> 'success can only be achieved when financial performance and societal performance of an organization are above average in the particular population in which the organization is operating.'

Large MNCs have learned their lessons in the last decade not to ignore societal issues that affect other stakeholders other than the traditional shareholders of the organization. Shell has had its Brent Spar incident and nowadays works closely together with an important external stakeholder and former 'enemy', Greenpeace. There is a growing willingness among MNCs to look beyond financial results and take into account the interests of multiple stakeholders. Heineken, for example, has a special Aids prevention and treatment programme for its employees and their families in African countries that are struck by the Aids epidemic. It is known as the Heineken HIV-Aids Policy Programme.

On the other side of the spectrum, there is a tendency towards management reforms in public sectors in some countries (e.g. in the UK and the Netherlands) that traditionally have social legitimacy (e.g. hospitals, local governments), but are now under pressure to become lean, provide high-quality services and meet the customer/client demands (Bach, 2000). In these public sectors the challenge is to rebalance the organization towards the economic side of organizing without losing sight of their societal performance.

The European Rhineland model and the British IR approaches have a much richer tradition in stakeholder acknowledgement (and a more balanced view on managing people) than the Anglo-American model, mainly because of differences in institutional contexts (Brewster et al. 2004; Legge, 2005). Coercive mechanisms – legislation, formal position of the trade unions, formal position of works councils and CBAs – are stronger and more deeply embedded in Europe than in the USA. At the same time, it is important to acknowledge fundamental institutional differences between European countries, as mentioned earlier on in this chapter (Gospel and Pendleton, 2003). Paauwe and Boselie (2003) make a case for the impact of coercive mechanisms on several levels of analysis in HRM, including sector level (in particular CBAs), national level (legislation) and international level (e.g EU laws on works councils in MNCs). An overview of different views on HRM is listed below:

- Human resources are more than just resources.
- HRM is not concerned solely with financial performance.
- HRM focuses on the exchange relationship between the employee and the organization.

- The shaping of the employment relationship takes place in an era of continuous tension between the added value and moral values.
- HRM covers all workforce groups.
- HRM involves line and specialist managers, and is not solely aimed at employees.
- HRM is focused on managing work and people, collectively and individually.
- HRM is embedded in industries and societies.

Boxall and Purcell (2003) and Paauwe (2004)

The definition of 'good' and 'bad' people management can be linked to the balanced approach. Taking into account multiple stakeholder interests and a broader societal view in the design of the employment relationship in an organization is likely to result in 'good' people management. From this point of view it means that using a narrow and unitarist perspective (e.g. only serving the interests of the shareholders) is likely to result in 'bad' people management. The recent financial and global economic crisis in 2008/2009 has proved the risk of shareholder dominance. This topic will be discussed in more detail in Chapter 9 on compensation.

Overview of the book

Chapters 2–5 are focused on the foundation of contemporary SHRM using a European multidimensional perspective. Chapter 2 highlights HRM and context. This chapter emphasizes the relevance of HR alignment with contextual factors inside and outside the organization. The HR strategy scan can be used to analyse the context of an organization, understand the shaping of the employment relationship in that organization and classify the degree of HR fit within the organization's context. The multi-actor perspective and the broad societal view of this book is highlighted in Chapter 2 with special attention to the theory of new institutionalism. Chapter 3 is devoted to the (potential) added value of HRM to the success of an organization. The RBV is the central theory in the search for creating an ideal HR value chain for an organization. Lessons learned from the ongoing HRM and performance debate are summarized in this chapter. Chapter 4 on HR metrics and measurement is an extension of Chapter 3 on the added value of HRM. The metrics chapter concretely focuses on the measurement of HRM and performance in order to value HRM in organizations. Chapter 5 is focused on blending insights from MHRM with SHRM in an attempt to integrate different approaches that are linked to different levels of analysis: MHRM mainly on individual employee level and SHRM mainly on organizational level. Achieving organizational agility (a form of flexibility) and employee vitality (representing optimal employee well-being) might be the key to long-term success for an organization. Multilevel issues are discussed in more detail in this chapter.

Chapters 6–11 are devoted to strategic design, implementation and the use of HR tools. Chapter 6 is focused on a special type of HRM called 'high-performance work systems' (HPWSs); these HPWSs represent a bundle of HR practices that increase performance. The underlying theory for the HPWS approaches is the AMO theory, which is discussed in more detail in this chapter. Five key HPWSs are identified in Chapter 6 that can be combined to form an ideal HPWS: selective recruitment and selection, appraisal and performance management, compensation, extensive training and development and employee participation. The content of these five HPWSs are discussed in Chapters 7–11.

Finally, the last three chapters incorporate general themes that are relevant to SHRM. Chapter 12 is concerned with the HR roles and competences required for becoming a business partner in HRM. Chapter 13 deals with IHRM and strategic employment relationship issues in an international setting. Chapter 14 summarizes the main issues discussed in the other chapters and provides reflection on relevant HR issues, for example with regard to the critical role of the front-line manager in the shaping of HRM in practice.

This book covers a wide range of topics and theories relevant to practice, including theories on HPWSs (AMO theory), organizational performance and long-term success (e.g. the RBV), employee well-being (e.g. critical HR studies and job demands model) and organizational context (e.g. strategic contingency approaches and new institutionalism). These theoretical frameworks are introduced not only for the sake of science, but as an instrument for structuring contemporary challenges organizations are confronted with in practice. These challenges might involve some of the following questions:

- How can we improve our long-term success (performance) through people management?
- Are we applying HR practices that will lead to a high-performance culture in our organization?
- How can we manage our workforce optimally in times of major organizational changes; for example, in case of a merger, reorganization or an acquisition?
- What do employees want and how can we use HRM to fulfil their needs and the organization's interests?
- How do we detect best practices and bad practices in HRM throughout our organization?
- What causes stress and high risks of decreased job performance among employees?
- How do we align our HR strategy and policies optimally to our organizational context?

And perhaps this might include other more specific challenges reflected in the following questions:

- Which qualities do HR professionals need to become and remain business partners to top management and line managers (HR roles and competences)?
- How do we attract and retain top talent (talent management)?
- How do we attract and develop our future leaders (LD)?
- Are we fishing in the right pond (recruitment and selection)?
- How much leeway and autonomy do employees need to do their job without any form of control and monitoring?

Table 1.1 presents an overview of the different possible stakeholders of an organization, their potential interests and the level of analysis with regard to the shaping of the employment relationship.

Stakeholder	Illustrations of their interests	Level
Shareholders	High profits, growth and increased market value	Strategic organization level
Employees	Security, fun, development and challenges	Individual employee level
Managers	Productivity, quality, innovation and status	Team and departmental level
Top management	Reputation, shareholder value and long-term success	Strategic organization level

Stakeholder	Illustrations of their interests	Level
Works councils	Employment security and good working conditions	Strategic organization level and individual employee level
Trade unions	Employment, fairness and good working conditions	Strategic organization level and individual employee level
Financiers	Return on investment and financial health of the organization	Strategic organization level
Local government	Employment and environmental pollution	Strategic organization level
National government	Labour legislation and social legitimacy	Strategic organization level
Other interest groups	Environmental pollution	Strategic organization level
Suppliers	Reliability	Strategic organization level
Customers	Costs, quality and innovation	All levels

TABLE 1.1 Overview of potential stakeholders of an organization

CASE STUDY: ABN AMRO

2007 turned out to be a crucial year for ABN AMRO, an international financial services organization that employs around 110 000 people worldwide. Banking, asset management, insurance and leasing were the core business activities of ABN AMRO, ranked in the top ten banks in Europe and the top 20 banks in the world. The organization had three home markets (the Netherlands with its own brand ABN AMRO, Italy with Antonveneta and Brazil with Banco Real) and a substantial market in the USA with LaSalle Bank. It all began early in 2007 when one of the shareholders – the British hedge fund The Children's Investment (TCI) – proposed to the board of directors splitting the organization and selling the business units separately. According to TCI, ABN AMRO had failed to show competitive results within the global financial services population over a period of six years. ABN AMRO's CEO, Rijkman Groenink, reacted to TCI by announcing a merger between ABN AMRO and the British Barclays. However, other competitors were interested in a piece of the cake as well.

In particular, the consortium of three major players in the field – the Belgian/Dutch Fortis, the British Royal Bank of Scotland and the Spanish Banco Santander Centro Hispano – proposed a joint takeover of ABN AMRO in order to split the organization into three pieces; Fortis opting to buy the Belgian and Dutch business units, the Royal Bank of Scotland absorbing the US business units and Santander wanting to buy the Italian and Brazilian business units. Within a few months Barclays' offer turned out to be too low to convince the shareholders and the consortium of Fortis, RBS and Santander was able to take control of ABN AMRO. The transition had a major impact on the employment relationship within the organization. First, the process of a merger or takeover had resulted in feelings of insecurity among employees of ABN AMRO and the corporate reputation was damaged. There were even rumours of competitors hiring head-hunters to seduce ABN AMRO talents with new jobs.

Employee retention of the so-called 'regrettable losses' (the talent pool of an organization) is one of the major challenges in processes of mergers, acquisitions, reorganizations and takeovers. In times of perceived insecurity, we cannot expect full employee engagement, commitment, motivation and satisfaction. And young talents are easily persuaded to move to another organization that offers new challenges and better working conditions.

Second, the transitions took place on an international level with little or no influence of social partners such as trade unions and works councils representing the employees of ABN AMRO. The rationale in strategic decision making was dominated by economic considerations (profits, return on investments and competitiveness), while the interests of the individual employee and other stakeholders (trade unions, works councils and governments) were largely neglected.

Summary

- Organizational change is inevitable for most contemporary organizations, including MNCs, small and medium enterprises and not-for-profit organizations.
- Organizational change affects one of the most valuable assets of an organization: employees.
- HRM can be a source for gaining competitive advantage and supporting organizational change.
- HRM consists of three sub-fields: MHRM, IHRM and SHRM.
- MHRM is mainly focused on the shaping of the employment relationship on the individual employee level and has strong roots in organizational behaviour and occupational psychology.
- IHRM is focused on HRM in different countries and has a comparative nature.
- SHRM is mainly focused on the alignment between HRM and the organizational internal and external context and has strong roots in strategic management and organization studies.
- Anglo-American approaches mainly focus on the added value of HRM to create shareholder value (financial performance), while Rhineland approaches apply a much broader view of HR goals, including the interests of employees and trade unions.
- Some countries are more institutionalized with regard to labour than other countries. The degree of institutionalization in a country affects the shaping of the employment relationship in an organization and HRM.
- Stakeholders are internal and external groups that affect the strategic decision making of an organization, including its SHRM. Influential stakeholders potentially include, for example, shareholders, top management, trade unions, works councils, employees, line managers and the government.
- The balanced approach blends economic and institutional interests in an attempt to create sustained competitive advantage.

Glossary of key terms

Anglo-Saxon or Anglo-American model is an approach in IR and HRM that is typical for the USA, which mainly focuses on the added value of people management to shareholder value.

Balanced approach blends the insights from an economic perspective with the insights from an institutional perspective in order to create a balanced and sustainable position within the organization.

Competitive advantage is the relative stronger position of an organization in comparison to other organizations in the (geographical) region or in the same branch of industry.

Human resource management (HRM) involves management decisions related to policies and practices that together shape the employment relationship and are aimed at achieving individual, organizational and societal goals.

Micro HRM (MHRM) is the sub-field of HRM aimed at studying the shaping of the employment relationship at the individual employee level.

International HRM (IHRM) is the sub-field of HRM aimed at studying the shaping of the employment relationship in an international context, with special attention to HRM for expatriates, HRM in large MNCs and HRM in international governmental organizations (IGOs).

Organizational change represents the process between two different situations that affect an organization and its HRM.

Rhineland model is an approach used in IR and HRM that is typical for many Western European countries that acknowledges multiple stakeholders affecting the employment relationship in organizations.

Stakeholders are all relevant groups inside and outside an organization that affect strategic decision making and strategic HRM within an organization.

Strategic human resource management (SHRM) is the sub-field of HRM aimed at studying the shaping of the employment relationship taking into account the internal and external organization context.

Personal development

What aspects of HRM, for example in terms of personal development (PD) and compensation, do you find important for your career?

Individual task

Consider the ABN AMRO case study. Think of HR practices that could positively affect employee retention within ABN AMRO. In other words, what kind of HR interventions could ABN AMRO apply to avoid the loss of talented employees? You should keep in mind that the financial leeway for ABN AMRO is limited at this stage of the process, therefore offering much more money to talented employees as a form of compensation retention is not an option.

Team task

The strategic decision making with regard to ABN AMRO's future is taken on an international corporate level. Trade unions are mainly organized on national and sector levels, with only limited influence on an international level. Think of ways in which you as a 'local' trade union representative (e.g. from Belgium or the Netherlands) can affect the strategic decision making related to ABN AMRO on an international corporate level.

Learning checklist

After studying this chapter, you should be able to:

- Understand the impact of organizational change on the employment relationship.
- Outline MHRM, SHRM and IHRM.
- Discuss the concept of competitiveness.
- Understand the difference between Anglo-American and Rhineland models in managing employees.
- Identify the multiple stakeholders of an organization.
- Understand the balanced approach to HRM.

References

Bach, S. (2000) Health sector reform and human resource management: Britain in comparative perspective, *International Journal of Human Resource Management*, 11(5): 925–42.

Beer, M., Spector, B., Lawrence, P., Mills, D.Q. and Walton, R. (1984) *Human Resource Management: A General Manager's Perspective*. New York: Free Press.

Boselie, P. (2002) Human resource management, work systems and performance: a theoretical-empirical approach. Dissertation, Tinbergen Institute, Amsterdam: Thela Thesis.

Boxall, P. and Purcell, J. (2003) *Strategy and Human Resource Management*. New York: Palgrave Macmillan.

Boxall, P., Purcell, J. and Wright, P.M. (eds) (2007) *The Oxford Handbook of Human Resource Management*. Oxford: Oxford University Press.

Brewster, C. (2004) European perspectives on human resource management, *Human Resource Management Review*, 14(4): 365–82.

Brewster, C., Mayrhofer, W. and Morley, M. (2004) *Human Resource Management in Europe: Evidence of Convergence?* London: Butterworth-Heinemann.

Deephouse, D.L. (1999) To be different, or to be the same? It's a question (and theory) of strategic balance, *Strategic Management Journal*, 20(2): 147–66.

Delery, J.E. and Doty, D.H. (1996). Modes of theorizing in strategic human resource management: tests of universalistic, contingency, and configurational performance predictions, *Academy of Management Journal*, 39(4): 802–35.

DeLong, D.W. (2004) *Lost Knowledge: Confronting the Threat of an Aging Workforce*. Oxford: Oxford University Press.

Dex, S. and Scheibl, F. (2001) Flexible and family-friendly working arrangements in UK-based SMEs: business cases, *British Journal of Industrial Relations*, 39(3): 411–31.

Felstead, A., Jewson, N., Phizacklea, A. and Walters, S. (2002) Opportunities to work at home in the context of work–life balance, *Human Resource Management Journal*, 12(1): 54–76.

Fombrun, C., Tichy N.M. and Devanna, M.A. (eds) (1984) *Strategic Human Resource Management*. New York: Wiley.

Gospel, H. and Pendleton, A. (2003) Finance, corporate governance and the management of labour: a conceptual and comparative analysis, *British Journal of Industrial Relations*, 41(3): 557–82.

Guest, D.E. (1987) Human resource management and industrial relations, *Journal of Management Studies*, 24(5): 503–21.

Hayton, J. (2004) Strategic human capital management in SMEs: an empirical study of entrepreneurial performance, *Human Resource Management*, 42(4): 375–91.

Keegan, A. and Boselie, P. (2006) The lack of impact of dissensus inspired analysis on developments in the field of human resource management, *Journal of Management Studies*, 43(7): 1491–511.

Legge, K. (1995) *Human Resource Management, Rhetorics and Realities*. London: Macmillan Business.

Legge, K. (2005) *Human Resource Management: Rhetorics and Realities*. Basingstoke: Palgrave Macmillan.

Lepak, D.P. and Snell, S.A. (2002) Examining the human resource architecture: the relationships among human capital, employment, and human resource configurations, *Journal of Management*, 28(4): 517–43.

Paauwe, J. (2004) *HRM and Performance: Achieving Long-term Viability*. Oxford: Oxford University Press.

Paauwe, J. and Boselie, P. (2003) Challenging 'strategic HRM' and the relevance of the institutional setting, *Human Resource Management Journal*, 13(3): 56–70.

Porter, M.E. (1998) Clusters and the new economics of competition, *Harvard Business Review*, November–December: 77–90.

Sels, L., De Winne, S., Maes, J., Delmotte, J., Faems, D. and Forrier, A. (2006) Unravelling the HRM–performance link: value-creating and cost-increasing effects of small business HRM, *Journal of Management Studies*, 43(2): 319–42.

Wright, P.M. and Boswell, W.R. (2002) Desegregating HRM: a review and synthesis of micro and macro human resource management research, *Journal of Management*, 28(3): 247–76.

Further reading

Boxall, P. and Purcell, J. (2003) Human resource management and business performance, in P. Boxall and J. Purcell (eds), *Strategy and Human Resource Management*, pp. 1–24. New York: Palgrave Macmillan.

Boxall, P., Purcell, J. and Wright, P.M. (2007) Human resource management: scope, analysis, and significance, in P. Boxall, J. Purcell and P.M. Wright (eds), *The Oxford Handbook of Human Resource Management*, pp. 1–16 . Oxford: Oxford University Press.

Paauwe, J. (2004) Introduction, in J. Paauwe (ed.), *HRM and Performance: Achieving Long Term Viability*, pp. 1–7. Oxford: Oxford University Press.

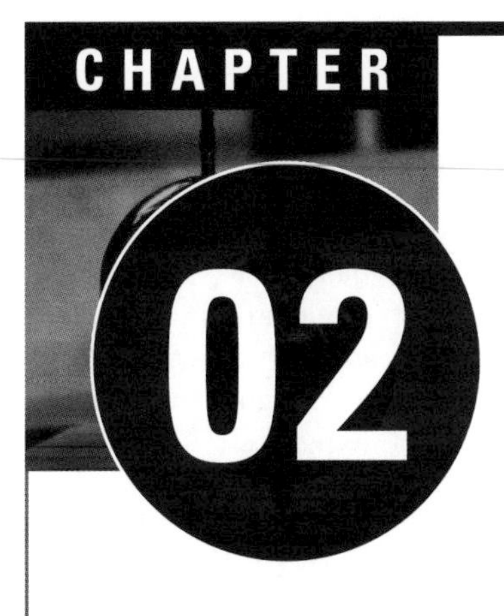

CHAPTER 02 Strategic Human Resource Management and Context

Learning Objectives

After studying this chapter, you should be able to do the following:

- ❖ Understand the concept of strategy in contemporary organizations
- ❖ Understand the difference between best-practice approaches and best-fit approaches in human resource management (HRM)
- ❖ Identify the four types of fit in HRM
- ❖ Recognize the impact of contextual factors (general environment and population environment; market mechanisms, institutional mechanisms and configuration) on the shaping of employment relationships in organizations
- ❖ Examine and analyse the context of an organization using the model presented in this chapter

CASE STUDY: EASYJET

Book a return flight from London to Geneva for just £40 (airport tax included). The only thing you need is a computer, a printer, an Internet connection and a (valid) credit card. The 1990s introduced budget airlines in Europe (e.g. easyJet, Ryanair) that started to offer cheap flights in line with the US Southwest Airlines model. easyJet is one of the most well-known budget airlines in Europe perhaps partly because of its striking orange colours and its popular real-life docusoap on television (Airline).

easyJet was founded in 1995 by Sir Stelios Haji-Ioannou. The underlying philosophy of the firm is formulated as follows: 'easyJet keeps costs low by eliminating the unnecessary costs and "frills" which characterize "traditional" airlines' (www.easyjet.com). The combination of web-based organizing, standardization of processes and cost-reduction practices at all levels of the organization has contributed to easyJet's success. The airline transported 30 000 passengers with two Boeing 737–200 aircraft in their first year. One decade later (in 2006) easyJet transported 33 million passengers with 122 airplanes to over 80 destinations or key cities in Europe and Northern Africa.

The success of the organization is reflected in numerous awards and tributes, including Top Management Team (British Telecom, 2002), Best Low Cost Airline (*Business Traveller Magazine*, 2003) and Best Airline Website (Travelmole Web Awards, 2006), together with a record profit in 2006 of £129 million before tax, a rise of 56 per cent over 2005. The profit per seat increased from 332p to 430p in 2007. Cost reduction and optimal service quality in terms of reliability and customer ease represent the overall organizational goals of easyJet. To keep the costs low easyJet uses the Internet – the so-called web-based organizing method – for selling tickets. The food and drinks on board are not free and in most cases easyJet makes use of relatively small airports that are cheaper and more flexible. It only offers direct flights and takes no responsibility for connecting flights. This way it can avoid additional expenses for passengers missing a connecting flight (e.g. hotel costs and additional ground personnel).

The standardization of processes includes the use of only two types of aircraft up until 2007: the Boeing 737 and the Airbus 319. This way both pilots and cabin crew can be trained to work in the two aircraft types, thus creating company flexibility. Maintenance is also relatively cheaper with a limited number of aircraft types. Reliability represented in on-time performance (83 per cent of all flights arrived on time in 2007 and 96 per cent of all flights arrived within one hour in 2007) and low baggage loss are crucial customer quality standards, together with the ease of booking a flight.

There are a couple of serious challenges for easyJet linked to managing people. First, attracting and retaining pilots is one of the major challenges for easyJet. The costs for training pilots are high and high employee turnover rates among pilots may cause disruptions to their organization. It is a well-known fact that pilots start working for easyJet because of the opportunity to extend their flight hours. The formal pilot training in combination with the number of flight hours makes these pilots extremely valuable to other airline companies, including British Airways (BA) and Air France-KLM.

Second, the career opportunities of the cabin crew are limited and therefore cause human resource (HR) challenges in retaining good personnel and keeping them motivated. Internal promotion opportunities are restricted as a result of the nature of the business.

Third, increased competition between airline carriers forces easyJet to continuously improve its business activities, expand the market (new destinations and market penetration) and reduce costs, putting more and more pressure on employees to improve performance. Overall, easyJet has turned out to be one of the most successful low-cost carriers, partly caused by its first-mover advantage and its corporate reputation (the latter is, for example, reflected in the brand name).

? Discussion questions

- easyJet is a performance-driven organization. Find out what the key performance indicators for airline companies are in general and easyJet in particular.
- Find out whether easyJet uses any other performance indicators that are non-financial and not directly linked to efficiency, sales (including number of passengers and destinations) and profits.
- easyJet operates in a highly competitive environment. How can easyJet compete with other low-cost carriers (e.g. Virgin, Ryanair, Transavia, Corendon) using HRM?

Introduction

easyJet illustrates the alignment of the organization's strategy and the work design in terms of web-based organizing, standardization of processes and cost-reduction practices at all levels of the organization. The company's cost-effectiveness and quality service strategy through the application of technology (the Internet) and the standardization of processes is reflected in its HR strategy and policies. For example, employees of easyJet receive a yearly budget for company clothing and if they ruin their clothing they have to pay for new clothing themselves. This is in line with easyJet's cost-efficiency focus emphasizing employee responsibility aligned with the company philosophy. This is called 'strategic fit' in HRM. Another illustration of the alignment between the overall strategy and HRM is reflected in the standardization of work processes. Using a limited number of airplane types enables the firm to standardize employee development (two airplane types require only two training programmes) and increases employee flexibility. This is called 'organizational fit' in HRM. We return to these two forms of fit in HRM (strategic and organizational) later on in the chapter.

The notions of *fit* or alignment are important features of strategic human resource management (SHRM) and are therefore key issues in this chapter. Two things that go well together represent fit; for example, two magnets attracting each other. This phenomenon can also be applied to HRM: HR practices can fit together and HRM can fit with other factors including the strategy and the production system. A misfit represents two things that oppose each other.

'The more HR fit the better.'

The aim of this chapter is to emphasize the idea that a better fit between HRM and the context of an organization will lead to more success. In other words, the more HR fit the better (Boon, 2008). Part of easyJet's success might be created by a good fit between its people management practices (e.g. web-based recruitment) and the business of the organization. For a better understanding of an organization's context and business we need to find out more about the business model of that organization. The *business model* is the way an organization manages its business to make money. The Internet and the web-based organizing principles in combination with the standardization principles (e.g. only two airplane types) are fundamental organizing principles of easyJet that determine its business model. Other airline organizations might have different business models, for example working with travel agencies and having a more intercontinental focus. An optimal fit between HRM and the context can positively affect the business model and the organization's success. A better fit can be achieved through strategic decision making.

Strategy is generally defined by an organization's *intention* to achieve certain *goals* through *planned alignment (or fit)* between the *organization* and its *environment* (De Wit and Meyer, 1998). The two words 'intention' and 'planned' indicate that the organization has some kind of strategic plan for current and future actions. Therefore, the concept of a strategic plan, often a written-down document, is used as an indicator for the strategy of an organization. We can find the strategy of an organization in the strategic plan and documents such as the annual report and the president's letter. Contemporary developments in both strategic management (e.g. Regner, 2008) and SHRM (e.g. Becker and Huselid, 2006) stress the importance of strategy in practice and the implementation strategy as crucial parts of the overall organization strategy, meaning strategy is much more than just a written-down plan from the top echelon of an organization. According to these new insights, strategy is also about the embeddedness and implementation of plans at lower levels of the organization and with involvement of multiple actors, including middle-line managers (Regner, 2008), works councils and employees (Paauwe and Boselie, 2003). An optimal strategy includes a fit between HRM and the context. This strategy contributes to the organization's business model and its performance. In Chapter 3 more specific attention is paid to the potential added value of HRM to firm performance.

Another important concept in the strategy definition is 'goal'. Organizations aim for the achievement of certain goals. These goals can be defined in narrow terms; for example, aiming at exclusively satisfying shareholder interests, concretely aiming for increasing sales, profits and market value. The goals can also be defined in much broader terms, including organizational goals (increasing efficiency, quality and flexibility), societal goals (satisfying trade union interests, complying with national and EU legislation) and individual employee goals (creating opportunities for an optimal work–life balance, career opportunities and involvement). This much broader view of goals is also reflected in some of the theoretical HRM models, including Beer et al. (1984) (see Figure 2.1), Paauwe (1991) and Boselie (2002). The Anglo-American approaches tend to use a narrow definition of goals, while the continental European approaches tend to apply a much broader definition including multiple stakeholders and interests. The German chemical organisation BASF, for example, emphasizes the importance of employee consultation through employee representatives inside the organization (works councils). Their model is not only used in Germany, but is also exported in adapted versions to the UK, the USA and Asia. Employee and societal goals in terms of employee consultation are a key element in the organization's strategy.

The Beer et al. (1984) model heavily influenced the Paauwe approach (2004). The six-component model in this chapter builds on notions described by Beer et al. (1984) and by Paauwe (2004), and is extended by insights from Baron and Kreps (1999).

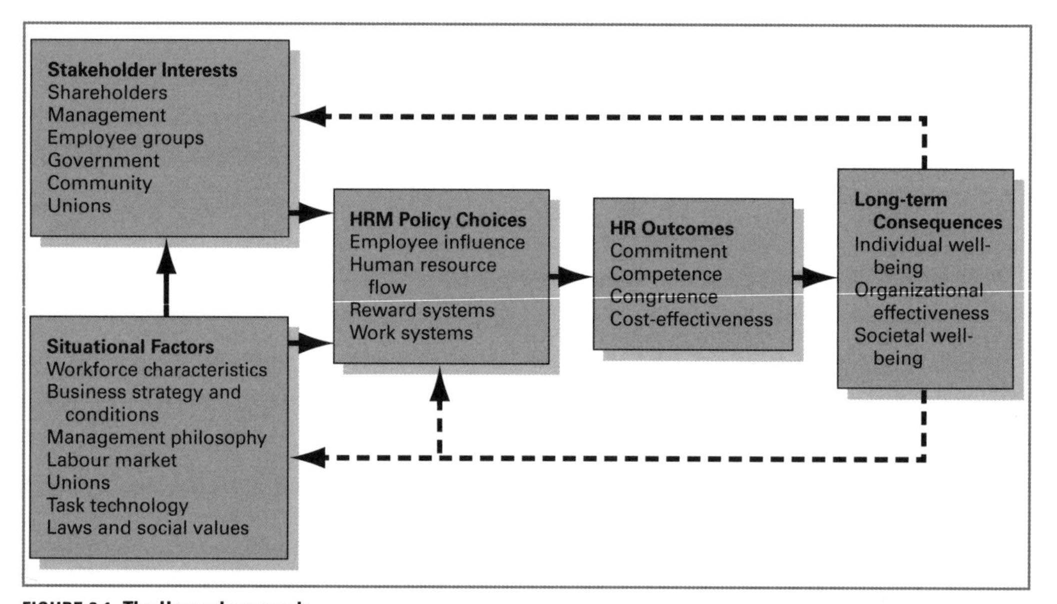

FIGURE 2.1 The Harvard approach

Source: Reproduced with permission from Beer et al. (1984, Figure 2-1, p. 16).

Alignment or fit are two other concepts in the strategy definition; more specifically the alignment or fit between the organization and its environment. Alignment and fit refer to the principle of matching elements, which in this case is the organization and its context (or environment). The organization refers to the social, legal and economic entity that exists for a certain purpose; for example, delivering services, manufacturing products or transporting goods. The environment or context of an organization refers to its internal and external constitution. The internal and external context of an organization is discussed in more detail later in this chapter.

SHRM is focused on the alignment or fit between the strategy of an organization and the HR strategy of that organization. Boxall and Purcell (2008) call the overall strategy of an organization the business strategy or competitive strategy. The business strategy is composed of multiple strategies 'covering the various "functional silos" of the business: marketing, operations, finance and human resources' (Boxall and Purcell, 2003: 35). They define the **business strategy** as 'the system of the firm's important choices, a system that could be well integrated around common concerns or which might have various links and foul-ups' (Boxall and Purcell, 2003: 35). The **HR strategy** is one of the functional silos and the linkage between the business strategy and the HR strategy is one of the central themes in this chapter, with a key focus on notions of HRM and fit.

There is an ongoing debate about the relevance and necessity of fit between HRM and other aspects of an organization (Boxall and Purcell, 2008). *To fit or not to fit* appears to be one of the key points of attention in the field of SHRM over last two decades. For example, should an organization align its HR strategy with the overall business strategy? Does a strategic fit between the business strategy and the HR strategy add value to the organization? Linked to this is the question of whether HR practices that are successful in one context (e.g. in the budget airline industry) can be copied and be equally successful in any other branch of industry. The theoretical debate linked to this issue of fit (or not) is known for its two competing schools: the *best-fit school* versus the *best-practice school*. The 'best-fit' school argues that HRM is more effective when it is aligned with its internal and external context. The 'best-practice' school advocates a universalistic perspective (Delery and Doty, 1996): 'It argues that all firms will be better off if they identify and adopt "best practice" in the way they manage people' (Boxall and Purcell, 2003: 47). Pfeffer's (1998) seven HR practices for 'building profits by putting people first' is representative of the 'best-practice' school. His seven practices are employment security, selective hiring, self-managed teams or teamworking, high pay contingent on organizational performance, extensive training, reduction of status differences and sharing information.

Illustrations of Pfeffer's seven best practices 'in practice'

1 *Selective recruitment and selection* of a management trainee might involve a combination of different techniques, including intelligence tests, integrity tests, assessment centres and structured interviews with HR managers, line managers and employees with whom trainees are supposed to work in their first assignment. The focus within this HR practice is on the 'selective' part of it and refers to a sophisticated way of trying to recruit and select the best person for the job and the organization.

2 *Extensive training* may involve employee development through training programmes outside the organization (e.g. an MBA programme in a business school), training on the job, eLearning (Strohmeier, 2007) through training programmes via an intranet (e.g. a yearly compliance training to get updated on the latest rules and regulations on health and safety in the production plant), and coaching by another manager other than the direct supervisor.

3 *Performance-related pay* (PRP) linked to the profits of an organization (e.g. 8–10 per cent profit-related pay for workers), PRP linked to individual and team performance, and the use of yearly bonuses for the best-performing employees in a department.

4. *Teamworking* with autonomy and self-responsibility in work design and planning for a group of employees. Teamwork is a way to break through the hierarchical model and decentralize responsibility.
5. *Information sharing and communication* using the intranet, Internet, newsletters, direct supervisor talks and, last but not least, top management presentations. The latter refers to the importance of the chief executive officer's (CEO's) involvement with and commitment to major organizational changes. Top management support and involvement in communication is crucial in the change process of an organization.
6. *Reduction of status differences* through avoiding status symbols linked to hierarchical positions such as executive parking spaces (in place in most organizations), separate elevators for top executives as is the case in a large multinational bank, and employees at higher positions located at higher levels of a building as is the case in one of the United Nations (UN) related organizations.
7. *Employment security* in terms of employee benefits providing insurance for unemployment, disability and death for employees and their families. In most European countries employment security is institutionalized and embedded through legislation. The possibility of fewer restrictions on employee dismissals has been placed on the political agenda. In some continental European countries there used to be very strict rules on firing workers. New labour legislation tends to strengthen the employers' interests (more leeway) and weaken the employees' position (less employment security).

! *Stop and reflect*

Can you think of other concrete illustrations of Pfeffer's seven best practices?

! *Stop and reflect*

Which of Pfeffer's seven best practices are important for you? What are your personal preferences and interests? Use a realistic perspective, because your best-practice list might be too demanding for an organization to fulfil. For example, high pay might be a preference, but is the organization willing and able to offer that to you?

Pfeffer (1998) claims success for all companies that apply these seven practices in HRM. The question remains how much impact the context of an organization has on the success of a certain HR practice. Pfeffer's **best-practice proposition** ('one size fits all in HRM') is both supported by empirical research (Delery and Doty, 1996) and criticized for its lack of attention to contextual factors, including national differences with respect to labour legislation, sector differences, the nature of the business (e.g. manufacturing focused on manufacturing products versus services organizations delivering services), the size of a firm and different employee groups (Boxall and Purcell, 2008). The strength of the 'best-practice' model is its simplicity and clarity.

In contrast, the **best-fit proposition** (HRM's success depends on the alignment of it with the organizational context) stresses the contextual embeddedness of HRM in organizations. According to this proposition success can only be achieved through the appropriate fit between HRM and its context. **Context** represents the set of facts or circumstances that surrounds the organization. A distinction can be made between the internal and external organizational context. The *internal context* represents the organization's unique history (founding father(s) and 'zeitgeist' or time period of foundation), the administrative heritage (organizational structures, production systems and practices installed) and organization culture. easyJet was founded in the 1990s, a decade in which global communication via the World Wide Web changed our society. Without any doubt, these global information technology (IT) developments have had their impact on easyJet's strategy, tactics and operations. The web-based organizing principles of easyJet are fully in line with the IT developments in the 1990s, and easyJet was one of the first to apply them in the airline business. The founding father (Stelios Haji-Ioannou), the foundation period of the 1990s and its culture represent crucial aspects of easyJet's blueprint or organizational DNA.

'Context matters.'

The *external* context reflects the outside mechanisms that affect the organization or even interact with it. The external context puts pressure on an organization and forces it to adapt its strategy and decision making. There are two general mechanisms that determine the external context of an organization: **market mechanisms** and **institutional mechanisms** (DiMaggio and Powell, 1983). Market mechanisms include the degree of competition between organizations in terms of products, services, technology and people. Paauwe (2004) defines this part of the external context of an organization in terms of products, markets and technology (PMT dimension). The way these market mechanisms work is explained in more detail later in this chapter.

? Discussion questions

Determine the PMT dimension of easyJet:

- What are the product/services provided by easyJet?
- Describe easyJet's market characteristics.
- What technology does easyJet use?

Institutional mechanisms represent several pressures that stem from legislation (e.g. collective bargaining agreements (CBAs)), protocols and procedures (e.g. agreements between organizations and works councils), routines, habits, norms and values (e.g. linked to certain professions such as accountants and lawyers), and social-cultural issues (e.g. societal attitudes towards work–life balance and labour participation of women) (see Figure 2.2). Paauwe (2004) also pays special attention to this part of the external context of an organization and calls it the social, cultural and legal (SCL) dimension. Returning to the easyJet case, institutional mechanisms that affect the company include: European Union (EU) legislation on environmental pollution and safety measures, maximum flying hours regulation for pilots, and CBAs on wages and other working conditions. The Paauwe (2004) model for both the internal and external context of an organization stresses the notion that organizations do not operate in a vacuum. The 'best-fit' models can become quite complex when taking into account all potential contextual factors, an issue that should be borne in mind when applying this approach in theory and practice.

Deephouse (1999) makes a valuable contribution to this debate, making a further distinction between the **general environment** and the **population environment**. The general environment represents all the market and institutional mechanisms that affect all organizations in a country;

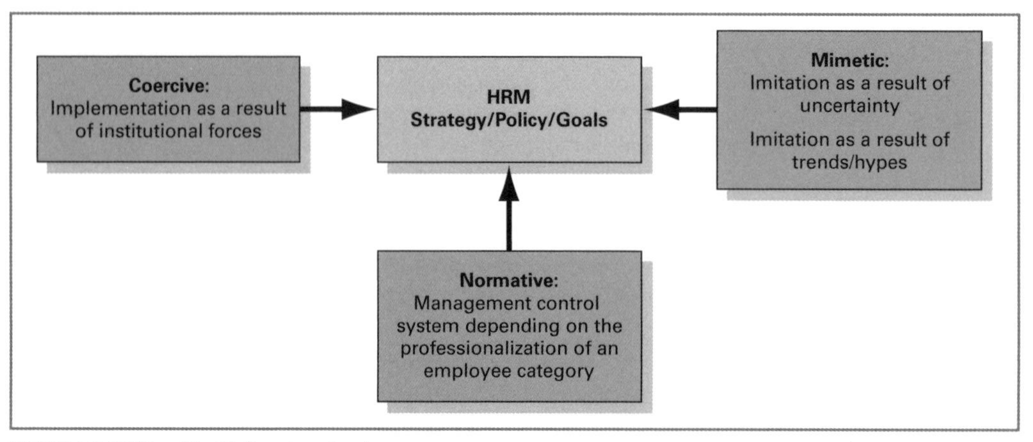

FIGURE 2.2 HRM and institutional mechanisms
Source: Reproduced with permission from Paauwe and Boselie (2003).

for example, the macroeconomic situation of a country at a certain time and the general labour legislation on unemployment and disability.

Illustration of general and population environments in practice

The Dutch-British Shell, the French Total and British Petroleum (BP) all operate in the same population environment manifested through their main business activities (oil and chemicals), with both their headquarters and their significant operations based in Europe. Therefore Shell, Total and BP belong to the same population based on the nature of their business and the geographical location of activities. The latter is particularly relevant because of national and EU legislation placed on all three companies. However, Shell, Total and BP are also part of a more general community of large multinationals (MNCs) operating on a global scale. Recent corporate scandals within Enron (in the USA), Parmalat (in Italy) and Ahold (in the USA and the Netherlands) affected the general environment of MNCs all over the world, including Shell, Total and BP. New legislation, for example the US Sarbanes–Oxley Act 2002, influences all three companies independently of their business.

Stop and reflect

Find out more about the Sarbanes-Oxley Act 2002 (SOX):

- What is the background and aim of this US Act?
- What kinds of organization are affected by the Act?
- What is the impact of SOX on HRM?
- Are there similar Acts in place in Europe?

An organization operates in an **organizational field or population**, which is 'a community of organizations that partakes of a common meaning system and whose participants interact more frequently or fatefully with one another than with actors outside the field' (Scott, 1994: 6). The population in which an organization operates is mainly the sector with its competitors (e.g. the airline industry in the case of easyJet), but it may also include suppliers and other types of organization (e.g. organizations that provide onboard food and drinks for easyJet). Deephouse's (1999) distinction is relevant because it acknowledges potential external factors that affect all organizations in a country (e.g. shortages of labour supply as a result of an ageing population in many European countries) versus potential external factors that only affect the organizations in a population (e.g. environmental pollution and the public image of airline organizations in the case of easyJet).

SUMMARY

- 'best-practice' school: universalistic best practices in HRM
- 'best-fit' school:
  - *internal context* (history, administrative heritage and culture)
  - *external context* (market mechanisms and institutional mechanisms; general environment and population environment)

In the early days of the HR discipline some academics stressed the impact of context on HRM (e.g. Beer et al., 1984), while others did not or to a lesser degree (e.g. Fombrun et al., 1984). These early 'best-fit' models were grounded on *strategic contingency approaches* from the 1960s and 1970s that emphasize the impact of internal contingencies (e.g. firm size, firm history and capital intensity) and external contingencies (e.g. degree of unionization and legislation) on the shaping and structuring of organizations (Woodward, 1965; Lawrence and Lorsch, 1967; Mintzberg, 1979). Together with the strategic management typology of competitive strategies by Porter (1980, 1985) – distinguishing cost leadership, differentiation and focus strategies – these strategic contingency approaches resulted in multiple 'best-fit' models in HRM in the 1980s, including the ones by Miles and Snow (1984) on competitive types in HRM distinguishing defenders, prospectors and analysers and Schuler and Jackson (1987) on linking HR practices to Porter's three competitive strategies.

Strategic contingency approaches showed that certain contextual factors affect the shaping of an organization. For example, organization size affects the (financial) resources available for investment. Large organizations are known for their capability of creating economies of scale. In other words, large organizations can be more efficient than small organizations because of their size and therefore create more financial leeway for future investment (e.g. in human resources). Another example of contextual factors affecting the shaping of an organization relates to the influence of trade unions through the degree of unionization of employees within an organization. When a substantial number of an organization's workforce are members of a trade union, this generally indicates a significant influence of trade unions on the organization and its HRM.

Illustration of strategy and practice by Schuler and Jackson

According to Schuler and Jackson (1987), cost leaders' strategies can be translated in HRM characterized by few and simple tasks, few skills required to do the job, narrow career paths, training few employees, evaluation on short-term criteria and individual incentives. In contrast, organizations with a differentiation strategy translate their strategy in HRM characterized by many and complex tasks (little or no labour division), many skills required to do the job, broad career paths, training all employees, evaluation on long-term criteria and group incentives.

The two most common forms of fit in these HR approaches are strategic or vertical and internal or horizontal. **Strategic or vertical fit** refers to that part of the 'best-fit' school that assumes a necessary alignment between the overall business strategy and the HR strategy. Strategic fit has many faces and is modelled in different ways, including the model by Golden and Ramanujam (1985) in which a distinction is made between four linkages (see Figure 2.3):

1 An *administrative linkage* between strategy and HRM represents the lowest level of integration. Actually, it could be argued that organizations that incorporate this format have no linkage between the business strategy and their HR strategy. The HRM department, if in place at all, is merely engaged in administrative work such as salary administration. Small and medium-sized enterprises (SMEs) often show the administrative linkage as a result of a lack of economies of scale for installing an HR department with HR professionals. In fact, this level indicates little or no linkage between strategy and HRM.
2 A *one-way linkage* can be found in organizations where the HR strategy is derived from the overall business strategy. In this ideal type, the HR strategy is affected by the overall business strategy, but the relationship is only one way. A cost-reduction strategy might result in certain HR interventions for goal achievement (e.g. individual performance-related pay and minimum training expenses).
3 A *two-way linkage* represents a potential model in which HR experts determine certain external (or internal) developments that are put on the table of the board of directors. These two-way HR issues (e.g. noticing future labour shortages of knowledge workers) can become part of the overall business strategy, reflected in the focus on employee attraction and retention. The new business strategy in return pushes the HR strategy towards certain HR interventions that help the organization to achieve its goals.
4 An *integrative linkage* represents full alignment of HRM and strategy. Part of an integrative linkage is the position of the HR director, who has a seat at the 'high table' (board of directors). Only a few organizations can be characterized by this type of linkage in which people management is such a crucial part of the strategy, tactics and operations of an organization.

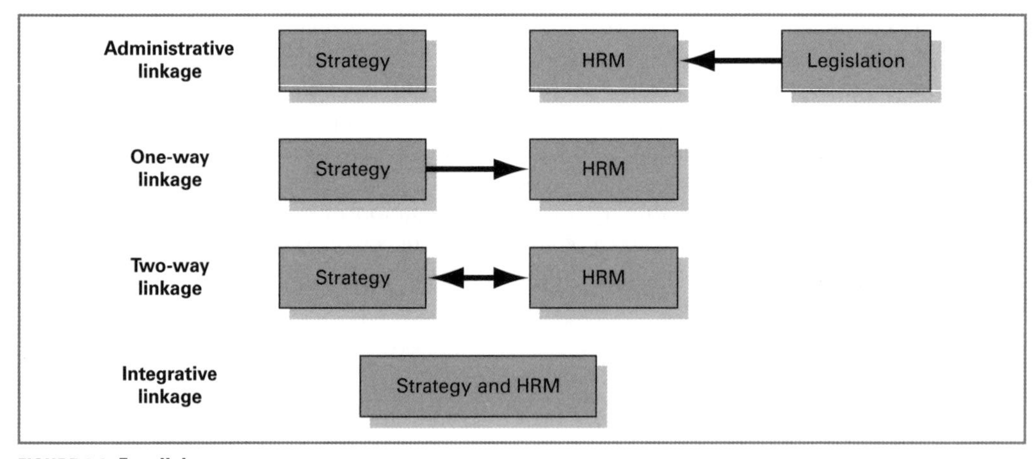

FIGURE 2.3 Four linkages

Internal or horizontal fit reflects the link between individual HR practices and is thought to be crucial for gaining success as well as the strategic fit. There is a general school of thought within HRM that builds on the ideas of internal fit called *HR system approaches*. An HR system is defined as a coherent and consistent set of HR practices that combined together results in higher organizational performance than the sum of the effects of using each HR practice separately. The underlying idea of the system approach is that linking HR practices strengthens the HR strategy and philosophy of an organization, signalling the organization's intentions and aims through the different elements of people management (see Chapter 6 on high-performance work systems). For example, *recruitment and selection* can be used to signal the type of desired new employees in terms of their qualities (e.g. in search of employees with the highest grades at high school and university level) and their attitudes (e.g. willing to work more than 40 hours per week). After the selection process, the newcomers can be *socialized* in a way that fits the organization's strategy and culture. The socialization process can be strengthened by firm specific *training* and a *reward system* (e.g. individual PRP based on achieving targets) that matches the strategy. The above illustration of aligning recruitment and selection, socialization, training and rewards is an HR system that might lead to organizational success according to the literature. The empirical evidence for HR system approaches is very weak (Boselie et al., 2005), but the rationale behind it is actually pretty plausible.

Delery (1998) warns us of so-called *deadly combinations* of HR practices. Deadly combinations are the result of a misfit between HR practices. These deadly combinations represent combinations of HR practices that affect each other negatively. An example of a deadly combination is the application of teamwork and individual PRP. Individual PRP does not stimulate cooperation and teamwork in most situations. It would therefore be more logical to combine extensive teamwork with team PRP. A very specific form of the HR systems approach is discussed in Chapter 6, HPWSs.

Stop and reflect

Discuss at least one other potential deadly combination between two HR practices.

Next to strategic (vertical) and internal (horizontal) fit, Wood (1999) stresses the importance of at least two other types of fit in SHRM: organizational and environmental. **Organizational fit** refers to the necessary fit between the HR strategy, policies and practices on the one hand and the other organizational systems on the other. The other organizational systems include the production system, the communication and information system (both hardware in terms of the communication channels and software in terms of the computer language and programs used), the technological system, for example embedded in the research and development (R&D) department, the marketing system, the financial system and the legal system (including procedures and compliance). Traditionally, organizational fit has received a lot of attention in management research within manufacturing industries (e.g. the car industry). The work-design related practices such as teamwork, job rotation, job autonomy and job enrichment were put on the agenda in the 1960s to increase workers' motivation and commitment in manufacturing firms. The organizational systems (e.g. an assembly line in a mass-production process of electronic devices) can have a big impact on the work design in terms of how employment is shaped in an organization (teamwork or not, level of job autonomy, etc.), but also on the nature of HR practices. Alignment between HR practices and other organizational systems is the essence of organizational fit (Verburg et al., 2007). In some cases the organizational systems are extremely determinative with little or no leeway for HR practices. An assembly line in a mass-production organization often puts restrictions on HRM, for example with respect to the degree of teamwork that can be applied and the degree of job autonomy that can be given to employees. In those cases the production line simply determines the leeway for HRM variety.

! Stop and reflect

Call centres are commonly used to sell products and services to customers, but also help clients who have a problem that needs to be solved. Employees of a call centre operate behind a computer and use a headphone with a microphone to communicate with clients. They are often physically located with other employees in one big room, but some do their work from home. There is no face-to-face contact between the call centre employee and the customer. The computer and the telephone are the devices that enable the contact between the two actors. The computer linked to the organizational databases and the telephone connections are characteristic for the organizational system. Think about the potential interaction between these organizational systems and the HR practices that can be used in this call centre. For example, how can the individual PRP of call centre employees be linked to their performance?

Environmental fit is focused on the link between the HR strategy and the institutional environment of an organization. Organizations operate in different institutional contexts (DiMaggio and Powell, 1983, 1991; Oliver, 1997). The strategic contingency approaches, although very popular within SHRM research, together with the resource-based view (RBV) (see Chapter 3) and AMO theory (see Chapter 6), tend to neglect the institutional organizational environment (Deephouse, 1999). For a better understanding of the concept of environmental fit, an alternative theoretical framework is required: *new institutionalism*. This socio-economic theory has become popular since the 1980s and 1990s in strategic management in contrast to the Porter-like strategies that mainly take an economic perspective. DiMaggio and Powell (1983) argue that organizations are confronted with both *market mechanisms* and *institutional mechanisms*. The market mechanisms reflect the elements of competition between organizations operating in the same market. Organizations compete for resources, customers, financiers, shareholders and employees. From a micro-economic perspective competition creates more homogeneity among the competing organizations, because successful practices will be copied and implemented resulting in a new equilibrium. New institutionalism claims there are other reasons for homogeneity among organizations than competition: institutional mechanisms. DiMaggio and Powell (1983) make a distinction between three types of institutional mechanism:

1. *Coercive mechanisms* that stem from legislation and procedures.
2. *Normative mechanisms* that have their origins in the professions of employees (e.g. the professional education of lawyers and accountants, but also the professional networks that operate to develop and protect certain professions).
3. *Mimetic mechanisms* that are the result of uncertainty or fashion.

The institutional framework and the three institutional mechanisms can be applied to HRM (Paauwe and Boselie, 2003, 2007) (see Figure 2.2). Coercive mechanisms that affect the HR strategy include national labour legislation, for example on working hours and working conditions; CBAs with trade unions and/or works councils; norms and values in a given country or continent; the role of the government or larger entities such as the EU; and the role of trade unions in the shaping of the employment relationship in an organization. The coercive mechanisms are manifested in the event of a new labour law (e.g. new national labour legislation with regard to health, safety and working hours), yearly CBAs and reorganization with massive layoffs. Normative mechanisms are generally embedded in the employees' professional norms and routines. In other words, these mechanisms determine to a large extent how an employee does the job. Medical specialists, for example, are educated and trained in a very specific way. Their routines are not easily changed and influenced by the organization's new strategy focused on, for example, cost reduction and service quality. The potential tension between the medical specialists and new public reforms can be found in many hospitals, creating a major challenge for HRM in bridging the two perspectives.

Stop and reflect

Think of at least two other professions that are likely to reveal normative mechanisms in an organization. Also discuss how the normative mechanisms for these two professions affect the HRM of those professionals.

The third institutional mechanism is focused on the general tendency of organizations to copy/imitate others in times of uncertainty or as a result of hype. Mimetic mechanisms can be the result of consultancy interference or the development of a new fashion in management. The learning organization, the balanced scorecard (BSC), benchmarking, competence frameworks, lean production principles and the HR scorecard are all potential guru management principles that might lead to mimetic behaviour among organizations in a population. Once several, often leading, organizations in a population have adopted such a practice, it is likely that other organizations in the population will follow (Paauwe and Boselie, 2005). The imitation of a best practice might be done because of competitive considerations; then, however, it is not an institutional mechanism, but a competitive mechanism that drove the organization to implement the practice. The imitation of a best practice because others are doing it as well reflects mimetic behaviour potentially caused by legitimacy considerations. In other words, if others are doing it we must do it as well, otherwise we run the risk of reputation damage for not doing it.

Given the internal and external context of an organization, there is room to manoeuvre for those in charge of that organization. This leeway enables different choices; for example, whether an organization applies a more cost-driven focus or a more service-oriented focus (or both) given the market conditions, institutional environment and the internal organizational characteristics. Child (1972) was one of the first to introduce the concept of **strategic choice**, referring to the degree of leeway in strategic decision making given the organizational context. The notion of strategic choice was picked up by leading scholars in SHRM, including Paauwe (1991) and Boxall and Purcell (2003). The extent of choice available to organizations is further discussed by Child (1997) in his reformulation of the strategic choice perspective in the late 1990s, when he introduced the concepts of *hyper-determinism* and *hyper-voluntarism*. These two concepts represent the two extremes of the strategic choice perspective. Hyper-determinism represents the situation in which an organization has absolutely no leeway for strategic choice, because the choices are fully determined by the contextual conditions. The hyper-voluntarism concept takes an opposite position, stating that an organization is free to do whatever the organization wants to do. In other words, there are no restrictions for strategic decision making. Boxall and Purcell (2008) apply Child's (1997) concept in strategic HRM, arguing that organizational reality in strategic choices is probably somewhere between hyper-determinism (everything is determined and therefore no leeway) and hyper-voluntarism (everything is possible and there are no restrictions for strategic decision making). Paauwe (1991, 2004) also applies the concept of strategic choice and he shows that there is always leeway (room to manoeuvre) for strategic choices even if an organization is confronted with severe legislation. Paauwe (2004: 96) argues that the HRM room to manoeuvre of an organization is larger when:

- There is market growth (in contrast to market decline).
- There are a limited number of relevant stakeholders (in contrast to multiple relevant stakeholders).
- There are limited laws, rules, procedures and protocols (in contrast to extensive legislation and procedures).
- The ratio of labour/total costs tends to be close to zero, implying a capital intensive organizational context (in contrast to a ratio of labour/total costs that tends to be close to one).
- The organization has large financial buffers (in contrast to the absence of available financial resources).
- The organization is a monopolist (in contrast to an organization with multiple competitors).

Determining an organization's leeway is relevant because it gives insights into the factors that should be taken into account when decisions are being made (strategic decision making). easyJet's leeway, for example, is determined by the situation in the market (growth, stagnation or decline), the number of relevant external stakeholders including trade unions, airline regulations and procedures (e.g. after the 9/11 attacks), the total labour costs versus the total aircraft costs indicating capital intensity, easyJet's financial reserves, and its position in comparison to competitors reflected in easyJet's market share and number of destinations.

The SHRM context model: the HR strategy scan (six-component model)

The model presented in this chapter can be used to perform a context analysis of an organization. This analysis can be used for several purposes, including the determination of the major factors for the development of a new HR strategy and the evaluation of the existing HR strategy and practices in a given organization. The strategy scan is relevant for determining the degree of fit between HRM and the context of an organization. The underlying assumption is that better fit leads to better performance (Boon, 2008). The model is based on theoretical building blocks and prior SHRM models for contextual analysis, including the model by Beer et al. (1984), Baron and Kreps (1999) and Paauwe (2004). The model stresses the importance of the organizational context for designing the HR strategy of an organization. The alignment between the organizational context and the HR strategy will be discussed using the four different types of fit (strategic, internal, organizational and environmental) summarized earlier in the chapter.

The strategy scan is built on an external and internal contextual analysis. And the model contains six components that can be summarized as follows:

1. *The external general market context* includes the macroeconomic situation and the labour market conditions in the country or region in which the organization is operating.
2. *The external population market context* includes the competition (e.g. number of competitors), the maturity of the market and new developments in technology.
3. *The external general institutional context* includes country legislation, EU legislation if the organization operates within the EU, and societal norms and values (e.g. general attitudes towards part-time work, work–life balance issues and diversity).
4. *The external population institutional context* includes the nature of the CBAs (for example, branch of industry CBAs or company CBAs), the influence of social partners (works councils

and trade unions), the influence of other relevant sector-specific stakeholders (e.g. Greenpeace in the case of an oil company), and sector-specific regulations, for example related to health and safety procedures in the work design.

5 *The internal organization context (configuration)* includes the history of the organization, the organizational culture, the technology and systems used, the ownership structure and the people employed (workforce).
6 *The HR strategy* relates to managing employees through the HR practices of: (1) selection and recruitment, (2) appraisal and performance management (PM), (3) compensation, (4) training and development, and (5) employee participation.

These six components are discussed in more detail in the next sections.

The external general market context

The external general market context represents the market mechanisms that affect all the organizations in a specific country or region. The most important elements for the strategy scan are the *macroeconomic situation* and the labour market situation. *The macroeconomic situation* is, for example, reflected in the economic growth or decline of a country. Economic growth generally creates opportunities for companies to invest in new products and markets, while a market decline often goes hand in hand with decreasing consumer trust and therefore decreased consumption, and less willingness of financiers (banks and shareholders) to invest in an organization. Nowadays, other macroeconomic conditions can seriously affect an organization; for example, oil prices and value of the dollar or euro. Increasing oil prices as a result of global shortages have a negative effect on airline companies and a positive effect on oil companies' profits. The high value of the euro in comparison to the US dollar has a potential negative effect on EU exports, simply because EU products and services become too expensive for US consumers.

The financial crisis of 2008/2009 and the following global economic crisis of 2009 have had a major impact on organizations and the markets in which the organizations operate: for example, in early 2009 the sales of some car companies such as Toyota decreased by 20–40 per cent in various countries worldwide. Dramatically low sales resulted in record losses, causing workforce reductions (downsizing). The financial crisis also resulted in less leeway for company investments, directly affecting R&D, innovation and HR investments in employee training and development. The first thing organizations are most likely to do in times of crisis is to stop recruitment and cut training expenses.

Another important factor is *the labour market situation* in a country or region. The ageing population in Europe has created enormous challenges for attracting and retaining qualified personnel in the next couple of decades. Labour shortages can result in wage increases (higher labour costs), labour intensification because some vacancies cannot easily be filled so those employed have to work harder to do the job (e.g. in health care), and the selection of less qualified employees because there is no other alternative for an organization. The latter outcomes can have a direct impact on the performance of an organization in terms of efficiency (cost-effectiveness) and quality.

In Europe there is an organization tendency that can be labelled 'downgrading of occupations' (or jobs) in specific branches of industry as a result of increased competition. The mail and express delivery industry, often formerly owned by national governments, has undergone a tremendous change through privatization and increased competition created by new entrants. The TNT Group and Deutsche Post have proposed lower wages and employee benefits for postal staff to keep up with the competition, directly affecting employment security and family incomes. These tendencies may represent a further distinction between valuable core employees (e.g. skilled workers, managers and specialists) and less valuable peripheral employees who are often unskilled and easily replaced.

Eurofound – the European Foundation for the Improvement of Living and Working Conditions, an official EU body – reports on employment, working conditions, work–life balance, industrial relations (IR) and partnership, social cohesion and other labour market characteristics within the EU. Eurofound emphasizes the following important trends in the European labour market:

- An increased attention to flexicurity, representing the employer's need for flexibility which has to be balanced with the workers' need for security.
- Europe's coming of age, emphasizing that European citizens are now living longer than ever before in combination with fewer children being born, puts pressure on social systems and those employed. Stimulating workers to work longer and to increase the pension entitlement age are realistic options that are being studied and suggested to solve some of these issues.
- The need for further increasing labour market participation of women through flexible work arrangements (e.g. those returning to work and for those who are willing to expand their contract).

(www.eurofound.europa.eu)

The external population market context

The analysis of the external population market context of an organization first requires the determination and definition of the population of a specific organization. In most cases, the population of an organization consists of the *direct competitors* of the organization. These competitors usually constitute the branch of industry in which an organization is operating. In other words, the population probably overlaps the branch of industry by 80–90 per cent. However, the population of an organization can also include suppliers and customers since the organizational boundaries between suppliers, producers and consumers are disappearing. Therefore, we need to take a good look at the *suppliers* and the *consumers* of the organization as well to fully determine this component in the strategy scan.

The nature of the component is actually closely related to what Paauwe (2004) calls the PMT dimension company (as previously discussed). The *market* of an organization in a population can be determined by:

- the number of competitors in the market;
- the maturity of the market in which the organization is operating;
- the growth or decline of the market;
- the prospects for the market in terms of growth opportunities and market share.

Another crucial element is the *technology* used in the sector or business. The technology in a given industry represents the type of hardware (e.g. machines), software (e.g. certain types of management information system) and communication systems used. The leading principle here is the way the production or services are set up. For example, whether farmers still milk their cows by hand (the old-fashioned way), with a milking machine (the more common way), or with a fully automated and computer-steered milking machine (the future way?).

Finally, it is important to study the nature of the *products* produced or *services* delivered; for example, in terms of how many products or services (fast-moving consumer products versus cars) are made/created by an organization. Furthermore, it is relevant to study the nature of the organization's output since some of the output is semi-product/semi-service as a result of developments in IT. The latter issue refers to the trend of products becoming more service-like and services becoming more product-like.

The external general institutional context

The third component in the strategy scan is focused on the general external institutional environment of an organization. An important distinction related to the features of this component can be made between laws/legislation and norms and values; the latter being less concrete and often not written down, while legislation is on paper and can be used in court. There are often major differences between countries with respect to legislation. In one country there can be laws on works councils; for example, the obligation to have a works council installed for every organization with more than 50 employees as is the case in the Netherlands, while in other countries there are no laws on works councils whatsoever (e.g. the USA). Multinational companies operating in different institutional contexts are confronted with and challenged by these rule diversities. General *legislation* potentially affecting the HR strategy and policies of an organization in a given context is often related to:

- working conditions (e.g. maximum number of working hours);
- employment security (e.g. unemployment or disability);
- legal position of employees (e.g. legislation on discrimination).

It is important to note that there is a shift from national to EU legislation in Europe. This means that the majority of general laws are no longer determined on a national level, but on an EU level. On the one hand, this makes life a lot easier for MNCs because of an apparently converging labour legislation tendency throughout the EU. However, on the other hand, there is also a tendency to increase the number of laws passed by the EU, making it more complicated for organizations operating in Europe.

The other part of the external general institutional context refers to the *societal norms and values* in a given context. A good work–life balance (e.g. reflected in both partners working part time; dual-career couples), in combination with extensive leisure time of up to four- to six-week vacations per year, is generally seen as very important by many employees in continental northern Europe (in particular in countries such as the Netherlands, Denmark, Sweden and Norway), in contrast to the Anglo-American countries where building a career and working almost the whole year through is much more important than leisure time and long vacations. In the USA, for example, a yearly ten-day vacation for employees is quite common, whereas in the Netherlands employees have a minimum of 23 days per annum. This issue reflects differences in norms and values related to work based on institutional differences between countries embedded in societies. Societal norms and values can have many faces and are therefore often difficult to grasp, in particular when you are an outsider from another society. The notions on culture shock, relevant when sending employees abroad (expatriates), refer to issues that have to do with being confronted with other societal norms and values. Organizations that neglect the societal norms and values run the risk of frustrating local employees, local stakeholders (e.g. trade unions), local government and consumers. Chapter 13 on IHRM contains further discussion on global and local HR strategies of MNCs and expatriate management.

The external population institutional context

Organizations are also confronted with specific institutional mechanisms linked to their population. These population-linked institutional mechanisms include:

- *CBAs* in terms of their scope (e.g. the percentage of employees that are affected by the CBA) and their nature (e.g. a sector CBA or a company-specific CBA);
- *sector-specific legislation* related to working conditions (e.g. rules on health and safety);
- *trade union and works council influence* (the role and legal position of the employee representatives);
- *other relevant stakeholders* that affect the nature of the business in the organization and the work of employees (e.g. patient interest groups in the context of health care).

It is important to take into account that all members of a population are more or less confronted with similar types of institutional mechanisms as described above. Some organizations can be better in dealing with these mechanisms than others because of a better adaptation or alignment to their institutional environment (Paauwe and Boselie, 2005). The (dynamic) capabilities may provide some organizations (sustained) competitive advantage in a given population, because these 'leaders' are better in dealing with institutional constraints than other organizations in the same population (Mirvis, 1997).

The internal organization context (configuration)

Beer et al. (1984) were among the first to acknowledge the importance of (internal) situational factors for HRM policy choices, including workforce characteristics, management philosophy, task technology and business conditions. Paauwe (1991) also acknowledges internal contextual factors, including technology and the organizational structure. Later on, Paauwe (2004) extended his model with the configuration as one of the three key dimensions determining strategic choices in HRM. Finally, Baron and Kreps (1999) make a distinction between four internal factors that affect the HRM strategy and policies: technology, workforce, culture and strategy.

The internal organization context is also called the *configuration* of an organization. Key elements in the strategy scan include the history of the organization, the organizational culture, the technology and systems used, the ownership structure and the people employed (workforce). The history of an organization is embedded in the 'organization DNA', which represents the way the organization is now as a result of historical events. This is called 'gestalt' in German and reflects the key characteristics of an organization. *The history of an organization* can be determined by an analysis of the following aspects:

- The year of the foundation of the organization and the related 'zeitgeist' (spirit of the time) of the foundation. For example, organizations founded in the 1940s are often heavily manufacturing-oriented, organizations founded in the 1970s marketing-oriented and organizations from the 1990s IT-oriented and technology-driven. An organization's 'blueprint' is heavily determined by its historical roots.
- The role and philosophy of the founding father(s). For example, IKEA's founding father's philosophy on the firm's cultural heritage and organizational culture.
- Critical incidents that affected the organization and its strategic decision making; for example, manifested in the case of a merger, acquisition, leadership crisis, company scandal and/or reorganizations.

Another important element of the configuration component in the strategy scan is the *organizational culture*. The culture of an organization is embedded in the values and belief systems within the organization that are often based on a management philosophy of how to run the business. Organizational culture is a difficult concept to grasp and many scholars have attempted to capture it in a model. There is a general consensus that the organizational culture is important for the success of an organization. However, there is no general framework available for defining the concept in detail. Hofstede's (1984) model is probably the best-known approach, but also Schein's (1988) model is broadly used and applied. The organizational culture includes the norms, values, habits, rituals and routines within an organization that are embedded in the heads and hearts of employees. Some of these elements are deeply embedded and difficult to grasp, while other elements are more superficial and therefore easier to identify.

The *technology* used within the organization represents the production systems, service systems, hardware and software systems, and communication systems applied in the organization. A large distribution centre supplying consumer goods for a network of over 300 warehouses uses a dynamic picking system (DPS). This DPS enables the distribution centre to store and collect consumer goods for specific stores when they run out of those products. The highly automated DPS determines the work design within this distribution store, requiring basic hardware and software skills of employees who are employed within the centre. The introduction of the DPS initially resulted in workforce reduction because fewer employees were required to do the job. At the same time, other requirements were needed for employees operating within the new system. This illustrates the relationship between technology used in an organization and its workforce.

The *ownership structure* of an organization is also an important element of an organization. Most large organizations operate on the stock market. The shareholders are the owners and the shares are traded via the stock market. In many cases, large financial institutions (e.g. pension funds, insurance companies and banks) are the main shareholders of an organization trading on the stock market. Some organizations are not traded on the stock market; instead, they are family-owned or owned by a foundation. Family ownership, for example family-owned organizations such as the Dutch brewery Bavaria, have no obligations to publicly publish strategy details about their business activities and organizational performance. This creates more leeway for managers of family-owned organizations. But there are many other forms of ownership structure; for example, the so-called cooperatives. The Dutch Rabobank is a leading bank in Europe in mortgages and Internet banking. It does not have shareholders because of its cooperative ownership structure. Instead, it has members who are organized locally (or regionally). Other examples of large cooperatives can be found in the agricultural sector, including flower auctions and milk product producers. Finally, there are the so-called public organizations. These public organizations are 'owned' by the government and indirectly by the citizens of a country. Actually, there is no real ownership in the sense of owning shares, but there is a governance responsibility linked to these organizations. And in most cases the national or local government is in charge of the governance. The ownership structure has a direct effect on strategic decision making and HR strategies. For example, cooperatives cannot be bought by others in contrast to organizations trading on the stock market. Agency theory (Jensen and Meckling, 1976) suggests a tension between those who own an organization (the principals) and those who run the organization (the agents). This theory suggests that the principals and agents can have opposite interests in the way the organization is managed. The principals, for example, might be interested in increasing profits for increasing their yearly dividends and value of shares, while the agents might be primarily interested in new investments in markets, products and R&D. The theory suggests there are ways to solve these conflicting interests by using performance incentives for the agents in line with the principals' interests. We return to this issue in Chapter 9 on compensation.

Beer et al. (1984) and Baron and Kreps (1999) both stress the importance of the *workforce* factor. The workforce of an organization is the pool of people employed in it at a certain time. Organizations with thousands of employees worldwide are not capable of simply substituting everyone employed. In other words, an organization is stuck with its current employees to a large extent. Reorganization and downsizing might result in a 10 per cent workforce reduction; 90 per cent of the employees will thus stay within that organization. The key characteristics of an organization's workforce will therefore heavily affect the organization and the shaping of HRM in that organization. These key characteristics can be summarized as follows:

- The average employee age and the distribution of people among the different age groups (employee age).
- The number and percentage of young employees within the organization (an ageing workforce measure).
- The number and percentage of female workers in the organization (gender).
- The level of education of all employees (employee education level).
- The different nationalities and ethnic minorities in the organization (diversity).
- The work experience of the employees in terms of number of years working experience and work experience itself (work experience).
- Trade union membership within the organization measured by a percentage of the total workforce (trade union membership).

Organizations with an average employee age of above 50 might run the risk of becoming too expensive in terms of labour costs, incapable of attracting new and young employees, and risk skilled losses when this generation of workers retires in the near future. These key characteristics can be used to help develop the right HR policies that take into account future developments.

HR strategy

The *HR strategy* is one of the functional silos related to the overall business strategy of an organization. There are different types of relationship between the business strategy and the HR strategy as, for example, suggested by Golden and Ramanujam (1985): administrative linkage (no strategic alignment whatsoever), one-way linkage (the business strategy determines the HR strategy), two-way linkage (there is a two-way interaction between the business strategy and the HR strategy) and the integrative linkage (there is a full alignment between the business strategy and the HR strategy). The HR strategy scan starts with defining the overall *business strategy*. What is the organization's approach and intention towards cost-effectiveness, quality, innovation, flexibility and social corporate responsibility? Is the organization's aim to be a cost leader or is the organization aiming to be the most innovative firm? easyJet's business strategy is mainly built on combing cost reduction and service quality principles in one overall business strategy. The strategy of easyJet is operationalized using the Internet (web-based organizing), the standardization of work processes (e.g. limited aircraft types) and high reliability (flights on time and low risks of luggage loss). However, a pharmaceutical company such as AstraZeneca might have a completely different business strategy, with much more focus on innovation and R&D for inventing new medicines.

List of business strategy characteristics

What are the organization's goals and how important are these goals with respect to:

- efficiency and cost reduction;
- product and service quality;
- growth (e.g. market, sales, firm size, profits);

- innovation and R&D (new products, services and markets);
- focus versus differentiation (niche market versus multiple markets);
- flexibility (capability to adapt and adopt);
- health and safety;
- environmental pollution;
- corporate social responsibility?

Next, the strategy scan focuses on determining the HR strategy using five key HR practices:

1 recruitment and selection;
2 training and development;
3 appraisal and PM;
4 compensation;
5 employee participation.

In other words, how are employees recruited and selected, how are they developed, how are they monitored and evaluated, how are they paid and how are they involved in decision making? These five key HR practices are discussed in detail in Chapters 7–11. After a description of both the overall business strategy and the HR strategy, the researcher is challenged to determine the linkage between the two using the framework of Golden and Ramanujam (1985) distinguishing four levels: (1) administrative linkage, (2) one-way linkage, (3) two-way linkage, and (4) integrative linkage. The administrative linkage is the lowest level of possible relationship between the business strategy and the HR strategy. The integrative linkage is the most advanced relationship, probably only found in a very limited number of organizations.

Now we have all the building blocks for the six-component model. The only thing left to do is to explain and discuss the link between the components using the concept of fit.

The model

The HR strategy scan contains six components. Four components are external factors representing the external context of an organization (the external general market component, the external population market component, the external general institutional component and the external population institutional component). Two components are internal factors representing the internal context of the organization. The configuration is one of the two internal factors; the HR strategy together with the business strategy is the other internal factor.

The model incorporates the following underlying assumptions:

- The four external factors/components and the configuration affect the HR strategy (whether or not through the overall business strategy).
- The external general market context affects both the external population market context and the HR strategy.
- The external general institutional context affects both the external population institutional context and the HR strategy.

The relationship between the six components can be characterized by the concept of fit. The fit between the configuration and the HR strategy is the organizational fit. The HR strategy scan is focused on determining the alignment (fit) between the HR strategy and the configuration of the organization as described earlier in this chapter. The alignment between the five HR practices in the model is the internal fit. The internal fit describes the degree to which the five practices are aligned with each other. For example, what is the fit between the selection (signalling certain firm expectations), the employee development and the rewards linked to employee performance?

The relationship between the external market components and the HR strategy is labelled the strategic fit. The relationship between the external institutional components and the HR strategy is the institutional fit. The model presented here is rooted in the work by Beer et al. (1984) (see Figure 2.1) and Paauwe (2004) (see Figure 2.4). The model of the HR strategy scan is presented in Figure 2.5.

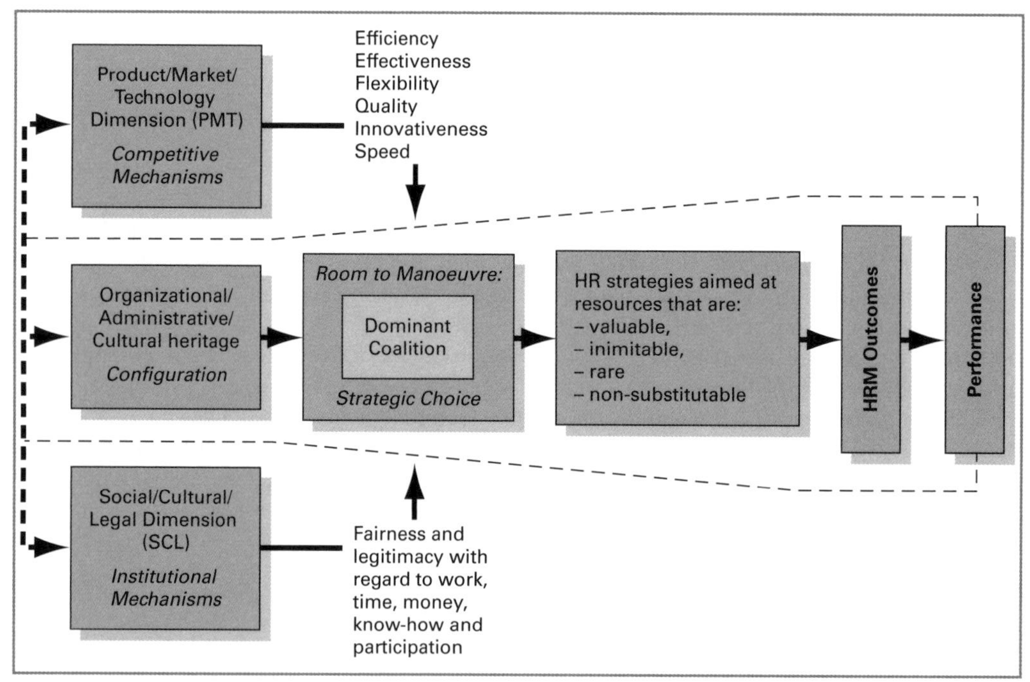

FIGURE 2.4 The contextually-based HR theory
Source: Paauwe (2004, Figure 5.1, p. 91).

For those who are interested in a more detailed and in-depth HR analysis of an organization the following other types of fit can be added to the analysis in the HR strategy scan. First, Baron and Kreps (1999) make a distinction between *single employee consistency* (similar to the concept of internal fit in the HR strategy scan), *among employee consistency* and *temporal consistency*. The latter two types of fit (or consistency) can be added to the analysis. Consistency among employees represents the extent to which the HR policies and practices are equally distributed among employees that have similar tasks and jobs in the organization. Inconsistency among employees may occur when, for example, employees with the same job, level of education, work experience and job performance get paid differently. This type of inconsistency may result in negative employee perceptions reflected in perceived distributive injustice (Baron and Kreps, 1999). Temporal consistency represents the degree to which HR policies and practices remain relatively stable over time. Promises made to employees (e.g. an internal promotion) in the past cannot simply be broken without negative impact on HR outcomes in terms of employee trust and commitment to the organization.

Second, Boon (2008) introduces the concept of *adaptation fit*. This concept reflects the dynamic component that is missing in the majority of fit models. Adaptation fit is focused on the

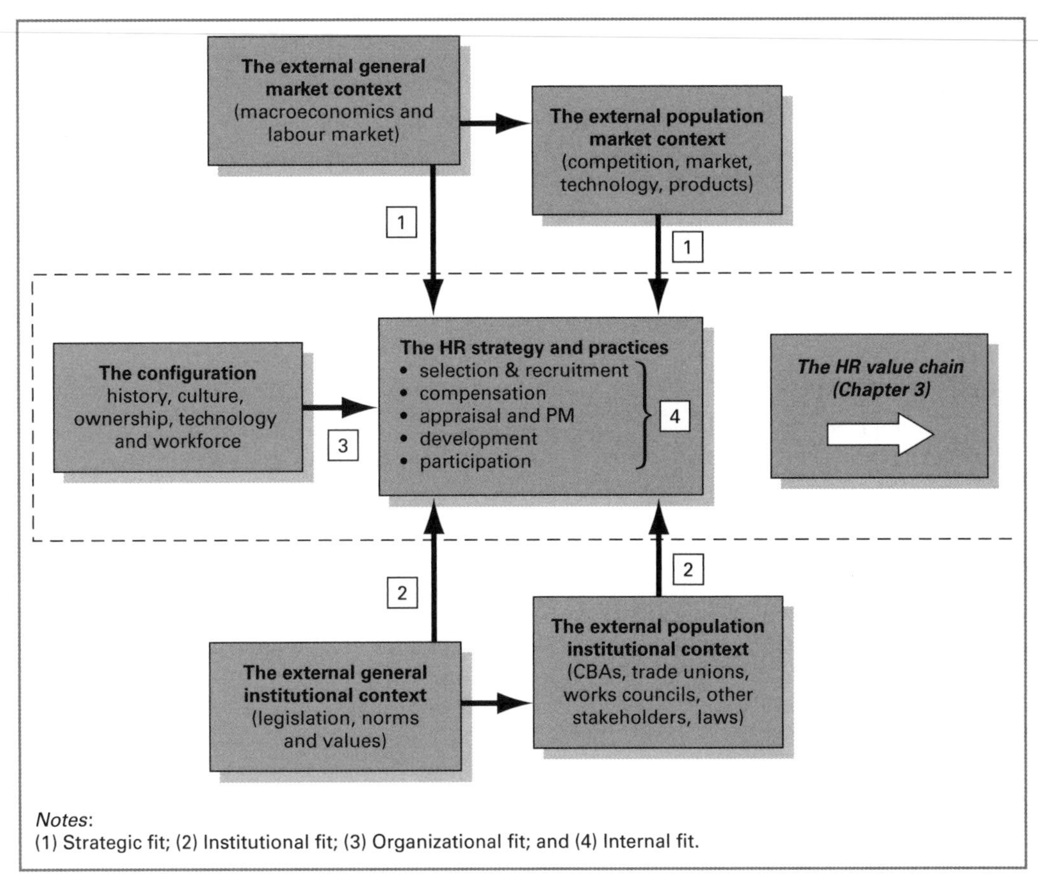

FIGURE 2.5 The strategy scan: the six-component model

degree to which an organization is capable of changing its HR strategy and policies to changes in the internal and external context.

Additional suggestions for the HR scan analysis

Look for *critical incidents* related to a specific organization in the archives of newspapers. These critical incidents may include corporate scandals (e.g. Enron and Siemens), mergers and acquisitions (e.g. the merger between Air France and KLM), and the appointment of a new CEO. Information on critical incidents can also be found on the Internet. However, always be very critical towards the reliability of Internet information.

Interviews with employees of an organization can be a rich source of data collection. There are a couple of issues that need to be taken into account when deciding to use interviews as an information source:

- Try to include different perspectives; for example, HR managers, line managers and employees, as suggested by Gerhart et al. (2000), in order to avoid a *single respondent perspective*.

- Try to avoid *socially desirable answers* by framing the interview questions in the right way. HR respondents, for example, tend to be more positive about themselves than non-HR respondents about HRM (Boselie and Paauwe, 2005).
- The latter issue is related to the notion of distinguishing *'ist'* and *'soll'* answers. The German concept of 'soll' refers to the desirable situation, while the concept of 'ist' refers to the actual situation. In the strategy scan the emphasis is on the actual situation ('ist').
- Try to make use of multiple sources in the analysis for *triangulation* purposes. The reliability and validity of research improves when multiple sources are used; for example, using interviews, annual reports, internal policy reports, president's letters, newspaper articles about the organization and observations.

Trends over time

Looking at the external environment of organizations, there have been some major shifts since the 1970s. In the 1970s the majority of Western European countries were characterized by a strong emphasis on employee democracy and the role of social partners in strategic decision making with regard to HRM. Social partners such as trade unions and works councils were very influential and the external institutional context played an important role in determining HRM in organizations through these social partners. The 1980s can be characterized by increased competition and globalization, with a strong emphasis on the external market context. Free market principles dominated the agenda of most organizations and competition became the central theme of attention. Downsizing (workforce reduction), reorganizations, mergers and acquisitions with major implications for workers became popular tools in an attempt to strengthen an organization's position.

In the 1990s IT and the Internet were added, resulting in further globalization and the rise of a new sector in IT products and services. Technological developments resulted in new ways of organizing using the intranet and the Internet for communication, but also as a way of delivering products and services. The rise of call centres is an illustration of this IT impact on organizing work in a totally different way.

Since 2000 the financial sector has dominated organizations' mindsets. The global financial crisis that started in 2008 could be an indication of a new trend characterized by more legislation affecting an organization's leeway and a stronger role of local governments in controlling organizations. Free market principles are now seriously debated. These trends have a direct impact on the strategy scan. In summary, the 1970s put most emphasis on the external institutional environment, the 1980s created a shift towards more emphasis on the external market, the 1990s led to the introduction of major technological changes affecting organizations and the work design within organizations; after 2000, financial services dominated the organization's agenda putting even more emphasis on the external market component, while the financial crisis of 2008 might result in a shift back towards more legislation and a bigger role of governments.

The next chapter focuses on the added value of HRM.

summary

- The shaping of an organization, for example reflected in its structure, culture, systems and HRM, is affected by the context of that specific organization.
- A better fit between the organization and its context is thought to be more effective than the lack of fit or a misfit.
- Fit is an important feature of strategic HRM aimed at the alignment of HRM with the organizational context.
- The strategy is an organization's intention to achieve certain goals through planned alignment (fit) between the organization and its environment (context).
- Strategic HRM is focused on the alignment or fit between the strategy of an organization and the HR strategy of that organization.
- The 'best-fit' school assumes that HRM is more effective when it is aligned with its internal and external organization context.
- The 'best-practice' school assumes that certain HR practices (best practices) are universally applicable and successful.
- Context represents the set of facts or circumstances that surround the organization.
- The internal organization context consists of the unique organization history, the administrative heritage and the organization's culture.
- The external organization context consists of market mechanisms and institutional mechanisms.
- A further distinction can be made between the general environment (or general external context) and the population environment (or external population context).
- There are three institutional mechanisms: coercive, normative and mimetic.
- The internal and external context determines the degree of leeway in the strategic decision making of an organization, including HR decision making. This is also called strategic choice.
- Strategic or vertical fit refers to the alignment between the business strategy and the HR strategy.
- Internal or horizontal fit refers to the alignment between individual HR practices towards a coherent and consistent HR system.
- Organizational fit refers to the alignment between HRM and other organizational systems.
- Environmental fit refers to the alignment between HRM and the institutional environment of an organization.
- The HR strategy scan can be applied to analyse the organization's context and the degree to which HRM is aligned to it. The model builds on the assumption that more fit(s) leads to better organization performance. In other words, better fit is associated with better organization performance.
- High performance of an organization according to the 'best-fit' school in HRM is reflected in: strategic fit + organization fit + internal fit + environmental fit.

Glossary of key terms

Best-fit proposition states that specific HR practices are not universally applicable and successful when used, but can only be successful in case of a fit between HRM and the context.

Best-practice proposition states that specific HR practices are universally applicable and successful when used.

Business strategy is the system of an organization's important choices; a system that could be well integrated around common concerns or which might have various links and foul-ups.

Configuration is the cultural administrative heritage of an organization.

Context represents the internal and external organizational environment.

Environmental fit is the alignment between the HR strategy and the institutional environment of an organization.

General environment represents the broad external context of an organization, for example represented in the macroeconomic situation in which an organization is situated.

HR strategy is one of the functional silos of the business strategy specifically aimed at achieving the organizational goals through optimal HRM.

Institutional mechanisms are mechanisms that stem from legislation (coercive), professional norms (normative) and imitation as a result of uncertainty or fashion (mimetic).

Internal or horizontal fit is the alignment between individual HR practices.

Market mechanisms are mechanisms that stem from the markets in which an organization operates, the products or services an organization creates and the technological developments.

Organizational fit is the alignment between HRM and other organizational systems and the configuration.

Population environment represents the external context of an organization that is directly linked to the population or organizational field.

Population or organizational field is a community of organizations that partakes of a common meaning system and whose participants interact more frequently or fatefully with one another than with actors outside the field.

Strategic choice is the degree of leeway organizations have in strategic decision making given the organizational context.

Strategic or vertical fit is the alignment between the business strategy and the HR strategy.

Strategic human resource management (SHRM) is focused on the alignment or fit between the strategy of an organization and the HR strategy of that organization.

Strategy is an organization's intention to achieve certain goals through planned alignment (fit) between the organization and its environment.

 ***Team task***

The HR strategy scan approach

First step: general description of the organization

- What is the core business of the organization in terms of products, services and markets?
- What are the most important developments of the last 5–10 years, both inside and outside the organization?
- Find out more about the history of the organization, for example through studying annual reports, searching for documents and books in the library, and/or searching for information on the Internet.
- What are the key characteristics of the organization in terms of size (number of employees), yearly sales and yearly profits?

Second step: description of the general environment

- What are the most important developments in the general market environment over the last couple of years in terms of macroeconomics (e.g. increased globalization) and the labour market (e.g. labour market shortages and the ageing population)?
- What are the most important developments in the general institutional environment over the last couple of years in terms of societal norms and values (e.g., attitudes towards part-time work, work–life balance, labour market participation of women and diversity) and legislation (e.g. related to employee protection)?

Third step: description of the population environment:

- What is the nature of the business and, related to that, the nature of the customers (e.g. regular consumers versus industrial customers)?
- Find out more about the nature of the competition within the population; for example, whether there are many competitors or not.
- What kind of products or services are delivered and, linked to that, what are the latest developments with respect to these products and services?
- What kind of technology is used?
- Find out more about the CBAs relevant to the organization. What is the scope of the CBAs, who is involved in the negotiation and what is the impact of them on the organization?
- What is the influence of trade unions on the organization?
- What is the influence of works councils on the organization?
- What other (external) stakeholders are involved that influence the organization, and the HR strategy in particular?
- What specific laws are operational for the population of the organization; for example, related to working conditions, work procedures, health and safety?

Fourth step: description of the business strategy and the HR strategy:

- What is the overall business strategy? (If available, include president's letters, annual reports and newspaper articles on the organization's strategy.)
- Describe the HRM in the organization in terms of its recruitment and selection, employee development, appraisal and PM, compensation and benefits and employee involvement.

Fifth step: analysis:

1. Determine the linkage between the business strategy and the HR strategy.
2. Determine the degree of fit between the four external components on the one hand and the HR strategy on the other hand (strategic fit and institutional fit).
3. Determine the degree of fit between the configuration and the HR strategy (organizational fit).
4. Determine the degree of fit between the five HR practices within the organization (internal fit).
5. Determine the overall alignment between the HR strategy and the (internal and external) context of the organization. The basic idea behind the overall analysis is 'the more fits, the better it is' in terms of performance (see Boon, 2008).

Learning checklist

After studying this chapter, you should be able to do the following:

- Understand the concept of strategy in contemporary organizations.
- Understand the difference between best-practice and best-fit approaches in HRM.
- Identify the four types of fit in HRM.
- Recognize the impact of contextual factors (general environment and population environment; market mechanisms, institutional mechanisms and configuration) on the shaping of employment relationships in organizations.
- Examine and analyse the context of an organization using the model presented in this chapter.

References

Baron, J.M. and Kreps, D.M. (1999) *Strategic Human Resources: Frameworks for General Managers*. New York: Wiley.

Becker, B.E. and Huselid, M.A. (2006) Strategic human resource management: where do we go from here?, *Journal of Management*, 32(6): 898–925.

Beer, M., Spector, B., Lawrence, P., Mills, D.Q. and Walton, R. (1984) *Human Resource Management: A General Manager's Perspective*. New York: Free Press.

Boon, C. (2008) HRM and fit: survival of the Fittest!? Dissertation, Rotterdam: Erasmus Research Institute for Management (ERIM).

Boselie, P. (2002) Human resource management, work systems and performance: a theoretical-empirical approach. Dissertation, Tinbergen Institute. Amsterdam: Thela Thesis.

Boselie, P. and Paauwe, J. (2005). Human resource function competencies in European multinational companies, *Personnel Review*, 34(5): 550–66.

Boselie, P., Dietz, G. and Boon, C. (2005) Commonalities and contradictions in HRM and performance research, *Human Resource Management Journal*, 15(3): 67–94.

Boxall, P. and Purcell, J. (2003) *Strategy and Human Resource Management*. New York: Palgrave Macmillan.

Boxall, P. and Purcell, J. (2008) *Strategy and Human Resource Management*, 2nd edn. New York: Palgrave Macmillan.

Child, J. (1972) Organisational structure, environment and performance: the role of strategic choice, *Sociology*, 6(1): 1–22.

Child, J. (1997) Strategic choice in the analysis of action, structure, organizations and environment: retrospect and prospect, *Organization Studies*, 18(1): 43–76.

Deephouse, D. L. (1999) To be different, or to be the same? It's a question (and theory) of strategic balance, *Strategic Management Journal*, 20(2): 147–66.

Delery, J.E. (1998) Issues of fit in strategic human resource management: implications for research, *Human Resource Management Review*, 8(3): 289–309.

Delery, J.E. and Doty, D.H. (1996) Modes of theorizing in strategic human resource management: tests of universalistic, contingency, and configurational performance predictions, *Academy of Management Journal*, 39(4): 802–35.

De Wit, B. and Meyer, R. (1998) *Strategy: Process, Content, Context – An International Perspective*, 2nd edn. London: Thomson.

DiMaggio, P.J. and Powell, W.W. (1983) The iron cage revisited: institutional isomorphism and collective rationality in organizational fields, *American Sociological Review*, 48(2): 147–60.

DiMaggio, P.J. and Powell, W.W. (eds) (1991) *The New Institutionalism in Organizational Analysis*. Chicago: University of Chicago Press.

Fombrun, C., Tichy, N.M. and Devanna, M.A. (eds) (1984) *Strategic Human Resource Management*. New York: Wiley.

Gerhart, B., Wright, P.M. and McMahan, G. (2000) Measurement error in research on the human resource and firm performance relationship: further evidence and analysis, *Personnel Psychology*, 53(4): 855–72.

Golden, K.A. and Ramanujam, V. (1985) Between a dream and a nightmare: on the integration of the human resource management and strategic planning processes, *Human Resource Management*, 24: 429–52.

Hofstede, G. (1984) *Culture's Consequences: International Differences in Work-related Values*. London: Sage.

Jensen, M. and Meckling, W. (1976) Theory of the firm: managerial behavior, agency costs, and ownership structure, *Journal of Financial Economics*, 3: 306–60.

Lawrence, J.W. and Lorsch, P.R. (1967) *Organization and Environment*. Boston, MA: Harvard University Press.

Miles, R. and Snow, C. (1984) Designing strategic human resource systems, *Organizational Dynamics*, Summer: 36–52.

Mintzberg, H. (1979) *The Structuring of Organizations*. London: Prentice Hall.

Mirvis, P.H. (1997) Human resource management: leaders, laggards, and followers, *Academy of Management Executive*, 11(2): 43–56.

Oliver, C. (1997) Sustainable competitive advantage: combining institutional and resource-based views, *Strategic Management Journal*, 18: 697–713.

Paauwe, J. (1991) Limitations to freedom: is there a choice for human resource management?, *British Journal of Management*, 2: 1–17.

Paauwe, J. (2004) *HRM and Performance: Achieving Long-term Viability*. Oxford: Oxford University Press.

Paauwe, J. and Boselie, P. (2003) Challenging 'strategic HRM' and the relevance of the institutional setting, *Human Resource Management Journal*, 13(3): 56–70.

Paauwe, J. and Boselie, P. (2005) HRM and performance: what's next?, *Human Resource Management Journal*, 15(4): 68–83.

Paauwe, J. and Boselie, P. (2007) HRM and societal embeddedness, in P. Boxall, J. Purcell and P.M. Wright (eds), *The Oxford Handbook of Human Resource Management*, Chapter 9, pp. 166–84. Oxford: Oxford University Press.

Pfeffer, J. (1998) *The Human Equation: Building Profits by Putting People First*. Boston, MA: Harvard Business School Press.

Porter, M.E. (1980) *Competitive Strategy*. New York: Free Press/Macmillan.

Porter, M.E. (1985) *Competitive Advantage: Creating and Sustaining Superior Performance*. New York: Free Press.

Regner, P. (2008) Strategy-as-practice and dynamic capabilities: steps towards a dynamic view of strategy, *Human Relations*, 61(4): 565–88.

Schein, E.H. (1988) *Organizational Culture and Leadership: A Dynamic View*. San Francisco, CA: Jossey-Bass.

Schuler, R.S. and Jackson, S.E. (1987) Linking competitive strategies with human resource management practices, *Academy of Management Executive*, 1(3): 209–13.

Scott, R. (ed.) (1994) *Institutional Environments and Organizations: Structural Complexity and Individualism*. Thousand Oaks, CA: Sage.

Strohmeier, S. (2007) Research in e-HRM: review and implications, *Human Resource Management Review*, 17(1): 19–37.

Verburg, R.M., Den Hartog, D.N. and Koopman, P.L. (2007) Configurations of human resource management practices: a model and test of internal fit, *International Journal of Human Resource Management*, 18(2): 184–208.

Wood, S. (1999) Human resource management and performance, *International Journal of Management Reviews*, 4(1): 367–413.

Woodward, J. (1965) *Industrial Organization: Theory and Practice*. Oxford: Oxford University Press.

Further reading

Beer, M., Spector, B., Lawrence, P., Mills, D.Q. and Walton, R. (1984) *Human Resource Management: A General Manager's Perspective*. New York: Free Press.

Fombrun, C., Tichy, N.M. and Devanna, M.A. (eds) (1984) *Strategic Human Resource Management*. New York: Wiley.

Paauwe, J. (2004) *HRM and Performance: Achieving Long-term Viability*. Oxford: Oxford University Press.

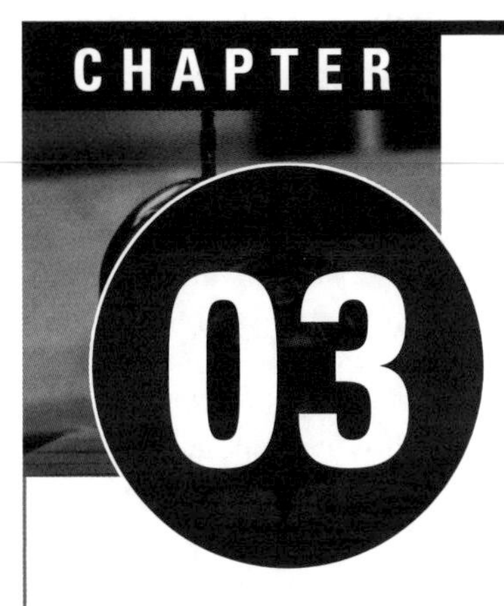

CHAPTER 03 Human Resource Management and Performance: Adding Value through People

❖ LEARNING OBJECTIVES

After studying this chapter, you should be able to do the following:

- ❖ Identify the potential impact of human resource management (HRM) on performance
- ❖ Review the concept of competitive advantage and sustained competitive advantage of an organization
- ❖ Outline the ultimate business goals of an organization
- ❖ Discuss human resource (HR) practices, HR outcomes and performance (the HR value chain)
- ❖ Understand the different stages of the HR value chain, including intended, actual and perceived HR practices

CASE STUDY: NOKIA

Nokia is a leading company in the mobile phone and telecommunications industry. The firm as we know it today is the result of a merger in 1967 between three businesses: Nokia Ab (paper industry and electricity generation), Finnish Rubber Works and Finnish Cable Works. A major crisis in the 1970s and 1980s forced the company to revise their business activities (a so called strategic reorientation). In the late 1990s major challenges and new business opportunities were identified mainly related to the emerging attention for mobile phones and the network industry (Merriden, 2001; Haiko, 2002). A national Finnish economic crisis (linked to a transition from a highly regulated economy to deregulation, liberalization and privatization) and an internal company crisis created a momentum for organizational change. General support from top management, government, social partners (trade unions) and employees enabled Nokia's transition in the 1990s to become a global player in telecommunications. Nokia today is a global market leader in mobile phones and telecommunications, ranked in *Business Week*'s Best Global Brands list of 2007 reflecting its global brand value. The firm is ranked 20th in *Fortune*'s World's Most Admired Companies list of 2007 and ranked 8th in *Business Week*'s top 100 Most Innovative Companies in 2006.

The success is also reflected in excellent financial performance and their market share worldwide. The organization is technology driven and its culture appears to be fully assimilated with networks and information technology. Nokia's corporate philosophy is focused on 'The Nokia Way' reflecting equality amongst employees, openness to people and sharing new ideas. Selective recruitment and selection, training and development, employee involvement and compensation are the key HR practices applied to achieve the organizational goals. Applicants are selected on the basis of their skills and knowledge in relationship to the job's technical requirements (person–job fit) and on the basis of the fit between a candidate and Nokia's culture (person–organization fit). Diversity management and the inclusion of minorities are key issues in the recruitment and selection process, because it is a corporate belief that a diverse workforce (different nationalities, men and women, different ethnic minorities) contributes to creativity, innovation and success. Training and development is mainly facilitated through intranet with eLearning opportunities and personal coaching by more experienced Nokia employees. Promotion opportunities are available online and called internal job market intranet. Employee involvement is reflected in job autonomy, self responsibility for personal development, regular feedback sessions, coaching new employees, regular employee surveys (called 'listening to you survey') and general participation in decision-making. The HR department operates a forum for all personnel management questions raised by employees (called 'ask HR' feedback channel). Every answer from the HR department on these questions is openly published on the intranet. Compensation within Nokia is mainly focused on two aspects: financial compensation in terms of high salaries, bonuses and stock options and compensation in terms of a variety of possibilities to create a personal work–life balance reflecting special attention to flexible working arrangement in line with employees' interests and preferences. Teleworking, mobile working, flexible working hours, study leaves and sabbaticals are illustrations of the latter HR practices applied to motivate Nokia's employees.

Overall, the firm can be characterized by a flat organizational structure and a culture that is highly affected by the technological nature of the business. The HR practices appear to be aligned with the technological environment and the company's culture. The downside of Nokia's success are the regular reorganizations and layoffs (e.g. in the Spring of 2003 downsizing 1800 jobs worldwide) in order to remain efficient and effective, at that time resulted in a 10 per cent job loss and several court cases, negatively affecting the corporate image, in particular at the home market in Finland.

Kloeg (2007)

? Discussion questions

Nokia applies specific HRM practices that focus on attracting and retaining good employees. These HR practices include selective recruitment and selection, extensive employee development, internal promotion opportunities and career development, employee involvement in decision making and pay for performance. Empirical research shows that these practices enhance employee satisfaction, organizational commitment, employee retention, employee presence (obverse of absenteeism) and loyalty (Boselie et al., 2005). In other words, part of Nokia's success might be caused by good people management. However, how do reorganizations and massive layoffs, for example in the spring of 2003, affect Nokia's employees in terms of their attitude and behaviour? And how do these critical incidents affect the employees' perception of Nokia's HR practices listed above? Finally, discuss how certain HR practices can overcome problems caused by reorganizations and massive layoffs. In other words, how can HRM contribute to firm performance and general employee well-being in times of organizational change (reorganization, downsizing)?

Introduction

According to Christian mythology, the Holy Grail was the cup used by Jesus at the Last Supper. It is said that this cup possesses special powers and those who drink from it will gain everlasting life and/or knowledge. Over time, the Grail myth has been an inspiration for numerous legends, including that of King Arthur, and more recently best-selling books such as J.R.R. Tolkien's *Lord of the Rings*, J.K. Rowling's *Harry Potter and The Philosopher's Stone* and Dan Brown's *The Da Vinci Code*. The Holy Grail was lost and the everlasting search for it has made the myth even stronger. The added value of HRM, also known as the HRM and performance debate, is often linked to 'the search for the Holy Grail', in a symbolic way of course, representing potential unique ways of managing people to gain organizational success. Some companies might have found their grail for success in people management and perhaps the Finnish Nokia is one of them. The unique organizational culture, the specific technological environment and the Finnish model of industrial relations (IR) in which multiple stakeholders (including trade unions and government) have a significant impact on the organization have contributed to Nokia's success. But how did they do it? What are their secrets of success, in particular with respect to people management? More than 15 years of worldwide empirical research on the added value of HRM and performance in different sectors shows that HRM matters. This chapter focuses on the contribution of HRM to the success of an organization using illustrations from practice and literature.

The majority of articles and books on HRM and performance start off with discussing HRM first and then link HRM to performance (Boselie et al., 2005). This book applies a reversed technique that is much more in line with goal-setting and strategic decision making. Firm performance is the starting point, reflected in organizations' search for competitive advantage and **sustained competitive advantage**. Determining (sustained) competitive advantage for an organization enables us to reveal the critical success factors that lead to success. These critical success factors – later on specified in critical HR goals and critical non-HR goals – are thought to be affected by employee attitudes (e.g. employee commitment and motivation) and employee behaviours (e.g. low employee absence rates). Finally, these employee attitudes and behaviours can be influenced by HRM. The reversed approach of what I will call 'the human resource value chain' can be summarized as follows (see also Figure 3.1):

1. Determine the competitive advantage and sustained competitive advantage of an organization.
2. Determine the critical factors that create (sustained) competitive advantage (e.g. high service quality, productivity, innovation, flexibility and social legitimacy).
3. Determine the employee attitudes, behaviours and cognitive factors that positively affect the critical success factors (e.g. high organizational commitment, motivation and overall job satisfaction).
4. Determine the HR **practices** that positively affect employee attitudes and behaviours (e.g. selective recruitment and selection, extensive training and development, performance-related pay (PRP), performance management (PM) and evaluation, employee participation and teamwork).

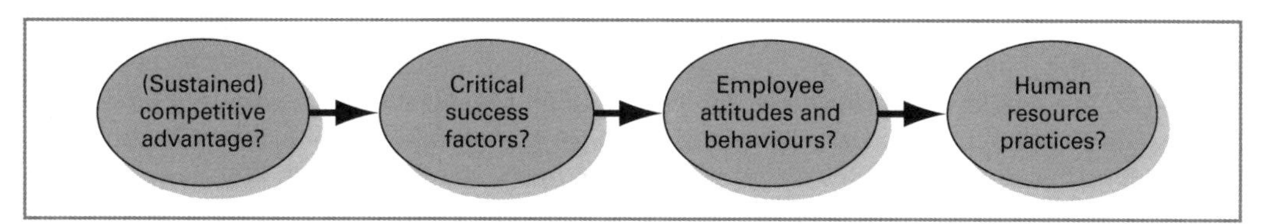

FIGURE 3.1 A reversed approach to creating an HR value chain

Stop and reflect

Can you think of any factors that created the (sustained) competitive advantage of Nokia in the last two decades?

The reversed approach in the creation of an HR value chain, starting with the **ultimate business goals**, pushes us to the heart of the performance debate and the search for the grail in HRM: the organization's search for (sustained) competitive advantage.

According to Delery and Shaw (2001), there is general agreement that (1) human capital can be a source of competitive advantage, (2) that HR practices have the most direct influence on the human capital of an organization, and (3) that the complex nature of HR systems of practice can enhance the inimitability of the system. Human resources are among an organization's most valuable assets. Since the late 1990s there has been a growing body of literature focused on creating (sustained) competitive advantage for organizations through the development of core competences, tacit knowledge and dynamic capabilities. One of the dominant theories in the debate on the added value of HRM is the *resource-based view (RBV) of the firm* (Boselie et al., 2005). The RBV has its roots in the early work of Penrose (1959) and was picked up and applied by Wernerfelt (1984) and Barney (1991) in the 1980s (Boselie and Paauwe, 2009). The RBV led to a change in strategic management thinking from an *'outside-in' approach* – with an emphasis on external, industry-based competitive issues (Porter, 1980) – to an *'inside-out' approach* (Baden-Fuller and Stopford, 1994), in which internal resources constitute the starting point for organizational success. Barney (1991) argues that sustained competitive advantage of an organization is determined by internal resources that are *valuable, rare, inimitable* and *non-substitutable*. Financial resources (equity, debt and retained earnings), physical resources (e.g. machines, a factory or cranes in a harbour), organizational resources (e.g. information technology (IT) systems, organizational design and management information systems) and human resources (in terms of their knowledge, skills, abilities and social network) are potential sources of organizational success when Barney's (1991) four criteria are met.

'Human resources are among an organization's most valuable assets'

The concept of *'value'* in the RBV represents the economic condition of a resource. For example, a supermarket chain owns property in terms of the local supermarket stores. The buildings and the building plot can be considered resources of an organization and represent economic value. Sometimes this value can be enormous as a result of the scarcity of building plots in villages and cities where the supermarket chain operates. The concept of *'rare'* in the RBV reflects the scarcity of a resource. Supermarket stores potentially possess economic value, for example, and can be rare when the property is built on a scarce building plot, in the centre of a big city. Banks and financiers will take these issues into account when an organization wants additional capital (loans, mortgages, etc.). The concept of *'inimitability'* in the RBV focuses on the degree to which resources are very hard to copy or imitate. Complex chemical production processes (e.g. within the German BASF) and oil refineries (e.g. within BP and Shell) are difficult for competitors and potential new entrants in particular to imitate. Inimitability can also be embedded in non-tangible resources; for example, the culture of an organization based on specific values, a unique history, the potential role of founding fathers and all other aspects that contribute to a social setting that influences the way an organization operates. The Swedish IKEA is an example of an organization with a unique organizational culture. The concept of *'non-substitutability'* in the RBV represents resources that 'are very hard to neutralize with other resources which will meet the same ends' (Boxall and Purcell, 2003: 75). Chemical engineers with both general and company-specific knowledge, skills and abilities are often very difficult to replace by others or by other resources (e.g. computers and IT systems).

RBV illustrations in practice

The US Black & Decker company, the world's largest producer of home improvement products including drills and sanders, created sustained competitive advantage through continuous innovation built around the same reliable electro motor, found in different home improvement products. The valuable and difficult to imitate resource of Black & Decker is the basic electro motor.

The Dutch amusement park *Efteling* – winner of the Applause Award for best park in the world (1992), winner of the Big-E Award as best park shows in the world (1999, 2001 and 2003) – continues to build its success on exploiting the heritage of illustrator Anton Pieck, who was the inspiration for the Fairy Tale Forest. The valuable, rare and difficult to imitate resource of the Efteling is embedded in Anton Pieck's heritage.

Barney and Wright (1998) discuss the **VRIO framework** – **v**alue, **r**areness, **i**nimitability and **o**rganization – based on earlier literature, consulting activities and input from executive training. This is a hierarchical framework for determining potential organizational success through internal resources. The first level in the framework focuses on the question of whether a resource is valuable or not. According to the model, internal resources without value are a source of competitive *dis*advantage. When resources are valuable the model suggests the possibility of competitive parity linked to normal performance. Valuable and rare resources can take an organization to the next level, creating temporary competitive advantage and above-average performance. The highest level is achieved when resources are valuable, rare and difficult to imitate. According to the VRIO framework, this is caused by intensive organizational support. The highest level potentially creates above-average performance and sustained (or long-term) competitive advantage. Only a few companies are capable of reaching this highest level.

The VRIO framework makes a distinction between different sorts of **performance** (see Table 3.1). The lowest level represents resources that do not have any value and are therefore likely to result in below-average performance. This does not automatically mean that these resources will have a dramatic negative impact on firm performance. Some resources need to be installed or in place because of legislation without any potential added-value effect; for example, health and safety procedures. Linked to the key business processes of an organization, the VRIO framework suggests it is best to avoid the use of resources that have no (economic) value and therefore do not contribute to firm performance. Nowadays, these types of resource are often outsourced to other organizations in order to reduce costs and focus on the core business activities of the organization. For resources that are valuable without being rare, for example in terms of labour supply or raw materials available for production processes, the framework suggests normal performance outcomes.

The RBV is mainly focused on the next two levels of the VRIO framework: the creation of (temporary) competitive advantage and (sustained) competitive advantage. The framework suggests that above-average performance can be created when resources are valuable, rare and difficult to imitate. Without any structural support by the organization, the framework suggests these three resource qualities are not likely to result in long-term success (sustained competitive advantage). For example, an organization that is first with the introduction of a new

Is a resource ...					
Valuable?	**Rare?**	**Difficult to imitate?**	**Supported by organization?**	**Competitive implications**	**Performance**
No	–	–	↕	Competitive Disadvantage	Below average
Yes	No	–		Competitive Parity	Normal
Yes	Yes	No		Temporary Competitive Advantage	Above average
Yes	Yes	Yes		Sustained Competitive Advantage	Above average

TABLE 3.1 The VRIO framework
Source: Barney and Wright (1998).

product (think of the introduction of the digital camera) might be quite successful, generating above-average performance for a couple of years (temporary competitive advantage). However, eventually competitors introduce their own products in response to the leading organization. The leader then runs the risk of losing the initial position and above-average performance outcomes if the unique resources are not 'nurtured' or supported by the organization. Therefore sustained competitive advantage is not merely the result of valuable, rare and inimitable resources, but is also the result of how these resources are acquired, managed, developed and supported by other organizational systems.

! *Stop and reflect*

Can you think of organizations that have gained temporary competitive advantage through valuable, rare and difficult to imitate resources (e.g. related to the emergence of digital photography, mobile phones, software and/or the Internet)? Was their temporary competitive advantage sustained? If so, do you have any idea how the organization created long-term success (sustained competitive advantage)?

Inimitability is one of the most important 'qualities of desirable resources' (Boxall and Purcell, 2003: 75) in the RBV theory. That is why Barney and Wright (1998) put it on the third level of their VRIO framework. An organization's resource can be imperfectly imitable (and difficult to substitute) for one or a combination of three reasons (Dierickx and Cool, 1989): the ability of an organization to obtain a resource is dependent on unique historical conditions (*path dependency*) (see Figure 3.2), the link between resources possessed by an organization and its sustained competitive advantage is causally ambiguous (*causal ambiguity*) (see Figure 3.3), and the resource generating an organization's advantage is socially complex and difficult to understand (*social complexity*) (see Figure 3.4). Path dependency captures the idea that valuable resources are developed over time and the fact that their competitive success does not simply come from making choices in the present but have their origin and starting point in a chain of past events, incidents and choices. According to Barney and Wright (1998), 'resource support by organization' is linked to the concept of path dependency. The chain of events and managerial choices over time in combination with the complexity of social interactions of the actors involved form the basis of the second barrier to imitation according to the RBV: social complexity (Dierickx and Cool, 1989). Unique networks of internal and external connections are natural barriers for imitation by rivals. The third type of barrier in RBV is causal ambiguity: it is difficult for people who have not been involved in the decision-making process to assess the specific cause–effect relationships in organizations.

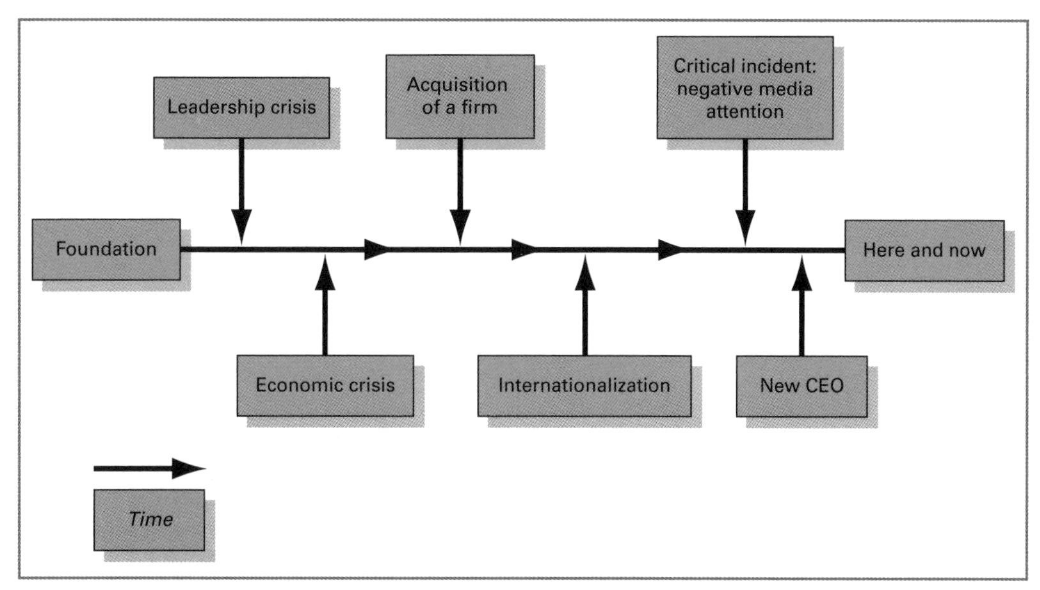

FIGURE 3.2 Path dependency illustration: history, incidents and decisions

SUMMARY

Temporary competitive advantage can be created by resources that are valuable, rare and difficult to imitate. Sustained competitive advantage can be created by resources that are valuable, rare, difficult to imitate and supported *by organization.*

The next step in the creation of a value chain in HRM is linking the notion of competitive advantage to firm performance. Boxall and Purcell (2003) provide a very useful approach in which they link competitive advantage to (1) ultimate business goals and (2) organizational performance represented by critical HR goals (e.g. labour productivity) and critical non-HR goals (e.g. market share). In this approach we also find a concrete link to HRM. Boxell and Purcell (ibid.) consider the ultimate business goals of an organization to be twofold:

1 Creating and maintaining viability with adequate returns to shareholders.
2 Striving for sustained competitive advantage.

Level two (average performance through valuable resources) and level three (above-average performance through valuable, rare and difficult to imitate resources) in the VRIO framework potentially create and maintain viability with adequate returns to shareholders. If organizations do not meet these criteria, they run the risk of going bankrupt. The second ultimate business goal is only for those organizations that are capable of managing and maintaining valuable, rare and difficult to imitate resources in a structural way. In reality, this might only be the case for the top 5–10 per cent of organizations in a sector or population. The majority of organizations in reality

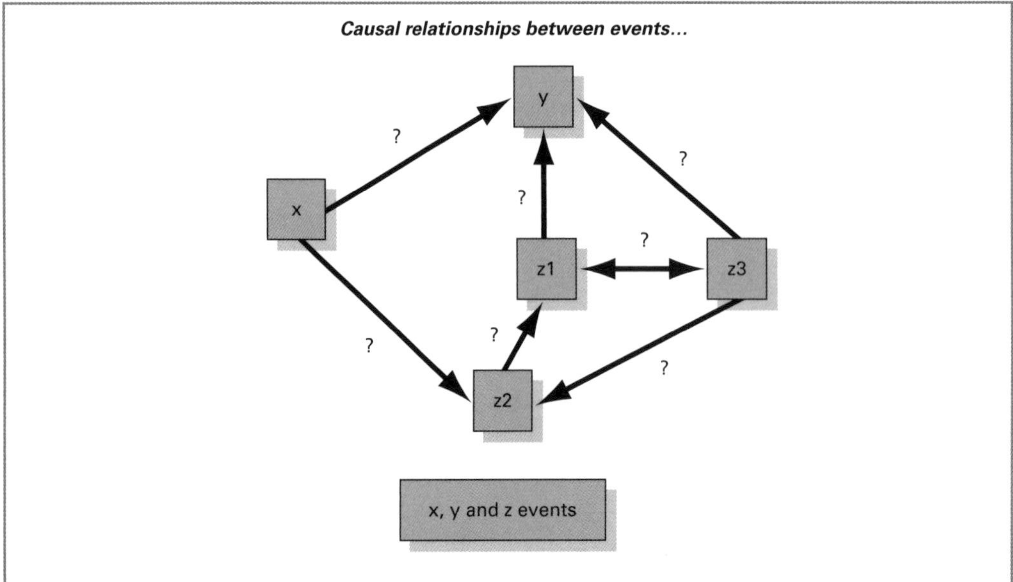

Note: For example: What is the impact of performance-related pay (x) on employee commitment (y) in an organization? The figure suggests an impact of PRP (x) on commitment (y). However, PRP (x) can also affect perceived distributive (in)justice (z2) among employees. Perceived distributive (in)justice (z2) has an impact on employee satisfaction (z1), and this employee satisfaction (z1) can affect employee commitment (y). Other factors, including employee trust (z3), can influence commitment (y), satisfaction (z1) and perceived justice (z2). Therefore, multiple 'events' can effect an apparently simple relationship between pay and commitment suggesting potential causal ambiguities.

FIGURE 3.3 Causal ambiguity illustration

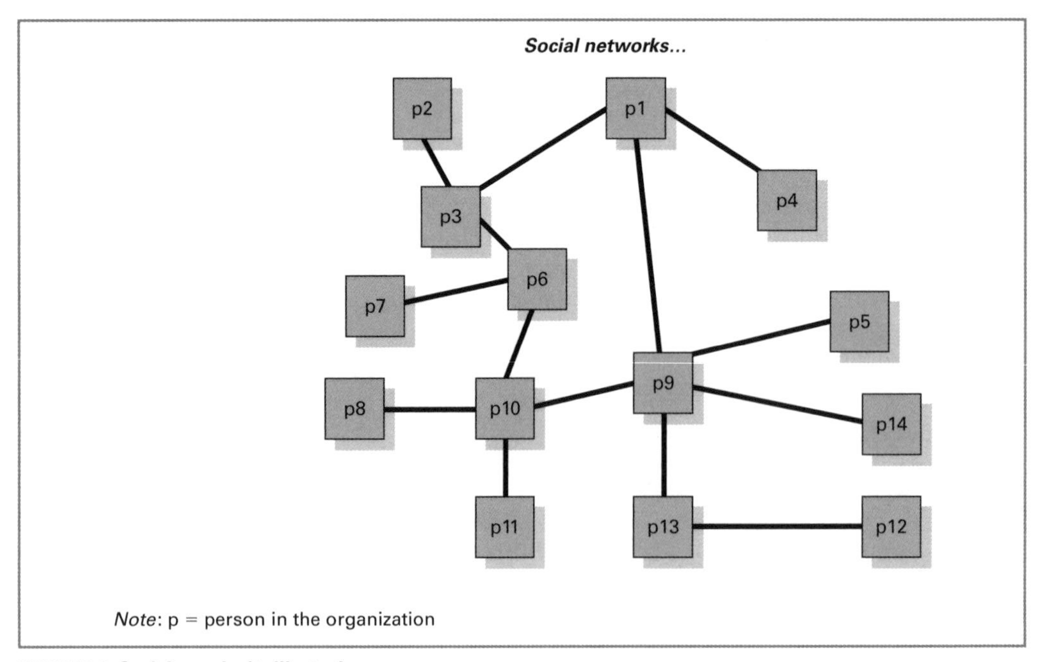

Note: p = person in the organization

FIGURE 3.4 Social complexity illustration

strive for survival in meeting the standards according to the first ultimate business goal in Boxall and Purcell's (2003) approach.

The approach has one disadvantage and that is related to the fact that it only focuses on profit organizations ('adequate returns to shareholders'). Public organizations do not have shareholders; however, there are good arguments for general application of Boxall and Purcell's (2003) twofold distinction to a much broader range of organizations in different sectors. For example, hospitals are under pressure to perform according to the standards of financiers (health insurance companies) and other actors (government). When hospitals do not meet the viability standards according to these actors, they run the risk of decreasing financial support and negative publicity. Therefore the ultimate business goals approach can easily be adapted to a broad range of organizations.

The next step is linking the ultimate business goals to critical HR and critical non-HR goals. From an HR perspective it is important to be modest and realistic. Though it is tempting to attribute general organizational success to employees, it is important to realize that much success has little or nothing to do with employees and good people management. Excellent sales of an organization as a result of a growing economy or because of a big sports event (e.g. a World Cup football match and the number of flat screen televisions sold) have hardly any relationship with employees or HRM. Therefore the concept of *critical non-HR goals* is introduced. These goals might include desired outcomes for sales, market share, and so on (Boxall and Purcell, 2003). An excellent brand name, for example Coca-Cola, Heineken or Mercedes, can produce economic value and therefore be a critical non-HR goal. Interestingly enough, there is a growing awareness of the potential negative impact employees on the shopfloor and at the highest levels of the organization can have on the organization's reputation. Recent organization scandals, including Enron, Parmalat and Ahold, have shown how employees can affect firm performance negatively and damage corporate reputation. Some of Boxall and Purcell's (ibid.) critical non-HR goals (e.g. reputation, corporate image) might become the domain of the critical HR goals in the years to come.

The *critical HR goals* in Boxall and Purcell's (ibid.) basic framework focus on three desired types and levels of outcome:

1. labour productivity (cost-effectiveness);
2. organizational flexibility;
3. social legitimacy and employment citizenship.

Of all the outcome variables in HRM and performance research over the last decade, productivity has proved to be the most popular outcome variable overall (Boselie et al., 2005). In general, productivity represents the amount of output per unit of input (labour, equipment and capital). Strangely enough, Boxall and Purcell (2003) do not include quality as a critical HR goal. Quality represents the effectiveness of the organization's services and products, often directly linked to customer demands and satisfaction. From this point of view, quality can be linked to the concept of productivity. If we combine the two, cost-effectiveness (productivity and quality) represents an efficient and optimal way of delivering products or services that meet the demands of customers. In this book, *cost-effectiveness* is a combination of labour productivity and product/service quality for customers.

The second critical HR goal is *organizational flexibility*, defined as the capacity to change and/or adapt. A further distinction can be made by three types of flexibility related to employees:

1. *Numerical flexibility* representing flexibility in the use of employees; for example, during different shifts and during fluctuations in production output. An ice cream producer, for example, can be affected by extremely warm weather (meaning above-normal ice cream

consumption) versus extremely cold and wet weather (meaning below-average consumption). In both situations the producer's numerical flexibility of employees is important (more employees in case of warm weather and less employees in case of structural bad weather).

2 *Functional flexibility* representing the degree to which employees are capable of performing multiple tasks and functions. This type of flexibility is often manifested in organizations through job rotation, teamwork, job enlargement and job enrichment.
3 *Mental flexibility* representing the employees' ability and willingness to change without resistance. This concept is also linked to *agility*, reflecting the organization's capability of adapting easily to changes in its external environment. Agility has its roots in ballet and in that context refers to the flexibility of dancers' bodies to bend in all directions as necessary in a performance. Willingness and ability are two key necessary conditions for mental flexibility.

The third critical HR goal is *social legitimacy*. This concept is manifested on a more macro-level, referring to the legitimacy of an organization to the outside environment; for example, in relation to society, consumers, trade unions and the government. But it is also manifested in a more micro-level, reflecting the organization's legitimacy to its own employees. Paauwe (2004) labels this micro element 'fairness to individuals'. He considers the macro element (legitimacy) and the micro element (fairness) to be part of the moral side of managing people in organizations, essential for creating unique approaches through HRM in organizations and not just an obligatory part (due to, for example, legislation) of the critical HR goals. Social legitimacy is highly underdeveloped in the majority of SHRM literature (Paauwe and Boselie, 2007). The main focus has always been on firm performance in financial terms, with an increased emphasis on flexibility. Legitimacy issues are often considered a necessary evil from the employer's perspective, necessary because of labour legislation and the influence of trade unions. Paauwe (2004) places much more value on the social legitimacy aspect, emphasizing the potential added value of it to the organization's success. To some extent, Boxall and Purcell (2003) do acknowledge and subscribe to this notion as well. Scandals related to child labour used for the production of an organization's products, for example in the case of Nike several years ago, directly affect the social legitimacy of an organization, with a potential negative impact on corporate image. This might have serious effects on consumer behaviour and the organization's reputation for potential future employees. Social legitimacy is a serious business, although most organizations do not see its full potential in relationship to employees and HRM yet. It is worth noting that the approach by Boxall and Purcell (2003) on the three critical HR goals can be extended with other potential critical HR goals, for example innovation.

! *Stop and reflect*

Can you think of any other critical HR goal linked to a specific organizational context? For example, innovation within the chemical German company BASF (www.basf.com) and health and safety within the British-Swedish pharmaceutical company AstraZeneca (www.astrazeneca.com).

Boxall and Purcell (2003) make an important remark about the three critical goals mentioned above (productivity/cost-effectiveness, flexibility and legitimacy). There is a natural tension between these three in organizations. High cost-effectiveness might be negatively associated with flexibility because of its efficiency focus and negatively associated with social legitimacy because of its potential neglect of human issues (e.g. work–life balance practices). Too exclusive a focus on flexibility might damage the financial performance from an efficiency point of view. And too much focus on social legitimacy does not meet efficiency and flexibility standards, as seems to be the case in some public organizations. There appears to be an optimum point at which the three critical goals are balanced. Chapter 5 of this book is partly devoted to tensions and balanced approaches in HRM.

SUMMARY

- Ultimate business goals cover two types of goal; the first focused on viability of adequate returns to shareholders, financiers and/or other relevant parties (e.g. the government) and the second focused on achieving sustained competitive advantage.
- Ultimate business goals can be affected by (1) critical non-HR goals and (2) critical HR goals.
- Critical HR goals consist of three parts: labour productivity (cost-effectiveness), flexibility and social legitimacy.
- There is a natural tension between the three critical HR goals.

HRM and performance: lessons

How do critical HR goals become affected by employees? In other words, what kinds of employee attitude and behaviour have a positive impact on cost-effectiveness, flexibility and/or social legitimacy? For example, highly committed and motivated employees are potentially more productive and more flexible (think of eagerness to learn different functions through job rotation) than employees that score very low on employee commitment and motivation. Perceived organizational justice by employees of, for example, the appraisal and compensation systems potentially have a positive impact on the social legitimacy of an organization. The issues above can be linked to the extensive HRM and performance debate that started some 15 years ago with publications by Arthur (1994), Huselid (1995) and MacDuffie (1995).

Before we get to the heart of this discussion, we need to link Boxall and Purcell's (2003) critical goals to **HR outcomes**. According to Guest (1997), these HR outcomes are much closer to actual HR practices and interventions than, for example, performance indicators such as sales, profits and market value. The latter are called *distal outcomes* because of their distance from managerial practices, including human resource practices. The risk of linking distal measures to HRM is an overestimation of the HR effect caused by other potential factors outside HRM influencing these outcomes. For example, global oil prices directly affect Shell's yearly profits without any HRM interference. Guest makes a plea for using *proximal outcomes* in studying the impact of HRM. Proximal outcomes are directly or almost directly affected by HR interventions or practices. The so-called HR outcomes are proximal outcomes. For an overview of these HR outcomes, see Paauwe and Richardson (1997). These outcomes include employee satisfaction, commitment, motivation, trust, loyalty, retention and turnover, absence due to illness and social climate between employees and managers. In Chapter 4, the performance indicators and HR outcomes are discussed in more detail and in more concrete terms.

The HRM and performance debate of the last 15 years is actually threefold. First, the majority of HR research in this area is focused on empirically testing the impact of HRM on performance. These studies were performed in different countries, in different branches of industry, with input from different respondents (including HR professionals, line managers, employees and employee representatives), on different levels of analysis (including the individual employee level, the team level, strategic business unit level and company level), in profit and non-profit organizations, using different theories and a diversity of outcome measures. For an extensive overview and critical review of over 104 empirical journal articles in international academic journals on HRM and performance, see Boselie et al. (2005). Second, there is a stream of HR research from 2000 onwards on the methods used to determine the added value of HRM; for example, reflected in the article by Gerhart et al. (2000) on measurement error in previous empirical HR research. Finally, recently overview articles and meta-analyses on HRM and performance were published, including the studies by Wall and Wood (2005), Paauwe and Boselie (2005), Combs et al. (2006), Becker and Huselid (2006) and Fleetwood and Hesketh (2006).

The first and the third stream within the HRM and performance debate generated the most output, with empirical evidence that HRM mainly has a modest positive impact on performance and in some cases no impact at all (Purcell, 1999). Huselid and Becker (2000) suggest that the effect of one standard deviation change in an HR system (a statistical way to describe the variation in HR variety and intensity among organizations) is 10–20 per cent of an organization's market value. Combs et al.'s (2006) meta-analysis on 92 empirical studies found that an increase of one standard deviation in the use of a special type of HRM called 'high-performance work practices' (HPWP) (See Chapter 6 of this book) is associated with a 4.6 per cent increase in return on assets (ROA). Therefore these authors conclude that the relationship between HRM and performance is not just statistically significant, but also managerially relevant (Paauwe, 2007).

Overall, there is general agreement among HR scholars that HR practices are at least weakly related to firm performance (Purcell, 1999; Wright and Gardner, 2003; Paauwe and Boselie, 2005; Wall and Wood, 2005); however, the results should be treated with caution (Boselie et al., 2005; Wall and Wood, 2005). The second stream is much more critical towards the findings because of serious doubts about the research designs (e.g. surveys sent to organizations to fill in), the quality of the data (e.g. input from single HR respondents; cross-sectional data), the research methods (e.g. using simple regression analysis) and the interpretation of the data (e.g. neglecting contextual factors such as the organization's size, sectoral differences and country differences caused by institutional differences). Boselie et al. (2005) conclude that there is no general agreement and consensus about (1) what constitutes HRM, (2) what performance is, and (3) what the link is between the two, although much progress has been made since Guest (1997) noted the need for good theory on these three issues.

Empirical evidence for the added value of HRM

Below are some illustrations of findings from empirical studies on the relationship between HRM and performance. *HR planning* is positively associated with labour productivity (Koch and McGrath, 1996). *Selective recruitment and selection* of new employees is positively related to labour productivity (Huselid, 1995; Koch and McGrath, 1996) and negatively related to employee turnover (Huselid, 1995). Selective recruitment and selection is often considered to be one of the key best practices in HRM and this is discussed in more detail in Chapter 7. Excellent *rewards* and *PRP* are positively related to product quality (Kalleberg and Moody, 1994), labour productivity (Lazear, 1996), customer satisfaction (Banker et al., 1996), employee motivation (Dowling and Richardson, 1997), organizational commitment and employee trust (Appelbaum et al., 2000), and negatively related to employee turnover (Arthur, 1994). PRP and compensation is another important best practice in contemporary HRM and is further discussed in Chapter 9. *Employee involvement, participation* and *consultation* are positively associated with employee commitment (Wallace, 1995) and negatively related to employee turnover (Arthur, 1994) and employee absence due to illness (Boselie et al., 2003). Employee participation is discussed as a best practice (or HPWP) in more detail in Chapter 11. *Training and development* decreases employee turnover (Arthur, 1994), increases the social atmosphere between managers and employees, also known as social climate (Kalleberg and Moody, 1994), and increases employee trust in an organization (Appelbaum et al., 2000). Employee development is another best practice that is discussed in more detail in Chapter 10. Creating *internal promotion opportunities* is positively related to organizational commitment and job satisfaction (ibid.). *Employee autonomy*, for example in job planning and decision making, increases job satisfaction (Wallace, 1995). The illustrations above indicate a positive impact of certain HR practices on performance.

There is also an enormous body of empirical evidence suggesting significant and relevant relationships between outcome variables. Job satisfaction is positively related to organizational commitment (Wallace, 1995). In other words, employees who are happy about their job are more committed to the organization and vice versa. Employee turnover is negatively related to labour productivity (Huselid, 1995), although we have to be very careful with the employee turnover outcome measure because turnover often shows a so-called non-linear relationship with other factors. High turnover rates are not good for an organization, for example because of the loss of valuable (human) resources, but extremely low turnover rates might also be bad for the organization, indicating little or no flexibility and mobility of employees. Employee trust and employee motivation decrease job stress in organizations (Appelbaum et al., 2000). Employee commitment increases productivity and quality (Guest, 2001). Overall, these illustrations indicate potential relationships between outcome variables, in particular significant relationships between HR outcomes (e.g. commitment, trust, motivation) and critical HR goals (e.g. productivity and quality).

The evidence for a relationship between HR practices, HR outcomes and critical HR goals is also visually presented in the model by Paauwe and Richardson (1997). The overview and framework by Paauwe and Richardson (1997) synthesizes the results of previous empirical research (see Figure 3.5). HRM practices give rise to HRM outcomes that influence the performance of the organization. A further distinction between distal financial performance indicators such as profits and market value versus more proximal critical HR goals such as productivity, flexibility and legitimacy is not made in this framework. The model does acknowledge potential *reversed causality* reflecting the possibility that excellent firm performance or poor firm performance affects HRM and vice versa. Excellent profits in a given year can have a strong positive effect on HRM in terms of top managers being more willing to invest in employees (higher budgets for employee development) and higher compensation for all employees. Poor firm performance, for example as a result of a country's economic crisis, might result in decreasing training budgets and a cessation of recruitment. The Paauwe and Richardson (1997) framework also acknowledges the impact of contextual factors on the relationship between HRM and performance. Contextual factors include the type of industry, the organization's size, age and history, capital intensity and the degree of unionization, but also include the employees' background (gender, level of education, age, etc.). Some HRM activities or practices influence the performance of the employees directly. PRP, for example, can have a direct positive effect on labour productivity (Lazear, 1996) without any mediating role of HRM outcomes such as employee motivation and commitment.

Looking back at the Nokia case, we might conclude that the success of that company may be at least partly based on the positive impact of its selective recruitment and selection practices, extensive training and development, the creation of internal promotion and career opportunities,

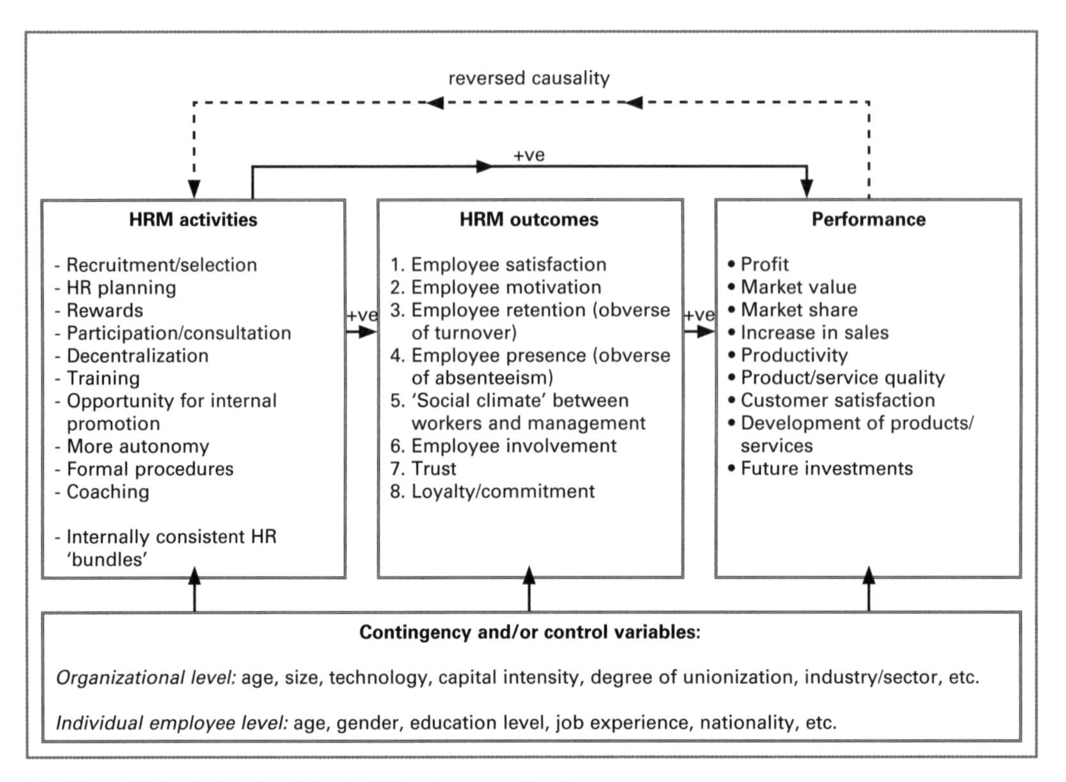

FIGURE 3.5 HRM activities in relation to HRM outcomes and performance
Source: Reproduced with permission from Paauwe and Richardson (1997).

employee involvement, job autonomy principles, good communication throughout the organization and information sharing. However, if it was that simple competitors could easily copy Nokia's success if they had the money available for HR investment for these HR practices and if they knew how to do it.

The potential competitive advantage of an organization, as discussed, uses the concepts of ultimate business goals, critical HR goals, critical non-HR goals and HR outcomes. This brings us to the next step in the model: the HR activities.

HR activities

Guest (1999), Purcell (1999) and Wright and Boswell (2002) were some of the first authors to acknowledge the lack of attention paid to the individual employee in the HRM and performance debate. The research was dominated by organization-level research focused on studying the impact of HR policies and practices reported by HR professionals on firm performance. The enactment or implementation of HR practices was almost completely ignored. Policies and reports full of ideas of excellent HR practices are just a first small step towards HR success. As suggested by Becker and Huselid (2006) and Wright and Boswell (2002), the implementation and perceptions of HRM are probably much more important.

To fully understand HR practices, a further distinction can be made between (Wright and Nishii, 2007):

1. *Intended HR practices* (policies and intended new HR practices).
2. *Actual HR practices* (practices implemented mainly by line managers).
3. *Perceived HR practices* (employees' experiences and perceptions of HR practices implemented by their direct supervisor).

'line managers (direct supervisors) are the hands that rock HRM's cradle.'

Perceived HR practices are thought to directly influence HRM outcomes. For example, if employees have a very positive perception about the performance appraisal (PA) and compensation linked to it, this will probably affect their job satisfaction, organizational commitment and trust in their direct supervisor. A systematic and strategic approach in creating excellent scores on perceived HR practices in an organization is at the heart of building an HR strategy within an organization, because incidental good scores on perceived HR practices do not guarantee organizational success in the long run. Wright and Nishii (ibid.) emphasize the crucial role of line managers in the success of HRM. The line managers are the ones enacting or implementing HR practices. Employee development can only be successful if direct supervisors acknowledge and stimulate talent within their own teams of employees. An appraisal system for evaluating individual performance can be effective when applied in the right way by the line manager. In other words, line managers (direct supervisors) are the hands that rock HRM's cradle. The HR department (or HR function) is mainly responsible for the HR design and the development of new intended HR practices. After the initial design the HR professionals mainly become business partners and facilitators of line managers in the HR enactment process. The new roles and positions of contemporary HR professionals are discussed in further detail in Chapter 12.

Intended, actual and perceived HR practices 'in practice'

A new 360-degree feedback system for monitoring and evaluating employees has been set up by HR professionals to increase employees' business awareness (e.g. reflected in increased customer focus, cost reduction and willingness to work harder when required). This is an intended HR practice developed and designed to link the performance management of an organization to the new corporate strategy, which is much more focused on creating shareholder value through sales, profits and market share. The HR professionals will then train all line managers and coach them in using the tool in all parts of the organization. An HR expert centre is set up for line management assistance during their use of the 360-degree feedback system on their employees. The data from this appraisal are centrally collected and stored at this HR expert centre. The HR department in close cooperation with top management communicates the introduction and relevance of the new system to all employees of the organization. Top management support in these situations appears to be crucial as well. If the CEO continuously tells employees and managers that this is very important, the chances of success will increase. After the introduction of the new system, it is entirely up to the line managers to make it work (actual HR practices). If applied correctly there is a good chance that employees will perceive these HR practices positively (perceived HR practices), resulting in a potentially positive impact on firm performance. Therefore, the best intentions in HRM will not automatically result in organization success.

It is crucial to make a distinction between the three different types of HR practice (intended, actual and perceived). This automatically implicates the awareness and involvement of multiple actors in the creation of an HR value chain in an organization, including HR professionals, line managers and employees. Intended HR practices are determined by the HR strategy and the overall organizational strategy. These two strategies were discussed in Chapter 2. In the next section the HR value chain is discussed.

SUMMARY

- Empirical research shows a positive impact of HRM on firm performance.
- HR outcomes are the employee attitudinal, behavioural and cognitive factors that mediate HR practices and critical HR goals.
- There are three types of HR practice: intended, actual and perceived.

The HR value chain

The ideas described in this chapter are combined with what is called the *'HR value chain'*. See Figure 3.6 for a visual presentation of the chain of events described earlier in the chapter. The competitive advantage position of an organization was the starting point of the discussion. Temporary or sustained competitive advantage is represented by the ultimate business goals in the model (inspired by Boxall and Purcell, 2003), which are affected by the critical HR and non-HR goals. The critical HR goals (productivity/cost-effectiveness, flexibility and social legitimacy) in turn are affected by HR outcomes in terms of attitudes, behaviours and cognitive aspects of employees. These HR outcomes can be positively influenced by HR practices through a mini-chain defined by Wright and Nishii (2007) in terms of intended, actual and perceived HR practices. It is noteworthy that the nature of practices, outcomes, critical HR goals and ultimate business goals is highly affected by (1) the nature of the business of an organization (e.g. manufacturing or services) and (2) the strategic choices made by an organization as discussed in Chapter 2. Below is an illustration of the latter notion.

Employee turnover and retention

The United Nations (UN) is a very popular employer because of its corporate image and excellent working conditions (including wages and other employee benefits). On average, 1500 people respond to a vacancy within the UN, in particular if the vacancy is an office job in New York. The popularity of the UN as an employer is not only reflected in the large number of respondents to a vacancy, but also in the very low employee turnover rates. In other words, nobody wants to leave the organization. To maintain flexibility and mobility within the UN, in combination with the ability to attract enough young newcomers, employee turnover might be a good thing for the UN. For most other organizations (both profit and non-profit), employee retention will become one of the biggest HR challenges in the next 10–15 years in Europe. There will be a serious labour shortage in Europe (and other parts of the world) as a result of an ageing population. Employee retention in contrast to employee turnover, where employee retention is defined as attracting and retaining valuable human resources for the organization, will probably be a key indicator for organizational success within the next couple of years. The sustainability of an organization will be in danger if it is unable to attract and retain talent. In contrast to the UN case, most organizations aim for retention and minimizing employee turnover. This, of course, all depends on the specific context.

The next chapter focuses on HR metrics and measurement. This chapter continues with a discussion on the measurement of HRM and performance in more detail and in a more concrete way.

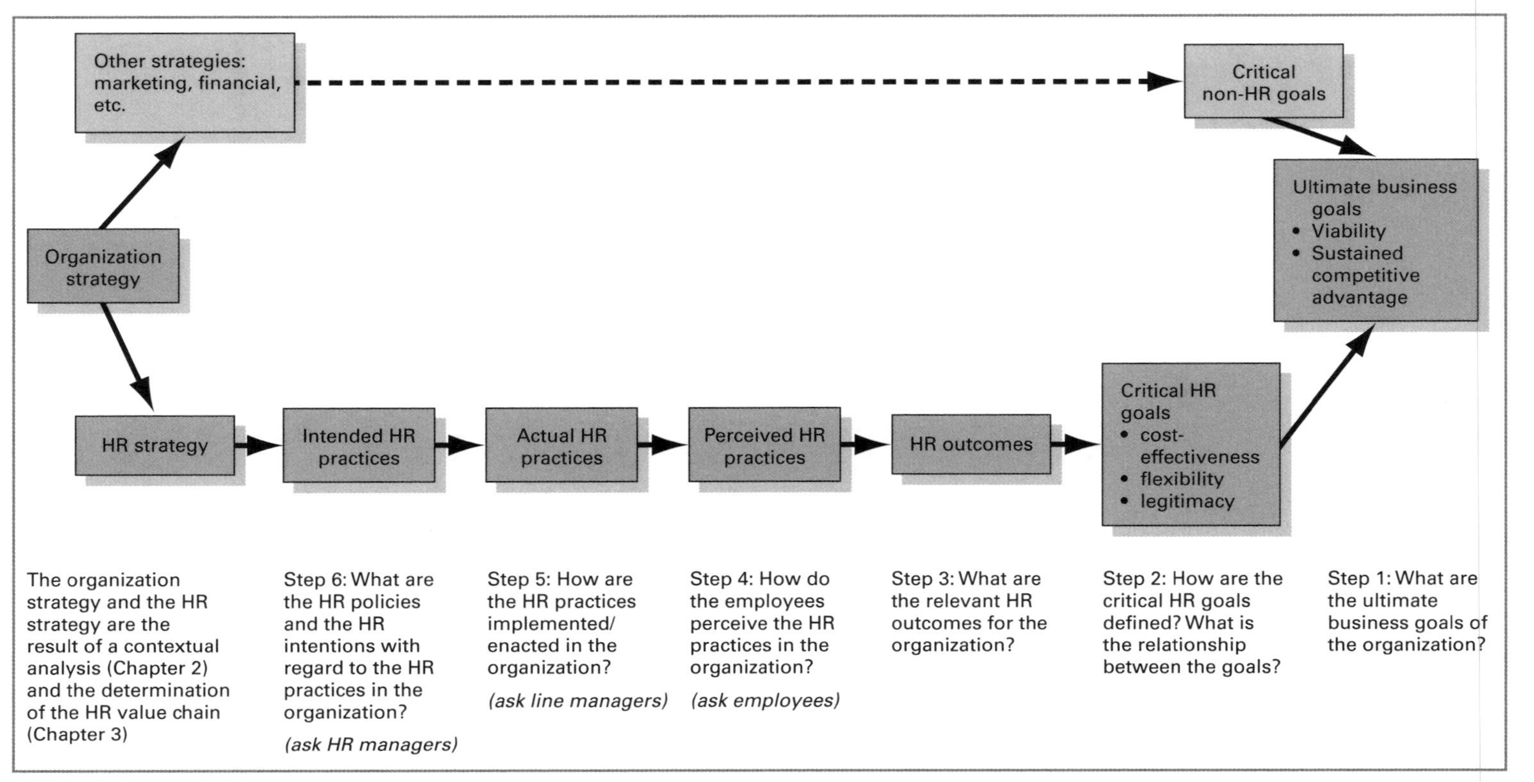

FIGURE 3.6 The HR value chain

summary

- Employees can be a source of competitive advantage for an organization.
- Internal resources that are valuable, rare, inimitable and non-substitutable can be a source of sustained competitive advantage when supported by organization.
- HRM can contribute to employees becoming a source of long-term organizational success.
- The HR value chain uses a reversed approach beginning with the organization's ultimate business goals. Next, the critical HR goals and the critical non-HR goals are determined, followed by the HR outcomes. Finally, the HR practices (intended, actual and perceived) need to be mapped, and linked to the strategy of the organization.
- The three main critical HR goals are labour productivity (cost-effectiveness), organizational flexibility and social legitimacy.
- The three types of HR practice can be linked to three different employee groups: employees (perceived HR practices), line managers (actual HR practices) and HR professionals (intended HR practices).

Glossary of key terms

Human resource (HR) outcomes are the results of people management in terms of employee attitudes, behaviours and cognitive aspects.

Human resource (HR) practices are personnel interventions or actions that contribute to shaping the employment relationship in an organization.

Performance is the final outcome of business actions.

Sustained competitive advantage is long-term organizational success reflected in continuously outperforming competitors as a result of unique resources and qualities.

Ultimate business goals are organizational targets for relevant stakeholders aimed at (1) creating and maintaining viability with adequate returns and (2) creating sustained competitive advantage.

Personal development

- What does or did your formal education (e.g. a BA degree and/or MA degree) cost you? And what are the revenues from it?
- What kind of HR practices have a positive impact on your personal HR outcomes in terms of, for example, satisfaction, motivation and retention?

Individual task

- Think of yourself as a human resource for an organization. What can you do to become valuable, rare, difficult to imitate and difficult to substitute?
- What kind of actions do you need to take?
- And if you are already in this position, you can ask yourself the question, 'How do I maintain this position?'

Team task

1 Determine the key performance indicators (KPIs) of an organization.
2 Determine the HR practices that affect these KPIs in that specific organization.

Learning checklist

After studying this chapter, you should be able to:

- Identify the potential impact of HRM on performance.
- Review the concept of competitive advantage and sustained competitive advantage of an organization.
- Outline the ultimate business goals of an organization.
- Discuss HR practices, human resource outcomes and performance (the HR value chain).
- Understand the different stages of the HR value chain, including intended, actual and perceived HR practices.

Appendix 1 HR Practices in HRM & Performance Research

HR practices:

1 Training & development
2 Performance-related pay, contingent pay & rewards
3 Performance appraisal & performance management
4 Recruitment & selection
5 Team working & collaboration
6 Participation (direct participation), empowerment, employee involvement & suggestion schemes
7 Good wages (e.g. high wages/salaries, remuneration and fair pay)
8 Communication & information sharing
9 Internal promotion opportunities & internal labour market (ILM)
10 Job design & job rotation (also job enrichment and broad jobs)

11 Autonomy & decentralization
12 Employment security
13 Employment benefits
14 Formal procedures (grievances)
15 HR planning (also career planning & succession planning)
16 Financial participation (employee stock ownership)
17 Symbolic egalitarianism (single status & harmonization)
18 Attitude survey
19 Indirect participation (trade unions, works councils, consultation committees, voice mechanisms)
20 Diversity & equal opportunities
21 Job analysis
22 Socialization & social activities
23 Family-friendly policies & work life balance (WLB)
24 Employee exit management, layoff and redundancy policy
25 Professionalization & effectiveness of the HR function – HR department
26 Social responsibility practices

Source: Boselie et al. (2005), based on 104 empirical articles, 1994–2003.

Appendix 2 Outcomes and Performance in HRM & Performance Research

Outcomes and performance:

1 Productivity
2 Employee turnover (versus retention)
3 Profits (profitability)
4 Product/service quality (e.g. scrap rate)
5 Sales
6 Organization performance (overall) & organization's competitiveness
7 Commitment
8 Market growth & growth
9 Efficiency of process (cycle time; throughput time; delivery; clerical accuracy)
10 Employee absence (sickness)
11 Satisfaction
12 Conflict (grievances) & social climate
13 ROA – return on assets
14 Intention to quit (or stay)
15 Flexibility (e.g. ability to move between jobs; adaptability)
16 Innovation (e.g. product development)
17 Costs (e.g. production, overhead, unit)
18 Motivation
19 ROI – return on investment
20 Labour costs
21 Market share
22 Quality of staff (competence)
23 Tobin's q
24 ROE – return on equity
25 Market value

26 Trust
27 OCB – organizational citizenship behaviour
28 Stress (workload; fatigue)
29 Morale
30 Effectiveness of HR department
31 GRATE – gross rate of return on assets
32 ROS – return on sales
33 Perceived security
34 Perceived fairness
35 Earnings
36 Staffing
37 Customer satisfaction
38 Attitude to change (e.g. resistance)
39 Death rates

Source: Boselie et al. (2005), based on 104 empirical articles, 1994–2003.

References

Appelbaum, E., Bailey, T., Berg, P. and Kalleberg, A. (2000) *Manufacturing Advantage: Why High-performance Work Systems Pay Off*. Ithaca, NY: Cornell University Press.

Arthur, J.B. (1994) Effects of human resource systems on manufactoring performance and turnover, *Academy of Management Journal*, 37(3): 670–87.

Baden-Fuller, C.W.F. and Stopford, J.M. (1994) Creating corporate entrepreneurship, *Strategic Management Journal*, 15(7): 521–36.

Banker, R.D., Lee, S.Y., Potter, G. and Srinivasan, D. (1996) Contextual analysis of performance impacts of outcome-based incentive compensation, *Academy of Management Journal*, 39(4): 920–49.

Barney, J.B. (1991) Firm resources and sustainable competitive advantage, *Journal of Management*, 17: 99–120.

Barney, J.B. and Wright, P.M. (1998) On becoming a strategic partner: the role of human resources in gaining competitive advantage, *Human Resource Management*, 37: 31–46.

Becker, M.A. and Becker, B.E. (2000) Comment on 'measurement error in research on human resources and firm performance: how much error is there and how does it influence effect size estimates?, *Personnel Psychology*, 53(4): 835–54.

Becker, B.E. and Huselid, M.A. (2006) Strategic human resource management: where do we go from here?, *Journal of Management*, 32(6): 898–925.

Boselie, P. and Paauwe, J. (2009) Human resource management and the resource based view, in A. Wilkinson, T. Redman, S. Snell, S. and N. Bacon, *The SAGE Handbook of Human Resource Management,* Chapter 25. London: Sage.

Boselie, P., Dietz, G. and Boon, C. (2005) Commonalities and contradictions in HRM and performance research, *Human Resource Management Journal*, 15(3): 67–94.

Boselie, P., Paauwe, J. and Richardson, R. (2003) Human resource management, institutionalization and organizational performance: a comparison of hospitals, hotels and local government, *International Journal of Human Resource Management*, 8(14): 1407–29.

Boxall, P. and Purcell, J. (2003) *Strategy and Human Resource Management*. New York: Palgrave Macmillan.

Combs, J., Liu, Y., Hall, A. and Ketchen, D. (2006) How much do high-performance work practices matter? A meta-analysis of their effects on organizational performance, *Personnel Psychology*, 59(3): 501–28.

Delery, J.E. and Shaw, J.D. (2001) The strategic management of people in work organizations: review, synthesis, and extension. Paper presented at the Academy of Management Meeting 2001, Washington, DC, August.

Dierickx, I. and Cool, K. (1989) Asset stock accumulation and sustainability of competitive advantage, *Management Science*, 35(12): 1504–11.

Dowling, B. and Richardson, R. (1997) Evaluating performance-related pay for managers in the National Health Service, *International Journal of Human Resource Management*, 8(3): 348–66.

Fleetwood, S. and Hesketh, A. (2006) Beyond measuring the human resources management–organizational performance link: applying critical realist meta-theory, *Organization,* 13(5): 677–99.

Gerhart, B., Wright, P.M. and McMahan, G. (2000) Measurement error in research on the human resource and firm performance relationship: further evidence and analysis, *Personnel Psychology*, 53(4): 855–72.

Guest, D.E. (1997) Human resource management and performance: a review and research agenda, *International Journal of Human Resource Management*, 8(3): 263–76.

Guest, D.E. (1999) Human resource management: the workers' verdict, *Human Resource Management Journal*, 9(3): 5–25.

Guest, D.E. (2001) Human resource management: when reality confronts theory, *International Journal of Human Resource Management*, 12(7): 1092–106.

Haiko, M. (2002) *Nokia, the Inside Story*. London: Prentice Hall.

Huselid, M.A. (1995) The impact of human resource management practices on turnover, productivity, and corporate financial performance, *Academy of Management Journal*, 38(3): 635–72.

Kalleberg, A.L. and Moody, J.W. (1994) Human resource management and organizational performance, *American Behavioral Scientist*, 37(7): 948–62.

Kloeg, M. (2007) Nokia: the global success and the role of HRM. BA thesis. Tilburg: Tilburg University.

Koch, M.J. and McGrath, R.G. (1996) Improving labor productivity: human resource management policies do matter, *Strategic Management Journal*, 17: 335–54.

Lazear, E.P. (1996) Performance pay and productivity. NBER working paper 5672, Cambridge.

MacDuffie, J.P. (1995) Human resource bundles and manufactoring performance: organizational logic and flexible production systems in the world auto industry, *Industrial and Labor Relations Review*, 48(2): 197–221.

Merriden, T. (2001) *Business the Nokia Way*. Oxford: Capstone Publishing Limited.

Paauwe, J. (2004) *HRM and Performance: Achieving Long-term Viability*. Oxford: Oxford University Press.

Paauwe, J. (2007) HRM and performance: in search of balance. Inaugural lecture. Tilburg: Tilburg University.

Paauwe, J. and Boselie, P. (2005) HRM and performance: what's next?, *Human Resource Management Journal*, 15(4): 68–83.

Paauwe, J. and Boselie, P. (2007) HRM and societal embeddedness, in P. Boxall, J. Purcell and P.M. Wright (eds), *The Oxford Handbook of Human Resource Management*, Chapter 9, pp. 166–84. Oxford: Oxford University Press.

Paauwe, J. and Richardson, R. (1997) Introduction: special issue on HRM and performance, *International Journal of Human Resource Management*, 8(3): 257–62.
Penrose, E.T. (1959) *The Theory of the Growth of the Firm*. Oxford: Blackwell.
Porter, M.E. (1980) *Competitive Strategy*. New York: Free Press/Macmillan.
Purcell, J. (1999) Best practice and best fit: chimera or cul-de-sac?, *Human Resource Management Journal*, 9(3): 26–41.
Wall, T.D. and Wood, S.J. (2005) The romance of human resource management and business performance, and the case for big science, *Human Relations*, 58(4): 429–62.
Wallace, J.E. (1995) Corporatist control and organizational commitment among professionals: the case of lawyers working in law firms, *Social Forces*, 73(3): 811–40.
Wernerfelt, B. (1984) A resource based view of the firm, *Strategic Management Journal*, 5: 171–80.
Wright, P.M. and Boswell, W.R. (2002) Desegregating HRM: a review and synthesis of micro and macro human resource management research, *Journal of Management*, 28(3), 247–76.
Wright, P.M. and Gardner, T.M. (2003) The human resource–firm performance relationship: methodological and theoretical challenges, in D. Holman, T.D. Wall, C.W. Clegg, P. Sparrow and A. Howard (eds), *The New Workplace: A Guide to the Human Impact of Modern Working Practices*. London: Wiley.
Wright, P.M. and Nishii, L.H. (2007) Strategic HRM and organizational behavior: integrating multiple levels of analysis. Working paper 26, Ithaca, NY: CAHRS at Cornell University.

Further reading

Boselie, P., Dietz, G. and Boon, C. (2005) Commonalities and contradictions in HRM and performance research, *Human Resource Management Journal*, 15(3): 67–94.
Boxall, P. and Purcell, J. (2008) *Strategy and Human Resource Management*, 2nd edn. New York: Palgrave Macmillan.
Fleetwood, S. and Hesketh, A. (2006) Beyond measuring the human resources management–organizational performance link: applying critical realist meta-theory, *Organization*, 13(5): 677–99.
Guest, D.E. (1997) Human resource management and performance: a review and research agenda, *International Journal of Human Resource Management*, 8(3): 263–76.
Huselid, M.A. (1995) The impact of human resource management practices on turnover, productivity, and corporate financial performance, *Academy of Management Journal*, 38(3): 635–72.
Paauwe, J. & Boselie, P. (2005). HRM and performance: What's next?, *Human Resource Management Journal*, 15(4): 68–83.
Wright, P.M. and Gardner, T.M. (2003) The human resource–firm performance relationship: methodological and theoretical challenges, in D. Holman, T.D. Wall, C.W. Clegg, P. Sparrow and A. Howard (eds), *The New Workplace: A Guide to the Human Impact of Modern Working Practices*. London: Wiley.
Wright, P.M. and Nishii, L.H. (2007) Strategic HRM and organizational behavior: integrating multiple levels of analysis. Working paper 26, Ithaca, NY: CAHRS at Cornell University.

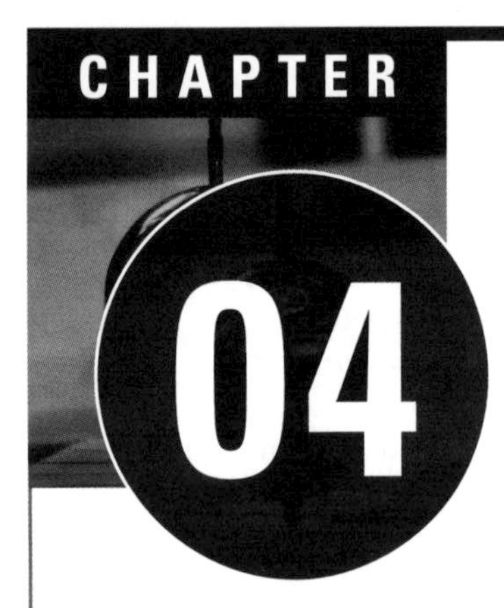

Human Resource Metrics and Measurement

Learning Objectives

After studying this chapter, you should be able to do the following:

- Discuss the advantages and disadvantages of human resource accounting (HRA) approaches
- Understand the concepts of human, social and organizational capital
- Identify different ways of measuring human resource (HR) input (presence, satisfaction, intensity, coverage and importance)
- Discuss the distinction between concepts, indicators and measurements in human resource management (HRM)
- Outline the core characteristics of an HR scorecard
- Identify the key performance indicators (KPIs) of an organization
- Review proximal outcome measures and distal outcome measures in HRM
- Recognize the potential tensions between organizational, employee and societal goals also reflected in the different outcomes (HR outcomes, organizational and financial outcomes)

CASE STUDY: NESTLÉ

Henri Nestlé set up a company to provide infant food in 1866 in Switzerland. The firm now employs over 275 000 people and operates on a global scale in the food processing industry. Recently, the company shifted its attention from 'food and beverages' to 'nutrition, health and wellness' mainly as a result of the increased obesity problems in contemporary Western countries. The firm is one of the most profitable companies in the European food, drink and tobacco industry. The firm's products include baby food, coffee, dairy products, breakfast cereals, confectionery, bottled water, ice cream and pet foods. Illustrations of some of its brands are Nestlé Corn Flakes, Nescafé, Mövenpick Ice Cream, Maggi, Milkybar, and Felix. Nestlé's headquarters are located in Vevey, Switzerland.

The firm's objective is to manufacture and market products that create economic value and meet ecological and societal requirements. Environmental performance and potential pollution, for example reflected in waste production, are high on the agenda with a direct linkage to reputation management. The company's good name should not be negatively affected by news in the media. Part of the new strategy aimed at 'nutrition, health and wellness' is a program called Globe. Globe is focused on increasing efficiency through bringing Nestlé much closer to the consumer using best practices, data standards and management, standardized information systems, and information technology. Another part of the new strategy is the Global Nestlé Business Service (GNBS) program aimed at concentrating the core business on a global scale. Globe and GNBS are the main drivers for improving growth and profitability.

One of the big challenges for Nestlé is the translation of the new strategy to people management. In other words, how can the organization create a high performance culture among its workforce aimed at achieving the new organizational goals (building a global reputation in nutrition, health and wellness products)? In order to achieve these new goals the company applies certain human resource practices aimed at building trust among employees, stimulating integrity and honesty, nurturing respect, encouraging employee development, offering employee career opportunities, providing competitive compensation, and creating safe and healthy working conditions. The HR practices within the organization include selective recruitment and selection with an emphasis on the match between a candidate and the core values of the firm, employee training and development on a continuous basis, performance management including regular feedback sessions and individual goal setting linked to Globe, individual performance-related pay linked to job performance and development, and employee involvement in decision making and innovations.

The Globe program is an important performance management tool for measuring and evaluating the outcomes of Nestlé's intervention including the measurement of the success of the HR interventions. If everything goes as planned these HR practices will contribute to the organization's goals in terms of growth and profitability through an ideal high performance culture among employees (employee trust, integrity, honesty, safety, citizenship behaviour and motivation).

(Loven, 2008)

? Discussion questions

Think of ways in which Nestlé can measure their ideal high-performance culture among employees in terms of trust, integrity, safety and employee motivation:

- What kind of measures can be used?
- How can Nestlé collect and store the data?

Introduction

Chapter 2 presented HRM in the organizational context and highlighted strategic decision making with regard to personnel issues. Chapter 3 presented the potential added value of managing human assets. This chapter deals with HRM issues. In order to create an HR value chain, as discussed in Chapter 3, measurement is inevitable. The organization's strategy is linked to strategic objectives and these objectives need to be translated into concrete *KPIs*. These KPIs reflect the organization's success or failure in goal achievement. On a regular basis, an organization is required to justify its performance and goal achievement for relevant stakeholders (e.g.

shareholders, financiers, trade unions, customers and employees). These goals can be represented by financial outcomes (e.g. profits and the concrete goal of a net profit increase of 10 per cent within the next year) and non-financial outcomes (e.g. service quality and the concrete goal of 90 per cent of trains arriving and departing on time in the specific case of a railway company).

First, organizations, however, tend to measure 'hard' outcomes to evaluate managerial interventions, including HR practices (Cascio, 2006). Hard outcome indicators are, for example, labour productivity, efficiency ratios, labour costs, sales volumes and net profits. 'Soft' outcomes, in particular employee satisfaction, are measured, but generally these scarce outcomes receive far less attention. In fact, employee satisfaction is often only measured on a yearly basis through employee surveys mainly because of institutional obligations towards social partners (trade unions and works councils). Ignoring soft outcomes (e.g. employee commitment) can be costly in the end (Benkhoff, 1998).

> 'Organizations ... tend to measure 'hard' outcomes to evaluate managerial interventions including HR practices'

Second, the soft outcome scales used in practice are often artificial and lack reliability and construct validity. Companies that collect and analyse employee survey data often apply self-designed scales on, for example, satisfaction, commitment and trust. These scales have not been properly tested. I regularly encounter employee surveys claiming the measurement of employee commitment and motivation, while in fact these scales all measure some kind of employee satisfaction.

Third, linking interventions (e.g. HR practices) to soft and hard outcomes requires the inclusion of both input (the intervention) and output (the outcome). The input generally receives less attention and is often not sufficiently measured. Employee surveys, for example, often contain items such as 'how satisfied are you with the opportunities for employee development in your organization?' It is unclear whether this type of question measures the HR practice (or intervention) employee development, the soft HR outcome employee satisfaction or a combination of both. In summary:

- There is a dominance of hard outcome measures for evaluating HR effectiveness and a lack of attention paid to soft outcome measures.
- The soft outcome scales lack reliability and construct validity mainly because the scales used have not been properly tested using scientific statistical procedures.
- Outcomes generally receive much more attention in actual measurement than input variables including HR practices; however, for a full measurement of HR effectiveness measuring both HR practices and outcomes is required.

These three general notions on measurement are the starting point of an alternative HR scorecard approach presented in this chapter.

Tension between HR-related, organizational and financial outcomes

The dominant school in strategic HRM (SHRM) builds on a hidden assumption that what is best for the employee is automatically best for the employer, and vice versa. In other words, highly satisfied, committed and motivated employees are likely to contribute to productivity, quality, sales and profits. Organizational outcomes (e.g. productivity) and financial outcomes (e.g. market value) are also assumed to be positively related to HR outcomes. Thus, high profits and market value of an organization are thought to be positively associated with a satisfied and motivated workforce. There is empirical evidence for a positive relationship between HR outcomes and organizational outcomes (Paauwe and Richardson, 1997), between organizational outcomes and financial outcomes (Boselie et al., 2001), and between financial outcomes and HR outcomes, in particular between high profits and high levels of employee satisfaction (Schneider et al., 2003). However, there are also potential tensions between the three types of outcome (HR, organizational and financial) as a result of conflicting interests between the stakeholders involved (e.g. employees, managers and shareholders). The employee–employer distinction is further discussed in Chapter 5.

Employees potentially have different needs and wants (e.g. self-esteem, a good work–life balance, a nice social atmosphere, employee development opportunities and responsibility) than the needs and wants of the employer represented by managers and the shareholders (owners) of an organization (e.g. market growth, increased profits and higher market value). An ideal HR measurement system or HR scorecard takes into account the interests of the different stakeholders, including the employees' and the employer's perspective.

> 'there are potential tensions between ... human resource, organizational and financial outcomes as a result of conflicting interests between the stakeholders involved'

Excellent financial performance might go hand in hand with low employee satisfaction and commitment, because employees simply have to work too hard to get their job done. Sweatshops in China and India can be very profitable, but what about their employees' well-being reflected in terms of employee satisfaction, motivation, commitment and trust? In contrast, excellent scores on HR outcomes, reflecting general employee well-being within an organization, might go hand in hand with a lack of business awareness (e.g. cost and quality awareness) and therefore result in low organizational outcomes in terms of productivity and quality. As a result, an ideal HR scorecard explicitly acknowledges the need for balancing the interests of the different actors involved in line with the strategic balance theory (SBT), as discussed in Chapter 2 (Deephouse, 1999). This theory suggests that high-performing organizations show above-average HR, organizational and financial outcomes.

Figure 4.1 is a representation of the alternative balanced HR scorecard, including:

1 Employee and employer interests.

2 HR, organizational and financial outcomes.

3 The underlying assumption that successful organizations show balanced scores on all outcome types.

4 The notion that organizations are out of balance when (1) HR outcome scores are low and organizational and financial outcome scores are high; and (2) HR outcome scores are high and organizational and financial outcome scores are low.

5 The most ideal situation in the balanced HR scorecard is high scores on all three outcome types; however, it is unlikely that there are many organizations that can achieve this situation, in particular for a long-term period.

6 The notion that the scorecard can be extended with other outcome variables that are relevant to the specific context of the organization.

In one of his lectures, Jaap Paauwe[1] presents the notion that unbalanced organizations – (a) high on employee interests and low on employer interests or (b) low on employee interests and high on employer interests – can restore the balance, for example through:

[1] Lectures of Jaap Paauwe at Tilburg University, the Netherlands (part of the HR Studies programme).

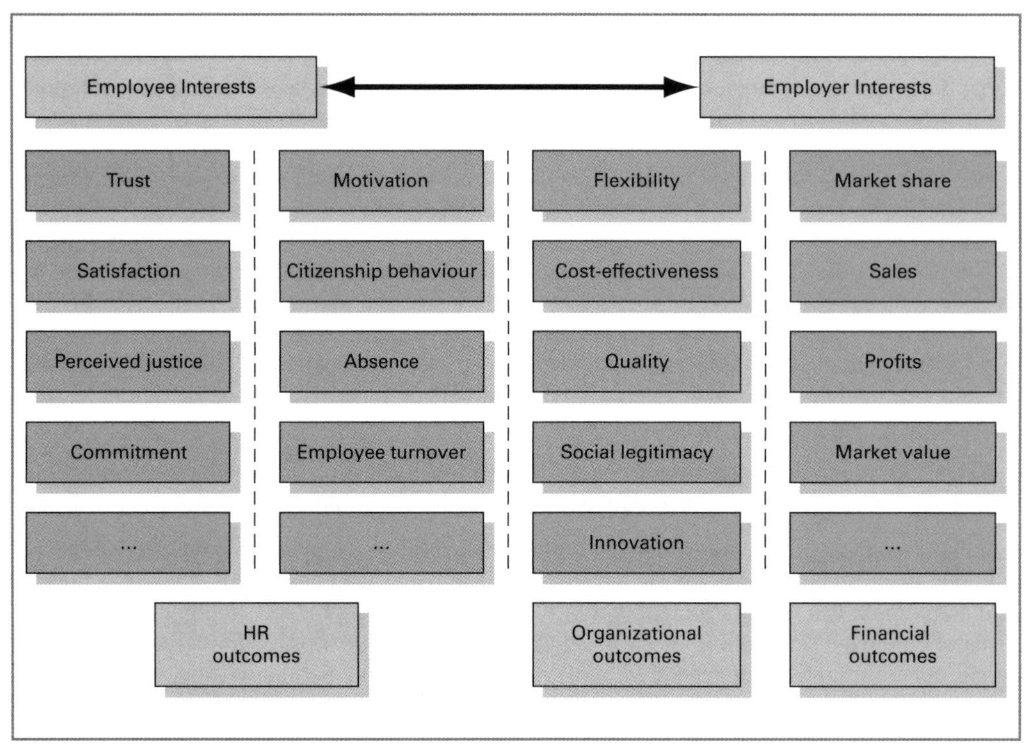

FIGURE 4.1 A balanced HR scorecard

- creating cost-awareness among employees, information sharing about the business activities and the organization's position in the market, and putting emphasis on service quality standards in relation to customers in the unbalanced situation (a) (high on employee interests and low on employer interests);
- providing employee autonomy, employee training and development, good communication and employment security in the case of the unbalanced situation (b) (low on employee interests and high on employer interests).

In practice the unbalanced situation (b) (low employee–high employer) is far more often found in organizations than situation (a). The HR interventions or practices will be linked to the outcomes discussed in the balanced HR scorecard presented above later in this chapter as a first step towards building your own scorecard using the dashboard technique.

'unbalanced organizations can restore the balance'

This chapter focuses on the measurement of HRM and performance using insights from human capital valuation and HR metrics. Chapter 3 presented the foundation of the HR value chain, but this chapter goes one step further in making the value chain more concrete, in particular aiming at building your own balanced HR scorecard. Measurement is crucial for organizations, because it represents the effectiveness of certain managerial decisions. The outcomes of the measurement can be used to continue the interventions, modify the practices or terminate managerial actions. Therefore measurement can be seen as part of an evaluation. This chapter also presents concrete HR outcome scales (e.g. commitment, justice and trust) that are validated and can be used to measure soft outcomes in organizations. There is a general trend of continuous evaluating (monitoring) managerial practices and therefore measurement has become one of the most important attention points within organizations.

For the last three decades there has been an ever-increasing focus on performance improvements reflected in the popularity of **HRA** (Elias, 1976; Fitz-enz, 1984) and the **balanced scorecard** (**BSC**) in the 1990s (Kaplan and Norton, 1992). The last ten years have witnessed the emergence of **HR scorecards** (Becker et al., 2001) in reaction to Kaplan and Norton's BSC. HRA is discussed first.

HRA has been a popular technique to measure and rate employees in an organization (Fitz-enz, 1984). HRA focuses on issues such as measuring human resources and return on investments (Elias, 1976), the measurement of the value of an organization's workforce (Sangeladji, 1977) and the measurement of management decisions with respect to HRM (Hendricks, 1976). HRA was a first attempt to quantify human capital in an organization for management accounting (control and monitoring costs) and financial purposes (e.g. as input for investment decisions). How much money does an organization invest in training and development, and what are the returns, for example, in terms of productivity and sales?

HRA was popular in the 1970s, but fell into disuse in the 1980s. The advantages of this approach are:

- it improves the quality of information with regard to human capital;
- personnel expenditures are interpreted as investments rather than costs;
- HRA provides information to stakeholders (management, shareholders, financiers, etc.);
- HRA systems are measurement systems (performance management (PM) systems), which can optimize decision-making processes.

The disadvantages of HRA are: employees are human beings, who from an ethical point of view should not be treated as assets; there are numerous measurement complications; and employees are not legally owned by organizations and therefore cannot be treated as human assets from an accounting point of view (Lybaert, 1990). However, times changed in the 1990s with the introduction of the BSC (Kaplan and Norton, 1992) and the empirical HRM and performance research from 1994 onwards (Boselie et al., 2005). Nowadays, the ethical issues mentioned before do not seem to be a problem in academia and in practice. Apparently, we have all accepted the business model and the fact that employees are human assets that are valuable to organizations.

The BSC provides a framework for mapping an organization's assets. Kaplan and Norton (1992) introduced a new approach for goal-setting and monitoring an organization. The authors make a distinction between four dimensions, with four key questions linked to each perspective:

1. *The innovation and learning perspective.* Key question: Can we continue to improve and create value?
2. *The customer perspective.* Key question: How do customers see us?
3. *The internal business perspective.* Key question: What must we excel at?
4. *The financial perspective.* Key question: How do we look to our shareholders?

The financial perspective is considered the most important one. However, the BSC also assumes that the other three perspectives affect the financial dimension of the model in the end. In other words, innovation, learning, good internal business processes and meeting customers' expectations will create shareholder value and organizational success. The introduction of multiple perspectives has been a major contribution to the field and a foundation for other scorecards to come, including the HR scorecards. Other characteristics of the BSC are the focus on (1) determining concrete goals and (2) measures for all four perspectives. The BSC unifies goal-setting

(setting targets) and defining concrete measures for evaluating to what extent the goals have been achieved (see Figure 4.2).

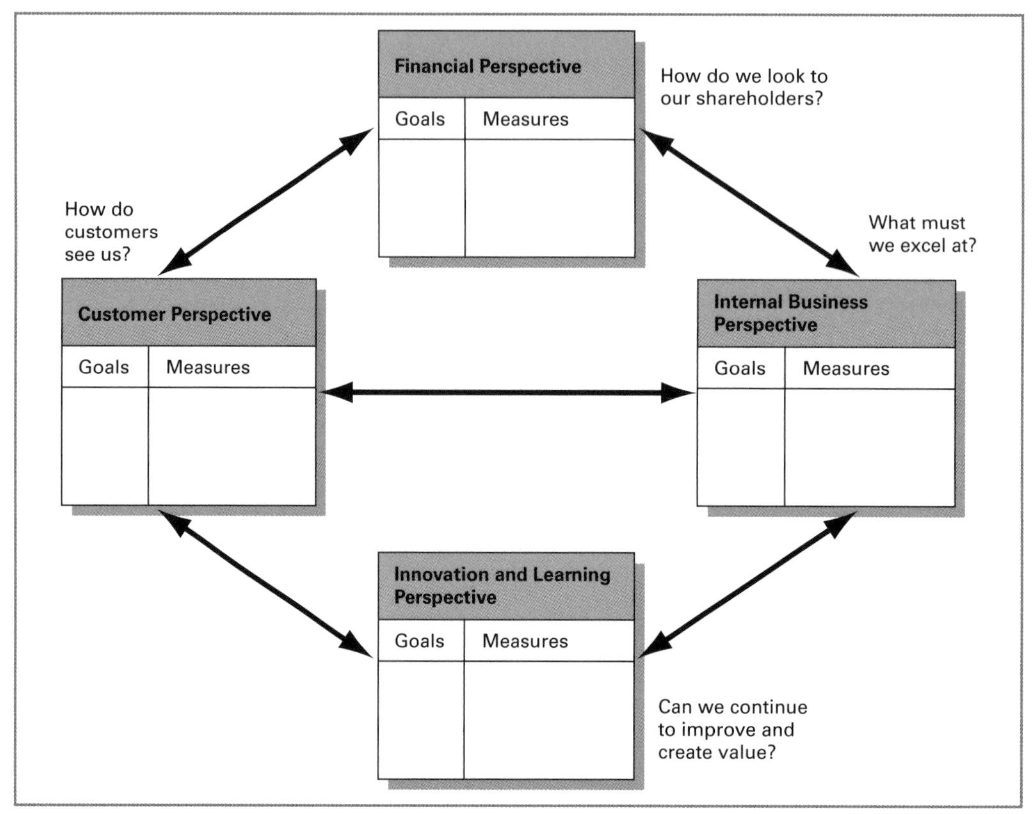

FIGURE 4.2 The balanced scorecard
Source: Reproduced with permission from Kaplan and Norton (1992).

The BSC has been adopted in thousands of organizations all over the world, including profit and non-profit organizations, but also both SMEs (small and medium enterprises) and large multinational companies (MNCs). However, in the late 1990s it was argued by some scholars, including Yeung and Berman (1997), that the BSC lacked room for the employee perspective. The HR function (including the HR professionals), the HR practices and the employee attitudes and behaviour do not fit in the BSC model easily. This called for an alternative approach, eventually resulting in the development of HR scorecards (Becker et al., 2001). The HR scorecards are part of the HRA and HR measurement debate. Part of the aim of this chapter is to build your own HR scorecard using the insights from existing literature.

Overview of HR scorecards

Early HR scorecards

- Yeung and Berman (1997) 'Adding value through human resources: reorienting human resource measurement to drive business performance'
- Becker et al. (2001) 'The HR scorecard: linking people, strategy and performance'
- Philips et al. (2001) 'The human resources scorecard: measuring the return on investment'

'Next-generation' HR scorecards

- Paauwe (2004) 'Changing HRM roles: towards a real balanced HRM scorecard'
- Huselid et al. (2005) 'The workforce scorecard: managing human capital to execute strategy'

The special issue in the *American Human Resource Management Journal* (Volume 36, Number 3, 1997) on measuring HR effectiveness and impact contains multiple articles that highlight: (1) the relevance of HR measurement, (2) the lack of HR models for measuring the added value of human assets, (3) the difficulties and challenges with regard to HR measurement, and (4) the potential of an adapted BSC for the HR discipline. Yeung and Berman (1997) were among the first to suggest the further development of an HR scorecard including organizational capabilities and employee satisfaction for the creation of customer satisfaction and shareholder value.

The early HR scorecards mainly focused on HR measurement from the HR function perspective (see Chapter 12). In other words, the first HR scorecards in both theory and practice mainly focused on:

1. the HR roles and competences (e.g. strategic partner, administrative expert, employee champion and change agent);
2. the HR practices in place (e.g. staffing, compensation and development);
3. the HR systems in place (e.g. the HR infrastructure).

Becker et al. (2001) present one of these early HR scorecards in their book with the HR function (e.g. HR department and HR professionals) as the main starting point for measuring HRM in an organization. Their scorecard contains five key elements:

1. The workforce success: 'Has the workforce accomplished the key strategic objectives for the business?'
2. The right HR costs: 'Is our total investment in the workforce appropriate (not just minimized)?'
3. The right types of HR alignment: 'Are our HR practices aligned with the business strategy and differentiated across positions, where appropriate? '
4. The right HR practices: 'Have we designed and implemented world class HR management policies and practices throughout the business?'
5. The right HR professionals: 'Do our HR professionals have the skills they need to design and implement a world-class HR management system?'

Figure 4.4 (below) presents the HR scorecard (left part of the figure), the workforce scorecard (the middle part of the figure) and the BSC (the right part of the figure). This visualization by Huselid et al. (2005) suggests the linkages between the three scorecards, including the BSC of Kaplan and Norton (1992).

Another early HR scorecard is presented by Philips et al. (2001), emphasizing evaluation planning, data collection (e.g. on satisfaction, learning, application implementation and business impact), data analysis, and the calculation of the return on investment (ROI), the intangible benefits and the general programme costs. They identify three potential user groups: HR professionals, senior managers and consultants (or evaluation researchers). There is, however, no clear linkage between HRM and strategy in this HR scorecard.

The 'next-generation' HR scorecards (e.g. Paauwe, 2004; Huselid et al., 2005) are much broader than the early models presented above, including not only the HR function and practices but organizational elements as well. Paauwe's (2004) 4logic HRM scorecard contains:

- a professional logic;
- a strategic logic;
- a societal logic;
- a delivery logic.

The professional logic is focused on the expectations of line managers, employees, works councils and colleagues of HR departments (Paauwe, 2004). This logic represents the traditional personnel management domain also highlighted in the early HR scorecards (Chapter 12 is mainly focused on this area). The strategic logic incorporates the expectations of the board of directors, chief executive officer (CEO), shareholders and financiers (Paauwe, 2004). This is where HRM can contribute to achieving strategic goals, for example with regard to talent management and leadership development (LD) (see Chapter 10). The societal logic is focused on the expectations of works councils, trade unions, the government, and other interest groups or stakeholders relevant to the organization (Paauwe, 2004). This logic makes it a typical continental European approach through acknowledging multiple stakeholders (see Chapter 2). The HR delivery logic represents the cost-effectiveness of the possible HR delivery channels, including HR departments (and HR professionals), line management, teams, employees themselves, outsourcing and self-service through e-HRM (ibid.). The real strength in this model is the stepwise approach for creating an HR scorecard offering opportunities for contextual alignment. Paauwe's (2004) 4logic HRM scorecard is presented in Figure 4.3.

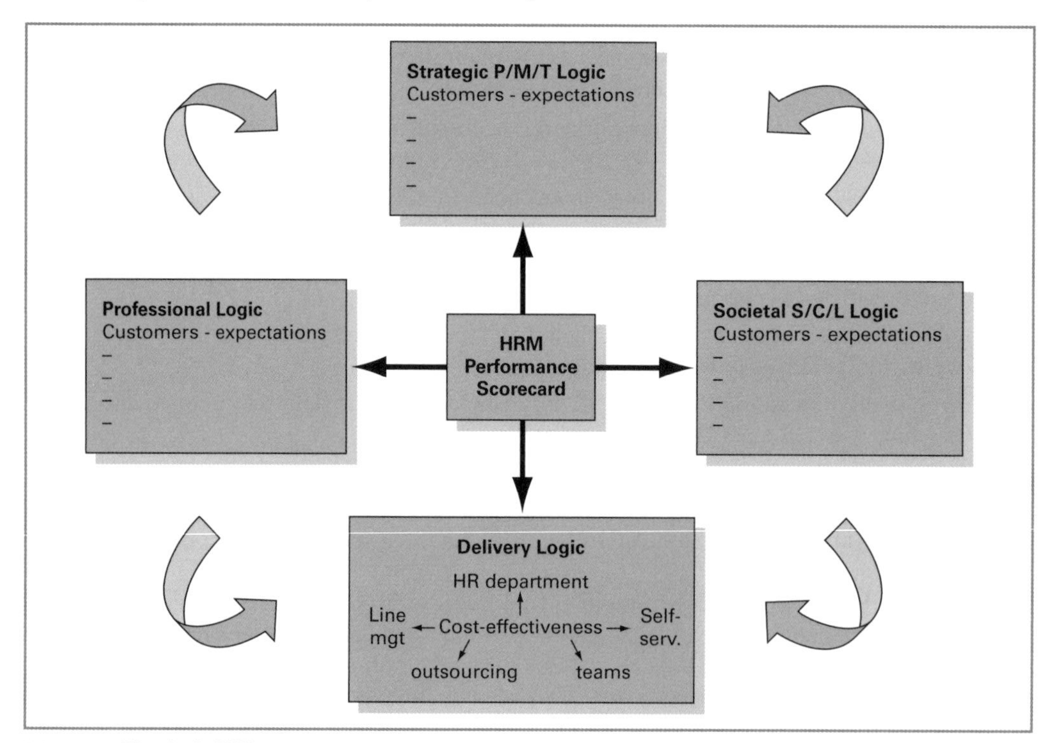

FIGURE 4.3 The 4logic HRM scorecard

Source: Reproduced with permission from Paauwe (2004, Figure 9.7, p. 196).

The workforce scorecard by Huselid et al. (2005) is another illustration of the 'next-generation' HR scorecards (see Figure 4.4). The workforce scorecard approach intends to bridge the narrow

HR scorecard approaches that are mainly focused on the HR function itself (see Chapter 12) and the general BSC presented by Kaplan and Norton (1992). The four key dimensions in the workforce scorecard are: (1) the mindset and culture of the workforce in an organization, (2) workforce behaviour with specific attention paid to the leadership team, (3) the competences of the workforce, in particular for the core employees, and (4) the workforce success in achieving strategic goals. The latter dimension is a replacement of Kaplan and Norton's (1992) innovating and learning perspective.

Huselid et al. (2005) pay a lot of attention to organizational culture (e.g. corporate values), leadership, the implementation process (strategy implementation), metrics (measurement), the distinction between 'superior' and 'marginal' employees and the actual translation of the scorecard into practice. The latter aspect is definitely a strength of their approach. The ultimate business goal in terms of financial success (shareholder value) makes the workforce scorecard a typical Anglo-Saxon approach in contrast to, for example, Paauwe's (2004) 4logic HRM scorecard.

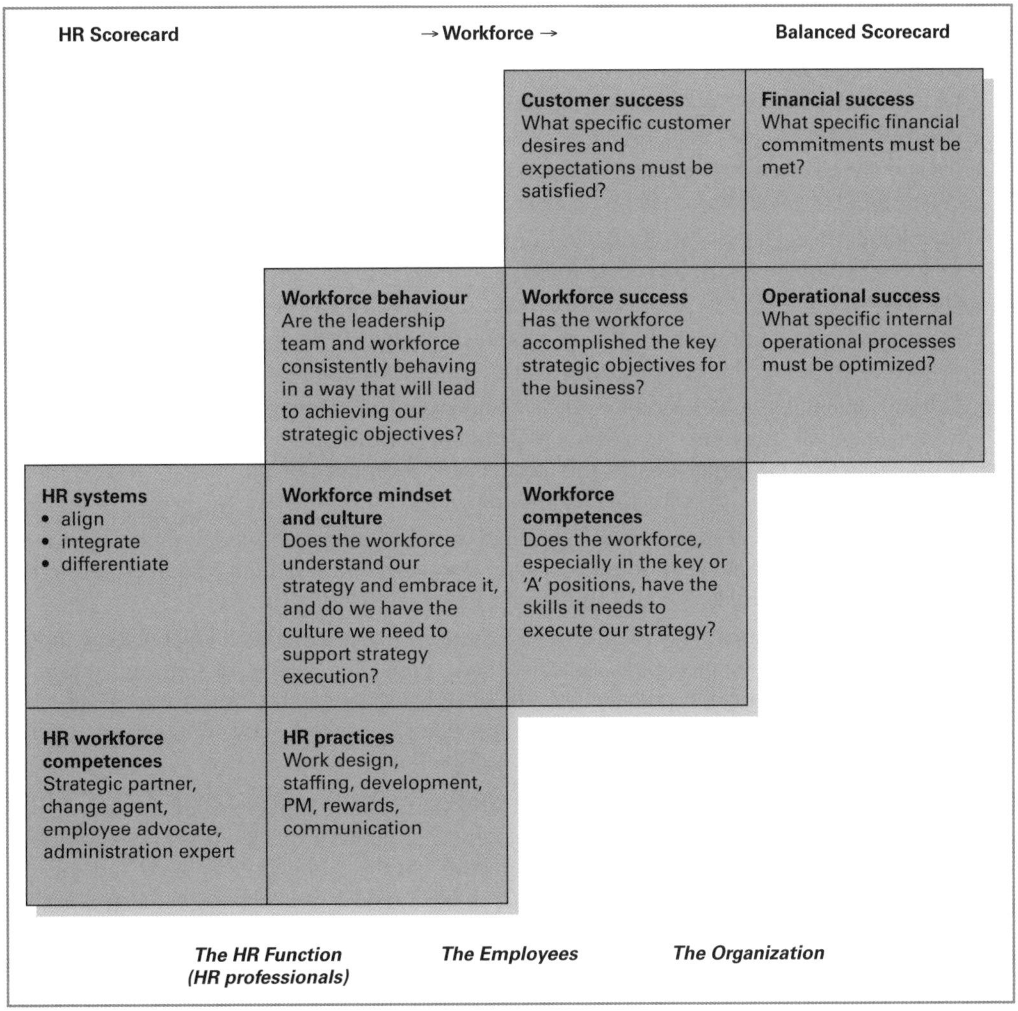

HR Scorecard	→ Workforce →		Balanced Scorecard
		Customer success What specific customer desires and expectations must be satisfied?	**Financial success** What specific financial commitments must be met?
	Workforce behaviour Are the leadership team and workforce consistently behaving in a way that will lead to achieving our strategic objectives?	**Workforce success** Has the workforce accomplished the key strategic objectives for the business?	**Operational success** What specific internal operational processes must be optimized?
HR systems • align • integrate • differentiate	**Workforce mindset and culture** Does the workforce understand our strategy and embrace it, and do we have the culture we need to support strategy execution?	**Workforce competences** Does the workforce, especially in the key or 'A' positions, have the skills it needs to execute our strategy?	
HR workforce competences Strategic partner, change agent, employee advocate, administration expert	**HR practices** Work design, staffing, development, PM, rewards, communication		
The HR Function (HR professionals)	***The Employees***	***The Organization***	

FIGURE 4.4 The HR scorecard, the workforce scorecard and the BSC

Source: Adapted version of the model reproduced with permission from Huselid et al. (2005).

Accounting and control literature

In recent years in the field of accounting and control, more substantial attention is paid to non-financial indicators that represent the performance and value of an organization. Starovic and Marr (2003), for example, provide an overview of managing and reporting intellectual capital. They conclude that many organizations across Europe already publish intellectual capital statements including intangibles that are directly related to human resources and HRM. Starovic and Marr define intellectual capital in terms of: (1) human capital (e.g. know-how, education and work-related competences), (2) relational capital (e.g. brands, customers and customer loyalty), and (3) organizational capital (e.g. patents, copyrights, corporate culture, management philosophy and networking systems).

Starovic and Marr (ibid.) also provide an overview of both generic and individual company models that measure intellectual capital, including:

1. the BSC (Kaplan and Norton, 1992) – a generic model;
2. the performance prism of the Cranfield School of Management in collaboration with consultancy firm Accenture – a generic model presenting a hierarchy of knowledge assets, including stakeholder relationships, human resources, physical infrastructures and virtual infrastructures;
3. the knowledge assets map approach (Marr, 2003) – a generic model with human resources as the central point of value creation linked to stakeholder relationships, culture and financial success;
4. the Skandia Navigator – an individual organization model developed in the mid-1990s, including a human focus, a process focus, a renewal and development focus, and a financial focus;
5. Ericsson's Cockpit Communicator – an individual organization model incorporating the five perspectives: innovation, employee, process, customer and financial;
6. Celemi's Intangible Assets Monitor – an individual organization model focused on the customers (external structure), the internal structure and the people (competence). Illustrations of the concrete measurements in this model are 'revenues per customer', 'rookie ratio', 'expert turnover' and 'people satisfaction index';
7. Ramboll's Holistic Company Model – an individual organization model, including values and management, strategic processes (human resources and structural resources), customer results, employee results, societal results and financial outcomes;
8. Bates Gruppen CompanyIQ Measurement Systems – an individual organization model incorporating: (a) human capital indicators (e.g. educational level of staff and image of company from employees' perspective), (b) organizational capital indicators (e.g. number of patents and number of times database has been consulted), and (c) customer capital indicators (e.g. brand loyalty and customer satisfaction).

In summary, the eight models presented by Starovic and Marr (2003) incorporate both hard (financial) and soft often intangible indicators. Some of the presented models explicitly build on stakeholder notions, including not only the shareholder perspective but the customer, employee and societal perspective as well. The employee dimension in these eight models is integrated in the approaches and embedded in human capital notions, human resources and processes. The overview represents contemporary views from HRA on measuring intangible assets, including those related to employees.

In the HR field, HRA is nowadays called **human capital valuation (HCV)** or **human resource (HR) metrics**. HCV and HR metrics are focused on HR measurement. Measuring and monitoring HR interventions have become crucial activities in creating added value through people. Like any other discipline (finance, marketing and operations), it is important that the HR function is capable of providing data on the effectiveness of HR activities. Human capital valuation and HR metrics include the measurement, monitoring and evaluation of HRM necessary for improving the performance of an organization.

What needs to be measured?

There are different ways of looking at measurement. The traditional measurement approach focuses on performance outcomes, often mainly financial outcomes (Cascio, 2006). These performance outcomes can be represented through, for example, sales figures, quality measures (number of defects), productivity, profits, market share and value. However, performance appears to be much broader than these typical organizational outcomes. In the HR value chain presented in Chapter 3, other outcomes were described, including HR outcomes reflecting employee attitudes and behaviours (e.g. employees' satisfaction, motivation, commitment, citizenship, trust and loyalty). In summary, the relevant outcomes for HR measurement might include a broad range of indicators as presented in the HR value chain in Chapter 3. Relevant outcome measures that represent the organization's success or the degree of goal achievement are often called KPIs. We return to these notions on performance later in this chapter.

The text above focuses on measuring the *output* of an organization. What about measuring the input? *Input* represents the interventions or managerial practices (including HR practices), but also the **human capital management (HCM)** available to the organization. The latter is discussed in more detail by Wright et al. (2001), who argue that there are three types of capital relevant for measuring the added value of HRM:

1. *Human capital* reflected in the knowledge, skills and abilities of the organization's employees. This factor can be strengthened by HR practices such as selective recruitment and selection and employee development (more employee knowledge represents more value).
2. *Social capital* reflected in the valuable social networks and relationships between employees within the organization and social networks of employees with the outside world. This factor can be influenced by stimulating cooperation (teamwork) and employee autonomy.
3. *Organizational capital* embedded in the practices and systems in place. For example, a management information system that enables employees to tap knowledge and expertise throughout the organization.

Human capital can be measured by the level of education, the work experience employees have and the abilities of employees. The latter are more difficult to measure, but regular tests for monitoring individual employee development and for measuring the organization's development can be carried out. You could, for example, also calculate the number of employees who have attended training in a given year. Unfortunately, training attendance does not tell us if the participant has learned anything from it and thus contributed to the human capital of an organization. The knowledge, skills and abilities (KSA) framework is often used to classify human capital. Illustrations of knowledge are business knowledge, HRM knowledge (e.g. with regard to labour law), information technology (IT) and accountancy knowledge. Illustrations of skills are negotiation, presentation, language, diplomacy and social. Finally, examples of abilities are analytic abilities (e.g. reflected in abstract thinking and the ability to shift between strategy and operations), managerial abilities (e.g. motivating subordinates) and the ability to adapt to changing circumstances.

Social capital is much more difficult to measure because it is focused on the relationships between people. However, the nature of the contacts employees have in the organization can be calculated. For example, how many people does an individual work with given a certain task? Do employees consult other employees for advice or knowledge? And to what extent do employees use their social network outside the organization for task performance? Account managers and sales representatives build their success on their external network with customers. This network and the employee's ability to successfully manage this network is a valuable asset for an organization. If an employee leaves an organization, this can potentially affect the value of the network to it.

Organizational capital represents the HR practices and systems that shape the employment relationship in an organization. HR practices incorporate a certain value themselves. A training programme costs time and money to develop and therefore represents capital. This rule applies to almost all HR practices. Organizational capital also includes systems such as SAP for monitoring and evaluating employees. These systems are often quite expensive and challenging to implement and therefore also represent capital. Measuring organizational capital by just calculating the initial investment costs is one way of presenting it. This can be extended by including the time needed for implementation and the investments in training employees to work with it.

The three forms of capital represent a rather hard approach to measuring the input. There are other ways of measuring the HR input. We can ask the opinions of multiple actors involved; for example, employees, line managers and HR professionals. This is often done with questionnaires. There are different perspectives that should be taken into account. First, we can simply ask whether a certain practice (e.g. performance-related pay (PRP)) or phenomenon (e.g. extended social networks for task performance) exists or not within the organization. The *presence* or *absence* of a factor is one way of measuring HR input. Second, we can ask respondents *how satisfied* they are with a practice or phenomenon. For example, indicate how satisfied you are with the cooperation within your department on a five-point scale, with 1 representing very dissatisfied, 3 neutral and 5 very satisfied. Third, we may ask people to what extent they are subject to a practice or phenomenon. For example, to what extent do you have opportunities for internal promotion presented on a five-point scale, with 1 being very little and 5 being very much. This is also called *intensity*. Fourth, another way of measuring HR input is to focus on how many people are covered by a practice. For example, how many employees are subject to an annual bonus? This is also known as *coverage* and often presented as a percentage of the total workforce. Finally, HR input can be measured by asking respondents about the *importance* of certain practices or phenomena. For example, how important is development for you personally?

Presence, satisfaction, intensity, coverage and importance are different ways of measuring HR input through questionnaires (Boselie et al., 2005). We also need to take into account who we ask. Coverage questions are probably more difficult to answer for employees than HR professionals, while satisfaction, intensity and importance questions are typically best asked of employees instead of HR professionals. The study of Gerhart et al. (2000) shows that we need at least four respondents per organization in order to measure HRM in a reliable way.

Summary of measuring HR input

- *Presence* (yes or no)
- *Intensity* (very little – very much)
- *Importance* (not important at all – very important)
- *Satisfaction* (very dissatisfied – very satisfied)
- *Coverage* (percentage of the total workforce)

The HR value chain was described in Chapter 3. In this value chain a distinction has been made between intended, actual and perceived HR practices. The distinction between intended, actual and perceived is also directly linked to three different types of group within the organization: HR professionals, line managers and employees. The HR professionals are closely related to the intended HR practices, because they will mainly be in charge of designing new HR policies and practices. The actual implementation of the HR practices is mostly done by the line managers and therefore called 'actual practices'. Finally, the implemented HR practices are perceived by employees in a certain way. Organizations tend to focus too much on the intended practices in their HR measurement with little or no attention paid to their implementation (Becker and Huselid, 2006) and employee perception (Wright and Boswell, 2002). It is of course best when we measure all three aspects (intended, actual and perceived) using different ways of measuring (presence, satisfaction, intensity, coverage and importance). Illustrations of measuring HR input are described below.

Presence

Promotion opportunities: 'I will eventually have the opportunity to move into a supervisory position at this company.' (scale: yes or no) (Appelbaum et al., 2000: 120)

Satisfaction

Compensation: 'I am very satisfied with my salary.'
(scale: totally disagree – disagree – neither agree nor disagree – agree – totally agree)

Intensity

Participation: 'Organization X offers me participation in developing strategic plans.' (scale: not at all – to a small extent – to a moderate extent – to a great extent – to a very great extent) (Boon, 2008: 252)

Coverage

Teamwork: 'What is the percentage of the total workforce working in teams?'
(scale: percentage with 0 per cent representing nobody and 100 per cent representing everybody of the workforce of the organization)

Importance

Employee participation: 'Involvement in decision making with respect to selecting a new colleague is important to me.'
(scale: totally disagree – disagree – neither agree nor disagree – agree – totally agree)

Measuring outcomes

Dyer and Reeves (1995) provide an overview of the different outcomes relevant for the HR field. They make a distinction between three types of outcome:

1. *financial outcomes* (e.g. profits, sales, market share, Tobin's q and GRATE);
2. *organizational outcomes* (e.g. productivity/cost-effectiveness, product and service quality, innovation and flexibility);
3. *HR-related outcomes* (e.g. attitudinal, cognitive and behavioural outcomes among employees such as job satisfaction, organizational commitment, trust in management, intention to quit and absence due to illness).

Guest (1997) argues that financial and organizational outcomes are *distal outcome measures* with regard to HRM. In other words, the distance between an HR intervention (e.g. skills training) and organizational outcomes (e.g. increased service quality) and financial outcomes (e.g. increased sales) is large and therefore effects of the intervention are difficult to measure when using distal outcome measures. Guest suggests the focus on HR-related outcomes being much closer to the actual intervention and therefore labelled *proximal outcome measures*. Distal outcome measures are potentially also affected by other factors that are non-HR related; for example, external market changes (economic recession or an increase in oil prices). However, the organizational and financial outcomes are much more closely related to the ultimate business goals of an organization and important indicators for the competitive position of an organization (see also Chapter 3, p. 57, on the proximal–distal notions suggested by Guest, 1997). We should take into account all three outcome types suggested by Dyer and Reeves (1995) when studying the added value of HRM, but at the same time take notice of Guest's (1997) plea for focusing on outcomes that are closely related to the HR interventions.

> 'the distance between an HR intervention ... organizational outcomes ... and financial outcomes ... is large and therefore effects of the intervention are difficult to measure when using distal outcome measures.'

Financial outcomes are in particular relevant for shareholders, because the owners want to know how the organization is doing in terms of sales, market share, potential growth, profits and market value. Financial outcomes in the non-profit context are relevant for financiers; for example, health insurance companies and the government in case of health care organizations such as hospitals. Organizational outcomes such as productivity and quality are in particular relevant for internal purposes; for example, monitoring the production process and the quality of the products or services. In Chapter 3 these organizational outcomes were called critical HR goals and critical non-HR goals in the HR value chain. The HR-related outcomes reflect the direct impact of people management practices on the attitudes, cognitive aspects and behaviour of employees. Selective recruitment and selection can lead to lower employee turnover, because selecting the right person for the job decreases the chance of newcomers leaving within the first two years. Another example of the direct impact of HR interventions on HR-related outcomes is the potential positive relationship between employee involvement and the organizational commitment of employees. In other words, employee involvement in decision making can increase employee commitment and loyalty to the organization.

Next, we need to clarify the nature of these outcomes. For research and managerial purposes, we need to specify what an outcome is. A distinction can be made between *concepts*, *indicators* and *measurements* (see Figure 4.5). A concept is a very broad notion involving multiple, more specific elements called indicators. Economic performance of an organization is an example of a performance concept. Economic performance contains indicators such as productivity and sales. Employee well-being is another example of a concept, which can contain more specific indicators such as stress and burn-out. Indicators can be measured using very specific items. For example, if we are interested in the economic performance of an organization, we can look at the indicator of productivity. In a hospital productivity is often measured by the percentage of beds occupied. This is just an illustration of how the economic performance of a hospital can be translated into a concrete indicator (productivity) and measured by the percentage of beds occupied at a certain time.

This threefold distinction can also be applied to the measurement of HRM. A high-performance work system (HPWS) or system of aligned best practices in HRM (see Chapter 6 on this subject) represents a concept that contains several indicators, including the HR practices selective recruitment, extensive employee development and pay for performance. Each of these HR practices can be measured using multiple items; for example, counting the number of

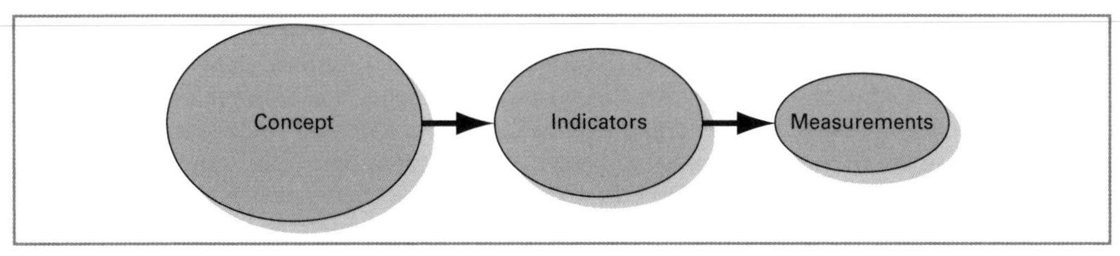

FIGURE 4.5 Concepts, indicators and measurements

HR techniques (e.g. interviews, assessment centres, psychological tests and reference checks) applied as part of the recruitment and selection process.

Policy-makers, including HR professionals, tend to focus on concepts and indicators. However, often the real challenge is in designing good measurements that are easily applied and collected. Measuring HR-related outcomes, for example motivation or employee trust, is difficult because of a lack of consensus on how to measure these indicators in combination with limitations on measuring these concepts on a regular basis (e.g. daily or weekly).

HR-related outcomes

One of the most popular and oldest HR outcomes is probably *employee satisfaction*. This indicator represents the employee's contentment with, for example, the job, the direct supervisor and the organization as a whole. The yearly employee surveys in organizations are often mainly focused on general employee satisfaction in a specific organization.

> ***'Overall, how satisfied are you with the job?***
>
> 1 = very dissatisfied; 2 = dissatisfied; 3 = neither dissatisfied nor satisfied; 4 = satisfied; 5 = very satisfied
>
> (Cooper-Thomas et al., 2004)

There are a couple of interesting notions related to satisfaction. First, it is often assumed that employee satisfaction and labour productivity are positively related. In other words, we often assume that a happy worker is also a productive worker. Unfortunately, as argued by Peccei (2004), this is often not the case. Very unhappy workers can be highly productive and very unproductive workers can be very satisfied. We should therefore not automatically assume positive relationships between satisfaction and other performance indicators. Second, aggregating employee satisfaction scores to organization level often results in average scores of around 7 on a 10-point scale, with 1 being extremely low satisfaction and 10 representing very high levels of satisfaction. Probably scores below an average of 6 indicating low employee satisfaction levels and scores above 8 indicating high employee satisfaction have meaning, while average scores for an organization between 6–8 on a 10-point scale do not tell us a lot. A possible explanation for this phenomenon is the respondent's tendency to score between 6–8 when it is about satisfaction.

Stop and reflect

- Think of two HR practices that potentially positively affect employee job satisfaction.
- Think of two HR practices that potentially negatively affect employee job satisfaction.
- How satisfied are you with your study (as a student) or with your job (as an employee)?

Another classic HR outcome is *employee motivation* focused on the employee's drive to perform the job. Traditionally, a distinction is made between intrinsic and extrinsic motivation (Ryan and Deci, 2003, in Porter et al., 2003). Intrinsic motivation represents 'the inherent tendency to seek out novelty and challenges, to extend and exercise one's capabilities, to explore, and to learn, (Ryan and Deci, 2003: 51). The employee's drive to do something comes from inside and the employee's behaviour is self-determined. In contrast, extrinsic motivation is mainly externally determined through rewards (e.g. pay for performance), punishments and compliance regulation. Highly motivated employees are assumed to deliver better job performance (see below).

Motivation scale

Motivation measured as effort/importance:

- 'I put a lot of effort into this.'
- 'I didn't try very hard to do well at this activity.' (reversed)
- 'I tried very hard on this activity.'
- 'It was important to me to do well at this task.'
- 'I didn't put much energy into this.'

1 = not at all; 4 = somewhat true; 7 = very true (7-point scale)

(Intrinsic Motivation Inventory, 2008)

The outcome of motivation has received less and less attention throughout the last decade, probably because of the following reasons. Although highly relevant, motivation is difficult to measure and difficult to interpret. There is no consensus on the actual measurement of motivation and the existence of the clear-cut intrinsic–extrinsic distinction is heavily debated (Ryan and Deci, 2003). Finally, motivation lacks the incorporation of actual employee behaviour. This was picked up by some scholars in organizational behaviour and led to the development of organizational citizenship behaviour.

Stop and reflect

Do high wages motivate employees to work harder? Think of situations in which high wages cause high employee motivation and situations in which high wages cause extremely low employee motivation.

When employees are willing to go the extra mile (willingness to put extra effort into their job without additional rewards or payments), it is called *organizational citizenship behaviour* (*OCB*). OCB has gained popularity since the 1990s because it is considered a good indicator for the workforce's willingness to perform in the interest of the organization and/or the department of an employee, especially when the organization or department is under pressure. In contrast to employee motivation, OCB is seen as a form of employee behaviour, as shown below.

The OCB scale

- 'I help orient new employees even though it is not required/I am willing to take time out of my busy schedule to help with recruiting or training new agents.'

- 'I am always ready to help or to lend a helping hand to those around me.'
- 'I willingly give of my time to help others.'
- 'I "keep up" with developments in the company.'
- 'I read and "keep up" with the company announcements, messages, memos, etc.'
- 'I attend functions that are not required, but that help the company image.'
- 'I attend training/information sessions that agents are encouraged but not required to attend.'
- 'I consider the impact of my actions on others.'
- 'I "touch base" with others before initiating actions that might affect them.'
- 'I try to avoid creating problems for the other employees.'

1 = strongly disagree; 2 = disagree; 3 = neither disagree nor agree; 4 = agree; 5 = strongly agree

(MacKenzie et al., 1991; Boon, 2008)

! *Stop and reflect*

Discuss why employees might be willing to put more effort into their job without any additional rewards. Can you think of occupations/professions in which organizational citizenship behaviour is extremely important?

Another popular HR outcome is *employee commitment.* Allen and Meyer's (1990) Three-Component Model of Commitment is the most commonly used framework for defining employee commitment. This model suggests the distinction of three components of commitment: affective, normative and continuance. *Affective commitment* can be defined by the identification with, involvement in and emotional attachment to the organization (Allen and Meyer, 1996). *Continuance commitment* reflects the attachment to the organization because of a lack of alternatives. In other words, employees have no alternatives and are committed to an organization because they cannot find a similar job elsewhere. *Normative commitment* is the employee's attachment to an organization (or department) because of a perceived moral obligation to stay with the organization because of attachment to, for example, colleagues in a team or clients. Empirical evidence suggests that affective commitment is positively associated with other desirable outcomes (e.g. intention to stay, employee presence, OCB, employee health, employee well-being), while the other two commitment components in some cases reveal negative associations with outcome measures (Meyer et al., 2002). Continuance commitment might be caused by excellent compensation, a phenomenon also known as 'golden chains' or 'the golden cage'. High levels of continuance commitment might result in decreasing mobility of employees, in particular too low levels of employee turnover. Normative commitment potentially reflects attachment to the organization, colleagues and/or customers not because of motivation and inspiration, but as a result of a perceived moral obligation to continue the job even under poor working conditions. There is a general consensus that affective commitment is a desirable HR outcome for organizations, while the other two forms of commitment might reflect negative employee attitudes. Affective commitment is considered extremely important in case of labour market shortages and the retention of knowledge workers and other core employees (representing the most valuable workers). Affective commitment is sometimes also labelled 'organizational commitment'. An effective way of measuring this type of commitment is offered by Ellemers et al. (1998) (see below).

Organizational commitment scale

Organizational commitment is:

- 'This organization has a great deal of personal meaning for me.'
- 'I feel emotionally attached to this organization.'
- 'I would be very happy to spend the rest of my career with this organization.'
- 'I feel "part of the family" in this organization.'

1 = strongly disagree; 2 = disagree; 3 = neither disagree nor agree; 4 = agree; 5 = strongly agree

(Ellemers et al., 1998; Boon, 2008)

! *Stop and reflect*

Discuss the downside of high continuance commitment levels in combination with very low affective commitment levels among employees in an organization.

In times of increased competition, globalization and continuous organizational change, *employee trust* is increasingly seen as a crucial indicator for the employee–employer atmosphere in an organization (Gillespie and Dietz, 2008). When employees trust their direct supervisor, the organization, their colleagues and top management, organizations have a much easier job of achieving goals because less management control (e.g. direct supervision and continuous monitoring) is required.

Large corporate scandals caused by mismanagement of top managers including the Enron, Parmalat and Ahold cases have had a huge negative impact on employees' trust within those organizations. Trust can be considered the organization's motor oil that enables a smooth ride towards a determined destination (see below).

Employee trust scale

- 'I believe my employer has high integrity.'
- 'I can expect my employer to treat me in a consistent and predictable fashion.'
- 'My employer is not always honest and truthful.' (reversed)
- 'In general, I believe my employer's motives and intentions are good.'
- 'I don't think my employer treats me fairly.' (reversed)
- 'My employer is open and upfront with me.'
- 'I'm not sure I fully trust my employer.' (reversed)

1 = strongly disagree; 2 = disagree; 3 = neither disagree nor agree; 4 = agree; 5 = strongly agree

(Robinson, 1996; Dietz and Den Hartog, 2006)

Stop and reflect

Major organizational changes (e.g. reorganization) can negatively affect employee trust levels within an organization. Think of two or three HR practices that can be applied to restore employee trust levels in times of major organizational change.

Perceived employee justice represents the employee's perception of the fairness of HRM in an organization (Baron and Kreps, 1999). Do I get a fair amount of payment for the efforts I put into my job? Am I being evaluated in a fair way by my direct supervisor? Do I get the same promotion opportunities as my fellow colleague who is doing exactly the same job as me? These are just a couple of questions employees can ask themselves on a regular basis that reflect perceived justice or perceived injustice. A further distinction can be made between *distributive justice* and *procedural justice*. Distributive justice concerns people's perception of outcomes or rewards and the way they are allocated (Baron and Kreps, 1999: 107). This form of justice is relevant for workers' satisfaction with decisions concerning their jobs and pay. Procedural justice, on the other hand, deals with the fairness of the procedures used to determine outcome distributions or allocations (Colquitt et al., 2001). Procedural justice is often related to workers' perception of the supervisor, their attachment to the organization, and their willingness to engage in various kinds of organizational citizenship behaviour (Paauwe and Boselie, 2007). When organizations fail to meet objectives of social legitimacy and fairness, perceived injustice is likely to increasingly be felt by those involved (e.g. employees) and this is likely to affect employee behaviour and social relations negatively within an organization (Greenberg, 1990).

Perceived justice scales: distributive and procedural justice

Distributive justice is:

- 'My work schedule is fair.'
- 'I think that my level of pay is fair.'
- 'I consider my work load to be quite fair.'
- 'Overall, the rewards I receive here are quite fair.'
- 'I feel that my job responsibilities are fair.'

1 = strongly disagree; 2 = disagree; 3 = neither disagree nor agree; 4 = agree; 5 = strongly agree

(Niehoff and Moorman, 1993)

Procedural justice is:

- 'Job decisions are made by the general manager in an unbiased manner.'
- 'My general manager makes sure that all employees' concerns are heard before job decisions are made.'
- 'To make job decisions, my general manager collects accurate and complete information.'
- 'My general manager clarifies decisions and provides additional information when requested by employees.'
- 'All job decisions are applied consistently across all affected employees.'

- 'Employees are allowed to challenge or appeal job decisions made by the general manager.'

1 = strongly disagree; 2 = disagree; 3 = neither disagree nor agree; 4 = agree; 5 = strongly agree

(Niehoff and Moorman, 1993)

! *Stop and reflect*

A CEO is dismissed because of poor financial firm performance. As a result the organization is in a crisis and needs to reorganize. The reorganization includes a downsizing of the workforce by 10 per cent of the employees. The CEO gets a €10 million bonus for his dismissal, whereas the average employee who is dismissed receives four months' salary (approximately €12 000). How do you think the employees will react to the CEO bonus and the payment of dismissed employees? What can the organization do to avoid employees perceiving this situation as a major injustice?

Employee turnover represents the percentage of the workforce that leaves the organization in a given year. People may leave the organization as a result of many different reasons, including retirement, dissatisfaction with their direct supervisor, seeking new challenges outside the organization, getting a better job offer elsewhere, disability, quitting the job because of children and even death. Employee turnover is an indicator that can only be measured at an aggregated level, including the turnover rates at team, departmental, business unit and organization level. Some organizations are confronted with very low turnover rates, for example the United Nations (UN) in New York. People who enter the UN are unlikely to leave the organization. This might result in a lack of employee mobility inside and outside the organization, because if employees do not leave, there are also constraints on attracting new employees from outside. Other organizations, for example supermarkets (consider Walmart in the USA and Aldi in Western Europe), are confronted with relatively high turnover rates of up to 50 per cent, showing that half of all the current employees will have left the organization within one year. In other words, too low employee turnover and too high turnover rates potentially have a negative impact on performance (Boselie et al., 2005). On an individual employee level, organizations tend to measure *intention to quit* as a predictor of employee turnover. Intention to quit can be measured by Colarelli's (1984) three items on a five-point scale, with 1 representing 'strongly disagree' and 5 representing 'strongly agree':

- 'I frequently think of quitting my job.'
- 'I am planning to search for a new job during the next 12 months.'
- 'If I have my own way, I will be working in this organization one year from now.' (reversed)

Stop and reflect

Discuss the positive and negative aspects of employee turnover for an organization.

Employee turnover and intention to quit are nowadays often linked to the employee retention debate. The retention debate focuses, broadly speaking, on two issues. First, there is an increased labour shortage in, for example, Europe and therefore it is important to attract and retain good employees. Second, in the war for talent and future leaders, it is considered crucial to devote special time and money to talent management and LD. Employee turnover rates and employee scores on intention to quit can be indicators of the organization's success in retaining valuable employees.

Employee absence represents whether or not employees are available to do their job. Again, there are many potential reasons for employee absence, including absence due to illness, parental leave, unpaid leave, an employee–employer conflict and sabbaticals. Vacation and public holidays are usually excluded from the employee absence data. Employee presence can be measured in three different ways (Boselie et al., 2005). First, employee absence can be measured as a percentage of the total workforce being absent in a given year. An 8 per cent employee absence represents a loss of 8 per cent of all the working days available in a given year caused by employees not being present. Incidentally, an 8 per cent employee absence figure is a relatively high negative HR outcome in most contexts. Second, employee absence can be measured by the average absence frequency in a given year. A score of 1.8 represents the situation that every employee is 1.8 times not present in a given year. Some employees are always present, but others might be absent every other month. If the average frequency is close to one, this is probably acceptable for most organizations, because every employee can get sick in a year with a cold or the flu. However, scores above 2 might indicate that there is something wrong in the organization. Finally, employee absence can be measured through the average working days lost due to employees not being present in a given year. This figure is calculated using the total days lost divided by the number of employees in a given year:

$$\text{Average duration of employee absence} = \frac{\text{Total number of days lost due to employee absence in year t}}{\text{Total number of employees in year t}}$$

High scores on duration can be caused by poor working conditions resulting in injuries or employee stress causing burnout. When the average duration is low, but the frequency is high, this might indicate that employees too easily call in sick. Absence due to illness is an important indicator for the general employee well-being in an organization.

Stop and reflect

Discuss the possible impact of employee absence on the employees who are present.

Organizational outcomes

The most popular organizational outcome in HR measurement is *productivity* (Boselie et al., 2005). Productivity represents the amount of output per unit of input and can be measured in different ways, mainly depending on the nature of the business and the branch of industry. In a hospital and in a hotel, the percentage of beds occupied in a given period reflects productivity, although the bed percentage outcomes in hospitals are completely different from the bed percentage scores in hotels. Thus, comparing hotels with hospitals on this productivity outcome does not make any sense. In a retail context, productivity can be measured by the total sales (e.g. in terms of the number of products sold or the total sales of a store) divided by the total square size of the store. This way productivity represents the sales per square metre. In HRM and performance research productivity is often measured dividing the total sales of an organization by the total number of employees. The number of employees can be measured using the absolute number of employees or using the full-time equivalent (FTE) data that take into account part-time contracts (e.g. 1.0 FTE is a full-time contract, while 0.6 FTE represents a three-day contract). The total sum of FTEs in an organization represents the total employee potential input in an organization. This measure is more valid than using the absolute number of employees. Illustrations of measuring productivity in different branches of industry are shown below:

- The percentage of beds occupied in a given year? (hospitals and hotels)
- The total sales of a store divided by the total number of square metre store size? (supermarkets)
- The total number of academic publications of a scholar divided by the research time available to the scholar? (universities)
- The number of telephone calls handled by a call centre operator per hour? (call centres)
- The number of notes played by a musician in an orchestra divided by the number of concerts of the musician in a given time period? (orchestra)

Another popular and important organizational outcome in HR measurement is *quality*. There are basically two types of quality: product quality and service quality. Both types can coexist depending on the nature of the business and the branch of industry. Quality is highly related to meeting customers' expectations given a certain price. easyJet's strategy (see Chapter 2) is focused on low costs and high reliability (a representative of quality). easyJet's service quality is reflected in the easiness to buy a ticket using the Internet, the flight schedule reliability of the company (e.g. 90 per cent of flights arriving within one hour of the schedule) and luggage reliability. Illustrations of measuring quality in different branches of industry are as follows:

- The number of mistakes made by a department on a daily and weekly basis?
- The number of customer complaints linked to a product or service in a given time period?
- The customer satisfaction scores related to a product or service?
- The average time spent on checking the products and services for mistakes?
- The percentage of flights arriving within one hour of the schedule in a given time period? (airline industry)
- The number of suitcases that do not arrive on time at the destination of a flight divided by the total number of customers transported in a given time period? (airline industry)

In Chapter 3 it was concluded that productivity and quality are often interwoven. Therefore the concept of *cost-effectiveness* was introduced, taking into account the quality of a product or service given the costs of it. Thus, McDonald's might provide an excellent product (e.g. a hamburger) in a cost-effective way, balancing optimal product quality and process efficiency.

Stop and reflect

Discuss the concept of cost-effectiveness for a very specific branch of industry and business (e.g. mobile phones in the telecommunications sector).

Flexibility shows the capacity to change and/or adapt. The concept was discussed in Chapter 3 where three types of flexibility were summarized:

1 numerical flexibility;
2 functional flexibility;
3 mental flexibility.

All three types of flexibility are relevant for the overall flexibility of an organization. Illustrations of measuring flexibility are as follows:

- The percentage of temporary contracts within an organization? (numerical)
- The total number of seasonal workers divided by the total number of employees in a year? (numerical)
- The percentage of employees that rotate between jobs on a regular basis? (functional)
- The number of employees working in teams divided by the total number of employees in a year? (functional)

! *Stop and reflect*

Think of the downside of organizational flexibility goals for individual employees.

Organizational legitimacy relates to the organization as a whole and can be defined as 'a generalized perception or assumption that the actions of an entity are desirable, proper, or appropriate within some socially constructed system of norms, values, beliefs, and definitions' (Suchman, 1995: 574). A further distinction can be made between three types of social legitimacy that can be applied in HRM (Paauwe and Boselie, 2007):

1 pragmatic legitimacy;
2 moral legitimacy;
3 cognitive legitimacy.

Pragmatic legitimacy mainly rests on the self-interested calculations of an organization's most immediate audiences (e.g. the media, the government and customers). Organizations that only apply pragmatic legitimacy are often accused of 'window-dressing'. An organization abandoning child labour because of potential negative publicity is an illustration of pragmatic legitimacy. *Moral legitimacy* builds on the question of whether a given activity is the right thing to do and not on judgements about whether a given activity benefits the evaluator. Whistle-blowers – employees that contact the media because of an internal organization's misbehaviour – often act on the basis of moral legitimacy notions. They feel that certain organizational activities (e.g. internal accounting scandals) are wrong and therefore choose to tell the media the real story. *Cognitive legitimacy* is based on acceptance of the organization as necessary or inevitable based on some taken-for-granted cultural account. In this type of legitimacy people's attitudes and behaviours are deeply embedded in the core values of the organization. Ben & Jerry's and the Bodyshop represent organizations with strong core values that link to forms of cognitive legitimacy; for example, reflected in good people management and organic products. Social legitimacy is difficult to measure because of its link to other relevant outcomes such as corporate image, reputation, conflicts with trade unions and publicity. Illustrations of measuring social legitimacy are as follows:

- The number of occasions of negative publicity regarding the organization in the media in a given time period?
- The number of conflicts between the organization and trade unions in a given time period?

- The number of strikes within the organization in a given time period?
- The number of external stakeholder protests (e.g. Greenpeace) against the organization in a given year?

! Stop and reflect

Can you think of any recent corporate scandals that potentially affected the social legitimacy of an organization?

Innovation represents the organization's capability to renew the organization and its products/services. Innovation has many different faces and includes the following outlets:

- *Business model innovation*: involves changing the way business is done in terms of capturing value.
- *Marketing innovation*: the development of new marketing methods with improvement in product design or packaging, product promotion or pricing.
- *Organizational innovation*: involves the creation or alteration of business structures, practices and models.
- *Process innovation*: involves the implementation of a new or significantly improved production or delivery method.
- *Product innovation*: involves the introduction of a good or service that is new or substantially improved.
- *Service innovation*: is similar to product innovation except that the innovation relates to services rather than to products.
- *Supply chain innovation*: where innovations occur in the sourcing of input products from suppliers and the delivery of output products to customers.

Illustrations of measuring innovation are as follows:

- Time to market of a product or service?
- The number of patents in a given year?
- The new product or service revenue?
- The number of new HR practices divided by the total number of HR practices in a given year?

Stop and reflect

Discuss the relevance of innovation measurement for an organization.

Financial outcomes

A huge number of potential financial outcomes can be used in HR measurement. Therefore, the focus of the financial outcomes overview is on the general financial concepts. *Sales* represents the number of products (or services) sold or the total income that stems from selling products or services by an organization in a given year. *Market share* represents the percentage of the total market that is in the hands of an organization. In other words, 5 per cent of market share of company X shows that out of every 20 products sold in a specific market, 1 product stems from organization X. *Growth* is often linked to sales (presented as an increase in sales from year 1 to year 2) and market share (presented as the increase in percentage in a certain time period). Growth represents the organization's ability to expand and increase profits over time. *Profits* are a very broad term for the organization's income after deducting all costs (or expenses). Often a further distinction is made between profits before taxes and profits after taxes. The outcome measure of profits represents the potential shareholder's payment and the leeway for new investment. Profits are of course only relevant for profit organizations. *Market value* is the total value of an organization. There are roughly two ways of calculating the value of an organization: (1) the market value of an organization based on the accountancy data and (2) the market value of an organization based on the stock market.

The value based on accountancy data is measured using accountancy standards that focus on past performance, while the value based on stock market data uses current and future information about the company and its markets (e.g. calculations of future net cash flows). In some cases, the market value on the stock market is five times higher than the value based on accountancy data.

There are many typical financial outcome measures used in HR measurement, including return on sales (ROS), return on equity (ROE), ROI and GRATE (Boselie et al., 2005). However, these outcomes will not be subject to further investigation in this book. For now, we stick to our scorecard model using the more general financial outcome measures.

The balanced HR scorecard and dashboard

A successful implementation of an HR scorecard depends on many other factors that have not been discussed in this chapter. The necessary conditions for a scorecard implementation can be summarized as followed:

- The introduction of a scorecard requires full top management support, for example through general meetings in which the CEO and/or chief HR director publicly declare the importance of the scorecard.
- A well-operating IT infrastructure is required for measuring, monitoring and evaluating the different aspects of HR measurement. Existing management information systems (MIS) can be the basis for such an infrastructure.
- The involvement of all relevant actors (including line managers, employees and HR professionals) is very important to make it work. Involvement includes participation in the design of the scorecard, but also skills training in how to use the tool.
- A clear responsibility structure is necessary with regard to who is doing what and who is in charge of the different aspects of the measuring, monitoring and evaluation. For example, HR professionals might be in charge of the data warehousing (collecting the data and performing analyses on it) and line managers might be in charge of the monitoring and evaluation of their subordinates.
- Priorities must be set and HR interventions determined that are subject to the HR measurement (e.g. the amount of training).
- The HR input data (human capital, social capital and organizational capital) must be linked to the outcome measures (HR outcomes, organizational outcomes and financial outcomes).

- The time period for HR measurement must be determined, monitoring an evaluation (start and finish).
- The reporting intervals (e.g. on a daily, weekly or monthly basis) must be established.
- The concepts, indicators and measurements must be defined in a clear and concise way that can be understood by all actors involved (e.g. employee well-being represented by satisfaction and commitment, and measured using employee survey scales).
- The targets for each of the indicators must be clarified (e.g. an absence due to illness decreases from 7 per cent on a yearly basis to 4 per cent within the next 12 months).
- The action that is taken in case of failure to achieve targets must be determined (e.g. the line manager organizes a feedback session and action is taken with respect to employee support, and rewards are adjusted).

The balanced HR scorecard in your organization might end up as a dashboard, with crucial HR information being part of a much broader system of performance management (PM). PM is discussed as one of the key high-performance work practices (HPWPs) in Chapter 8. An illustration of an HR dashboard is shown in Table 4.1.

	Human capital	Social capital	Organization capital	HR outcome	Organization outcome	Financial outcome
Concept	Skills	Social network	New pay system	Employee well-being	Quality	Economic performance
Indicator	Statistics	External contacts	Pay system operating	Job and organization satisfaction	Product quality	Profits
Measure	% employees participated in SPSS training	Average number of external contacts per employee	% employees being paid worldwide using the new pay system	Regular employee survey using intranet: 'how satisfied are you …'	Number of defects and number of mistakes on a daily basis	Net profits before tax
Target	75% within 1 year's time	Minimum of 10 in 2 years' time	50% within next 4 months	Minimum scores of 8 on a 10-point scale	Zero defects on a daily basis	€1 billion this year
Responsible	HR department and line managers	Line managers	HR department	HR department and line managers	Line managers	Top management
Start	Next month	In three months' time	Next week	Spring next year (yearly employee survey)	Next month	Last January
Finish	Within 12 months	In 27 months	Within 4 months	Within 4 weeks of the survey send around	Within 6 months' time	December of this year

TABLE 4.1 Illustration of an HR scorecard and dashboard

Reflection

Part of the outcomes discussion has a universalistic character. In other words, in general organizations are better off when high scores are achieved on, for example, employee satisfaction, employee motivation, employee commitment, labour productivity, quality and profits. There are two important notions that need to be taken into account. First, some outcome measures might be more important for an organization given a specific situation than other outcomes. Labour market shortages, for example, in the health care sector put pressure on hospitals to attract and retain qualified personnel. Employee commitment and turnover are therefore extremely important KPIs in most hospitals nowadays and even more important than other outcome measures.

Second, achieving high scores on all outcome measures (HR, organizational and financial outcomes) might be achieved temporarily, but seems to be a mission impossible in the long term. In practice, organizations go through cycles of prosperity (success) and 'poverty', potentially causing unbalanced situations. Financial losses, for example, often result in downsizing with significant effects on those who have to leave and those who stay (e.g. perceived employment insecurity and deteriorating institutional trust in management). Organizations always have some room to manoeuvre (leeway) in strategic decision making with regard to dealing with people management issues in difficult times (see Chapter 2). Strategic decision making in balanced approaches suggests the search for restoring the balance through HR practices, as discussed earlier in this chapter.

The next chapter focuses on the balance between what employees want and what employers want using insights from psychology (micro HRM or MHRM) and blending these with notions from strategic HRM (SHRM). The concept of employee well-being is extended using insights from critical HR approaches, organizational behaviour (OB) and organizational health psychology.

Our quest for success through good people management has just started.

Summary

- HRA was a popular technique for measuring the value of employees in an organization in the 1970s. Ethical considerations, measurement problems and the legal position of the employee (not being owned by an organization) decreased the significance of HRA.
- The BSC focused new attention on measuring assets (including human resources) in the early 1990s.
- The renewed attention on HR measurement is reflected in the growing popularity of human capital valuation and HR metrics in the 1990s.
- HR measurement can be focused on input (human, social and organizational capital) and output (HR, organizational and financial outcomes).
- HR input can be measured focused on presence, satisfaction, intensity, coverage and importance of an HR intervention or HR practice.
- HR input and output can be defined in terms of concepts, indicators and measurements.
- There is a potential tension between the three outcomes related to conflicting employee and employer interests.
- There is a list of necessary conditions for applying an ideal HR scorecard including top management support and involvement of all actors.

Glossary of key terms

Human resource accounting (HRA) is a school of thought developed in the 1970s focused on the measurement and rating of employees in an organization.

Human capital management (HCM) is a new school of thought that was developed in the 1990s and focuses on HR measurement and the determination of human, social and organizational capital in an organization.

Human capital valuation (HCV) or human resource (HR) metrics is closely related to HCM, with a strong emphasis on the quantification and statistics of HRM.

The balanced scorecard (BSC) is a framework for mapping an organization's assets using four different dimensions and emphasizing goals and measurements in an organization.

The human resource (HR) scorecard is a framework for mapping all assets that are directly linked to the employment relationship in an organization reflecting human, social and organizational capital.

Personal development

- What kind of skills do you need for building an HR scorecard in practice?
- What is your current knowledge of statistics (which statistical software programs)?
- What is your experience with information communication systems (ICT) and the use of IT programs?

Individual task

Find out different ways of measuring labour productivity within at least three different branches of industry (e.g. financial services, the food processing, construction or steel industries). You can use the Internet to find out more about productivity measures in branches of industry, but you can also look for information in financial annual reports or company information in newspapers and branch reports.

Team task

Build your own HR scorecard

Step 1: Choose an organization (e.g. the one that you are working for) – between 100–5000 employees preferably (if an MNC, focus on one of the organization units or subsidiaries).

Step 2: Determine the organization's ultimate business goals (UBGs) – see Chapter 3 for an explanation of UBGs.

Step 3: Translate these UBGs into concrete targets (e.g. a 10 per cent yearly profit increase or a market growth of 100 per cent within the next five years).

Step 4: Determine the critical HR goals (in terms of cost-effectiveness, flexibility and legitimacy) that positively affect the UBGs in this organization – see Chapter 3 for an explanation of the critical HR goals.

Step 5: Determine the HR outcomes – attitudinal, behavioural and cognitive – that positively affect the critical HR goals in the organization.

Step 6: Translate the HR outcomes and practices in concrete targets:
- concepts – indicators – measurements;
- presence – coverage – intensity – satisfaction – importance.

Step 7: Determine the actors involved in the measurement, monitoring and evaluation (e.g. line managers, HR professionals and employees); describe the responsibilities of those involved.

Learning checklist

After studying this chapter, you should be able to do the following:

- Discuss the advantages and disadvantages of HRA approaches.
- Understand the concepts of human, social and organizational capital.
- Identify different ways of measuring HR input (presence, satisfaction, intensity, coverage and importance).
- Discuss the distinction between concepts, indicators and measurement in HRM.
- Outline the core characteristics of an HR scorecard.
- Identify the key performance indicators (KPIs) of an organization.
- Review proximal outcome measures and distal outcome measures in HRM.
- Recognize the potential tensions between organizational, employee and societal goals also reflected in the different outcomes (HR, organizational and financial outcomes).

References

Allen, N.J. and Meyer, J.P. (1990) The measurement and antecedents of affective, continuance and normative commitment to the organization, *Journal of Occupational Psychology*, 63(1): 1–18.

Allen, N.J. and Meyer, J.P. (1996) Affective, continuance, and normative commitment to the organization: an examination of construct validity, *Journal of Vocational Behaviour*, 49: 252–76.

Applebaum, E., Bailey, T., Berg, P. and Kalleberg, A. (2000) *Manufacturing Advantage: Why High-performance Work Systems Pay Off*. Ithaca, NY: Cornell University Press.

Baron, J.N. and Kreps, D.M. (1999) *Strategic Human Resource Management: Frameworks for General Managers*. Danvers, MA: Wiley.

Becker, B.E. and Huselid, M.A. (2006) Strategic human resource management: where do we go from here?, *Journal of Management*, 32(6): 898–925.

Becker, B.E., Huselid, M.A. and Ulrich, D. (2001) *The HR Scorecard: Linking People, Strategy, and Performance*. Boston, MA: Harvard Business School Press.

Benkhoff, B. (1997) Ignoring commitment is costly: new approaches establish the missing link between commitment and performance, *Human Relations*, 50(6): 701–26.

Boon, C. (2008) *HRM and Fit: Survival of the Fittest!?* Dissertation, Erasmus Research Institute for Management (ERIM) Rotterdam.

Boselie, P., Dietz, G. and Boon, C. (2005) Commonalities and contradictions in HRM and performance research, *Human Resource Management Journal*, 15(3): 67–94.

Boselie, P., Paauwe, J. and Jansen, P.G.W. (2001) Human resource management and performance: lessons from the Netherlands, *International Journal of Human Resource Management*, 12(7): 1107–25.

Cascio, W.F. (2006) The New Human Capital Equation. Keynote address prepared for the 2006 Work–Life Conference, Global Economic Solutions: Framing Work–Life Contribution, New York, 13–14 June.

Colarelli, S.M. (1984) Methods of communication and mediating processes in realistic job previews, *Journal of Applied Psychology*, 69: 633–42.

Colquitt, J.A., Conlon, D.E., Wesson, M.J., Porter, C.O.L.H. and Ng, K.Y. (2001) Justice at the millennium: a meta-analytic review of 25 years of organizational justice research, *Journal of Applied Psychology*, 86(3): 425–45.

Cooper-Thomas, H.D., Van Vianen, A.E. and Anderson, N. (2004) Changes in person–organization fit: the impact of socialization tactics on perceived and actual P–O fit, *European Journal of Work and Organizational Psychology*, 13(1): 52–78.

Deephouse, D.L. (1999) To be different, or to be the same? It's a question (and theory) of strategic balance, *Strategic Management Journal*, 20(2): 147–66.

Dietz, G. and Den Hartog, D.N. (2006) Measuring trust inside organizations, *Personnel Review*, 35(5): 557–88.

Dyer, L. and Reeves, T. (1995) Human resource strategies and firm performance: what do we know, where do we need to go?, *International Journal of Human Resource Management*, 6(3): 656–70.

Elias, N. (1976) Behavioral impact of human resource accounting, *Management Accounting*, February: 43–5.

Ellemers, N., De Gilder, D. and Van Den Heuvel, H. (1998) Career-oriented versus team-oriented commitment and behavior at work, *Journal of Applied Psychology*, 83(5): 717–30.

Fitz-enz, J. (1984) *How to Measure Human Resources Management*. New York: McGraw-Hill.

Gerhart, B., Wright, P.M. and McMahan, G. (2000) Measurement error in research on the human resource and firm performance relationship: further evidence and analysis, *Personnel Psychology*, 53(4): 855–72.

Gillespie, N. and Dietz, G. (2008) Trust repair after organization-level failure, *Academy of Management Review*, 34(1): 127–45.

Greenberg, J. (1990) Organizational justice: yesterday, today, and tomorrow, *Journal of Management*, 16: 399–432.

Guest, D.E. (1997) Human resource management and performance: a review and research agenda, *International Journal of Human Resource Management*, 8(3): 263–76.

Hendricks, J.A. (1976) The impact of human resource accounting information on stock investment decisions: an empirical study, *The Accounting Review*, April: 292–305.

Huselid, M.A., Becker, B.E. and Beatty, R.W. (2005) *The Workforce Scorecard: Managing Human Capital to Execute Strategy*. Boston, MA: Harvard Business School Press.

Intrinsic Motivation Inventory (2008) www.psych.rochester.edu

Kaplan, R.S. and Norton, D.P. (1992) The balanced scorecard – measures that drive performance, *Harvard Business Review*, January–February: 71–9.

Loven, J.J.M. (2008) Using the right ingredients: the search for a HPWS in the successful organization Nestlé. BA thesis, Tilburg University, Tilburg.

Lybaert, N. (1990) Human resource accounting?, *Tijdschrift voor Economie en Management*, 35(2): 131–46.

MacKenzie, S.B., Podsakoff, P.M. and Fetter, R. (1991) Organizational citizenship behaviour and objective productivity: determinants of managerial evaluations of salespersons' performance, *Organizational Behavior and Human Decision Processes*, 50(1): 123–50.

Marr, B. (2003) Known quantities, *Financial Management*, Chartered Institute of Management Accountants, April.

Meyer, J.P., Stanley, D.J., Herscovitch, L. and Topolnytsky, L. (2002) Affective, continuance, and normative commitment to the organization: a meta-analysis of antecedents, correlates, and consequences, *Journal of Vocational Behavior*, 61(1): 20–52.

Niehoff, B.P. and Moorman, R.H. (1993) Justice as a mediator of the relationship between methods of monitoring and organizational citizenship behaviour, *Academy of Management Journal*, 36(3): 527–56.

Paauwe, J. (2004) *HRM and Performance: Achieving Long-term Viability*. Oxford: Oxford University Press.

Paauwe, J. and Boselie, P. (2007) HRM and societal embeddedness, in P. Boxall, J. Purcell and P.M. Wright (eds), *The Oxford Handbook of Human Resource Management*, Chapter 9, pp. 166–84. Oxford: Oxford University Press.

Paauwe, J. and Richardson, R. (1997) Introduction special issue on HRM and performance, *International Journal of Human Resource Management*, 8(3): 257–62.

Peccei, R. (2004) Human resource management and the search for the happy work place. Inaugural lecture, Erasmus Institute of Management (ERIM), Rotterdam.

Philips, J.J., Stone, R.D. and Philips, P.P. (2001) *The Human Resources Scorecard: Measuring the Return on Investment*. Woburn, MA: Butterworth-Heinemann.

Porter, L.W., Bigley, G.A. and Steers, R.M. (2003) *Motivation and Work Behavior*, 7th edn. Boston, MA: McGraw-Hill.

Robinson, S.L. (1996) Trust and breach of psychological contract, *Administrative Science Quarterly*, 41: 574–99.

Ryan, R.M. and Deci, E.L. (2003) Conceptual approaches to motivation at work, in L.W. Porter, G.A. Bigley and R.M. Steers, *Motivation and Work Behavior*, 7th edn., Chapter 2, pp. 45–65. Boston, MA: McGraw-Hill.

Sangeladji, M.A. (1977) Human resource accounting: a refined measurement model, *Management Accounting*, December: 48–52.

Schneider, B., Hanges, P.J., Smith, D.B. and Salvaggio, A.N. (2003) Which comes first: employee attitudes or organizational financial and market performance?, *Journal of Applied Psychology*, 88(5): 836–51.

Starovic, D. and Marr, B. (2003) Understanding corporate value: managing and reporting intellectual capital. Research report, Chartered Institute of Management Accountants, London.

Suchman, M.C. (1995) Managing legitimacy: strategic and institutional approaches, *Academy of Management Review*, 20: 571–610.

Wright, P.M. and Boswell, W.R. (2002) Desegregating HRM: a review and synthesis of micro and macro human resource management research, *Journal of Management*, 28(3): 247–76.

Wright, P.M., Dunford, B.D. and Snell, S.A. (2001) Human resources and the resource based view of the firm, *Journal of Management*, 27(6): 701–21.

Yeung, A.K. and Berman, B. (1997) Adding value through human resources: reorienting human resource measurement to drive business performance, *Human Resource Management*, 36(3): 321–35.

Further reading

Becker, B.E., Huselid, M.A. and Ulrich, D. (2001) *The HR Scorecard: Linking People, Strategy, and Performance*. Boston, MA: Harvard Business School Press.

Cascio, W.F. and Boudreau, J.W. (2008) *Investing in People: Financial Impact of Human Resources Initiatives*. Upper Saddle River, NJ: Pearson Education/FT Press.

Huselid, M.A., Becker, B.E. and Beatty, R.W. (2005) *The Workforce Scorecard: Managing Human Capital to Execute Strategy*. Boston, MA: Harvard Business School Press.

Paauwe, J. (2004) Changing HRM roles: towards a real balanced HRM Scorecard, in J. Paauwe, *HRM and Performance: Achieving Long-term Viability*, Chapter 9, pp. 179–212. Oxford: Oxford University Press.

Philips, J.J., Stone, R.D. and Philips, P.P. (2001) *The Human Resources Scorecard: Measuring the Return on Investment*. Woburn, MA: Butterworth-Heinemann.

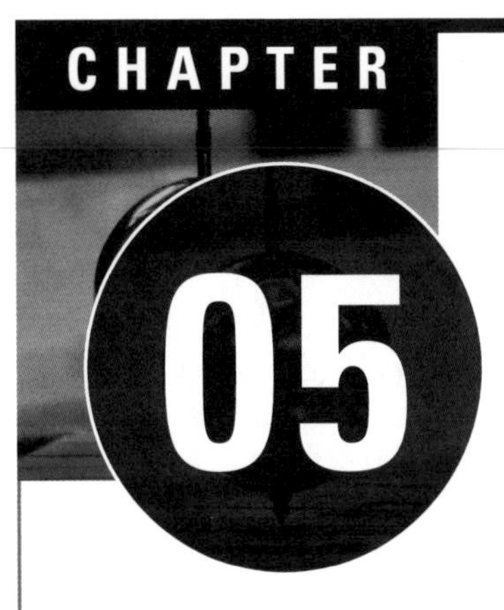

Achieving the Right Balance

❖ Learning Objectives

After studying this chapter, you should be able to do the following:

- ❖ Identify the possible different interests of the employer and the employee (what employers want and what employees want)
- ❖ Outline the consensus nature of mainstream human resource management (HRM)
- ❖ Evaluate the claims made by critical human resource (HR) studies
- ❖ Review the different types of HRM research using the level of analysis dimension (individual versus organizational) and the number of HR practices (single versus multiple)
- ❖ Evaluate the insights from organizational behaviour (OB) and organizational health psychology on HRM and employee well-being
- ❖ Consider the job demands–job control model of Karasek
- ❖ Discuss the potential effects of HR practices on stress and burnout
- ❖ Examine balanced approaches on individual employee and organization level
- ❖ Discuss the notions of agility and vitality

CASE STUDY: BMW

Bayerische Motoren Werke Aktiengesellschaft (BMW or Bavarian Motor Works) is one of the leading car companies in the world. This German firm, known for its 'gründlichkeit' (efficiency), was also the world's most admired motor vehicle company in 2007 (World's Most Admired Companies, 2007) and ranked 14th in the top 100 of the most powerful brands (Millward Brown Optimor, 2007). BMW produces cars – from the BMW 1 to 7 Series, sports utility vehicles such as X3 and X5, roadsters and coupes, and Mini – and motorcycles, and is headquartered in Munich, Germany. The company operates in the premium segment of the international car and motorcycle markets and employs over 100 000 people called 'associates' in more than 100 countries. The Quandt family owned about 48 per cent of the company's shares in 2007. Its influence is significant and a constant factor over time. Reliability, safety, style, speed and reputation are key characteristics of the BMW company.

The ageing workforce: Turning boomers into boomerangs

'LAST month the first baby-boomers turned 60. The bulky generation born between 1946 and 1964 is heading towards retirement. The looming "demographic cliff" will see vast numbers of skilled workers dispatched from the labour force ... The workforce is ageing across the rich world. Within the EU the number of workers aged between 50 and 64 will increase by 25% over the next two decades, while those aged 20–29 will decrease by 20%. In Japan almost 20% of the population is already over 65, the highest share in the world ... Given that most societies are geared to retirement at around 65, companies have a looming problem of knowledge management, of making sure that the boomers do not leave before they have handed over their expertise along with the office keys and their e-mail address. A survey of human-resources directors by IBM last year concluded: 'When the baby-boomer generation retires, many companies will find out too late that a career's worth of experience has walked out the door, leaving insufficient talent to fill the void.'

(*The Economist*, 16 February 2006)

BMW recently set up a factory in Leipzig that expressly set out to employ people over the age of 45

Leipzig – city of music and Johann Sebastian Bach's Thomas Kirche – is a former East German city hosting one of the most modern BMW factories. It is the factory's HR policy to attract and retain older workers, and nowadays is generally considered to be an example of best practices in managing an ageing workforce. In the factory, extra attention is paid to ergonomics and physical job demands. BMW offers fitness centre equipment to employees, additional instruments to avoid physical constraints and extra physiotherapy for those who need support. The HR policies and practices are mainly focused on managing the well-being of all employees, in particular the older worker. Voluntary yearly medical check-ups are also part of the people management in Leipzig's BMW factory. High unemployment rates of relatively highly skilled employees after the fall of the Wall in 1989 created these labour market opportunities for BMW in Leipzig about 15 years after the transition.

(*The Economist*, 2006)

? Discussion questions

Discuss the attractiveness of the older worker for an organization with regard to high commitment, knowledge, skills, experiences and productivity. Think about the lessons from the BMW case for other organizations; for example, knowledge-intensive organizations. Can you think about specific HR practices for managing the older worker?

Introduction

A lot of attention in both theory and practice is paid to *what employers want* in managing employees. It looks as if what is best for the employer and the organization is automatically in the interest of every individual employee. The Anglo-American approach, stressing the interests of the owners of an organization (shareholders) and emphasizing mainly financial outcomes in terms of sales, profits, market share and market value, can be characterized by this unitaristic perspective: What is good for the firm is also good for the employee. However, critical incidents, such as reorganizations, mergers and takeovers, show the negative effects on individual employees in the form of too much emphasis on shareholder interests. Downsizing an organization, for example with 10 per cent of the total workforce (see Nokia worldwide in 2003), to increase labour productivity and reduce costs goes hand in hand with unemployment, labour intensification for those who stay (Legge, 2005), feelings of insecurity and decreased employee commitment, satisfaction, trust and motivation (Baron and Kreps, 1999). What employers want (or, should we say, what shareholders want) is not always what employees want. Except for disciplines such as **organizational health psychology** (Bakker et al., 2004), **OB** (Rousseau and Schalk, 2000) and critical management (Legge, 2005), not much attention is actually paid to *what employees want.* My respected colleague, Dr Marc Van Veldhoven, stress expert at Tilburg University, contrasts the 'what employers want' question with the issue of 'what employees want' in one of the MA courses he teaches in university in a very nice and understandable way. The pictures he uses for illustrating the potential contrast between the interests of both groups (employers and employees) are presented in Figures 5.1, 5.2 and 5.3.

In times of continuous change in markets and societies, the average employer is in search of individual employees that possess:

1. the *willingness and capability to change* with whatever situation the individual is confronted with (different customers, different cultures, different languages, different managers, etc.), comparable with the adaptation of a chameleon to its environment; (Figure 5.1)
2. the *intelligence* of an Albert Einstein with above-average scores on knowledge, skills and competences (Figure 5.2);
3. the capabilities of an athlete in terms of *speed* (a working speed comparable with running the 100 metres in 10 seconds) and *endurance* (a working attitude comparable with running the marathon in less than two and a half hours) (Figure 5.3).

And there are of course young talents who possess these qualities. The question remains how many of them actually meet these criteria and, perhaps even more important, how many employees are willing to live by these standards? Research in organizational health psychology shows that employees want fun at work; social support from superiors; an acceptable work–life balance; employee development opportunities; a nice group atmosphere; and employment security. The employee perspective – *what employees want* – is often neglected, and the gap between what employers want and the employee perspective appears to have increased in the last few decades as a result of increased competition and globalization. It is therefore crucial to find the right balance between the employer's and employees' interests in order to achieve continuity and perhaps even long-term organizational success.

FIGURE 5.1 In search of the chameleon

This chapter focuses on the potential tensions, conflicting interests and balance issues that are related to employers and employees. Micro HRM (MHRM) insights from organizational health psychology and OB are summarized to give the reader a better understanding of the complexity and dynamic of HR issues in practice, taking explicitly into account the interests and needs of the employer on the one hand and the employee on the other hand. According to Boxall et al. (2007), MHRM represents one of the three building blocks of contemporary HRM (see Chapter 1). There is, however, another school of thought that is highly relevant for a full understanding of the tension, conflict and balance HR issues: the critical HR approach (Keegan and Boselie, 2006). The aim of this chapter is to apply a pluralist perspective to HR studies taking into account employees' interests; for example, with regard to employee well-being (vitality) and employee needs, and employer's interests; for example, in terms of long-term success through achieving organizational agility.

Critical HR studies: guess who's coming to dinner?

Not long ago my colleague, Dr Anne Keegan, and I had a discussion on the nature of the HR discipline. This resulted in the *Journal of Management Studies* (*JMS*) article published a couple of years ago (Keegan and Boselie, 2006). We asked ourselves an apparently simple question: If we were to throw a dinner party for representatives of the global academic HR community, who should be invited? The theme of our research project became *Guess Who's Coming to Dinner?*, referring to the 1967 movie with Spencer Tracey and Katharine Hepburn whose attitudes are

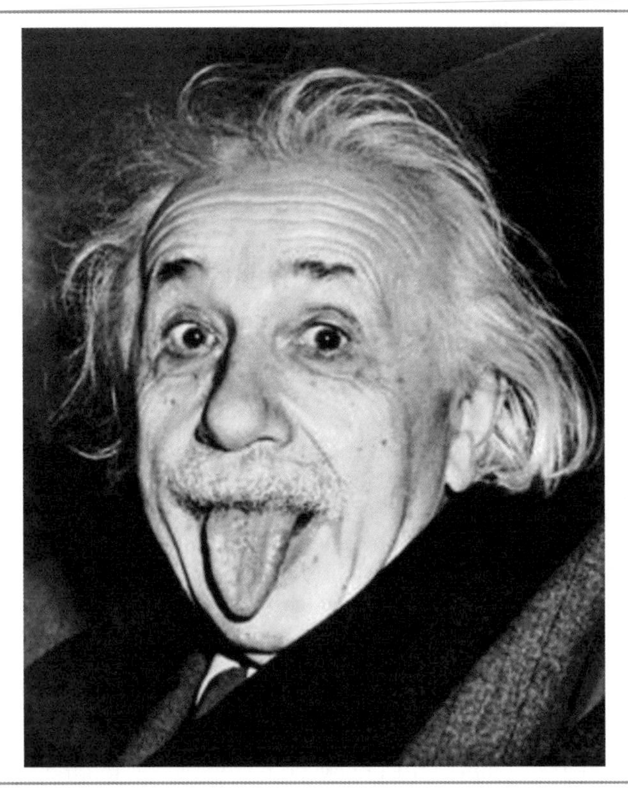

FIGURE 5.2 In search of the Einstein
Source: AFP-Getty Images File (1951).

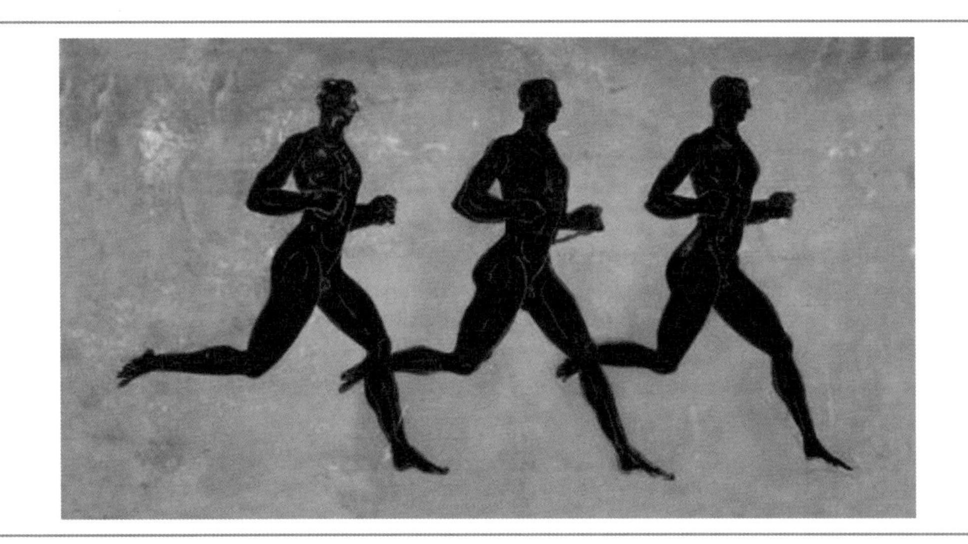

FIGURE 5.3 In search of the athlete
Source: Image © Trustees of the British Museum.

challenged when their daughter brings home her fiancé who is black. The usual suspects for our HR dinner party invitations were obviously HR scholars that had made a significant and substantial contribution to the HR field.[1]

This HR usual suspects' list is dominated by men (79 per cent) and by scholars from the UK and the USA. My colleague Dr Anne Keegan and I were puzzled about other scholars who are involved in HR debates, but it is not clear if they are fully part of the HR community. They perhaps do not consider themselves to be part of the academic HR community or the majority of the academic HR community do not take these scholars very seriously (Keegan and Boselie, 2006). 'The others' in our discussion were scholars such as Barbara Townley (1993), Tom Keenoy (1999), Tony Watson (2004), Bill Harley and Cynthia Hardy (2004), Paul Blyton and Peter Turnbull (1992), Paul Thompson and Bill Harley (2007), Rick Delbridge (2006) and Maddy Janssens and Chris Steyaert (2009).

In our 2006 *JMS* article (Keegan and Boselie, 2006), we presented an overview of a literature study on HRM and concluded that mainstream HRM journals (and the mainstream HR community) have largely ignored critical perspectives on HRM. HRM is a social construction: 'The use of language by theorists and researchers to describe HRM is a form of social action, creating understanding about what HRM is and the effects it is presumed to have on social life and in structuring employment relations' (Keegan and Boselie, 2006: 1492–93). The social constructivist perspective (e.g. Townley, 1993) is used to show that HRM as we know it from most of the books and the journal articles does not exist as a simple fact of the 'real' world, 'but is shaped by deeply embedded historical, political and discursive processes' (Keegan and Boselie, 2006: 1493). Another set of characteristic features of HRM, based on Deetz (1996) and Keegan and Boselie (2006), is related to the **consensus nature of mainstream HRM**:

- There is a general and common trust between the employer and the employee.
- The employer and the employee share the same interests ('what is good for the employer is also good for the employee and vice versa').
- The relationship between the employer and the employee is harmonious.
- The present is little or not affected by the past.
- The employee acknowledges the organizational hierarchy and the employer's power position.
- Science is neutral.
- The researcher is neutral, anonymous and out of time and space.

! *Stop and reflect*

Can you think of illustrations in practice ('in the real world') that seriously undermine one or more of the characteristic HR features summarized above? You may use the newspapers for finding illustrations.

[1] The usual suspects include, for example, Rosemary Batt (USA), Peter Boxall (New Zealand), Chris Brewster (UK), Lee Dyer (USA), Paul Evans (France), Barry Gerhart (USA), Lynda Gratton (UK), David Guest (UK), John Hollenbeck (USA), Mark Huselid (USA), Susan Jackson (USA), Bruce Kaufman (USA), Tom Kochan (USA), Karen Legge (UK), Mick Marchington (UK), Jaap Paauwe (Netherlands), John Purcell (UK), Denise Rousseau (USA), Sara Rynes (USA), Randall Schuler (USA), Keith Sisson (UK), Scott Snell (USA), John Storey (UK), Shaun Tyson (UK), Dave Ulrich (USA), Adrian Wilkinson (Australia), Stephen Wood (USA) and Pat Wright (USA).

We analysed 1674 articles in nine journals (e.g. *Human Resource Management*, the *International Journal of Human Resource Management* and the *Journal of Management Studies*) published in the period 1995–2000 (Keegan and Boselie, 2006). Our main focus was on Deetz's (1996) 'dissensus orientation' or 'consensus orientation'. The consensus orientation HR articles mainly build on the list of characteristics features summarized above. The **dissensus orientation in HRM** represents articles that apply a critical perspective, often highlighting the tensions between employers' and employees' interests. In the five general management journals (e.g. *Administrative Science Quarterly* and *Organization*), we identified 12 dissensus HRM articles; for example, in the 1999 special issue on HRM in *Organization*. In the four HR journals (e.g. *Human Resource Management Journal* and *Human Resource Planning*) we found eight dissensus HRM articles. Overall, we found that the HRM field is largely consensus-oriented, constituted as managerial, prescriptive and strategic, and biased in its focus on the development of core employees (the 'happy few') in large multinational companies (MNCs) (Keegan and Boselie, 2006). The narrative style of many HR articles is very much focused on 'strategy' and the search for 'added value through people'. The main strategic HRM themes are:

- HRM and performance;
- HRM and sustained competitive advantage, mostly using the resource-based view as the theoretical framework;
- HRM, strategy and fit (strategic fit between HRM and strategy).

The core employees in the studies include chief executives, HR professionals, expatriates, line managers, management trainees, MBA students and other white-collar employees. Executive selection, succession management, management development (MD) and performance-related pay (PRP) are popular best practices in HRM that are linked to these core employees in mainstream HR research.

The few and rare exceptions in HR research (20 articles in total and only eight articles in HR journals) that can be characterized by a dissensus orientation focus on the following issues (Keegan and Boselie, 2006):

- The struggle of line managers to make sense of proposed changes urged by HRM discourse of commitment, flexibility, rapid response to market conditions, etc. (Ezzamel et al., 1996).
- The mainstream (often implicit) HR assumptions that labour market deregulation and trade union abolition are required for organizational success (Black and McCabe, 1996).
- The continued marginalization of women in organizational life, in particular when concerned with promotion opportunities, career development and positions of managerial power (Edwards et al., 1999).
- The economic exploitation of workers, simultaneous with proposals for social partnerships between the employer and the employees, stimulating (false) employee involvement in decision making and promoting teamwork (Ackers and Payne, 1998).
- The political repression of weaker groups (mainly the workers on the shopfloor) by more powerful groups in an organization; for example, top management (Yun, 1999).
- The lack of ethical debates in HRM related to the concepts of flexibility, high commitment, empowerment and employability (Winstanley and Woodall, 2000).
- The exclusion, marginalization and repression of older workers (Taylor and Walker, 1998).

The **critical HR studies** (dissensus orientation) highlight the other side of organizational innovations and HR renewal; for example, with regard to work intensification, **job stress**, perceived employee insecurity and discrimination (e.g. age, gender, race and religion). The reader should be aware of the dominant managerial and unitarist perspective in many HR publications with a potential lack of the workers' and the pluralist perspective. Organizational reality is often full of conflicts, politics and tensions between the different stakeholders, including managers, employees and employee representatives (e.g. works council's members and trade union officers).

! *Stop and reflect*

A line manager in a hospital is confronted with the 'necessity' of introducing a new high-performance work system (HPWS) with an increased focus on employee involvement and autonomous teamwork. The line manager is not very enthusiastic about this organizational change because she can barely keep up with the current employee planning process. Employee planning for weekend and night shifts is the most challenging task for the manager. She is therefore very happy with a few colleagues that she calls 'mortgage workers', who prefer night and weekend shifts because of the additional payments and the better personal work–life balance which allows them to take care of their children during the daytime. The line manager is afraid that the new HPWS (with more explicit employee involvement) will dissatisfy 'mortgage workers' and cause an increase in problems with employee planning tasks. Discuss the downside of 'good' HRM in this particular case. Can you think of ways to solve the line manager's concerns?

If we were to throw a big dinner party inviting all 'the usual suspects' (e.g. Guest, Huselid and Wright) and 'the others' (e.g. Keenoy, Steyaert and Watson), imagine the table seating. Can, for example, Mark Huselid – famous for his HRM and performance article in the *Academy of Management Journal* (1995) – sit next to Tom Keenoy, who is an expert in HRM and discourses analysis? And, more importantly, is it likely that they will have an interesting conversation about HRM? Both Dr Anne Keegan and I agreed that some scholars, including Karen Legge, are more likely to bridge the difficult streams and schools in HRM than others.

The dissensus-oriented perspective presented above highlights the lack of critical HR studies. The previous rare critical HR studies often take the individual employee perspective as a starting point and reveal the opposite employer model that is dominant in the HR field. These previous critical studies, however, often do not fully incorporate the actual individual employee perspective in terms of what the employee experiences and how the managerial HR model affects employee well-being, for example, in terms of stress and **burnout**. Information about the actual individual experiences can be found in the fields of organizational health psychology and OB.

Organizational behaviour (OB)

Guest (1999) and Purcell (1999) make a strong plea for a more explicit focus on the individual employee in HR research because, at the time of their publications, the HRM and performance debate was dominated by organization level analyses using the employer's perspective exclusively. This issue is also discussed in Chapter 3 in the context of intended practices, actual practices and perceived practices. Traditionally, the employee perspective has received much attention in the field of OB, which is dominated by psychological research. OB is mainly focused on how people, individuals and groups act in organizations. This is what Boxall et al. (2007) call micro HRM (MHRM).

Wright and Boswell (2002) make a distinction between four areas of HRM and OB research based on two dimensions: (1) level of analysis, individual versus organizational; and (2) number of HR practices, single versus multiple.

Strategic HRM (SHRM) is mainly focused on the organization level and multiple HR practices, while OB or MHRM is mainly focused on the individual level and single HR practices. The empirical study by Huselid (1995) is a typical illustration of an organization level analysis including multiple HR practices. This study explicitly applies an employer's perspective aimed at improving firm performance through a specific type of HRM (HPWs) that will be discussed in more detail in Chapter 6. Single HR practices research on the individual employee level can be found on recruitment (e.g. person–job fit and person–organization fit), selection (e.g. personality studies), training and development (e.g. team learning), compensation (e.g. pay for performance), PM (e.g. accuracy issues), and employee participation and work design (e.g. flextime) (Wright and Boswell, 2002). The single HR practices studies on the individual employee level tend to include the individual perspective (the employee's interests), for example acknowledging employee well-being through job satisfaction; however, the majority of research in this area mainly focuses on the employer's interests, represented by outcomes such as employee motivation, employee turnover, organizational commitment and organizational citizenship behaviour.

Notions on differences in employee outcomes are also made in Chapter 4. In the balanced HR scorecard in Chapter 4, a distinction is made between HR outcomes that are more employee-oriented (e.g. trust, satisfaction and perceived justice) and HR outcomes that are more employer-oriented (e.g. motivation, citizenship behaviour and turnover). This dichotomy is of course disputable; however, the question remains whether all HR outcomes satisfy the needs and wants of the individual employee and those of the employer.

Stop and reflect

Think of the individual employee's interests with regard to the HR outcomes' satisfaction and organizational citizenship behaviour (OCB). Then think of the employer's interests with regard to satisfaction and OCB. The fundamental questions remain:

- Is a happy worker also a productive worker?
- Can an unhappy worker be productive?
- What's in it for individual workers if they show citizenship behaviour?

The single practice studies on organization level often use a focal HR practice (e.g. top management teamwork, work–life-balance practice, PRP and sophisticated staffing) and some measure of organizational effectiveness (Wright and Boswell, 2002) (see Figure 5.4). These studies mainly apply an employer's perspective in an attempt to show the added value of specific HR practices or interventions on, for example, labour productivity, service quality, product quality, organizational flexibility and innovation.

Wright and Boswell (2002) continue with highlighting multiple practice research on the individual employee level; for example, on psychological contracts (Rousseau and Schalk, 2000;

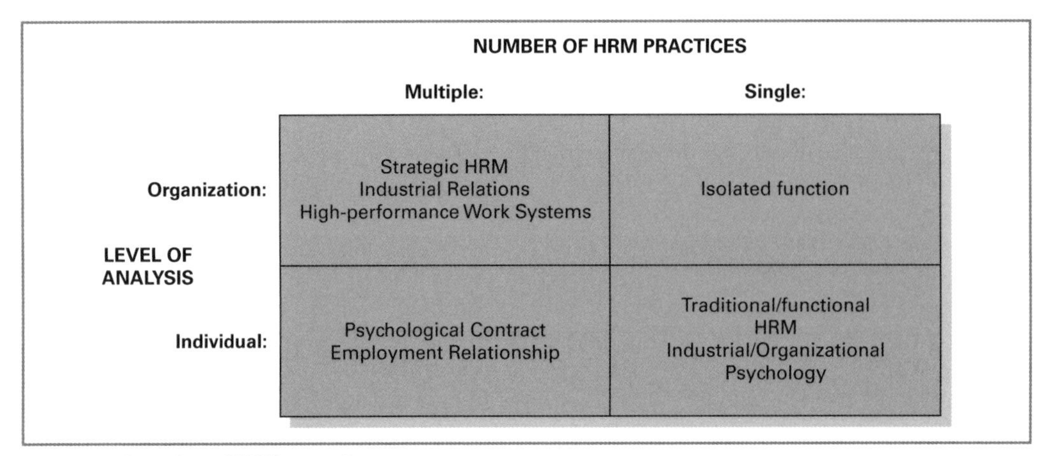

FIGURE 5.4 A typology of HRM research
Source: Reproduced with permission from Wright and Boswell (2002, Figure 1).

Coyle-Shapiro and Kessler, 2000). In general, the psychological contract research bridges the employer's interests and the employees' interests. A substantial amount of research in this area is focused on violation of the psychological contract and its potential effects on employee outcomes (Sonnenberg, 2006; Freese, 2007); for example, high employee turnover rates, employee dissatisfaction and decreased trust in the organization (Robinson and Rousseau, 1994).

Other research including multiple HR practices on individual employee level involves studies on the employment relationship (Tsui et al., 1997). These studies are related to macro HRM studies on HPWSs (e.g. Huselid, 1995), but the difference is in the focus on individual employee outcomes. The study by Tsui et al. (1997) is interesting because they acknowledge balanced (mutual investment and quasi-spot-contract) and imbalanced employment relationships (underinvestment and overinvestment) between employers and employees. The mutual investment employment relationship and the overinvestment employment relationship outperform the other two relationship models with regard to these multiple HR outcomes (Tsui et al., 1997):

- job performance;
- citizenship behaviour;
- continuance commitment;
- employee presence (in contrast to employee absence);
- affective commitment;
- perceived fairness;
- trust in colleagues.

The majority of these HR outcomes reflect the employer's interests; for example, high job performance, citizenship behaviour ('walking the extra mile'), continuance commitment and affective commitment. But what do these results tell us about the employee perspective?

In general, the OB research (or MHRM studies) on the individual employee level in the Wright and Boswell (2002) typology is focused on employee attitudes or *what an employee desires* (Sanders et al., 2008; Conway and Monks, 2008). Organizational health psychology is much more focused on employee well-being or *what an employee can handle* (e.g. with regard to stress).

Organizational health psychology

When workers are under continuous pressure, there is a high risk of job stress and burnout. The experience of long-term exhaustion at work can also result in burnout (Maslach and Jackson, 1981). Kroon et al. (2009) argue that burnout can emerge from any job in itself and from management practices. They also claim that the majority of previous research focuses on stress, burnout and the job. Only few empirical studies, however, actually look at the impact of management and HR practices on employee well-being in terms of stress or burnout (e.g. Ramsay et al., 2000; Godard, 2001). Overall, the research in organizational health psychology tends to be much more focused on potential negative effects of jobs and managerial practices on employees (e.g. in terms of employee satisfaction, job stress, fatigue and burnout) than the HRM discipline and the OB discipline.

Karasek (1979) developed a stress-management model of job strain commonly known as the job demand–job control model. In this job strain model a distinction is made between (1) job demands (low versus high) and (2) job decision latitude (low versus high). These two dimensions create four job types, according to Karasek (1979):

1. passive jobs (low job demands and low decision latitude);
2. low strain jobs (low job demands and high decision latitude);
3. high strain jobs (high job demands and low decision latitude);
4. active jobs (high job demands and high decision latitude).

Job demands measures stress sources (stressors) and refers to an internal state of an individual. **Job decision latitude** refers to job control or discretion, and represents individual employees' leeway or room to manoeuvre in their jobs. See Figure 5.5 for a visual representation of Karasek's model. The model predicts that, following diagonal A, strain increases as job demands increase, 'relative to decreasing job decision latitude' (Karasek, 1979: 288). The model also predicts that active jobs lead to 'the development of new behaviour patterns both on and off the job' (Karasek, 1979: 288). Passive jobs, however, induce a decline in activity in contrast to the active job type.

High strain jobs represent situations in which employees are under a lot of pressure without any leeway for solving the issues and therefore they are most likely to be stressed (mental strain) and dissatisfied with their jobs (Karasek, 1979). The findings also suggest that increasing job decision latitude leverages negative effects of high job demands. In other words, in the case of high job demands, it is essential that the individual employee has leeway and autonomy (job decision latitude, job control or discretion) to avoid high levels of job stress. The job demands model was revised and refined a decade after the *Administration Science Quarterly* publication in Karasek and Theorell (1990). Overall, these present interesting findings on jobs and job stress. Employees are not purely stressed (or frustrated) because of demanding jobs only. Their stress also depends on how much influence they have on their own jobs and their work. In this way, demanding jobs with a lot of leeway or room to manoeuvre can get the best out of certain employees. In contrast, low job demands, in combination with little or no individual leeway, can make employees passive and lazy. Van Yperen and Hagedoorn (2003), for example, find empirical support for Karasek's model with regard to the highly demanding jobs of nurses and their job control.

Interestingly enough, we may conclude that the HR discipline, the OB discipline and the organizational health psychology discipline show little or no interaction and knowledge-sharing on these people management issues, particularly in the context of adding value through people (HRM and performance debate). Employee burnout, for example, is a serious HR outcome, resulting from chronic emotional and interpersonal stressors on the job (Maslach et al., 2001), causing employee absence, employee turnover and/or additional labour costs (e.g. replacement costs and costs related to employee illness).

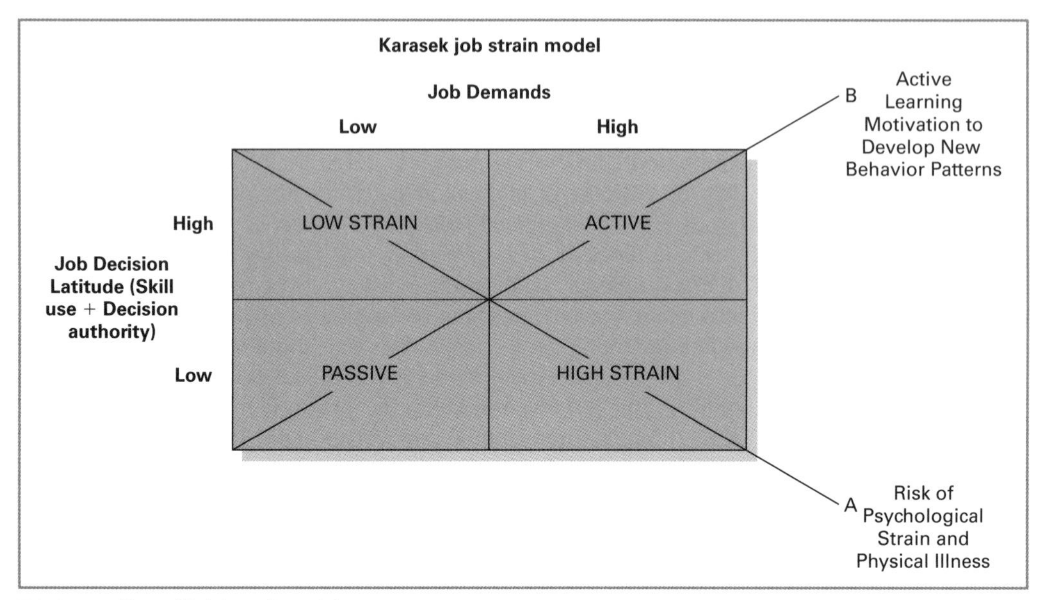

FIGURE 5.5 Karasek's job strain model
Source: Reproduced with permission from Karasek and Theorell (1990).

There are a few exceptions in this area. Ramsay et al. (2000) show that HPWPs (see Chapter 6) can negatively affect employee outcomes, in particular causing work intensification. In other words, the high commitment and involvement HR approaches (called HPWSs) not only imply more employee participation and learning opportunities, but potentially cause higher job demands and more stress. Godard (2001) shows positive relationships between HPWP and employee outcomes; however, more intensive HR systems caused decreased employee outcomes that are most likely as a result of work intensification. Peccei (2004) discusses the often assumed positive relationship between employee satisfaction and labour productivity. The basic idea is that a happy worker is automatically a productive worker. Peccei's (2004) mixed results and lack of statistically significant relationships between satisfaction and productivity tell us a more complex storey. Perhaps a happy worker can be very unproductive, while unhappy workers can be very productive. If this is true, this potentially creates a further but significant gap between the employer's interests (e.g. high productivity rates) and the employee's interests (e.g. employee well-being in terms of satisfaction). Van Veldhoven's (2005) findings in a longitudinal study suggest that: (1) work pressure and increased work intensity predict poor business unit financial performance, and (2) good financial performance (or financial success) predicts low job strain.

Kroon et al. (2009) find a positive relationship between HPWPs and burnout. Their findings support a critical 'employee exploitation'-oriented perspective on HPWPs and HPWSs. In other words, these new high commitment employee approaches are merely a disguise for getting more output or money from workers. In a way, these individual level HRM and organizational health psychology studies, summarized above (Ramsay et al., 2000; Godard, 2001; Peccei, 2004; Van Veldhoven, 2005; Kroon et al., 2009), support the claims made by critical HR researches mentioned earlier in this chapter, that HRM and HPWPs can have a negative effect on employee well-being. It is, however, not fully clear how these issues can be resolved in practice. Are employees and employers doomed to models of conflicting interests as suggested by some of the critical HR approaches, some OB approaches and some organizational health psychology approaches? Is there still hope for a more unitarist model in the search for harmony between employers and employees based on shared interests? Or is there a third way? The alternative might be a coalition approach or balanced approach in which the employer and the employees sometimes share similar interests, and in some cases bargain on differences of interest.

Balanced approaches

Balanced approaches with implications for people management have started to emerge in OB (e.g. Tsui et al., 1997), general management (e.g. Deephouse, 1999), organizational health psychology (e.g. Bakker et al., 2004) and HRM (e.g. Paauwe, 2004). Boselie et al., (2009) highlight the potential of balanced approaches for HR issues on different levels of analysis (e.g. individual, team and organization). They characterize the HR discipline by its *ambiguities* (e.g. in the roles of HR professionals; see Chapter 12 on HR roles and competences) and *potential conflicting interests* between employers and employees, and *dualities* in goals (economic value and moral values as argued by Paauwe, 2004).

Balanced approaches on the individual employee level

The study by Tsui et al. (1997), discussed earlier in this chapter, incorporates both notions on balanced employment relationships (mutual investment and quasi-spot-contract) and imbalanced employment relationships (underinvestment and overinvestment). Their findings suggest that the balanced mutual investment employment relationship model, which is comparable to the high commitment system and HPWSs on organization level analysis (see Chapter 6), is the optimal model with regard to HR outcomes. The overinvestment employment relationship, characterized by extensive employee development opportunities and high pay, also reveals positive effects on HR outcomes; however, the costs related to overinvestment in people are not taken into account. In other words, overinvestment might look interesting to please the employees and get good scores on employee outcomes, such as satisfaction and commitment, but the downside is most likely to be lower efficiency rates. The financial sector can be characterized by overinvestment in employment relationships; at least this was the case until the financial crisis started in late 2008.

Stop and reflect

Think of the potential negative effects of an overinvestment employment relationship in an organization, in which employees receive huge bonuses, profit-sharing schemes and extensive training budgets.

Bakker et al. (2004) present the job demands–resources model of burnout. This model proposes that job demands, defined in terms of work load, emotional demands and work–home conflict, positively affect exhaustion. The model also proposes that job resources, defined in terms of employee autonomy, possibilities for employee development and social support from colleagues and/or managers, negatively affect employee disengagement. In other words, job resources positively affect employee engagement. Another important set of propositions in the model is formulated as follows:

- Job demands and job resource are negatively associated.
- Exhaustion and disengagement are also negatively associated.
- Exhaustion is negatively associated with in-role performance (e.g. the expertise in job-related tasks; the achievement of goals of the job).
- Disengagement is negatively associated with extra-role performance (actions that go beyond what is stated in formal job descriptions; citizenship behaviour).

The job demands–resources model implicitly incorporates elements of a balanced approach on individual employee level taking into account:

- job demands versus job resources;
- exhaustion versus engagement/disengagement;
- in-role versus extra-role performance.

Balanced approaches on the organizational level

In the strategic balance model, organizational success can only be achieved when financial performance *and* societal performance of an organization are above average in the particular population in which the organization is operating (Deephouse, 1999). In this view, exclusive high scores on either financial *or* societal performance are bad for the long-term survival of an organization (see Chapters 1 and 2). Deephouse (1999) finds empirical evidence that successful organizations both conform to and differentiate from other organizations (mostly competitors) in the population. Some practices, including HR practices, need to conform to the population norms and regulations (e.g. minimum wages and working conditions related to safety), while other HR practices have more leeway for differentiation (e.g. selective recruitment and extensive employee development).

With regard to HR goals, Paauwe (2004) makes a distinction between *economic value* and *moral values* (see Chapters 1, 2 and 3):

- Human resources are something more than just 'resources'.
- HRM is not concerned solely with financial performance.
- HRM focuses on the exchange relationship between employee and organization.
- The shaping of the employment relationship takes place in an era of continuous tension between the added value and moral values.

Paauwe (2004) argues that organization can create unique approaches for long-term success when the economic and the moral side of organizing are fully taken into account. This requires a balanced approach. Evidence for his perspective is found in studies by Boon et al. (2009) and Boselie (2009).

Agility and vitality

Organizations that apply a balanced approach on both the individual and the organization level might find the Holy Grail through HRM as discussed in Chapter 3. The concept that perhaps best captures 'what employers want' is **agility**, reflecting the organizational capability to adapt easily to changes in its external environment (Dyer and Shafer, 1999). An HPWS, which is discussed in more detail in the next chapter, is thought to be the foundation for the creation of an agile organization by enhancing employee abilities, providing them the right incentive structure and creating opportunities for extensive employee involvement and participation. The critical HR studies, the OB studies and the organizational health psychology studies summarized in this chapter, however, show the potential downside of putting too much emphasis on the organization or the employer's interests. More attention on employee well-being, in particular employee **vitality**, is required to restore the balance between 'what employers want' and 'what employees want' (Dorenbosch, 2009). The concept of vitality captures elements of employee satisfaction, job demands, employee trust in the organization and the managers, job stress and the physical health of an individual employee. One of the major challenges for organizations is the persistency and consistency of a balanced approach towards employees focused on both agility and vitality in times of crisis (e.g. an economic crisis or a company crisis). Vitality notions are most likely to be dropped in times of crisis. This is, for example, reflected in higher job demands, organizational downsizing and longer working hours. In some cases these actions are inevitable. The argument for a balanced agility–vitality approach in times of organizational prosperity could then be that organizations build up reserves for bad times that might come. An agility–vitality approach is a long-term model that should be part of a more general organization philosophy and strategy. The challenges of long-term HR issues are discussed in more detail in Chapter 14.

Conclusion

The outcomes of this chapter have multiple implications for future HR research and HR in practice. First, balancing 'what employers want' with 'what employees want' suggests the relevance of a multi-actor approach explicitly including individual employee and employer input. The latter can be represented by line managers and top management. Second, blending and integrating insights from different theoretical lenses – critical HR perspectives, OB and organizational health psychology – can contribute to the full understanding of the shaping of successful HRM in organizations. Third, the proposed multi-actor and multiple lenses' approaches also imply multi-level analysis; for example, combining organizational level data with team level and individual employee level data.

The balanced theoretical framework proposed in this chapter builds on two important underlying assumptions:

1. Organizational success can be achieved when an organization is moderately different on social and economic performance from other organizations in the same population (or sector) (see Deephouse, 1999).
2. Long-term outstanding scores on both social and economic performance are unlikely for most organizations. Excellent economic performance (times of organizational prosperity) can contribute to social performance (e.g. HR investments in employee well-being). Excellent social performance can be the buffer for poor economic performance, for example, as a result of a macroeconomic crisis or a major internal reorganization.

Financial reserves or buffers can contribute to social aspects of shaping the employment relationship. And social reserves or buffers (e.g. reflected in an excellent atmosphere between employees and managers and in high employee trust levels) can contribute to the financial performance of an organization in the case of organizational crisis (e.g. market stagnation or market decline).

The proposed perspective explicitly builds on a multidimensional performance construct including both 'hard' financial indicators (e.g. cost-effectiveness, sales, market share and profits) and 'soft' social indicators such as general employee well-being (e.g. job stress, absence due to illness and job satisfaction), fairness towards organizational members (e.g. distributive and procedural justice), social legitimacy and corporate reputation. The notions of continuously balancing social and economic aspects represent the dynamic component of the approach. In a way, this approach is like a pendulum and HRM the mechanism for creating a new equilibrium.

The next step is to determine the exact nature of HRM in line with the proposed balanced framework presented in this chapter.

Summary

- The management and HRM literature is dominated by 'what employers want'.
- 'What employers want' is not necessarily the same as 'what employees want'.
- In general, employers search for employees who have the characteristics of a chameleon (adaptability skills), Einstein (intelligence and knowledge) and a top athlete (speed and endurance).
- The average individual employee is in search of a job that can be characterized by fun at work, social support from superiors, an acceptable work–life balance, employee development opportunities, a nice group atmosphere and employment security.
- Critical HR studies show the 'dark side' or downside of the dominant management and HRM approaches, for example with regard to the general managerial attitudes towards trade unions, the marginalization of women in organizational life, the economic exploitation of workers, the political repression of weaker groups in an organization, the lack of ethical debates in HRM and the exclusion, marginalization and repression of older workers.
- Mainstream HRM is focused on the added value of HRM, the search for sustained competitive advantage through 'good' people management and the alignment between HRM and strategy.
- OB pays more attention to the individual employee outcomes of which some (e.g. satisfaction and trust) may reflect what employees want, instead of the dominating 'what employers want' paradigm.
- Organizational health psychology highlights the negative effects of managerial and HR interventions on employee well-being, for example, with regard to job stress and burnout.
- The balanced approaches in HRM on individual and organization levels present a new school of thought.
- The balanced approaches acknowledge shared interests between the employer and the employee in some situations, but also pinpoint the often conflicting interests between the two. The relationship between the employer and the employees is therefore most likely to be a coalition instead of a harmony as proposed by mainstream HRM or a conflict as suggested by many critical HR studies.
- An agility–vitality approach is a model for long-term organizational success blending the employer's (agility) and the employees' interests (vitality).

Glossary of key terms

Agility is the organizational capability to adapt easily to changes in its external environment.

Balanced approaches in HRM take into account employers' and employees' interests on individual employee and organization levels of analysis.

Burnout represents a person's condition in which the individual is completely exhausted, lacks the energy to work, is extremely demotivated, is cynical towards the organization and colleagues, and perceives personal incompetence in job performance.

Consensus orientation in mainstream HRM builds on the core assumption 'what is good for the employer is also good for the employee and vice versa'.

Critical HR studies focus on the negative effects of organizational innovations and HR renewal in terms of work intensification, job stress, perceived employee insecurity and discrimination.

Dissensus orientation in HRM highlights the downside of people management practices in an organization.

Job decision latitude refers to job control or discretion, and represents individual employees' leeway or room to manoeuvre in their jobs.

Job demands measures stress sources (stressors) and refers to an internal state of an individual.

Job stress is a condition or feeling experienced when a person perceives that demands exceed the personal and social resources the individual is able to mobilize.

Organizational behaviour (OB) focuses on how people, individuals and groups act in organizations.

Organizational health psychology mainly focuses on what workers can handle given the working conditions; for example, in terms of job demands and stress.

Vitality is the emotional, the mental and physical well-being of employees.

Individual task

There is a growing body of literature acknowledging that job stress is related to stress at home, and vice versa. In other words, job stress and burnout caused by, for example, impossible requirements, lack of personal control and/or poor leadership, is most likely to affect the employee's home situation with possible negative effects on relationships and a desired work–life balance. But it also works the other way around. Personal stress caused by family-related issues (e.g. marriage problems, family members seriously ill and/or the death of family members) is most likely to affect somebody's work, possibly causing job stress and burnout. Can you think of practices that could be applied by an employer to decrease job stress caused by serious family issues of an employee? More concretely, what can a manager (supervisor) do to help a subordinate in the case of:

- an employee who is in the middle of a divorce;
- an employee who is confronted with the serious illness of a child who needs medical treatment in hospital for a long period;
- the death of an employee's partner?

This might not be a pleasant assignment, but remember that these issues occur in real life and line managers are confronted with them.

Team task

Discuss your personal scores as (a) a student or (b) a practitioner on the following HR outcomes:

(1 = extremely low and 10 = extremely high)

- student or job *satisfaction* ___
- trust in the teachers or *trust* in the managers of your organization ___
- student or job *stress* ___*
- student or employee *motivation* ___
- willingness to walk the extra mile for the school or the organization (*organizational citizenship behaviour*) ___
- willingness to walk the extra mile for your fellow students or your colleagues at work (*group citizenship behaviour*) ___
- *commitment* to the school or the organization ___
- *intention to quit* or *intention to leave* the organization ___*
- student presence or employee presence (opposite to *absenteeism*) ___
- *being proud* of your school or your organization ___

Total score ___
*Reversed item

For the 'reversed' items, you need to recalculate the score by applying this simple formula: 11 − your score (e.g. a score of 8 on 'student or job *stress*' will equal 3; that is, 11 − 8 = 3).

Discuss your total score with the others and think of practices that can increase and practices that can decrease your personal scores.

Learning checklist

After studying this chapter, you should be able to do the following:

- Identify the possible different interests of the employer and the employee (what employers want and what employees want).
- Outline the consensus nature of mainstream HRM.
- Evaluate the claims made by critical HR studies.
- Review the different types of HRM research using the level of analysis dimension (individual versus organizational) and the number of HR practices (single versus multiple).
- Evaluate the insights from OB and organizational health psychology on HRM and employee well-being.
- Consider the job demands–job control model of Karasek.
- Discuss the potential effects of HR practices on stress and burnout.
- Examine balanced approaches on individual employee and organization level.
- Discuss the notions on agility and vitality.

References

Ackers, P. and Payne, J. (1998) British trade unions and social partnership: rhetoric, reality and strategy, *International Journal of Human Resource Management*, 9(3): 529–50.

Bakker, A.B., Demerouti, E. and Verbeke, W. (2004) Using the job demands–resources model to predict burnout and performance, *Human Resource Management*, 43(1): 83–104.

Baron, J.M. and Kreps, D.M. (1999) *Strategic Human Resources: Frameworks for General Managers*. New York: Wiley.

Black, J. and McCabe, D. (1996) Mobilizing consent: paternalism and cellular manufacturing, *International Journal of Human Resource Management*, 7(2): 534–52.

Blyton, P. and Turnbull, P. (eds) (1992) *Reassessing Human Resource Management*. London: Sage.

Boon, C., Paauwe, J., Boselie, P. and Den Hartog, D.N. (2009) Institutional pressures and HRM: developing institutional fit, *Personnel Review*, 38(5): 492–508.

Boselie, P. (2009) A balanced approach to understanding the shaping of human resource management in organisations, *Management Revue*, 20(1): 90–108.

Boselie, P., Brewster, C. and Paauwe, J. (2009) In search for balance: managing the dualities of HRM – an overview of the issues, *Personnel Review*, Special Issue, 38(5): 461–71.

Boxall, P., Purcell, J. and Wright, P.M. (2007) Human resource management: scope, analysis, and significance, in P. Boxall, J. Purcell and P.M. Wright (eds), *The Oxford Handbook of Human Resource Management,* Chapter 1, pp. 1–16. Oxford: Oxford University Press.

Conway, E. and Monks, K. (2008) HR practices and commitment to change: an employee-level analysis, *Human Resource Management Journal*, 18(1): 72–89.

Coyle-Shapiro, J. A.-M. and Kessler, I. (2000) Consequences of the psychological contract for the employment relationship: a large scale survey, *Journal of Management Studies*, 37(7): 903–30.

Deephouse, D.L. (1999) To be different, or to be the same? It's a question (and theory) of strategic balance, *Strategic Management Journal*, 20(2): 147–66.

Deetz, S. (1996) Describing differences in approaches to organizational science: rethinking Burell and Morgan and their legacy, *Organization Science*, 7: 191–207.

Delbridge, R. (2006) The vitality of labour process analysis, *Organization Studies*, 27(8): 1209–19.

Dorenbosch, L. (2009) Management by vitality: examining the 'active' well-being and performance outcomes of high performance work practices at the work unit level. Dissertation, Tilburg University, Tilburg.

Dyer, L. and Shafer, R. (1999) Creating organizational agility: implications for strategic human resource management, in P.M. Wright, L. Dyer, J. Boudreau and G. Milkovich (eds), *Research in Personnel and Human Resource Management,* Supplement 4. Stamford, CT and London: JAI Press.

Edwards, C., Robinson, O., Welchman, R. and Woodall, J. (1999) Lost opportunities? Organizational restructuring and women managers, *Human Resource Management Journal,* 9(1): 55–64.

Ezzamel, M., Simon, L., Wilkinson, A. and Willmott, H. (1996) Practices and practicalities in human resource management, *Human Resource Management Journal*, 6(1): 63–81.

Francis, H. and Keegan, A. (2006) The changing face of HR: in search of balance, *Human Resource Management Journal*, 16(3): 231–49.

Freese, C. (2007) Organizational change and the dynamics of psychological contracts: a longitudinal study. Dissertation, Tilburg University, Tilburg.

Godard, J. (2001) Beyond the high-performance paradigm? An analysis of variation in Canadian managerial perceptions of reform programme effectiveness, *British Journal of Industrial Relations*, 39: 25–52.

Guest, D.E. (1999) Human resource management: the workers' verdict, *Human Resource Management Journal*, 9(3): 5–25.

Harley, B. and Hardy, C. (2004) Firing blanks? An analysis of discursive struggle in HRM, *Journal of Management Studies*, 41(3): 377–400.

Huselid, M.A. (1995) The impact of human resource management practices on turnover, productivity, and corporate financial performance, *Academy of Management Journal*, 38(3): 635–72.

Janssens, M. and Steayaert, C. (2009) HRM and performance: a plea for reflexivity in HRM studies, *Journal of Management Studies*, 46(1): 143–55.

Karasek, R.A. (1979) Job demands, job decision latitude, and mental strain: implications for job design, *Administrative Science Quarterly*, 24(2): 285–308.

Karasek, R.A. and Theorell, T. (1990) *Healthy Work: Stress, Productivity and the Reconstruction of Working Life*. New York: Basic Books.

Keegan, A. and Boselie, P. (2006) The lack of impact of dissensus inspired analysis on developments in the field of human resource management, *Journal of Management Studies*, 43(7): 1491–511.

Keenoy, T. (1999) HRM as a hologram: a polemic, *Journal of Management Studies*, 36(1): 1–23.

Kroon, B., Van De Voorde, K. and Van Veldhoven, M.J.P.M. (2009) Cross-level effects of high performance work practices on burn-out: two counteracting mediating mechanisms compared, *Personnel Review*, 38(5): 509–25.

Legge, K. (2005) *Human Resource Management: Rhetorics and Realities*. Basingstoke: Palgrave Macmillan.

Maslach, C. and Jackson, S.E. (1981) The measurement of experienced burnout, *Journal of Occupational Behavior*, 2: 99–113.

Maslach, C., Schaufeli, W.B. and Leiter, M.P. (2001) Job burnout, *Annual Review of Psychology*, 52: 397–422.

Paauwe, J. (2004) *HRM and Performance: Achieving Long-term Viability*. Oxford: Oxford University Press.

Peccei, R. (2004) Human resource management and the search for the happy workplace. Inaugural address. Erasmus Research Institute of Management (ERIM), Rotterdam.

Purcell, J. (1999) Best practice and best fit: chimera or cul-de-sac?, *Human Resource Management Journal*, 9(3): 26–41.

Ramsay, H., Scholarios, D. and Harley, B. (2000) Employees and high-performance work systems: testing inside the black box, *British Journal of Labour Relations*, 38: 501–31.

Robinson, S.L. and Rousseau, D.M. (1994) Violating the psychological contract: not the exception but the norm, *Journal of Organizational Behavior*, 15: 245–59.

Rousseau, D.M. and Schalk, R. (2000) *Psychological Contracts in Employment: Cross-national Perspectives*. Thousand Oaks, CA: Sage.

Sanders, K., Dorenbosch, L. and Reuver, R. de (2008) The impact of individual and shared employee perceptions of HRM on affective commitment: considering the climate strength, *Personnel Review*, 37: 412–25.

Sonnenberg, M. (2006) The signalling effect of HRM on psychological contracts of employees. Dissertation, Erasmus University, Rotterdam.

Taylor, P. and Walker, A. (1998) Policies and practices towards older workers: a framework for comparative research, *Human Resource Management Journal*, 8(3): 61–76.

Thompson, P. and Harley, B. (2007) HRM and the worker: labor process perspectives, in P. Boxall, J. Purcell, J. and P.M. Wright (eds), *The Oxford Handbook of Human Resource Management*, Chapter 8, pp. 147–65. Oxford: Oxford University Press.

Townley, B. (1993) Foucault, power/knowledge, and its relevance for human resource management, *Academy of Management Review*, 18(3): 518–45.

Tsui, A.S., Pearce, J.L., Porter, L.W. and Tripoli, A.M. (1997) Alternative approaches to the employee–organization relationship: does investment in employees pay off?, *Academy of Management Journal*, 40: 1089–121.

Van Veldhoven, M. (2005) Financial performance and the long-term link with HR practices, work climate and job stress, *Human Resource Management Journal*, 15(4): 30–53.

Watson, T. (2004) HRM and critical social science analysis, *Journal of Management Studies*, 41(3): 447–67.

Winstanley, D. and Woodall, J. (2000) The ethical dimension of human resource management, *Human Resource Management Journal*, 10(2): 5–20.

Wright, P.M. and Boswell, W.R. (2002) Desegregating HRM: a review and synthesis of micro and macro human resource management research, *Journal of Management*, 28(3): 247–76.

Van Yperen, N. and Hagedoorn, M. (2003) Do high job demands increase intrinsic motivation or fatigue or both? The role of job control and job social support, *Academy of Management Journal*, 46(3): 339–48.

Yun, H.A. (1999) Knowledge regimes and political power: the social construction of knowledge, *International Journal of Human Resource Management*, 10(6): 996–1005.

Further reading

Boselie, P., Brewster, C. and Paauwe, J. (2009) In search for balance: managing the dualities of HRM – an overview of the issues, *Personnel Review,* Special issue, 38(5): 461–71.

Keegan, A. and Boselie, P. (2006) The lack of impact of dissensus inspired analysis on developments in the field of human resource management, *Journal of Management Studies*, 43(7): 1491–1511.

Legge, K. (2005). *Human Resource Management: Rhetorics and Realities*. Basingstoke: Palgrave Macmillan.

Maslach, C., Schaufeli, W.B. and Leiter, M.P. (2001) Job burnout, *Annual Review of Psychology*, 52: 397–422.

Thompson, P. and Harley, B. (2007) HRM and the worker: labour process perspectives, in P. Boxall, J. Purcell and P.M. Wright (eds), *The Oxford Handbook of Human Resource Management*, Chapter 8, pp. 147–65. Oxford: Oxford University Press.

Wright, P.M. and Boswell, W.R. (2002) Desegregating HRM: a review and synthesis of micro and macro human resource management research, *Journal of Management*, 28(3): 247–76.

CHAPTER 06

High-performance Work Systems

❖ Learning Objectives

After studying this chapter, you should be able to do the following:

- ❖ Review the history of the systems approaches, including scientific management, human relations, revisionism and socio-technical systems (STS) theory
- ❖ Understand systems approaches in general
- ❖ Review the high-performance work system (HPWS) approaches
- ❖ Understand the emergence of human resource management (HRM) in the early 1980s
- ❖ Recognize the five main high-performance work practices (HPWPs) (selective recruitment and selection, appraisal and performance management (PM), compensation, training and development and employee participation)
- ❖ Outline the differences and similarities between the best-practice approaches in HRM and the contemporary HPWS approaches in HRM
- ❖ Understand the AMO model
- ❖ Examine the added value of HPWS in the creation and maintenance of a high-performance culture in an organization

CASE STUDY: FERRARI

In sports car racing the colour red is generally associated with one specific brand: Ferrari. Though other colours are used for Ferrari cars, such as the black Ferrari Daytona Spyder 365 GTS/4 in the popular 1980s television series *Miami Vice* (later on replaced by the white Testarossa), there are people who argue that only *rosso corsa* ('race red') matches a Ferrari car. The Italian organization was founded by Enzo Ferrari in 1929 and there has always been a close link between the production cars and racing, in particular Formula 1 racing. It is the oldest team in Formula 1 racing and has won more than 14 World Drivers' Championship titles, including huge success with Michael Schumacher until he retired in 2006. Since 1969 Ferrari has been part of the Italian Fiat Group. Ferrari's success as an organization is much more than selling sports cars and participating in race events. The merchandising of Ferrari products, including eyewear, pencils, cell phones, clothing and perfume, all contribute to the secret of the organization's success.

The organization was ranked number one on the 2007 list of a hundred best workplaces in Europe by the *Financial Times*. The Ferrari brand itself definitely attracts employees with a passion for cars (annually about 4000 application letters for less than 200 vacancies; on average 20 candidates for every vacancy). The close interplay between racing and sports car production has strengthened the company's image, but that is surely not enough to become successful. Building high-performance cars for decades is only possible in a high performance organization where people management is aligned with the high standards of the products: very expensive and powerful automobiles (prices between €200 000–400 000 for production cars; over 600 horsepower in one engine). However, with a four or six-litre engine, these monsters consume about one litre of gasoline every five kilometres, which is almost five times higher than the consumption of the hybrid Toyota Prius. From an environmental pollution point of view the Ferrari car is an absolute nightmare; for the sports car fan it is the ultimate fantasy (e.g. those who love the television series *Top Gear*).

In 2007 the company employed about 2800 people producing nearly 6000 cars on a yearly basis. Selective recruitment and selection, continuous extensive employee development of both employees on the shopfloor and managers, employee involvement in product development (e.g. with the Creativity Club project that mixes employees from different units and different hierarchical levels), employment security practices (e.g. linking the employees' well-being to personal growth in the Formula Uomo project), performance-related pay (PRP) and information sharing. The company can also be characterized by some degree of hierarchy and status differences between employees, probably linked to the premium position of the product (status) and the hierarchical family tradition implemented by Enzo himself. In general, employees are proud of their work. However, just a few months after the award by the *Financial Times* for its great workplace, Ferrari employees went on strike.

Workers put the brakes on Ferrari

'The Ferrari factory in Modena, which is annually voted the best place in Italy to work, has suffered the first strike on its production line in more than 20 years. "Around 80pc of our workers, who build our Gran Turismo models, went on strike," said Renzo Ferri, the head of Ferrari's union. "Several office workers did go in but none of the engineers." The workers on the picket line sang: "We have a dream in our hearts – to see Cordero driving a tractor." They were referring to Luca Cordero di Montezemolo, the company's president. The strikers said the Ferrari factory, where the F430 and F599 models are produced, increasingly resembled one of the mass-market factories run by Fiat, which owns Ferrari. They complained that they had been fined for "disturbing a tour of journalists" and that they were asked to cover up when they had injuries. They are also upset at not receiving a larger pay rise after upping their productivity'.

(Malcolm Moore, *Telegraph*, 7 May 2007, cited in Maessen, 2007)

? Discussion questions

- Discuss the impact of the Ferrari brand name on the recruitment and selection of new employees. What are the advantages and disadvantages of a strong brand for the recruitment and selection of new personnel?

- Discuss the potential best practices in HRM within Ferrari. To what extent are these HR practices aligned to each other within Ferrari?
- Discuss the risks of a high-performance work environment for employee well-being within Ferrari.

Introduction

An HPWS is a bundle or cluster of HRM practices that increases organizational performance; for example, in terms of labour productivity, service quality and flexibility (Kepes and Delery, 2007). Part of the success of an HPWS (e.g. based on selective recruitment and selection, employee involvement, employee monitoring and some kind of PRP) is the ideal combination of individual HR practices, also called **internal fit** (see Chapter 2). An internal fit between the individual HR practices into a coherent and consistent HR leads to a higher performance than the sum of the individual HR practices. Kepes and Delery (2007: 385) argue that 'one of the defining characteristics of SHRM [strategic human resource management] has been the proposition that HRM systems and not individual practices are the source of competitive advantage.' An HPWS can be defined as a bundle of specific HR practices that create employee abilities in terms of knowledge and skills, employee motivation through a sophisticated incentive structure, and employee opportunity to participate in decision making.

> 'the past is often neglected or ignored perhaps partly caused by our human nature to forget about our history and partly caused by the rat race for organizational survival.'

Severe competition and globalization in the 1980s and 1990s caused increased dynamics and complexity issues for most organizations. Product life cycles are shortened, new competitive technology is easily adopted by others, knowledge is being transferred through the Internet and customer demands are higher than ever before. In a reaction to these new developments the management approaches in both theory (e.g. resource-based view (RBV), see Chapter 3) and practice (e.g. balanced scorecard (BSC), see Chapter 4) started focusing more and more on the future and the central question 'How do we achieve long-term organizational success?' Economics and business became the centre of attention in contrast to, for example, sociology, history and industrial relations (IR). The latter three disciplines got far more attention in the 1960s and 1970s. Nowadays, the past is often neglected or ignored perhaps partly caused by our human nature to forget about our history and partly caused by the rat race for organizational survival. History and historical models of the employment relationship, however, are very important in understanding the shaping of the employment relationship in different contexts, including branches of industry, countries and organizations.

The configuration notions, for example, made earlier in Chapter 2 highlight the relevance of the organization's DNA or roots for the creation of HRM in the present and near future. Companies founded in the 1940s are most likely to be affected by operations management and manufacturing principles that are characteristic for that time period. Companies founded in the 1990s are most likely to be affected by technological DNA related to the emergence of the Internet and information technology (IT).

> 'it is most likely that China and India will also make a leap forward in their employment relationship models, perhaps even faster than most Western countries ever did.'

Companies (e.g. call centres, factories) in emerging countries such as China and India are often being judged from a contemporary Western point of view suggesting the majority of these organizations are (still) applying old-fashioned scientific management principles (e.g. labour division, direct supervision and financial incentives). Not long ago, however, these same principles were applied in many Western countries and it is most likely that China and India will also make a leap forward in their employment relationship models, perhaps even faster than most Western countries ever did. The point I want to make here is that the main management models of the last century, starting with Taylor's approach, are still relevant for today's discussions on shaping the employment relationship. Scientific management and Fordism, for example, are linked to contemporary discussions on total quality management (TQM) and performance management. This is reflected in concepts such as Toyotaism. Boje and Winsor (1993), for example, discuss the 'resurrection of Taylorism' through TQM principles in many organizations, including Toyota. In their view, neo-Taylorism is an individualistic version of Taylor's (1911) model in which direct supervision and close monitoring is replaced by self-management and self-control.

The classic management models (e.g. Taylorism) incorporate systems notions and elements that are picked up by contemporary HPWS approaches. The HPWSs contain the 'flavours of the past models'; however, the contemporary HPWSs go beyond these classic approaches, including other HR practices in particular aimed at achieving high employee commitment levels through internal labour market principles, autonomous teamwork and advanced PRP. HPWSs are a special type of HRM that has received a lot of attention since the mid-1990s (Appelbaum et al., 2000; Wall and Wood, 2005; Boxall and Macky, 2009).

> 'The classic management models incorporate systems notions and elements that are picked up by contemporary HPWS approaches'

First, four classic management models are summarized with a focus on the systems notions made in these models. Second, the emergence of HRM in the early 1980s is discussed linked to the classic management models. Third, the early HR models in the 1980s are closely related to the control and commitment models of Walton (1985) and Arthur (1994), and these control and commitment approaches follow. Fourth, the HPWS approaches are summarized and specific attention is paid to the **AMO** theory. AMO is the acronym for 'abilities', 'motivation' and 'opportunity to participate'. Fifth, the five main HPWSs of this book are discussed briefly related to selection and recruitment, development and training, PM and appraisal, compensation and employee participation. Finally, an overview of the latest developments and insights on HPWSs is presented using the model by Boxall and Macky (2009).

Classic management models and systems approaches

For the introduction of the main topic, we have to go back in history to another car manufacturer (other than Ferrari) from the USA: Ford Motor Company. In 1908 Henri Ford delivered the first mass-produced car called the T-Ford, applying assembly-line principles from slaughterhouses in order to build cheap cars. The automated assembly line was combined with what Taylor (1911) would later call *scientific management* principles such as division of labour, direct supervision and improved working conditions. Actually, Taylor created one of the first systems approaches in theory and Ford did it in practice. At about the same time (late 1800s) a Frenchman called Henri Fayol (1949) also created new ways of organizing work using similar scientific management principles inspired by the French mining industry. Taylor's (1911) combination of division of labour, direct supervision, improved working conditions and financial incentives, linked to individual performance for creating a high-performance organization, is one of the first systems approaches in the field of management and organization.

> 'Taylor's (1911) combination ... is one of the first systems approaches in the field of management and organization.'

Both Taylor and Fayol's approaches are based on the following assumptions: employees are only motivated by financial incentives; employees are lazy by nature; and finally, employees are not willing to assume any form of responsibility. According to these views, strong leadership (direct supervision) is required to improve labour productivity and increase employee satisfaction. Nowadays, these systems are often heavily criticized on the basis of our current expectations about work and work design, but we should keep in mind that the working conditions at the beginning of the twentieth century in most factories were very poor. People often had to work for more than 10 hours a day and for more than 5 days a week without holidays and mostly without any kind of employment security. One hundred years after the start of the industrial revolution, most employees were probably much better off in one of Ford's factories with scientific management regimes than employees in any other manufacturing organization.

In the 1930s some scholars continued working on Taylor's scientific management principles in the so-called Hawthorne studies comparing the impact of light intensity in factories on employee productivity. The results, representing an increased performance in all factories in the study (both with high and low-light intensity on the production level), were surprising and could not be explained with existing models, including Taylor's approach. During a field research study, Mayo (1933) and colleagues discovered that paying personal attention to employees conditions overall enhanced employee performance and led to an increase in productivity. And the performance increases had nothing to do with the field experiment of variation in light intensity. This hidden effect caused by researchers is known as the *Hawthorne effect*. The Hawthorne experiments or studies reveal the importance of employees' emotions, feelings and sentiments and the influence of these on employee behaviour. The study itself is the foundation of a new school of thought known as the *Human Relations Movement* (Mayo, 1933). The basic assumptions of this school have been:

- organizations consist of social relationships;
- labour is a group activity;
- informal groups have an enormous impact on the organization;
- financial incentives are not the only motivators – social relationships are also very important;
- there are no real controversies between employees and their employer;
- conflicts are caused by problems in communication.

The Hawthorne studies started off as a Tayloristic approach, but the findings led to a new school of thought – the Human Relations Movement (HRM) – and this new school grew up to become the opposite of scientific management in the years to come. The special attention paid to the employee perspective in the Human Relations Movement is often seen as one of the building blocks or early foundations of HRM. A high-performance organization, according to the Human Relations Movement, consists of special personal attention of direct supervisors to employees, motivation through financial and non-financial incentives, emphasis on cooperation and social aspects of cooperation, and good communication and information sharing throughout the organization.

! Stop and reflect

- Can you think of ways in which an HR researcher or research consultant can affect the research setting and object in an unintended way (the Hawthorne effect)?
- Can you think of ways to avoid unintended research effects when studying HRM practice?

In the 1950s and 1960s the *revisionistic perspective* focused on the integration of different aspects of labour relations and their mutual dependence (e.g. Herzberg, 1968 on vertical job loading and early notions of job enrichment). McGregor (1960), whose work was heavily influenced by Maslow (1943), rejects the traditional view of the nature of employees, a view he labelled 'Theory X' in his argument. In his opinion, motivation by financial incentives only, employee laziness and their unwillingness to assume responsibility are the results of conventional organization structures and managerial policies, practices and programmes. In other words, people are naturally passive or resistant to organizational needs; they have become so as a result of their experiences in organizations (McGregor, 1957). The author assumes that the motivation, the potential for development, the capacity for assuming responsibility and the readiness to direct behaviour towards organizational goals are all present in people. The alternative view, also known as 'Theory Y', relies heavily on notions of self-control and self-direction. A system of decentralization and delegation, job enlargement, employee participation and consultative management, and performance appraisal (PA) all fit Theory Y in practice. In essence, McGregor's Theory Y reflects his critiques on scientific management almost 50 years after its birth. However, Theory Y is often mistakenly linked to the Human Relations Movement. Mayo's (1933) movement is far too 'soft' according to McGregor (1960), putting too much focus on employee attitudes without linking employee behaviour to organizational goals. McGregor's Theory Y has a more functional orientation with regard to the performance of an organization. The underlying assumptions and ideas of this revisionistic approach are closely related to notions of HRM made at the beginning of the 1980s (Porter et al., 2003). A high-performance organization, according to McGregor's (1960) revisionistic approach, applies decentralization of decision making, increasing employee autonomy and involvement, job enlargement and job enrichment and PA.

The 1960s also introduced the so-called *STS theory*, combining production elements with social elements in order to enrich employees' jobs and to create more organizational flexibility (Emery and Trist, 1960). The rise of STS theory is closely related to developments in the oil, mining and textile industries, followed by the car industry. Mass production, the use of assembly lines and process industry have resulted in extreme labour division and monotonous jobs. Solutions were thought to be found in new work designs stressing a system of practices, including job enlargement (multiple tasks), job enrichment (diversity in tasks), teamwork, job rotation and employee involvement in decision making. The STS theory is built on social and technological considerations that are characteristic of manufacturing companies, although some of these principles (e.g. teamwork and rotation) have found their way to other types of organization such as services organizations. In fact, some of the STS practices, such as teamwork, are more easily implemented in non-manufacturing contexts because of the sometimes restrictive production systems in manufacturing contexts. For example, assembly lines may limit the scope and application of teamwork and job rotation as a result of the nature of the system. The STS theory has been an inspiration for the quality of work–life approaches (Katz et al., 1983) and the TQM movement in the 1980s and 1990s. Even today STS theory is applied in HR research, including the work of MacDuffie (1995) and Appelbaum et al. (2000). A high-performance organization, according to the STS theory, applies good employment conditions, teamwork, job enlargement, job enrichment, employee autonomy and integrating production systems with work systems.

The scientific management school (Taylor, 1911; Fayol, 1949), *the Human Relations Movement* (Mayo, 1933), *the revisionistic approach* (McGregor, 1960) and *the STS school* (Emery and Trist, 1960) represent four different schools of thought on creating a high performance organization (see Table 6.1). The emergence of the HRM discipline in the 1980s was heavily influenced and affected by these schools and from that point in time you can see the debate on HPWSs and HRM often go hand in hand. This, is for example, reflected in the work by Bailey (1993), Huselid (1995), Appelbaum et al. (2000), Boselie (2002) and Combs et al. (2006).

The contemporary HPWS approaches contain 'the flavours' of the past models (e.g. good working conditions, good communication, employee involvement and job enrichment). The HPWSs, however, go beyond these practices, including selective recruitment and selection, extensive employee development, career planning and internal labour market practices, and autonomous teamwork aimed at high employee commitment levels that are most likely to positively affect organizational performance (e.g. cost-effectiveness).

	Scientific management	Human relations	Revisionism	Socio-technical systems
Main focus	Strong leadership and close employee monitoring	Personal attention and employees in their social context	Creation of autonomy, challenging jobs and employee involvement	New work design for technical production settings
Practices	■ labour division ■ direct supervision ■ good working conditions (e.g. safety) ■ financial incentives	■ personal attention for employees by supervisor ■ cooperation ■ good communication ■ information sharing ■ financial and non-financial incentives	■ decentralization ■ employee autonomy ■ employee involvement ■ job enlargement ■ job enrichment ■ performance appraisal	■ teamwork ■ job enlargement ■ job enrichment ■ job rotation ■ employee autonomy ■ good working conditions ■ integration of production and work systems
System approach	Direct control system	Social integration system	High involvement system	Enrichment system

TABLE 6.1 Overview characteristics of systems for each school

HRM approaches in the 1980s

Before we discuss the contemporary HPWS paradigms, we have to take a closer look at the emergence of HRM as a discipline in the early 1980s. The classic books by Beer et al. (1984) and Fombrun et al. (1984) mark the introduction of a serious and relevant new discipline called HRM. Before the 1980s all issues referring to managing employees in organizations were called personnel management (Guest, 1987) with a major emphasis on the administrative part of personnel management (e.g. salary administration) and on translating labour legislation into personnel practices in the organization (e.g. applying the new collective bargaining agreements (CBAs) to the organization with regard to wages, employee benefits, pension schemes and working conditions). What made it all change from traditional personnel management to HRM?

Legge (1995) argues that the major transitions in personnel management were caused by developments in Asia; first, in Japan and later on in other Asian countries such as South Korea and Singapore. The Japanese were the first to manufacture products that were cheap in combination with high-quality standards. The combination of low-cost and high-quality products resulted in increased global competition and a direct attack on the US and European hegemony of most big organizations. Toyota, for example, managed to build a reputation in the car industry with relatively cheap cars that were far more reliable and sustainable than European (e.g. Citroën) and US cars (e.g. General Motors). The secret of the Japanese success was the introduction of TQM, introduced by experts such as Deming and Juran in the 1960s and 1970s, combining new production techniques with the Japanese way of working. The HPWSs, according to the TQM model, exists of teamwork, employee monitoring through regular appraisals, PRP based on individual and team performance, goal-setting (e.g. zero defects), employee development, and employee involvement in decision making but more importantly in continuous improvement.

'the major transitions in personnel management were caused by developments in Asia'

The ultimate goal of the TQM approaches in the 1970s and 1980s was to continuously improve products (based on the Kaizen principle of continuous small improvements) and reduce costs where ever possible. Legge (1995) argues that these developments led to increased global competition and a huge pressure on Western companies in Europe and the US. A lot of traditional industries (e.g. the textiles) were no longer capable of competing with Asia, because of this low-cost, high-quality competition. The competition was strengthened by the relatively low labour costs in most Asian countries. Therefore Western organizations were forced to focus their business on knowledge-intensive markets and abandon traditional industries (Legge, 1995). The more knowledge-intensive markets such as the oil industry, the chemical industry, and the more exclusive car industry require a different type of employee (often highly educated) and a different type of management. The latter became the cradle for HRM, a new way of personnel management focused on recruiting good employees, developing them in terms of skills and knowledge, paying employees according to their performance, involving employees in decision making and evaluating them to achieve individual and organizational goals. According to Legge (1995), HRM is a reaction to TQM developments in Asian companies. Since the early 1980s HRM has been considered as an instrument for creating a **high-performance culture** in an organization, necessary to compete in the global arena. A high-performance culture can be defined as an organizational culture where the corporate values for achieving the organization goals are deeply embedded in the minds and hearts of all employees. The contemporary HPWSs are thought to be the foundation for creating such a high-performance culture (Combs et al., 2006).

Control and commitment work systems

For a full understanding of the HPWSs of today's organization, we need one more element: control. Management control theory is focused on the way management is organized in an organization. Some of the control theories are highly relevant for our HPWSs debate. Walton (1985), for example, starts out by distinguishing *control strategies* from *commitment strategies* (see Table 6.2). Control strategies are characterized by 'division of work into small, fixed jobs for which individuals could be held accountable' (Walton, 1985). The HPWS in Walton's control strategy consists of specialization, narrowly defined jobs, pay by specific job content, evaluation by direct supervision, work closely supervised, little or no career development opportunities, status symbols used to reinforce hierarchy and employees having little input. In contrast, commitment strategies create leeway for employees, provide challenges for employees (e.g. multiple tasks and job rotation), extensive teamwork, and involvement in decision making.

High-commitment work systems contain broadly defined jobs, job rotation, pay by skills mastered, evaluation by peers, team assignments, extensive concern for learning and growth, business data widely shared and broad employee participation.

'Traditional Work System's (control strategy)	'High-commitment Work System's (commitment strategy)
narrowly defined jobs	broadly defined jobs
specialization of employees	rotation of employees through jobs
pay by specific job content	pay by skills mastered
evaluation by direct supervision	evaluation by peers
work is closely supervised	evaluation by peers
overtime or transfer assigned by rule book	team assigns members to cover vacancies in flexible fashion
no career development	concern for learning and growth
employee as individual	employee as member of a team
employee is ignorant about business	teams run a business; business data shared widely
status symbols used to reinforce hierarchy	status differences minimized
employees have little input	broad employee participation

TABLE 6.2 Traditional versus high-commitment work systems
Source: Reproduced with permission from Walton (1985).

Walton's (1985) control versus commitment strategy model was explicitly applied and empirically tested in HRM by Arthur (1994) using input from US steel mills (see Table 6.3). Arthur's (1994) analysis shows that the high-commitment HR system outperforms the control HR system with respect to employee turnover and labour productivity. Similar HPWSs were developed and tested in the field of HRM in the 1990s, including the studies by Osterman (1994), Huselid (1995) and MacDuffie (1995). The control–commitment distinction in Walton's (1985) work builds partly on McGregor's (1960) distinction between Theory X (more control-oriented) and Theory Y (more commitment-oriented).

Control HR Systems	Commitment HR Systems
centralization	decentralization
no participation	participation
no general training	general training
no skills training	skills training
no social activities	social activities
no due process	due process
low wages	high wages
no employee benefits	employee benefits
direct supervision	no direct supervision
individual bonus or incentive payments	group bonus or incentive payments

TABLE 6.3 Control versus commitment HR systems
Source: Adapted version of Arthur's model (1994) by Boselie (2002).

High-performance work systems and the AMO model

The 1990s revealed multiple systems approaches in HRM often using different names, including 'high-involvement work systems' (Lawler et al., 1998), 'high commitment human resource systems' (Arthur, 1994; Boselie, 2002), 'high-performance work systems' (Huselid, 1995; Luna-Arocas and Camps, 2008; Guthrie et al., 2009), 'bundles of HR practices' (Gooderham et al., 2008) and 'high-improvement work systems' (Pil and MacDuffie, 1996). There is a substantial overlap between these systems approaches and therefore we stick to the general term of **HPWS** when referring to a consistent and coherent system of HR practices that enhance the high-performance culture of an organization to achieve the organizational goals.

In Chapter 2 Pfeffer's (1998) best practices in HRM were discussed. To a large extent these best-practices overlap the list of potential HR practices that can create an HPWS: selective recruitment and selection, extensive training, PRP, teamworking, information sharing and communication, reduction of status differences and employment security. Pfeffer (1998) argues that the application of these seven best practices will increase performance. And there is empirical evidence for this thesis (Delery and Doty, 1996); in other words, implementing one or more of these practices will improve organization performance. The HPWS approaches go one step further. The HPWSs thesis builds on the notion that individual best practices can have a positive effect on performance, but integrating these practices (internal or horizontal fit) with each other will be even more successful (Kepes and Delery, 2007). For example, linking a certain type of selective recruitment and selection to specific employee development programmes will have a higher impact than applying recruitment and development without any alignment. For a better understanding of the HPWS we need a theory: the AMO theory.

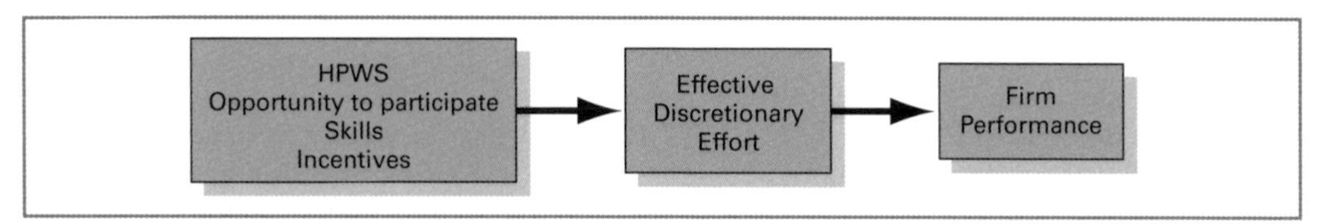

FIGURE 6.1 The AMO model

Source: Reproduced with permission from Appelbaum et al. (2000: 27).

The underlying principles of the **AMO** model were first presented by Bailey (1993) and extended by Appelbaum et al. (2000) (see Figure 6.1). The AMO model is one of the three most commonly used theoretical frameworks in strategic HRM research according to the 1994–2003 analysis by Boselie et al. (2005). The other two popular theories are the strategic contingency approaches discussed in Chapter 2 and the RBV discussed in Chapter 3. The AMO model argues that organizational interests are best served by an HR system that attends to employees' interests, namely their skill requirements, motivation and the quality of their job. Overall performance is considered to be a function of employees' abilities, employees' motivation and employees' opportunity to participate.

Boxall and Purcell (2003: 20) argue that according to the AMO model 'people perform well when:

- they are able to do so (they can do the job because they possess the necessary knowledge and skills);
- they have the motivation to do so (they will do the job because they want to and are adequately incentivized);

- their work environment provides the necessary support and avenues for expression (e.g. functioning technology and the opportunity to be heard when problems occur).'

The AMO model builds on the notion that HR practices can be bundled to enhance ability, motivation and opportunity. Concrete practices linked to the three dimensions of the AMO model can be summarized as follows (Appelbaum et al., 2000; Wall and Wood, 2005):

- Ability practices include selective recruitment and selection (getting the right people) and training and development (development of skills, knowledge and abilities).
- Motivation practices include PA (evaluation and feedback), PRP, coaching and mentoring, employment security, internal promotion opportunities, fair pay and employee benefits.
- Opportunity practices include autonomy, employee involvement, job rotation, job enlargement, job enrichment, self-directed teamwork, communication and decentralization of decision making.

Stop and reflect

Explain the essence of the AMO model and its three major components. How is the AMO model linked to the notions on HPWSs?

High-performance work systems

High-performance work systems (HPWSs) are bundles of well-integrated high-performance work practices (HPWPs). These HPWPs are closely related to the best practices discussed in Chapter 2. The five key HPWPs that can be used to build an HPWS are discussed in the next few chapters. According to the analysis of 104 prominent journal articles in strategic HRM by Boselie et al. (2005), the key practices have to do with: (1) selective recruitment and selection, (2) compensation and PRP, (3) appraisal and PM, (4) training and development, and (5) employee involvement. Apparently 'good HRM' is all about selecting the right people, developing them to do their job well, evaluating them on a regular basis for aligning their work with the organizational goals, rewarding them for excellence and involving them in decision making. The combination of these five HPWPs into an HPWS depends on the business and the context of the organization (Paauwe and Boselie, 2007).

Contemporary HPWS approaches incorporate elements that go back to the different schools of thought in management discussed earlier in this chapter (scientific management, human relations movement, revisionistic approach and STS). The five key HPWPs are now discussed briefly.

Stop and reflect

Discuss the differences and similarities between scientific management, the Human Relations Movement, the revisionistic approach and the STS theory. Discuss which elements of these four schools of thought are incorporated in contemporary HPWS models.

Selective recruitment and selection is discussed in Chapter 7. The emphasis is on 'selectivity'. All organizations have to select and recruit people once in a while. However, selective recruitment and selection goes beyond the regular job advertisements and interviews. Selective recruitment and selection is about finding people who not only fit the job (person–job fit), but also fit the culture and the team of an organization (person–organization fit). Value-based recruitment, focused on the person–organization fit, is becoming more and more important for organizations in practice since it is not only important that a person can do the job, but also that a person fits the performance culture of that organization. Another important aspect of selective recruitment and selection relates to the different selection techniques available, their reliability and validity and their costs.

Performance management (PM) is discussed in Chapter 8. The PM approach presented in that chapter goes beyond the traditional yearly employee appraisal. PM is about goal-setting and monitoring employees' performance. It is a strategic way to improve overall performance and create business awareness among employees throughout the organization. PM is one of the leading themes in multinational companies (MNCs) (Paauwe, 2007). Perceived justice with respect to the distribution of resources among employees (e.g. pay) and the procedures for appraising employees (e.g. by the direct supervisor) is discussed because of its potential impact on employee attitudes and behaviours in case of perceived injustice in relation to PM aspects.

The third **HPWP**, *compensation*, is discussed in Chapter 9 with special attention to pay for performance (variable payment) and employee benefits (e.g. with respect to health insurances, pension funds and employment security). There is a general deregulation tendency with respect to collective bargaining and payment in most European countries creating room for alternative HPWPs in compensation, including PRP and employee benefits.

Training and development is discussed in Chapter 10. This chapter focuses on strategic decision making with regard to employee development in an organization. Special attention will be paid to different types of learning; for example, focus on skills, knowledge and/or abilities (SKAs), but also to different learning environments, including on-the-job learning and eLearning. Finally, this chapter also focuses on the role of employee development in creating a flexible organization, in particular how to create an agile organization through development.

Finally, *employee participation* is the fifth HPWP that is discussed in Chapter 11. This chapter pays attention to both participation on the shopfloor (participation as a best practice as we know it from the HR literature) and participation at higher levels of the organization. The latter refers to institutionalized employee participation through trade unions and works councils. This is typical for the European context. Some MNCs in Europe see employee representatives as strategic partners in achieving organizational goals; for example, as in the case of major reorganizations, mergers, acquisitions, but also with respect to the yearly CBAs.

High-involvement work systems: an integrative framework

Boxall and Macky (2009) present an extended overview of the HPWSs literature. In their view the existing HPWS approaches are too narrow. Arthur's (1994) commitment HR systems and the AMO model (Appelbaum et al., 2000) cover work practices (e.g. employee participation) and employment practices (e.g. recruitment and selection) without a clear distinction between work design and HR practices. The STS theory discussed earlier in this chapter has a much richer tradition in distinguishing (a) work design (e.g. job design, job rotation, employee autonomy, employee involvement and teamwork) and (b) work systems (e.g. selection, training, pay and appraisal) (MacDuffie, 1995).

Boxall and Macky (2009) also highlight the relevance of what they call 'related management actions/investments', including production technologies in use and degree of product innovation. These elements interact with work practices and employment practices, but also affect perceived work and practices by employees.

The elements of the original AMO model can be found in Boxall and Macky's (2009) 'work and employment processes experienced by workforce group'. The abilities component is represented by skill enhancement, knowledge development, intra- and intergroup collaboration, and interpersonal communication. The motivation component is represented by perceived changes in intrinsic and extrinsic rewards. Finally, the opportunity to participate component contains involvement, empowerment and work intensification. The authors emphasize the employee perception dimension is comparable to the notions of perceived HR practices discussed in Chapter 3.

In the high involvement work systems model of Boxall and Macky (2009), high involvement HR systems and related management actions (investments) affect work and employment processes experienced by workforce groups. The next step in the model represents a direct and an indirect effect of the AMO components on operating outcomes such as cost-effectiveness, labour turnover and absenteeism. The indirect effect is called the 'motivational path' and the direct effect the 'cognitive path'. The direct effect of AMO or cognitive path builds on the notion that enhancing skills and knowledge has a direct effect on operating or organizational outcomes. The indirect effect of AMO or motivational path suggests that operating or organizational performance can be increased through high trust levels (e.g. in management and peers), high job and need satisfaction levels and high levels of organizational commitment. Providing extensive employee development opportunities and employee involvement, for example, potentially increases employee trust in managers and organizational commitment. High trust and commitment levels are most likely to be positively related to employee retention (in contrast to employee turnover) and employee presence (in contrast to employee absence due to illness). The Boxall and Macky (2009) approach is represented in Figure 6.2.

Stop and reflect

Discuss the differences and similarities between the model presented by Boxall and Macky (2009) and (1) the model by Walton (1985), (2) the model by Arthur (1994), and (3) the AMO model (Appelbaum et al., 2000).

Mini-bundles

The HPWSs presented in this chapter consist of multiple HR practices, including selective recruitment and selection, all types of employee development, excellent pay and employment benefits, continuous monitoring, coaching, employee involvement and teamwork. However, there is empirical evidence that *mini-bundles* can be effective in practice as well (Guest et al., 2004). A mini-bundle of HPWPs includes a limited number of HR practices; for example, only two or three HPWPs that are perfectly aligned and therefore increase the organization's performance. The alignment of individual PA with individual PRP and internal promotion opportunities is an illustration of a mini-bundle of HPWPs. The alignment of teamwork and employee training aimed at stimulating cooperation and knowledge exchange is another illustration of such a mini-bundle that can be applied in an organization. These mini-bundles are perhaps not as successful in increasing long-term success of an organization in comparison to the more sophisticated HPWSs presented in this chapter. However, the mini-bundles can still increase the organization's performance and outperform the situation in which individual HR practices are not aligned or fitted at all.

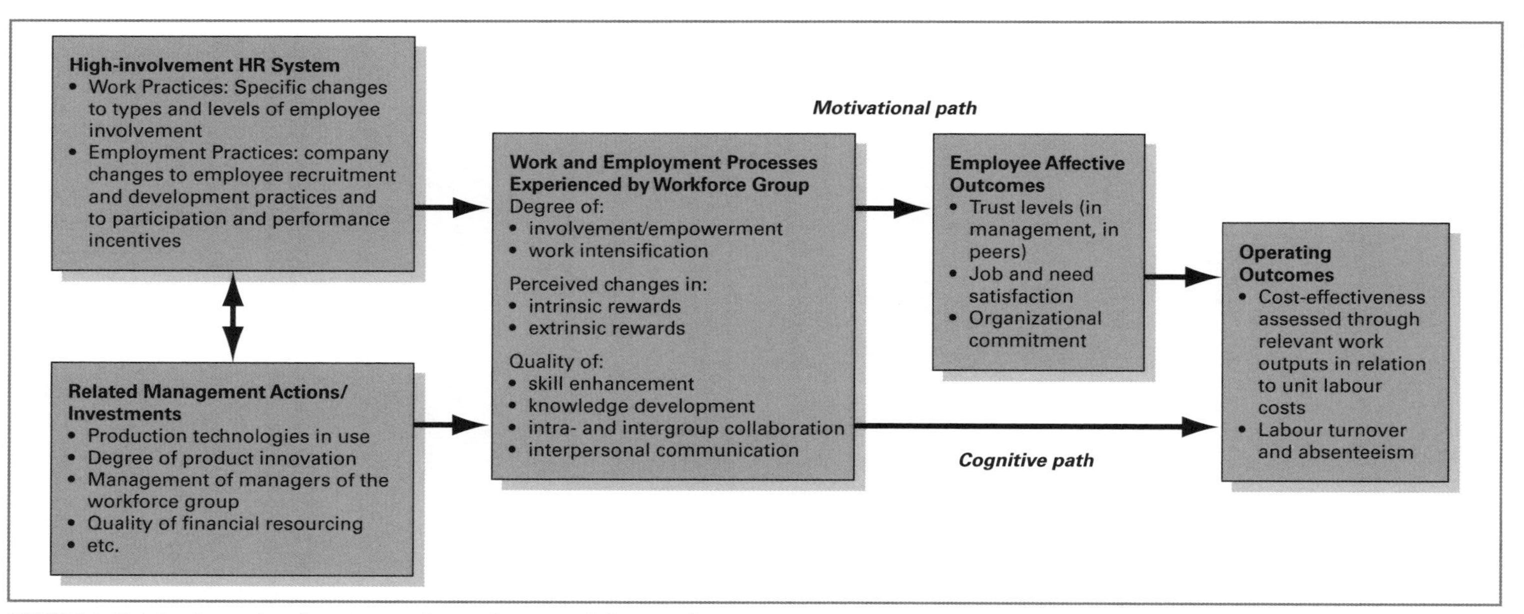

FIGURE 6.2 High-involvement work systems: an integrative research framework

Source: Reproduced with thanks from Boxall and Macky (2009, Figure 3, p. 18).

Guest et al. (2004) introduce a technique called 'sequential tree analysis' for determining bundles of HR practices that increase performance. Their findings support the mini-bundle notions:

1. Teamworking applied to 75 per cent of the workforce or more, in combination with training and development applied to 75 per cent or more, causes the highest scores on employee performance (mini-bundle: teamworking and training/development).
2. PA applied to all workers in combination with employee involvement practices applied to more than 75 per cent of the workforce and, in combination with job design applied to all employees, causes the highest scores on innovative employee behaviour (mini-bundle: PA, employee involvement and job design).
3. PA applied to all workers, in combination with all employees being kept well informed and in combination with job design applied to 75 per cent or more, causes the highest scores on employee relations (mini-bundle: PA, information sharing and job design).
4. The lowest labour turnover reported in the case of job design applied to the total workforce in combination with employee involvement applied to all employees (mini-bundle: job design and employee involvement).

These four potential mini-bundles relating to specific outcome measures also suggest that intensity and employee coverage (percentage of the workforce subject to the practice) are important for the success of a mini-bundle. A combination of teamworking applied to only 25 per cent and training applied to 25 per cent, for example, is not likely to cause increased employee performance as suggested by the notions on mini-bundle 1. Apparently a critical employee mass is required (in terms of intensity and coverage) to make the mini-bundles work.

The introduction of the concept of mini-bundles suggests at least three different ways of applying HPWPs:

1. The application of individual HPWP (best practices in HRM) with no further horizontal alignment or fit.
2. The application of mini-bundles that represent the alignment of two or three HPWPs.
3. The application of a sophisticated HPWS, including multiple HPWPs.

? Discussion questions

Can you think of other potential mini-bundles of HPWPs that can contribute to the organization's performance? What are the advantages and disadvantages of the mini-bundle approach in comparison to the sophisticated HPWSs approach?

CASE STUDY: MURRAY & ROBERTS

Murray & Roberts is South Africa's leading construction and engineering organization concentrated on delivering mining and general infrastructure, commercial buildings and industrial facilities. One of the organization's major projects is the Green Point Stadium in Cape Town for the 2010 FIFA World Cup. For over a hundred years this company has operated in South Africa; it also operates in the Middle East, Southeast Asia, Australasia and North America. Murray & Roberts employs more than 33 000 people working in different market segments. Seventy per cent of the organization's revenue comes from construction and engineering, around 20 per cent from materials and services, and the rest from fabrication and manufacture, and corporate and properties. Over 50 per cent of the organization's order book for the period to 2011 is based on the South African home market, 25 per cent on orders in the Middle East, 20 per cent in Australasia and 5 per cent in North America. The main construction projects are in the Middle East and South Africa. The Middle East projects include the Dubai International Airport, the Tameer Towers in Abu Dhabi and the Trump International Hotel Towers in Dubai.

Murray & Roberts have introduced a HPWS called 'leadership pipeline' with a strong emphasis on leadership, PM and teamwork. The recruitment of the majority of employees is decentralized except for newcomers at senior level. The latter group is recruited and selected according to the leadership pipeline standards. The recruitment and selection includes job interviews, reference checks and psychological tests. Diversity management and the recruitment of people with different cultural and racial backgrounds is one of the key personnel targets of the organization including 'a meaningful number of black senior executives throughout the Group' (*source*: www.murrob.com, 2008). Attracting and retaining talents from outside South Africa is considered essential by the company since the South African labour market is not sufficient to meet Murray & Roberts' demands.

The employee development within the company is focused on leadership development (LD), team development and individual development including an individual development plan (IDP) 'pushing people deeper into their jobs'. The overall employee development programs are aligned with the HPWS called 'leadership pipeline' aimed at improving performance awareness throughout the organization. The employee development also includes close cooperation with schools and universities to improve the knowledge and skills of the South African workforce.

The decision-making within Murray & Roberts is mainly top-down in order to 'avoid micromanaging'. The organization itself is hierarchical although the teams at the operational level have a lot of leeway and autonomy in their work. Employee participation is stimulated with respect to problem-solving and innovation. Tools for encouraging problem-solving and innovation are the organization's 'white spaces' and 'dialogue circles'.

PRP and compensation are fully in line with the leadership pipeline approach and closely linked to employee monitoring and evaluation across all levels of the organization. The key performance indicators (KPIs) are translated to all levels of the organization and linked to variable pay of the employees. The PRP is also related to the teamwork. Appraisal and compensation are highly integrated within the organization.

Overall, Murray & Roberts appear to apply certain HPWPs including selective recruitment and selection (in particular for the senior level), extensive employee development, employee appraisal and evaluation, and PRP linked to KPIs. Leadership and teamwork play a crucial role in the design and the alignment of the individual HPWPs into a HPWS.

(Peene, 2008)

? Discussion questions

- Discuss the relevance of diversity management for Murray & Roberts, for example reflected in their recruitment and selection targets.
- Discuss the degree of alignment between the different HPWPs within the organization.

Summary

- The HPWS is a special type of HRM.
- Historical schools of thought in management – scientific management (direct control system), human relations (social attention system), revisionism (high-commitment system) and STS theory (enrichment system) – each have their own ideal work system that has affected contemporary thinking in HPWSs.
- HRM and HPWSs in particular find their origins in the early 1980s as a result of competitive pressures from Asian countries such as Japan and South Korea, reflected in TQM and increased attention for creating a high performance culture through good people management.
- Management control theory inspired Walton's (1985) dichotomy on two different strategies: control and commitment strategies. This dichotomy is applied in HRM and represented in the distinction between control HR systems and commitment HR systems.
- The AMO theory is the foundation of the HPWS thesis and focuses on unique bundles of HPWPs that enable employee abilities, motivation and opportunity to participate.
- Five prominent HPWPs are selective recruitment and selection, compensation and PRP, appraisal and PM, training and development, and employee involvement.

Glossary of key terms

AMO represents the underlying theory for an HPWS reflecting employee abilities, employee motivation and employee participation.

High-performance culture is an organization's culture among employees sharing corporate norms and values aimed at achieving excellent performance.

High-performance work practices (HPWPs) are a special type of HR practice that enable employees' abilities, create the optimal incentive structure for employees and/or create opportunities to participate in decision making.

High-performance work systems (HPWSs) are bundles of consistent and coherent HPWPs that potentially create employee discretionary effort.

Personal development

- What are the three most important HPWPs for you?
- Think of your career as a path through different stages and phases:
- What kind of HPWPs are likely to be relevant to employees in their first job?
- What kind of HPWPs are likely to be relevant to employees in their thirties?
- What kind of HPWPs are likely to be relevant to employees close to retirement?

Individual task

Select an organization and summarize the best practices or HPWPs of that organization using the following checklist.

To what extent does the organization use or apply:

(1 = very little; 2 = little; 3 = neutral; 4 = intensive; 5 = very intensive)

Abilities						
1	Selective recruitment and selection (e.g. assessment and psychological tests)	1	2	3	4	5
2	General training (e.g. language training)	1	2	3	4	5
3	Skills training (e.g. presentation and negotiation)	1	2	3	4	5
4	Job rotation (e.g. every two years)	1	2	3	4	5
5	Coaching (e.g. coaching newcomers)	1	2	3	4	5
Motivation						
6	High wages	1	2	3	4	5
7	Performance-related pay	1	2	3	4	5
8	Internal promotion opportunities	1	2	3	4	5
9	Job security	1	2	3	4	5
10	Information and communication	1	2	3	4	5
Opportunity to participate						
11	Participation in decision making	1	2	3	4	5
12	Employee autonomy	1	2	3	4	5
13	Teamwork	1	2	3	4	5
14	Employee survey research	1	2	3	4	5
15	Regular employee/supervisor meetings	1	2	3	4	5

Calculate the total score by adding all the item scores.
Minimum score = 15
Maximum score = 75

Scores above 60 might indicate the existence of an HPWS in an organization. Scores between 50–60 might indicate a good HRM system and scores below 50 might indicate a mediocre HR system in the organization.

Team task

Pfeffer (1994) summarizes 16 best practices in HRM. Paauwe (1998) argued that a majority of these best practices are institutionalized in most European countries (e.g. employment security, employee benefits and high wages) (see table below). Study the potential impact of legislation on EU, country and sector level on the best practices presented by Pfeffer (1994). How does legislation affect Pfeffer's best practices in HRM? And how does EU deregulation after the year 2000 (e.g. on employment security) potentially affect HRM in organizations?

Best practices (Pfeffer, 1994)	HR practices that are common in the Netherlands (Paauwe, 1998)
1) Employment security	Yes
2) Selectivity in recruiting	–
3) High wages	Yes
4) Incentive pay	–
5) Employee ownership	Yes
6) Information sharing	Yes
7) Participation and empowerment	Yes
8) Self-managed teams	Yes
9) Training and skill development	Yes
10) Cross-utilization and cross-training	–
11) Symbolic egalitarianism	–
12) Wage compression	Yes
13) Promotion from within	Yes
14) Long-term perspective	Yes
15) Monitoring of practices	–
16) All-embracing philosophy	–

Pfeffer's 'best practices' and paauwe's comments

Source: Reproduced with permission from Pfeffer (1994) and Paauwe (1998).

Learning checklist

After studying this chapter, you should be able to do the following:

- Review the history of the systems approaches, including scientific management, human relations, revisionism and STS theory.
- Understand systems approaches in general.
- Review the HPWS approaches.
- Understand the emergence of HRM in the early 1980s.
- Recognize the five main HPWPs (selective recruitment and selection, appraisal and PM, compensation, training and development and employee participation).
- Outline the differences and similarities between the best-practice approaches in HRM and the contemporary HPWS approaches in HRM.
- Understand the AMO model.
- Examine the added value of HPWSs in the creation and maintenance of a high-performance culture in an organization.

References

Appelbaum, E., Bailey, T., Berg P. and Kalleberg, A. (eds) (2000) *Manufacturing Advantage: Why High-performance Work Systems Pay Off*. Ithaca, NY: Cornell University Press.

Arthur, J.B. (1994) Effects of human resource systems on manufacturing performance and turnover, *Academy of Management Journal*, 37(3): 670–87.

Bailey, T. (1993) Organizational innovation in the apparel industry, *Industrial Relations*, 32: 30–48.

Beer, M., Spector, B., Lawrence, P., Mills, D.Q. and Walton, R. (1984) *Human Resource Management: A General Manager's Perspective*, New York: Free Press.

Boje, D.M. and Winsor, R.D. (1993) The resurrection of Taylorism: total quality management's hidden agenda, *Journal of Organizational Change Management*, 6(4): 57–70.

Boselie, P. (2002) Human resource management, work systems and performance: a theoretical-empirical approach. Dissertation, Tinbergen Institute, Amsterdam: Thela Thesis.

Boselie, P., Dietz, G. and Boon, C. (2005) Commonalities and contradictions in HRM and performance research, *Human Resource Management Journal*, 15(3): 67–94.

Boxall, P. and Macky, K. (2009) Research and theory on high-performance work systems: progressing the high-involvement stream, *Human Resource Management Journal*, 19(1): 2–23.

Boxall, P. and Purcell, J. (2003) *Strategy and Human Resource Management*. New York: Palgrave Macmillan.

Combs, J., Liu, Y., Hall, A. and Ketchen, D. (2006) How much do high-performance work practices matter? A meta-analysis of their effects on organizational performance, *Personnel Psychology*, 59(3): 501–28.

Delery, J.E. and Doty, D H. (1996). Modes of theorizing in strategic human resource management: tests of universalistic, contingency, and configurational performance predictions, *Academy of Management Journal*, 39(4): 802–35.

Emery, F.E. and Trist, E.L. (1960) Sociotechnical systems, in C.W. Churchman and M. Verhulst (eds), *Management Science: Models and Techniques*, Volume II. Oxford: Pergamon Press.

Fayol, H. ([1916] 1949) *General and Industrial Management*. London: Pitman.

Fombrun, C., Tichy, N.M. and Devanna, M.A. (eds) (1984) *Strategic Human Resource Management*. New York: Wiley.

Gooderham, P., Parry, E. and Ringdal, K. (2008) The impact of bundles of strategic human resource management practices on the performance of European firms, *International Journal of Human Resource Management*, 19(11): 2041–56.

Guest, D.E. (1987) Human resource management and industrial relations, *Journal of Management Studies*, 24(5): 503–21.

Guest, D.E., Conway, N. and Dewe, P. (2004) Using sequential tree analysis to search for 'bundles' of HR practices, *Human Resource Management Journal*, 14(1): 79–96.

Guthrie, J.P., Flood, P.C., Liu, W. and MacCurtain, S. (2009) High performance work systems in Ireland: human resource and organizational outcomes, *International Journal of Human Resource Management*, 20(1): 112–25.

Huselid, M.A. (1995) The impact of human resource management practices on turnover, productivity, and corporate financial performance, *Academy of Management Journal*, 38(3): 635–72.

Katz, H.C., Kochan, T.A. and Gobeille, K.R. (1983) Industrial relations performance, economic performance, and QWL programs: an interplant analysis, *Industrial and Labor Relations Review*, 37(1): 3–17.

Kepes, S. and Delery, J. (2007) HRM systems and the problem of internal fit, in P. Boxall, J. Purcell and P.M. Wright (eds), *The Oxford Handbook of Human Resource Management*, Chapter 19, pp. 385–404. Oxford: Oxford University Press.

Lawler, E.E., Mohrman, S.A. and Ledford, D.E. (1998) *Strategies for High Performance Organizations: Employee Involvement, TQM, and Reengineering Programs in Fortune 1000 Corporations*. San Francisco, CA: Jossey-Bass.

Legge, K. (1995) *Human Resource Management, Rhetorics and Realities*. London: Macmillan Business.

Luna-Arocas, R. and Camps, J. (2008) A model of high performance work practices and turnover intentions, *Personnel Review*, 37(1): 26–46.

MacDuffie, J.P. (1995) Human resource bundles and manufacturing performance: organizational logic and flexible production systems in the world auto industry, *Industrial and Labor Relations Review*, 48(2): 197–221.

Maessen, F.J.H. (2007) To what extent do high performance work systems contribute to the success of Ferrari? Bachelor thesis, Tilburg University, Tilburg.

Maslow, A.H. (1943) A theory of human motivation, *Psychological Review*, 50: 370–96.

Mayo, E. (1933) *The Human Problems of an Industrial Civilization*. New York: Macmillan.

McGregor, D. (1957) The human side of enterprise, *Management Review*, November.

McGregor, D. (1960) *The Human Side of Enterprise*. New York: McGraw-Hill.

Osterman, P. (1994) How common is workplace transformation and who adopts it?, *Industrial and Labor Relations Review*, 47(2): 173–88.

Paauwe, J. (1998) HRM and performance: the linkage between resources and institutional context. RIBES working paper, Erasmus University, Rotterdam.

Paauwe, J. (2007) HRM and performance: in search of balance. Inaugural lecture, Tilburg University, Tilburg.

Paauwe, J. and Boselie, P. (2007) HRM and societal embeddedness, in P. Boxall, J. Purcell and

P.M. Wright (eds), *The Oxford Handbook of Human Resource Management,* Chapter 9, pp. 166–84. Oxford: Oxford University Press.

Peene, N. (2008) Strategic HRM: a case-study on high performance work systems – Murray & Roberts analyzed by the model of the contextually based human resource theory. BA thesis, Tilburg University, Tilburg.

Pfeffer, J. (1994) *Competitive Advantage through People*. Boston, MA: Harvard Business School Press.

Pfeffer, J. (1998) *The Human Equation: Building Profits by Putting People First*. Boston, MA: Harvard Business School Press.

Pil, F.K. and MacDuffie, J.P. (1996) The adoption of high-involvement work practices, *Industrial Relations*, 35(3): 423–55.

Porter, L.W., Bigley, G.A. and Steers, R.M. (2003) *Motivation and Work Behavior*, 7th edn. Boston, MA: McGraw-Hill.

Taylor, F.W. (1911) *Principles of Scientific Management*. New York: Harper.

Wall, T.D. and Wood, S.J. (2005) The romance of human resource management and business performance, and the case for big science, *Human Relations*, 58(4): 429–62.

Walton, R.E. (1985) From control to commitment in the workplace, *Harvard Business Review*, March–April: 77–84.

Further reading

Appelbaum, E., Bailey, T. Berg, P. and Kalleberg, A. (2000) Discretionary effort and the organization of work, in E. Appelbaum, T. Bailey, P. Berg and A. Kalleberg (eds), *Manufacturing Advantage: Why High-performance Work Systems Pay Off,* Chapter 2, pp. 25–46. Ithaca, NY: Cornell University Press.

Boselie, P., Dietz, G. and Boon, C. (2005) Commonalities and contradictions in HRM and performance research, *Human Resource Management Journal,* 15(3): 67–94.

Boxall, P. and Macky, K. (2009) Research and theory on high-performance work systems: progressing the high-involvement stream. *Human Resource Management Journal,* 19(1): 2–23.

Guest, D.E., Michie, J., Conway, N. and Sheehan, M. (2003) Human resource management and corporate performance in the UK, *British Journal of Industrial Relations,* 41: 291–314.

Kepes, S. and Delery, J. (2007) HRM systems and the problem of internal fit, in P. Boxall, J. Purcell and P.M. Wright (2007) *The Oxford Handbook of Human Resource Management,* Chapter 19, pp. 385–404. Oxford: Oxford University Press.

Wall, T.D. and Wood, S.J. (2005) The romance of human resource management and business performance, and the case for big science, *Human Relations,* 58(4): 429–62.

CHAPTER

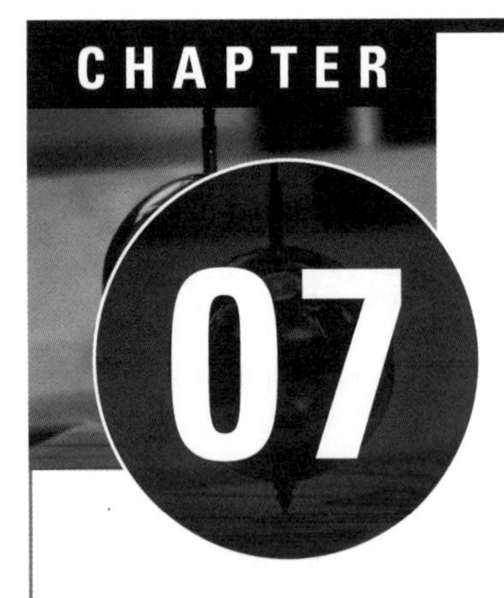

Selective Recruitment and Selection

Learning Objectives

After studying this chapter, you should be able to do the following:

- Be aware of the existence of different employee groups within an organization
- Understand the relevance of a realistic job preview
- Evaluate the concept of signalling both the organization and the candidate
- Outline the concept of employment branding
- Outline person–job fit and person–organization fit
- Identify the different selection techniques
- Review the different criteria for choosing selection techniques
- Recognize the strategic human resource management (SHRM) relevance of selective recruitment and selection

CASE STUDY: ADECCO

Adecco is a leading company in human resource (HR) services with roots in Switzerland and France. In 2008 it claimed that everyday it helped more than 700 000 people to find work through their network of 150 000 clients worldwide. Adecco operates in more than 60 countries and territories with a workforce of 36 000 focused on 'finding the right person for the client'. The clients are the organizations who are looking for employees. This way Adecco operates as an intermediary between individual people who are looking for a job and organizations that have a job vacancy.

The outsourcing of HR, including staffing (recruitment and selection), by organizations over the last decade is probably partly the success of a flexible organization such as Adecco.

? Discussion question

Can you think of strategic rationales for outsourcing recruitment and selection to an organization such as Adecco? The criteria behind the decision making can be linked to efficiency, effectiveness, reputation, quality and/or flexibility.

It is a challenge for Adecco to find the right person for the job and the organization. The right person for the job is someone who possesses the knowledge, skills and abilities to do the job. This is reflected in a person's education level, specialization, working experience and diplomas. However, it is also important to find a good match between a candidate and the organization in terms of norms and values. In other words, the potential employee also needs to fit in with the culture of the organization.

Adecco ponders job cuts as crisis bites

Adecco, the world's largest staffing company, will have to think about cutting jobs as the financial crisis bites, its chief executive was quoted as saying in an interview. 'First we will use our high employee fluctuation of 20 to 25 percent annually. When that is not enough, then we certainly have to think about redundancies,' Dieter Scheiff said in an interview with newspaper Sonntag, published on Sunday.

Adecco's sales would fall due to the crisis, Scheiff said, and the company's operations in the United States, a large part of Europe and Japan were hardest hit. Adecco's net profit fell 27 percent in the third quarter, and those difficult business conditions were continuing, he said. Adecco has cut its workforce by 3 percent in the last year and said in October it would cut up to 600 jobs in France and will merge about 75 branches. 'It is not possible to foresee what will happen in the next year. I know only one thing: We have to prepare ourselves for it to last longer and have more radical consequences than anything we have experienced until now,' Scheiff said.

(Reuters, 7 December 2008; reporting by Sam Cage, editing by Will Waterman)

? Discussion questions

- Discuss the possible implications of a financial or economic crisis on the recruitment and selection of organizations.
- How does the financial and economic crisis affect Adecco's activities?

Introduction

All organizations have to select and recruit employees once in a while because of, for example, expansion or employee turnover. Bloisi (2007: 107) defines **recruitment** as 'the different activities of attracting applicants to an organization'. **Selection** 'consists of sifting through the pool of applicants and making decisions about their appropriateness' (Bloisi, 2007: 107). In other words, job vacancy recruitment and selection is all about attracting potential candidates and choosing individuals who have the relevant qualifications for the job.

Selection and recruitment is often the starting point for organizational success through HRM. Selecting and recruiting the right people for the job and the organization increases the chances of success for both the individual employee in terms of employee well-being (e.g. job satisfaction) and the organization in terms of firm performance (e.g. productivity and high quality). This chapter is not focused on the pure instrumental part of recruitment and selection.[1] Instead, it applies a strategic approach to stimulate the reader's sensitivity for strategic issues related to getting the *right* people in an organization. The concept of 'right' in this context refers to the optimal fit or alignment of an individual employee and an employer from the employer's perspective and the employee's perspective (see Chapter 5).

This chapter is focused on *selective* recruitment and selection. 'Selective' refers to finding the right person for the job and the organization. Selectivity starts in the recruitment process and can vary among employee groups. The frameworks of Baron and Kreps (1999) and Lepak and Snell (2002) are presented to highlight the potential differences between employee groups that affect the recruitment process. Next, issues on target groups are discussed in more detail referring to the key question: 'Are we fishing in the right pond?' Ponds dry up and therefore new areas of the labour market need to be targeted. After the determination of the recruitment of specific employee groups and target groups, it is essential to present a **realistic job preview** (RJP)of what an organization has to offer. Employment branding and **signalling** are two important elements of recruitment as well, reflecting strategic HR issues on how to 'sell the organization' to (potential) employees in order to attract and retain talents. The recruitment part of this chapter is finalized by a section on the growing popularity of web-based recruitment, also known as eRecruitment.

'Ponds dry up and therefore new areas of the labour market need to be targeted.'

Selection is in the remaining sections of this chapter. The alignment between a person and the job and/or the organization is called the person–environment fit (Bretz and Judge, 1994). Two types of **person–environment fit (P–E fit)** are discussed in more detail in this chapter: **person–job fit (P–J fit)** and **person–organization fit (P–O fit)** using the overview of Boon (2008). 'Selective' selection also refers to the optimal choice of a technique for recruitment and selection. There are multiple techniques available, including job interviews, psychological tests and assessment centres. However, which techniques are most reliable, valid, applicable and cost-effective given a certain job vacancy? The recruitment and selection of a new chief executive officer (CEO) might require different techniques than the recruitment and selection of a plumber. Selective recruitment and selection assumes an optimal fit between a person and the organization's environment and an optimal fit through the application of the right techniques in order to increase the long-term success of an organization. In other words, the better the fit, the better the performance.

Stop and reflect

Search the newspapers for vacancies and study the nature of these jobs.

- What are the requirements?
- What is the procedure for the selection and recruitment?
- What does the organization offer?
- Finally, what kind of impression does the organization make on you after you have read the advertisement?

[1] For the basics in recruitment and selection, I recommend reading Chapters 4 ('Recruiting the right people') and 5 ('Selecting the right people') in Bloisi (2007). Another option for a more detailed overview of the instrumental side of recruitment and selection is offered in Chapter 6, 'Selection and placement' in Noe et al. (2008).

Recruitment

Different employee groups

Recruitment and selection can be significantly different between employee groups. Highly skilled jobs require a different type of recruitment and selection than unskilled jobs. Recruiting a specialized chemical engineer, for example, requires a thorough analysis of a candidate's qualifications (e.g. diplomas) and skills. In contrast, seasonal work in the agricultural sector (e.g. picking strawberries) often requires little or no extensive recruitment and selection. Baron and Kreps (1999) make a distinction between three employee groups:

1. *Stars:* employee stars are the core employees that can add value to the organization because of their knowledge, skills and abilities. The experts responsible for the development of a new successful medicine for fighting HIV are examples of stars within a pharmaceutical organization.
2. *Guardians:* employee guardians are also core employees; though not adding value to the organization they avoid major losses. Process operators in the oil refinery industry are examples of guardians who protect the business processes of organizations such as Shell, British Petroleum and Total.
3. *Foot soldiers:* foot soldiers are the more peripheral workers of an organization who are necessary to run the business and support other employee groups. Administrators, cleaners and employees working in the company's restaurant are all illustrations of foot soldiers, according to the model by Baron and Kreps (1999).

Lepak and Snell (2002) have built the so-called HR architecture model in which a distinction is made between peripheral and core employees. The core employees of an organization are those who represent the real human and social capital of the organization. Top managers, young high potentials, knowledge workers (e.g. technicians) and other professionals can be part of this elite group of core employees. The peripheral employees are less valuable to an organization in terms of economic value, scarcity, inimitability and substitutability (see the resource-based view (RBV) model in Chapter 3).

In their *HR architectural perspective* Lepak and Snell (2007) make a distinction between two dimensions: (1) the strategic value of a group of human capital and associated types of knowledge; and (2) the uniqueness of a group of human capital and associated types of knowledge.

These two dimensions create a matrix of four employee groups 'that differ in terms of employment sub-systems, employment relationships, and the HR systems used to manage employee groups' (Lepak and Snell, 2007: 213), including the recruitment and selection of employees. The skill sets of employees determine the strategic value of a specific employee group. The extent to which knowledge and skills are specialized or firm specific determine the uniqueness of a group (see Figure 7.1 for a visual presentation of the model).

Contract workers score low on strategic value and uniqueness in the Lepak and Snell (2007) model. These workers can be characterized by ancillary knowledge and the optimal employment system is labelled compliance-based HR. This HR system is closely related to Arthur's (1994) control HR system discussed in Chapter 6. The contract workers are mostly hired on a temporary basis with little or no employment security.

Job-based employees score low on uniqueness, however these workers do score high on strategic value (Lepak and Snell, 2007). According to the authors, they are characterized by compulsory knowledge and the ideal employment system is productivity-based HR.

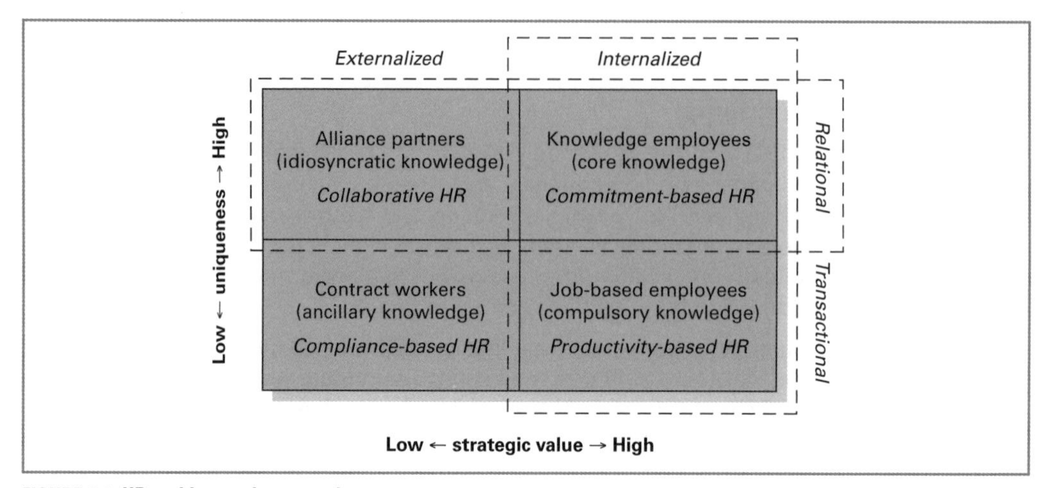

FIGURE 7.1 HR architectural perspective
Source: Reproduced with permission from Lepak and Snell (2007, Figure 11.1, p. 214).

The relationship between the employer (organization) and the latter two employee groups ('contract workers' and 'job-based employees') is often transactional and performance-oriented with little or no attention paid to a long-term perspective and employee development.

The *alliance partners* score high on uniqueness, but low on strategic value in the model. These employee groups represent the type of work that is required in organizations regularly, but has no direct link to the business processes and core business of the organization. According to Lepak and Snell (2007), management consultants (external) are illustrations of this employee group that is characterized by idiosyncratic knowledge and a need for collaborative HR.

Finally, the *knowledge employees* score high on both uniqueness and strategic value for an organization. These employees are characterized by core knowledge that is essential for the long-term success of an organization. The ideal employment system, according to the model, is a commitment-based HR system comparable to the high-commitment HR systems (Arthur, 1994) discussed in Chapter 6.

The employee groups scoring high on strategic value tend to be internalized (knowledge workers and job-based employees), while the other two are mostly externalized (outsourced).

From an egalitarian and continental European perspective the Baron and Kreps (1999) and the Lepak and Snell (2007) models may appear harsh, distinguishing (1) valuable core employees and (2) peripheral 'regular' workers. It is not just an employee group's uniqueness and strategic value that justifies a certain HR system (see Chapter 2). One way of looking at these models – an Anglo-American view – is that the 'foot soldiers', 'contract workers' and 'job-based employees' are less important and therefore require less attention from an HR perspective. Yet another way of looking at it is that an HR differentiation of different employee groups makes a lot of sense, starting with the recruitment and selection of employees. The European perspective is generally acknowledging values other than pure economic value (or strategic value as in the Lepak and Snell, 2002 model) and therefore using a less strict distinction between the knowledge workers and job-based employees in the HR policies and practices applied (see Chapter 2). The main contribution of the models presented here, however, is the explicit acknowledgement of different employee groups in an organization with potentially different HR practices and systems to achieve organizational goals.

'an HR differentiation of different employee groups makes a lot of sense'

Recruitment and selection from Lepak and Snell's (2007) point of view is aimed at 'knowledge employees' and 'job-based employees'. The other two employee groups ('alliance partners' and 'contract workers') are externalized.

Stop and reflect

Find job advertisements for each of the four employee groups presented in the Lepak and Snell (2007) model.

Are we fishing in the right pond?

Organizations run the risk of myopia in recruiting and selecting new employees. When an organization traditionally recruits and selects new employees (e.g. technicians) from its own home country, this organization might run the risk of not tapping sources from emerging countries with excellent candidates, such as India and China. Another example could be that an organization traditionally recruits and selects employees with a specific professional background (e.g. economists). However, the markets and businesses nowadays tend to change so fast that other professional backgrounds (e.g. in information technology (IT)) fit much better with the organization's current and future activities.

> 'Organizations run the risk of myopia in recruiting and selecting new employees.'

Those two illustrations refer to geographical and professional notions, but one can also think of other issues such as:

1. Are we recruiting employees from all age groups (in particular older workers)?
2. Are we focused on recruiting both women and men (gender sensitivity)?
3. Are we focused on employees with different cultural backgrounds (cultural diversity)?

These three issues are closely related to the concept of managing diversity (Ng and Burke, 2005). The Nokia case, presented earlier in this book (Chapter 3, p. 47), shows the strategy and vision of the Finnish organization towards attracting and retaining a diverse workforce. Nokia has a firm belief that diversity positively affects innovation and firm performance.

Some organizations attract new employees from a limited number of schools and universities. This can be the result of an alliance between an organization and a school. Such a strategic alliance enables the organization and the school to match the education system and the job requirements. It also creates opportunities for internships. These internships are one of the most valid and reliable ways of selecting new employees, because these internships often represent a type of work sample enabling the organization the chance to see an individual student's knowledge, skills, competences and motivation in practice.

Other organizations only select and recruit employees from top-ranking schools and universities; for example, students from Harvard, Cambridge and Oxford. Recruiting the best students with the highest grades is only feasible for a limited number of organizations. Not all organizations have the luxurious position, for example, reflected in its corporate image and reputation, to attract these top talents.

The RJP: when does it hurt to tell the truth?

The realistic job preview (RJP) provides applicants with honest information about a vacancy (Wanous, 1989). This helps applicants to develop clear expectations of what it will be like to work in the job and organization if they are hired. Organizations are most effective when both favourable and unfavourable information is presented. This way, hired candidates will not be disappointed after having started to work in their jobs. For example, an organization with limited employee autonomy and participation in decision-making should *not* present itself as an organization in search of new employees who search for extensive involvement in decision making and high degrees of self-responsibility. The hired new employee then expects full involvement and autonomy, although the organization will not be able to meet the individual employee's expectations. A violation of the employee's expectations is likely to result in employee dissatisfaction, mistrust about the organization and management, low motivation and a high intention to quit the job (Wanous, 1989).

> 'presenting an honest and realistic picture of the organization will increase job satisfaction, employee motivation, trust, commitment and employee retention after an applicant is hired.'

The Shell Case below illustrates a way to present a RJP in order to find an optimal match between an applicant and the organization. The idea behind the RJP here is that presenting an honest and realistic picture of the organization will increase job satisfaction, employee motivation, trust, commitment and employee retention (in contrast to employee turnover) after an applicant is hired. The more realistic the information is, the higher the chances are of a fit between the candidate and the organization. This is thought to be in the interest of both the employee and the employer. Shell, for example, is open about its bureaucracy because of the organization size and the global operations. It argues that forms of bureaucracy are inevitable within larger organizations and that procedures are necessary for running the business. This way applicants at least know that working within Shell might implicate having to work in bureaucratic circumstances. This probably counts for all large multinational companies (MNCs). However, Shell is one of the MNCs being open about it.

CASE STUDY: SHELL 

Realistic Job Preview

'As the title suggests, our Realistic Job Preview offers you an insight into exactly how well you'd fit in working for Shell. What are you looking for from Shell?' Here are two illustrations of Shell's online realistic job preview test for potential employees (available on the website). The participant is asked to choose one out of three options. After each choice the program provides Shell's view on the participant's choice.

Challenge and reward
Which of the following situations would most frustrate you when joining a new organization?

1 Not much guidance provided on where exactly to apply your efforts within your new role.
2 Being in a team with people who have low levels of motivation and morale.
3 Having a manager who is overly attentive and asks you to agree all your actions with them in great detail before implementing them.

If the participant's choice is 2:
[Shell's response] 'This situation would indeed be frustrating, but in big companies such as Shell this can sometimes happen. Think about whether or not you could view this as a chal-

lenge to try to tackle and change. As a new joiner with us, you can expect to be working with very diverse people with different backgrounds and approaches and, although this can place extra demands on you, ultimately it can be very rewarding'.

Bureaucracy and conservatism:
To what extent can you tolerate bureaucracy?

1 Only a little, I quickly find ways around it.
2 A moderate amount, I find ways within the system to minimize its effects.
3 I can tolerate it well. If you break the rules then there will be consequences for it later.

If the participant's choice is 1:
[Shell's response] 'Shell is a very large and complex organization so our culture could sometimes be described as bureaucratic. Because we have many different businesses operating in diverse markets in over 130 countries, it's vital that we have robust systems and procedures in place – and that these are followed. Think about how tolerant you could be of operating within a strong standards framework if you joined us'.

(Shell, 2008: www.shell.com)

Stop and reflect

Collect a number of job advertisements from the newspapers. See if the organizations are likely to present an RJP in the text.

Signalling: message in a bottle

An organization has several options to send messages to potential employees for creating an optimal P–E fit (P–J fit and P–O fit). In a job advertisement the organization can sell itself using reputation and corporate image (see the next section on 'Employment branding'). Several organizations, for example, explicitly advertise their past successes and/or their internationalization for attracting new talents.

Organizations can also offer excellent working conditions, high wages and employee training and development. The question is whether this will attract the right people? Offering high wages is not always the best tool for recruiting and selecting good employees. After the probation year, employees will be evaluated and when they meet the expectations of the employer, this will result in a contract with a salary far above average. This procedure is presented in Figure 7.2.

Candidates will be told that after the first year (at t = 1) they will get a pay increase that is above the average wage in the sector if they qualify for the organization. This sends a message to potential candidates that there is much to be gained if you are a good employee and that these gains will start after the first year. It is likely that only the best candidates are willing to take the risk of applying for this job and receiving the real gains after one year if they are evaluated positively. Average candidates are not likely to apply because they know in advance that they will probably be kicked out after one year. Their alternative is to apply for another job in the sector that offers the average sector salary right from the start. An organization proposing a model as presented in Figure 7.2 is therefore capable of sending messages to potential employees in order to preselect the best candidates.

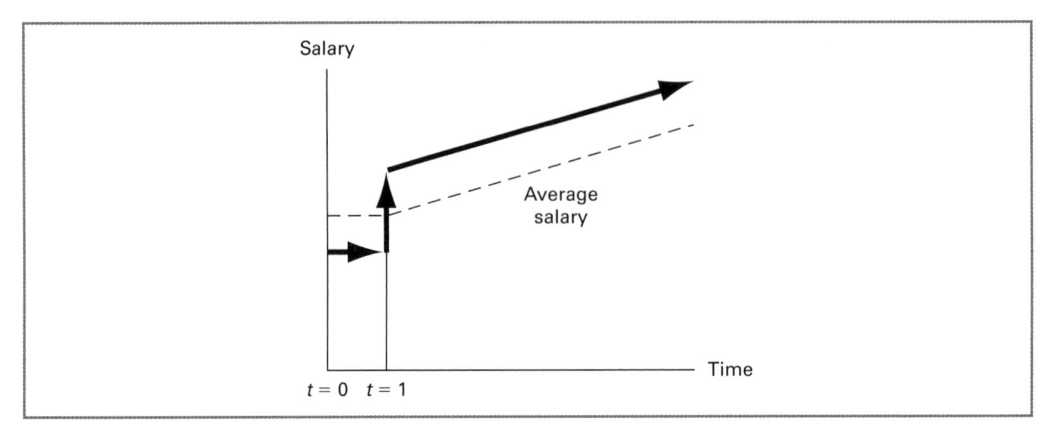

FIGURE 7.2 Sending salary messages to attract the best candidates

Candidates send messages to organizations as well. The education level of a candidate signals the quality and competences of an individual towards an organization (Spence, 1973). A university degree of an individual sends a message to an organization that this person is willing and able to successfully go through the highest learning experiences. Apparently, this individual is not only capable of acting on that level, but also willing to invest time and money in this education. Therefore, it signals to organizations that this is a qualified and motivated employee. The education level is considered to be proof of an individual's capabilities and motivation.

The downside of this signalling through education level is the increased complexity and lack of transparency with respect to the actual quality of the degrees linked to educational systems throughout the world. There are huge differences in quality between, for example, universities. Organizations should therefore be very cautious with the interpretation of the education levels and degrees of potential employees. In some countries there is a central system operating from where organizations can get information with regard to (1) whether the education really exists and is officially recognized as such (official accreditation or not) and (2) the quality of the teaching programme through assessment grades.

Accreditation and assessment of educational programmes is usually a governmental responsibility within a country, although there is a general tendency in Europe of increased European Union (EU) interference. Berry et al. (2006) warn against placing too much emphasis on educational attainment as a proxy for general mental ability, also referring to Schmidt and Hunter's (1998) relatively low predictive validity of educational attainment. The latter is discussed in more detail in the 'Selection' section of this chapter (p. 156).

Employment branding

Corporate brands of organizations represent value and act as magnets for customers, investors and suppliers but also potential employees. According to Interbrand, a company specializing in the valuation of corporate brands, the most valuable brands in 2008 were those listed in Table 7.1.

Rank	Brand	Country
1	Coca-Cola – $66 billion	USA
2	IBM – $59 billion	USA
3	Microsoft – $59 billion	USA
4	General Electric – $53 billion	USA
5	Nokia – $36 billion	Finland
6	Toyota – $34 billion	Japan
7	Intel – $31 billion	USA
8	McDonald's – $31 billion	USA
9	Disney – $29 billion	USA
10	Google – $26 billion	USA

TABLE 7.1 Top ten most valuable brands, 2008
Source: www.interbrand.com.

Other valuable brands are Mercedes Benz ($26 billion, Germany), BMW ($23 billion, Germany), Louis Vuitton ($22 billion, France), H&M ($13 billion, Sweden), IKEA ($11 billion, Sweden) and Philips ($8 billion, the Netherlands). The value of the brand is highly related to the long-term success of the organization and customers knowing the brand on a global scale. In other words, Coca-Cola represents long-term success in the food and beverages industry and is known for it worldwide.

> 'valuable human assets (talents) are more easily attracted and retained by an organization with a strong corporate identity and corporate brand name.'

In recent years organizations have increasingly started using the brand and corporate image to attract and retain employees. This is also known as **employment branding or employer branding**. Edwards (forthcoming) defines employer branding as 'an activity where principles of marketing, in particular the science of branding, are applied to HR activities in relation to current and potential employees as targets'. In the 'war for talent' employment branding is considered highly relevant. The underlying assumption here is that valuable human assets (talents) are more easily attracted and retained by an organization with a strong corporate identity and corporate brand name.

? Discussion question

Discuss specific features and characteristics of organizations with a strong corporate identity, image and brand. You can use the list of leading companies, with regard to brand names, presented above. Think of the impact of these features and characteristics on potential employees and current employees, and discuss how these aspects can be used in the recruitment and selection of employees.

Web-based organizing: eRecruitment

With the emergence of the World Wide Web (Internet), there is an increased use of web-based HRM or eHRM, including electronic recruitment (Strohmeier, 2007). Traditional advertisements in newspapers continue to exist but these advertisements are shortened through the use of website links in these advertisements. In other words, only the job title and the organization are mentioned in newspapers and the web link enables those who are interested to get more information on the website of the organization. The advantage of this method is that this is cost saving (less costs for newspaper space) and more information can be provided on the website of the organization. Organizations have to take into account that the majority of the world's population do not have access to the Internet or have serious limitations on getting access; for example, caused by governmental limitations on Internet use or technical limitations.

The use of the Internet for the recruitment and selection of employees also creates opportunities for on-line applications. Most large MNCs such as Shell and international governmental organizations (IGOs), such as the United Nations (UN), use some kind of system for on-line application. The advantage of this method is again linked to cost savings (the operating costs are relatively low). However, there are other advantages, including speed of communication, the standardization of the recruitment process making it easier to compare different candidates (everybody has to fill in the same electronic form and provide a standard format with personal information), and the possibility to build in filters that automatically exclude candidates that do not meet the basic criteria for the job vacancy (e.g. because they do not have the proper qualifications or education).

Selection

The right person for the job: P–J fit

Traditionally, much attention is paid to finding people who are qualified to do the job. This qualification can be represented by someone's diplomas, skills certificates, specific knowledge and former work experience. In some cases – for example, medical specialists, lawyers, accountants, judges and pilots – official diplomas, certificates or degrees are required for the job. The general idea behind the (P–J fit is that the most qualified candidate is most likely to show the best job performance. Hunter and Schmidt (1998) show that high scores on general mental ability (GMA) tests, conscientiousness and job experience result in high job knowledge of an individual employee. Job knowledge is positively related to job performance. Some organizations not only look at test scores, degrees and experience, but they also focus on candidates' high school and university grades. Berry (2006) finds empirical support for a positive relationship between educational attainment (e.g. years in college) and cognitive ability of potential applicants, meaning that educational attainment can be used for a cognitive screen of the best candidates.

'the most qualified candidate is most likely to show the best job performance.'

The concept of P–J fit contains two important components. First, does the candidate possess the right qualities for desirable job performance as described above? Second, is the job in line with the interests of the candidate? The latter notion refers to whether the individual employee is likely to be satisfied and engaged in the (new) job. This is supported by the empirical study of Villanova et al. (1994). In other words, P–J fit covers both (1) the aspects of the job and the candidate's qualities and (2) the nature of the job and the candidate's personal preferences and interests. Employee well-being and the employee perspective, as discussed in Chapter 5, are essential for optimal P–J fit.

A job analysis is often used for identifying the tasks and skills that are required for the job. The qualification criteria for the job vacancy in terms of, for example, formal education level, number of years work experience and language skills can be the result of the job analysis. The job analysis usually provides input for the job description that can be used in an advertisement. A job analysis can also be used for performance appraisal (PA) and PM. In the past the focus in the recruitment process was mainly on (1) *knowledge* and (2) *skills*. Illustrations of knowledge can be related to:

- knowing the business and the market in which an organization operates;
- knowing the laws and procedures of the sector in which an organization operates;
- knowing the right people inside and outside the organization (social network).

Illustrations of employee skills are:

- language skills (speaking multiple languages);
- technical skills;
- social skills (presentation, negotiation and convincing).

In the last decade there has been an increased focus on a third component called *competences* (Rychen and Salganik, 2001). Competences reflect the abilities of an employee with a focus on the individual's qualities for future desired attitudes, behaviour and job performance. Analytical abilities of an employee, for example, reflect the individual's capability to solve difficult problems when required. Overall, we can observe the need for knowledge, skills and abilities (KSAs) when recruiting and selecting a new employee, particularly when focused on P–J fit issues. P–J fit focuses on the needs and qualities that are directly linked to the characteristics of the job (Boon, 2008).

Value-based recruitment: P–O fit

The P–J fit is important when recruiting and selecting a new employee. However, recent global research has revealed the emergence of another type of P–E fit: value-based recruitment (Paauwe, 2007). Leading MNCs tend to put more emphasis on the person–organization fit than ever before. The idea behind this tendency is that people who match the organization's culture will outperform those that do not. There is, however, no empirical support for this proposition. It does seem plausible and logical that a match between the values of an individual and the organizational values is most likely to result in higher employee motivation levels and employee satisfaction. In times of continuous change and complexity, it is important for organizations to build and maintain a strong corporate culture, that is also in the heads and hearts of its employees, to keep up employee motivation and to avoid employee dissatisfaction.

> 'people who match the organization's culture will outperform those that do not.'

P–O fit can be defined as the compatibility between people and organizations 'that occurs when (1) at least one entity provides what the other needs, or (2) they share similar fundamental characteristics, or (3) both' (Boon, 2008: 128, based on Kristof, 1996). To put it differently, a match between an individual and an organization can be found when both parties share the same values, when one party lacks a certain value (e.g. assertive employees) while the other party possesses this value, or when both parties share certain values in combination with complementary values that are considered important. The P–O fit refers to the alignment between the person and the values and goals of the organization (Boon, 2008).

? Discussion questions

- Can you think of the *advantages* when organizations recruit and select new employees mainly on the basis of P–O fit?
- Can you think of *disadvantages* when organizations recruit and select new employees mainly on the basis of P–O fit?

P–J fit versus P–O fit

As mentioned earlier in this chapter, there has been a shift from attention paid to P–J fit to P–O fit, in particular to value-based recruitment. However, both types of fit are relevant for getting the right person for the job. Boon's (2008) empirical research within two large Dutch organizations (one retail and one in health care) shows a positive relationship between P–J fit and P–O fit. In other words, a P–J fit is likely to positively affect a P–O fit and the other way round.

The other interesting findings of Boon's (2008) empirical study on P–J and P–O fit are related to the effects of both types of fit on HR outcomes. The evidence suggests that P–O fit, in particular, positively affects organizational commitment and citizenship behaviour. In contrast, P–J fit positively affects job satisfaction and employee retention (in contrast to intention to leave). In other words, value-based recruitment, linked to creating a good P–O fit, creates the foundation for employee commitment to the organization and the employee's willingness to put an extra effort into that organization. This is important for the creation of a high-performance culture in the organization. A good match between an individual and a job results in job performance, employee satisfaction and retention. The latter two outcomes are relevant for the well-being of the individual employee and the business continuity of the organization (see Chapter 5 on balanced approaches in HRM).

Selection techniques, job performance and strategic decision making

The validity of a selection technique is one of the most important criteria, next to reliability and utility, given a job vacancy and a number of applicants. *Validity,* in the context of selection techniques, represents 'do we measure what we want to measure?'. The validity of a selection technique shows that the technique really measures what it is supposed to measure. This can be represented in terms of the applicant's technical job performance (e.g. in terms of productivity and quality).

Smith and Smith (2007) present an excellent overview of the validity of the different selection techniques in relationship to job performance based on the research by Hunter and Hunter (1984) and Hunter and Schmidt (1998). The most valid selection techniques according to their analysis are:

- work sample tests with a score of 0.54;
- GMAs with a score of 0.51;
- structured interviews with a score of 0.51;
- peer ratings with a score of 0.49;
- job knowledge tests with a score of 0.48;
- job tryout procedures with a score of 0.44;
- integrity tests with a score of 0.41.

A **work sample test** is a selection technique that tests candidates' knowledge, skills and/or abilities by asking them to perform certain tasks similar to the vacancy. For example, the candidate for a teaching position at a high school is asked to give a lecture for the selection committee or for a group of students. Work sample tests are an attempt to imitate the real job and to see how the potential employee responds to that (Roth et al., 2005). Work sample tests are mainly used for testing skills.

GMA tests focus on the intelligence of an individual. The outcomes of the GMA test reflect somebody's relative speed and accuracy of processing complex information (Schmidt and Hunter, 2004). Empirical research shows that GMA results are applicable in different contexts (e.g. in different countries) and to different employee groups (e.g. low-skilled workers and knowledge workers) (Salgado et al., 2003). GMA tests are mainly used for testing cognitive abilities.

Structured interview is a preplanned-based job interview mainly focused on knowledge and experiences. All candidates for a specific vacancy are confronted with the same set of interview questions under similar conditions. This interview type might cover a short business case that includes an issue that needs to be resolved by the candidate. The rating or scoring of the candidates on the basis of their responses is often part of this technique (Conway et al., 1995).

Peer ratings are a selection technique used for selecting internal candidates. The ratings of colleagues (peers) on a set of predetermined criteria (e.g. managerial skills, people skills and business knowledge) are used for selecting a candidate. The 360-degree feedback instrument, as part of an employee appraisal system, includes the ratings of peers.

Job knowledge tests are focused on specific knowledge that is required to do the job. Knowledge has different faces, including knowledge linked to a person's occupation (e.g. knowledge about legislation required for a lawyer), product knowledge (e.g. knowing certain software programs) and market knowledge (e.g. the degree of competition, main competitors, market opportunities and prospects). It is obvious that the emphasis of these tests is on an individual's knowledge.

Job tryout procedures represent a probation period for a candidate and an organization to find out whether there is a good P–E fit. These probation periods can be relatively short from one week to one month. However, in some countries it is quite common for candidates to have a probation period of one year with the option of getting a permanent contract right after that year following a satisfying relationship between the employee and the employer. Job tryout procedures are mainly applicable for entry-level positions (candidates from outside the organization).

Integrity tests measure the likeliness of future counterproductive behaviours of a potential employee (Berry et al., 2007). Recent organization scandals, including Enron, Ahold, Parmalat and Shell, show that employee misbehaviour can damage the reputation of an organization and lead to huge financial losses. Integrity is highly relevant in circumstances characterized by confidential information (e.g. the military and the secret services), privacy (e.g. patient health care files) and stock market sensitive information (e.g. information on a potential merger or acquisition). Consciousness tests measure the degree to which a person is able to inhibit impulses and direct behaviour along socially desirable lines (Smith and Smith, 2007). Consciousness test outcomes show high correlations with integrity test outcomes of individuals, representing construct similarity and therefore overlap between the two instruments.

The scores can be interpreted as follows: using work sample tests will lead to 54 per cent less uncertainty about an applicant's future performance in the job. The smaller the uncertainty, the more chance of choosing the most adequate person for the job and the organization, and thus the higher the expected output (Hunter and Schmidt, 1998; Smith and Smith, 2007). Scores below 0.2 are considered inadequate, scores between 0.2–0.34 are adequate, scores between 0.35–0.44 reasonable, scores between 0.45–0.54 good and scores above 0.55 are excellent.

Very poor selection criteria are employee age (score is −0.01) and number of years of job experience (score is 0.18) (Hunter and Schmidt, 1998; Smith and Smith, 2007). Job experience is important but appears to show a non-linear relationship. The latter implies that job experience is relevant up to a certain number of years of work experience; for example, five years for a difficult job. Reference checks result in an adequate score of 0.26 and conscientiousness tests in a score of 0.31. The findings of Hunter and Schmidt (1998) show two particularly interesting results: (1) assessment centres score 0.37, representing a reasonable but not a very good score; and (2) unstructured interviews score 0.38, revealing a big difference with the scores of a structured interview (0.51).

Assessment centres use a combination of different techniques, including psychological tests, observations, interviews, external experts and role plays (Arthur et al., 2003). This technique is time-consuming and very expensive. In theory, the assessment centre is the most valid instrument, because it combines different techniques. However, the analysis shows something different that might be caused by the poor application of assessment centres in practice.

A second remarkable finding is the difference in scores between structured and unstructured interviews. A structured interview is quite difficult and challenging and therefore in reality unstructured interviews are applied in the selection process. Using structured interviews requires good training of those using them to avoid, for example, the 'first impression' trap (also known as the halo effect). First impressions do not tell us much about an applicant's qualities, facts and figures do. Therefore, interviews should be focused on actual behaviour and facts linked to the candidate. Candidates, however, appear to prefer unstructured interviews.

'A structured job interview is difficult and challenging'

Smith and Smith (2007), using the analysis of Hunter and Schmidt (1998), also show the scores on incremental validity with respect to selection techniques. Incremental validity explains how adding a technique will change the total validity score of the procedure. The authors use the GMA test as a starting point because of its relatively high predictive validity score of 0.51, its relatively low developmental and administrative costs, its sensitivity, its relatively high reliability, and its general acceptability among those who use it. Adding work sample tests to GMA tests will increase the total validity score of the procedure (GMA plus work samples) from 0.51 to 0.66. The incremental validity in this example is 0.12. Applying GMA tests and work samples results in a maximum reduction of uncertainty about an applicant's future performance to 66 per cent. Organizations have to take into account that there is still an uncertainty of 34 per cent. In other words, a reduction of uncertainty is not a full guarantee of selecting and recruiting the best candidate. Another good combination is GMA tests with structured interviews resulting in a total validity score of 63 per cent.

Table 7.2 gives an overview of the validity scores, incremental validity scores and total validity scores of the different selection techniques (see Hunter and Schmidt, 1998 and Smith and Smith, 2007). Combining GMA and other selection techniques creates potential mini-bundles of high-performance work techniques.

Other criteria for judging selection techniques

The starting point for the optimal selection technique is its validity. However, there are many other criteria that are relevant for selecting a technique. The most important other criteria are: costs and utility, sensitivity, reliability, practicality and fairness (Russell et al., 1993; Ryan and Tippins, 2004; Hunter and Schmidt, 1998; Smith and Smith, 2007). The *costs* and *utility* of a selection technique include the costs of the technique itself, but also costs that are directly or indirectly linked to the selection technique; for example, the costs related to the training and development of those who are going the use the technique (direct costs) and costs linked to lost working hours of those who are involved in selecting a new employee (indirect costs). Utility refers to whether the instrument is applicable and relevant for achieving certain goals (e.g. selecting the best candidate for a vacancy). Costs and utility can be seen as one construct in recruitment and selection representing the relative gain in performance (e.g. in Euros) due to a better selection.

The *sensitivity* of a selection technique refers to whether the technique is actually good in differentiating between similar applicants. This criterion is highly relevant in situations where multiple applicants have more or less similar qualifications; for example, the same education level and working experience. *Reliability* as a criterion refers to whether repetition of the technique results in the same conditions with the same individual. In other words, if we repeat the technique on the same person, do we get the same results? Another relevant criterion for picking the optimal selection technique is *practicality*, referring to the notion that a technique should not be too time-consuming, require as little equipment as possible, be as flexible with

Selection technique	Validity	Incremental validity (GMA + other technique)	Total validity
General mental ability test (GMA) (psychological tests)	0.51	–	–
Work sample tests	0.54	0.12	0.66
Structured interview	0.51	0.12	0.63
Peer ratings	0.49	0.07	0.56
Job knowledge tests	0.48	0.07	0.55
Integrity tests	0.41	0.14	0.55
Job tryout procedure	0.44	0.07	0.51
Unstructured interview	0.38	0.04	0.42
Conscientiousness tests	0.31	0.09	0.40
Assessment centres	0.37	0.02	0.39
Reference checks	0.26	0.06	0.32
Job experience (years)	0.18	0.03	0.21
Age	−0.01	0.00	−0.01

TABLE 7.2 Selection techniques and job performance
Source: Reproduced with permission from Smith and Smith (2007).

respect to location as possible and require minimal amount of training. Finally, *fairness and acceptability of applicants* is a criterion that refers to whether applicants perceive the selection technique as being fair (Truxillo et al., 2004). This is in line with notions of perceived procedural justice in HRM. Perceived procedural injustice is likely to result in dissatisfaction and mistrust.

Table 7.3 gives an overview of four different techniques and the scores on the different criteria summarized above. It all depends on the vacancy and the type of applicants as to which technique is best. These criteria can be used in organizations to choose the optimal selection technique given a job and given the applicants. This way it becomes part of the strategic HR decision-making process.

Technique	Validity	Costs	Sensitivity	Reliability	Practicality	Fairness and acceptability
GMA test	Very good	Low	Very good	Very good	Very good	Good
Work sample	Very good	High	Poor	Reasonable	Very good	Very good
Integrity test	Good	Low	Good	Unknown	Very good	Poor
Structured interview	Very Good	High	Poor	Reasonable	Good	Good

TABLE 7.3 Four selection techniques and criteria for choosing them
Notes: Very poor represents the lowest score and very good the highest score; there are five possible scores presented in this table with the exception of the criterion 'costs' (low versus high); very poor – poor – reasonable – good – very good)
Source: Smith and Smith (2007), using Hunter and Schmidt (1998).

This practitioner list can be used for selecting the optimal selection technique given a certain situation. GMA tests show a very good predicting validity, the costs are relatively low, the outcomes can relatively easily be used for differentiation between candidates, the test proves to be reliable, it is not very difficult to apply the test (often presented in a short questionnaire handed to the applicant) and the test is generally accepted by those involved. The costs are low because of the high degree of standardization of the technique (standardized questionnaires, data collection, data analysis and results). Work samples show the best predictive validity (predicting the candidates' future job performance) in comparison to the other three selection techniques presented in Table 7.3. The costs of work samples are high because of the development of those who have to work with the tool and also because of supervision time. The sensitivity of work samples is not so good, meaning this tool does not easily differentiate between candidates. Work samples are easily applied, reasonably reliable and very well accepted by those involved. Internships of undergraduate and graduate students are often used as work samples for selecting starters.

Integrity tests are quite valid, the costs are low, the sensitivity is good and the tests are not very difficult to apply. However, the reliability of these tests is still unknown and the tests are not widely accepted by both employers and employees. Integrity tests appear to be highly relevant in circumstances where ethics and complaint behaviour are crucial for the business and the reputation of an organization. Part of the selection process of most financial institutions is integrity tests, because those employees are involved in financial activities involving very large sums of money. The validity of the structured interview is very good, the technique is easily applied and it is generally accepted by those involved. However, the costs can be high because of development costs for those doing the interview and because of lost working hours for those involved in the interviews (including preparation time). The sensitivity is poor and the reliability reasonable.

Overall, one may conclude that the GMA tests and the integrity tests reveal good scores on almost all criteria presented here. In comparison to the other two techniques (work sample and structured interview), both tests show much better scores on sensitivity. In other words, if an organization has multiple candidates for a vacancy, these tests can be used to differentiate between the candidates. On the other hand, we can see particularly good scores for work samples and structured interviews on predictive validity (job performance) and acceptability.

Values of the individual candidate and the organization (core values) are essential for the right P–O fit and can be tested in the selection process by using integrity tests. The GMA tests can be used to look for the right P–J fit with regard to the candidate's qualities and job requirements. Work samples and structured interviews can also be used to look for an optimal P–J fit, but in this case it is more specifically aimed at an alignment between the nature of the job and the candidate's personal preferences and interests.

What happens if there is a mismatch between the job/organization and the candidate?

Up until now this chapter has mainly focused on the search for a fit between (1) a person and a job, (2) a person and an organization, and (3) a vacancy and a selection technique. But what happens if an organization selects a candidate and after a while there is a mismatch between the two? There are several causes for a mismatch. The misfit or mismatch can be caused by the organization, for example, as a result of the selection technique used. Selection techniques are not perfect predictors of future behaviour and the overview of the techniques in this chapter shows there is always a measurement error possible even if an organization applies multiple techniques (e.g. GMA tests in combination with work samples and/or structured interviews). Not presenting a realistic job preview is another example of a potential cause for a mismatch caused by an organization. Finally, an unforeseen critical incident (e.g. a reorganization or a crisis) after an employee is selected can also lead to a mismatch because an organization might no longer be capable of meeting the expectations of the new employee; for example, with regard to giving a permanent contract after the first year or providing training and development facilities.

A mismatch can also be caused by the candidates themselves. In some cases the candidates have not been honest about their background and qualifications. A thorough check of a candidate's curriculum vitae, working experience, diplomas, certificates and references may be required to minimize the chances of fraud of a candidate. Fundamental changes in the social life of an employee after the recruitment are another example of a misfit caused by an employee. These changes in the social life of an employee may involve children, health of the employee or relatives and the career of a partner.

In a lot of cases these misfits are inevitable. The direct results of misfits can be summarized as follows:

- low motivation, satisfaction, commitment and citizenship behaviour of the recently recruited employees;
- the relationship between the recruited employees and their colleagues deteriorates;
- the relationship between the recruited employees and their direct supervisors deteriorates;
- the recently recruited employees leave the organization (employee turnover);
- potential high costs for terminating the contracts with the recruited employees;
- labour intensification for those who stay (the work of the recruited employee has to be done by others);
- potential reputation damage;
- new costs for recruiting and selecting new employees.

Optimizing the recruitment and selection of employees is therefore crucial for organizational success. Getting the right person for the job is a fundamental building block of SHRM and a key stone for creating high-performance work systems (HPWSs).

The strategic relevance of selective recruitment and selection

Finding the right person for the job and the organization is an important foundation for running a successful organization. A misfit between an individual worker and the job and/or organization potentially causes additional costs (e.g. costs with regard to recruiting a replacement), discontinuity of the work through employee turnover, work intensification for those who stay until the vacancy is filled again, reputation damage and extra time necessary for finding somebody else.

A structural fit between new starters and the job/organization can help strengthen the organizational culture and build a strategic climate. This is important for the employer in terms of employee retention through organizational commitment, business continuity, employment branding towards potential employees and organizational performance (e.g. productivity). But this structural fit is also important for the individual employee in terms of job satisfaction, perceived employment security and employee well-being (e.g. job stress).

summary

- Selective recruitment and selection is a crucial high-performance work practice (HPWP) and often the starting point of unique strategic HRM within an organization.
- Recruitment and selection can differ between employee groups in the organization depending on the HR architecture.
- Organizations should always aim for a realistic job preview to avoid employees' disappointments and decreased motivation.
- Organizations can send signals to potential employees offering excellent working conditions, high wages and employee development.
- Employment branding is an activity where principles of marketing, in particular the science of branding, are applied to HR activities in relation to current and potential employees as targets.
- e-Recruitment is gaining popularity as an instrument for attracting potential employees.
- P–E fit represents the alignment between a person and the job and/or the organization.
- There are two types of P–E fit: P–J fit and P–O fit.
- Finding the right person for the job (P–J fit) is often focused on the knowledge and skills of the right candidate.
- There is a tendency to emphasize recruiting and selecting people who fit the core values of the organization best (P–O fit). This is called value-based recruitment.
- Different selection techniques can be applied for decision making in recruitment, including work sample tests, GMAs, structured interviews, peer ratings, job knowledge tests, job tryout procedures, assessment centres, reference checks, job experience, conscientiousness tests and integrity tests.
- Criteria for choosing a selection technique are validity, costs (utility), sensitivity, reliability, practicality, fairness and acceptability of the specific technique.
- A mismatch between an employee and the organization can result in low motivation, dissatisfaction, low organizational commitment, intention to quit, replacement costs and reputation damage.

Glossary of key terms

Assessment centres are a bundle of different selection techniques, often including observations, GMA test, role play and interviews.

Employment branding or employer branding is an activity where principles of marketing, in particular the science of branding, are applied to HR activities in relation to current and potential employees as targets.

General mental (GMA) ability test reflects somebody's relative speed and accuracy of processing complex information.

Integrity tests measure the likeliness of future counterproductive behaviours of a potential employee.

Job knowledge tests are focused on specific knowledge that is required to do the job.

Job tryout procedures represent a probation period for a candidate and an organization to find out whether there is a good P–E fit.

Peer ratings are a technique that uses the judgements of colleagues for decision making with respect to selection or internal promotion.
Person–environment fit (P–E fit) is the degree of alignment between candidates on the one hand and the job and the organization on the other hand.
Person–job fit (P–J fit) is the degree of alignment between individual employees and their job.
Person–organization fit (P–O fit) is the degree of alignment between individual employees and their organizations in terms of sharing the same norms and values.
Realistic job preview (RJP) provides applicants with honest information about a vacancy.
Recruitment relates to the different activities of attracting applicants to an organization.
Selection consists of sifting through the pool of applicants and making decisions about their appropriateness.
Signalling refers to the information sent by a candidate to the organization (e.g. education level) or by the organization to the candidate (e.g. in terms of salary development).
Structured interview is a preplanned-based job interview, with job questions mainly focused on knowledge and experiences.
Work sample test focuses on the candidate's knowledge, skills and/or abilities through a real-life job assignment.

Personal development

What are the most important HRM aspects for you if you apply for a new job (personal development (PD), promotion opportunities, autonomy, flexibility, high wages, leisure time, responsibilities, cooperation with others, a good social atmosphere among colleagues, coaching and/or challenging projects)?

Individual task

The organization has a vacancy for an information and communication technology (ICT) specialist. The main task of this specialist is to install complex software programs on the computers of employees. There are two types of potential employee for this vacancy:

1 low educated ICT personnel who are capable of installing four computers per day (type 1);
2 high educated ICT personnel who are capable of installing six computers per day (type 2).

The average all-in hourly wage of a type 1 employee is £32, while the average all-in hourly wage of a type 2 employee is £40. The type 1 employee is less expensive but also less productive than the type 2 employee.

Can you think of a variable pay system – payment for every computer installed instead of a fixed payment per hour – that will only attract the type 2 employee? Justify your approach and suggest a concrete reward for every computer installed.

Team task

Search for four different job advertisements in the newspapers. Keep in mind that the bigger the differences between the four vacancies the better this team task. The differences can be related to the following aspects:

- level of education required for the job (low versus high);
- number of years of working experience required (no experience versus extensive working experience);
- salary (low versus high);
- different professions (e.g. a specialist or a manager).

Perform an analysis of all four vacancies and make a decision as to which selection technique is best for finding the right person for the job. You can make use of all selection techniques presented in this chapter. You are allowed to make combinations of the different techniques, but you have to justify your choices on the basis of the following criteria for technique selection:

- validity;
- costs;
- sensitivity;
- reliability;
- practicality;
- fairness/acceptability.

Learning checklist

After studying this chapter, you should be able to do the following:

- Be aware of the existence of different employee groups within an organization.
- Understand the relevance of a realistic job preview.
- Evaluate the concept of signalling of both the organization and the candidate.
- Outline the concept of employment branding.
- Outline P–J fit and P–O fit.
- Identify the different selection techniques.
- Review the different criteria for choosing selection techniques.
- Recognize the SHRM relevance of selective recruitment and selection.

References

Arthur, J.B. (1994) Effects of human resource systems on manufacturing performance and turnover, *Academy of Management Journal*, 37(3): 670–87.

Arthur, W. Jr., Day, E.A., McNelly, T.L. and Edens, P.S. (2003) A meta-analysis of the criterion-related validity of assessment center dimensions, *Personnel Psychology*, 56: 125–54.

Baron, J.M. and Kreps, D.M. (1999) *Strategic Human Resources: Frameworks for General Managers*. New York: Wiley.

Berry, C.M., Gruys, M.L. and Sackett, P.R. (2006) Educational attainment as a proxy for cognitive ability in selection: effects on levels of cognitive ability and adverse impact, *Journal of Applied Psychology*, 91(3): 696–705.

Berry, C.M., Sackett, P.R. and Wiemann, S. (2007) A review of recent developments in integrity test research, *Personnel Psychology*, 60(2): 271–301.

Bloisi, W. (2007) *An Introduction to Human Resource Management*. London: McGraw-Hill.

Boon, C. (2008) HRM and fit: survival of the fittest!? Dissertation, Erasmus Research Institute for Management (ERIM), Rotterdam.

Bretz, R.D. and Judge, T.A. (1994) The role of human resource systems in job applicant decision processes, *Journal of Management*, 20(3): 531–51.

Conway, J.M., Jako, R.A. and Goodmann, D.F. (1995) A meta-analysis of interrater and internal consistency reliability of selection interviews, *Journal of Applied Psychology*, 80(5): 565–79.

Edwards, M. (forthcoming) An integrative review of the links between employer branding and existing academic work from the field of organisational behaviour, *Personnel Review*.

Hunter, J.E. and Hunter, R.F. (1984) Validity and utility of alternative predictors of job performance, *Psychological Bulletin*, 96(1): 72–98.

Hunter, J.E. and Schmidt, F.L. (1998) The validity and utility of selection methods in personnel psychology: practical and theoretical implications of 85 years of research findings, *Psychological Bulletin*, 124(2): 262–74.

Kristof, A.L. (1996) Person–organization fit: an integrative review of its conceptualizations, measurements, and implications, *Personnel Psychology*, 49(1): 1–49.

Lepak, D.P. and Snell, S.A. (2002) Examining the human resource architecture: the relationships among human capital, employment, and human resource configurations, *Journal of Management*, 28(4): 517–43.

Lepak, D.P. and Snell, S.A. (2007) Employment subsystems and the 'HR architecture', in P. Boxall, J. Purcell and P.M. Wright (eds), *The Oxford Handbook of Human Resource Management*, Chapter 11, pp. 210–30. Oxford: Oxford University Press.

Ng, E.S.W. and Burke, R.J. (2005) Person–organization fit and the war for talent: does diversity management make a difference?, *International Journal of Human Resource Management*, 16(7): 1195–210.

Noe, R.A., Hollenbeck, J.R., Gerhart, B. and Wright, P.M. (2008) *Human Resource Management: Gaining Competitive Advantage*, 6th edn. London: McGraw-Hill.

Paauwe, J. (2007) HRM and performance: in search of balance. Inaugural lecture, Tilburg University, Tilburg.

Roth, P.L., Bobko, P. and McFarland, L.A. (2005) A meta-analysis of work sample test validity: updating and integrating some classic literature, *Personnel Psychology*, 58(4): 1009–37.

Russell, C.J., Colella, A. and Bobko, P. (1993) Expanding the context of utility: the strategic impact of personnel selection, *Personnel Psychology*, 46(4): 781–801.

Ryan, A.M. and Tippins, N.T. (2004) Attracting and selecting: what psychological research tells us, *Human Resource Management*, 43(4): 305–18.

Rychen, D.S. and Salganik, L.H. (eds) (2001) *Defining and Selecting Key Competencies*. Cambridge, MA: Hogrefe & Huber Publishers.

Salgado, J.F., Anderson, N., Moscosso, S., Bertua, C. and De Fruyt, F. (2003) International validity generalization of GMA and cognitive abilities: a European community meta-analysis, *Personnel Psychology*, 56: 573–605.

Schmidt, F.L. and Hunter, J.E. (2004) General mental ability in the world of work: occupational attainment and job performance, *Journal of Personality and Social Psychology*, 86(1): 162–73.

Smith, M.J. and Smith, P. (2007) *Testing People at Work: Competencies in Psychometric Testing*. Oxford: British Psychological Society/Blackwell.

Spence, M. (1973) Job market signaling, *Quarterly Journal of Economics*, 87(3): 355–74.

Strohmeier, S. (2007) Research in e-HRM: review and implications, *Human Resource Management Review*, 17(1): 19–37.

Truxillo, D.M., Steiner, D.D. and Gilliland, S.W. (2004) The importance of organizational justice in personnel selection: defining when selection fairness really matters, *International Journal of Selection and Assessment*, 12(1/2): 39–53.

Villanova, P., Bernardin, H.J., Johnson, D.L. and Dahmus, S.A. (1994) The validity of a measure of job compatibility in the prediction of job performance and turnover of motion picture theater personnel, *Personnel Psychology*, 47(1): 73–90.

Wanous, J.P. (1989) Installing a realistic job preview: ten tough choices, *Personnel Psychology*, 42(1): 117–34.

Further reading

Hunter, J.E. and Schmidt, F.L. (1998) The validity and utility of selection methods in personnel psychology: practical and theoretical implications of 85 years of research findings, *Psychological Bulletin*, 124(2): 262–74.

Kristof-Brown, A.L., Zimmerman, R.D. and Johnson, E.C. (2005) Consequences of individuals' fit at work: a meta-analysis of person–job, person–organization, person–group, and person–supervisor fit, *Personnel Psychology*, 58(2): 281–342.

Lepak, D.P. and Snell, S.A. (2007) *Employment subsystems and the 'HR architecture'*, in P. Boxall, J. Purcell and P.M. Wright (eds), *The Oxford Handbook of Human Resource Management*, Chapter 11, pp. 210–30. Oxford: Oxford University Press.

Philips, J.M. (1998) Effects of realistic job previews on multiple organizational outcomes: a meta-analysis, *Academy of Management Journal*, 41(6): 673–90.

Performance Management

Learning Objectives

After studying this chapter, you should be able to do the following:

- ❖ Understand the role of performance management (PM) in translating strategy and goals into concrete employee action
- ❖ Outline the key characteristics of PM
- ❖ Identify the different purposes of evaluation and PM
- ❖ Understand the relationship between human resource management (HRM) and PM
- ❖ Evaluate goal-setting theory
- ❖ Understand the relevance of goal setting in improving job and organizational performance
- ❖ Recognize the role of the direct supervisor in the application of successful PM
- ❖ Discuss performance and perceived justice (procedural and distributive)

CASE STUDY: SIEMENS

Siemens Belux is the Siemens group holding for the region Belux (Belgium and Luxembourg) and West and Central Africa. The organization's businesses are information and communications, automation in the industrial sector, building technologies, energy, transportation, medical solutions and lighting.

Strategy and PM: the role of the Management Cockpit War Room

Since 2002, Siemens Belux no longer operates on the basis of traditional financial reporting and variance analysis, but instead operates based on a strategy-oriented, KPI-based (key performance indicator-based) management process. In the following interview, conducted in March 2005, Guy Bourdon, the initiator of the new management process and person responsible for introducing the Management Cockpit War Room at Siemens Belux, speaks to Juergen H. Daum about the use and introduction of the Management Cockpit War Room concept, and the results that have been achieved.

Juergen H. Daum: What is the objective of the new Policy & Strategy process at Siemens Belux and how does it work?

Guy Bourdon: The objective of the Policy & Strategy process is to maintain a permanent overview within the management team of the current fiscal year plus two years, from a business and a strategic perspective. In this corporate planning process we create, monitor, and adapt our strategic business plan. The process begins with an analysis phase, in which we examine our internal and external situation. This is followed by the development or revision of the mission and vision and of our corporate values. We then adapt the strategic goals and the policies and strategies accordingly. This means that in the management team, we discuss the cause–effect relationships between the various strategic objectives in order to arrive, also at a detailed level, at a common understanding of the strategy and of the inner logic of the strategy. We then check the indicator targets of the Balanced Scorecard, break these down according to the responsibility hierarchy, define or revise the action plans, and then define the key performance indicators (KPIs) and performance indicators of the Management Cockpit.

Juergen H. Daum: Let us now talk about the Management Cockpit War Room. Why do you need a Management Cockpit War Room?

Guy Bourdon: The first and most important issue is to improve the quality of decisions and to accelerate decision-making processes. It enables us to gain an insight into the different and, sometimes contrasting, aspects at one glance in order to effectively and efficiently determine those areas where we have time, and areas in which no more time is available and immediate action is required.

Juergen H. Daum: For which type of management meeting is the Management Cockpit War Room used?

Guy Bourdon: On the one hand, we use the Management Cockpit War Room to manage ad-hoc crisis situations. Other meetings in the Management Cockpit War Room can result from the monthly performance analysis. In these meetings, we look at all the key performance indicators and, if necessary, schedule specific meetings for specific topics. On a quarterly basis we hold global reviews. These systematically cover all business divisions and support functions.

Juergen H. Daum: In summary, what are the most important improvements that you have achieved through the new strategy and performance management approach at Siemens Belux?

Guy Bourdon: Clearly the most important improvement is that the new Policy & Strategy process and the Management Cockpit War Room have enabled us to master the transformation from tactical to strategic management. Without this, mastering the business environment, which has been tricky since 2002, would have become even more difficult. You can't realize the full potential of a company or of an entity unless you have a complete and transparent view of opportunities, risks, possible synergies, and 'How-To'. Also, our controlling and controlling meetings have become much more efficient. Nowadays, the quarterly controlling meeting of business divisions typically takes 60 minutes. It used to take two to four hours. Now we need less time and are more effective, as we have a broader and more proactive approach to the different issues. Our approach to strategy, which now extends to operational management and day-to-day controlling, together with the focus on the management of strategic programs, simply generates far better results – for the business itself, in form of lower costs, a reduced capital lockup, and the creation of important competencies of employees. The Management Cockpit approach has also enabled us to make great progress in the area of Shared Services. Previously, Shared Services were only ever touched upon briefly in controlling meetings. Now, Shared Services are completely integrated and can therefore be more easily monitored. At the same time, they receive more information about the business of their internal customers and the development of the business, and so can proactively adjust their services accordingly. In the difficult business situation of the last few years, Shared Services were therefore in a situation to take the necessary steps themselves, in order to improve their efficiency and effectiveness. They have been able to reduce their overall costs by 35%.

Guy Bourdon was the Chief Consultant at Siemens s.a., Brussels, the Siemens holding group for the region of Belux and west and central Africa at the time of the interview.

(*Source*: Shortened and adapted version of Juergen Daum's (2005) Trend Report, 1 November: www.juergendaum.com)

? Discussion question

Discuss the advantages of the new PM system within Siemens for strategic decision making.

Introduction

Chapter 3 highlights the increased attention as the potential added value of human resources, also known as the HRM and performance debate. Human resources belong to an organization's most valuable assets. To get the best out of people, it is not enough to recruit and select the best candidates (see Chapter 7, 'Selective recruitment and selection'). Recruitment and selection are just the start of value creation through human resources. PM is another important high-performance work practice (HPWP) that can be applied to inform, guide, monitor and evaluate employees to achieve organizational goals. In other words, PM provides direction and stimulates employee motivation. Employees need to know the organization's strategy, the organizational goals and the corporate values for desired individual attitudes and behaviours. What is expected from individual workers with respect to their job performance? What kind of corporate norms and values are important for employees in their daily work? What are the targets of the department and what is the potential individual employee's contribution? And what are their KPIs? PM can act as a bridge between corporate strategy and concrete employee interventions in the process of goal achievement:

Strategy and goal-setting → HR strategy → PM → HR outcomes →
critical HR goals → ultimate business goals (UBGs)

A simple test for checking the PM system in an organization is to ask several individual employees about:

- the organization's strategy;
- the organizational goals;
- the KPIs of the organization;
- how the individual employee is expected to contribute to the strategy, goals and KPIs?

Creating a high-performance organization starts with an organization strategy and goals. The HR strategy is linked to the overall strategy and the goals (see Chapter 3). Together with other

HPWPs, such as selective recruitment, selection, compensation, development and employee participation, PM is an intervention that can positively affect HR outcomes, in particular employee motivation, organizational citizenship behaviour and organizational commitment. These HR outcomes positively affect critical HR goals (e.g. cost-effectiveness) and the UBGs of an organization.

'PM can act as a bridge between corporate strategy and concrete employee interventions'

In practice PM tends to represent the 'hard' HRM approach (see Legge (1995) in Chapter 5), which is mainly focused on the employer's and shareholder's interests. The 'hard' approach is mainly reflected in the attention to organizational goals (e.g. employee motivation, citizenship behaviour and labour productivity) and financial performance indicators. Performance-related pay (PRP), direct supervision and monitoring are key HR components of this 'hard' model in PM.

There is, however, a growing awareness of the importance of 'soft' elements in PM aimed at employee well-being (e.g. employee development and employee involvement). This chapter highlights these aspects and shifts; for example, represented in the shift from pay for performance to employee development and the shift from PM by the supervisor exclusively to PM by the supervisor, employees themselves and other relevant evaluators (e.g. colleagues and customers).

The Siemens case study at the start of the chapter highlights the importance of a PM system for both strategic decision making and practical operations. Monitoring and evaluation have become more important with an increased emphasis on performance of an organization (Latham et al., 2007). The traditional administrative appraisal systems have been replaced by extensive PM approaches (Armstrong and Baron, 1998; DeNissi, 2000; Den Hartog et al., 2004). One of the strengths of the new PM approaches is the crucial element of goal-setting (Locke and Latham, 1990). **Goal-setting theory** is a powerful theory on getting the best out of employees by setting challenging goals, communication and close monitoring.

This chapter contains an overview of the key elements of performance appraisal (PA) and PM with special attention focused on the role of the direct supervisor in the process of evaluation and monitoring, as suggested by Den Hartog et al. (2004). Linked to the latter notion are the concept of distributive justice, procedural justice (Greenberg, 1990) and the relevance of a fair system of appraisal among employees.

Successful contemporary organizations apply strong PM systems monitoring individual, group and business unit performance, but at the same time creating a corporate culture and a guideline for employees on how the work should be done. Modern PM is much more than the traditional administrative PA. Instead, PM is one of the key areas for achieving organizational success. PM is about goal-setting and monitoring employees' performance. It is a strategic way to improve overall performance and create business awareness among employees throughout the organization; for example, with regard to innovation and learning (Molleman and Timmerman, 2003). PM is one of the leading themes in leading multinational companies (MNCs) (Paauwe, 2007).

This chapter examines PM beginning with a definition of PA and PM. The different key characteristics, purposes and developments over time of performance management are then discussed. After PM is linked to HRM, you find out the similarities and differences between the two. The next section deals with goal-setting theory, which is considered a crucial foundation of PM. Next, the role of the direct supervisor in PM is discussed in more detail, followed by a section on 360-degree feedback systems. The chapter ends with sections on PM and justice and the future of PM.

Defining performance appraisal

According to Cardy and Dobbins (1998: 470), PA 'is the process of identifying, observing, measuring, and developing human performance in organizations'. Identification in this definition refers to the determination of what areas are to be focused on (Cardy and Dobbins, 1998), including performance indicators and the way these outcomes are going to be measured. For example, an employee is expected to deliver a given number of products per day with a certain quality level. The employee's performance in terms of productivity and quality will be checked on a daily basis. The observation in Cardy and Dobbins' (1998) definition refers to the monitoring and checking of the employee's performance. Measurement is one of the key aspects of PA. It refers to the actual testing of the individual employee's performance. This can be done at fixed times or through random inspections. The development component in the definition of Cardy and Dobbins (1998) suggests that PA goes beyond assessment of past performance. The outcomes of the assessment can, and should, be used to improve future performance. One way of doing this is employee development. In some cases employees may need additional skills training and in other cases knowledge development is required to improve performance. PM is a more sophisticated evaluation system built on the traditional PA systems (Bach, 2000). PM is defined as one of the five key HPWPs in this book together with selective recruitment and selection, compensation, employee development and participation. However, PM itself contains elements of other HPWPs; in particular, elements of PRP and employee development.

'PM is a more sophisticated evaluation system built on the traditional PAs'

Stop and reflect

Select two professions (e.g. a lawyer and a dentist).
What kind of criteria can be used to evaluate the performance of these two professions?

Definitions of PM[1]

First, PM can be seen as a broad range of activities that create a bridge between managing employee performance and enhancing overall organization performance. PM thus 'deals with the challenge organizations face in defining, measuring, and stimulating employee performance with the ultimate goal of improving organizational performance' (Den Hartog et al., 2004: 556). This view is upheld by DeNisi (2000), who maintains that PM refers to the range of activities an organization engages in to enhance the performance of a target person or group, with the ultimate purpose of improving organizational effectiveness.

Armstrong and Baron (1998: 38) emphasize the strategic and integrated nature of PM, which in their view focuses on 'increasing the effectiveness of organizations by improving the performance of the people who work in them and by developing the capabilities of teams and individual contributors'. However, they go further and start to describe more about the process and characteristics of PM (see Table 8.1). They see it as a continuous process involving performance reviews focusing on the future rather than the past. In their empirical research among British practitioners, they find that the key characteristics of PM (those identified by more than half of

[1] This section was inspired by Chapter 19 in Boselie et al., in Brewster and Mayrhofer (2010).

the respondents) are: goal-setting and evaluation (85 per cent of respondents); annual appraisal (83 per cent); and personal development (PD) programmes (68 per cent). Less frequently mentioned items include self-evaluation (45 per cent); pay for performance (43 per cent); coaching and mentorship (39 per cent); career management (32 per cent); competence management (31 per cent); two-yearly appraisal (24 per cent) and 180-degree feedback systems (20 per cent). In summary, goal-setting, employee monitoring and modification through employee development as necessary are the central characteristics according to Baron and Armstrong's (1998) analysis.

Characteristics of PM	Mentioned by ... % of the respondents
1. Goal-setting and evaluation	85
2. Yearly appraisal	83
3. Personal development (PD) programmes	68
4. Self-evaluation	45
5. Pay for performance	43
6. Coaching and mentorship	39
7. Career management	32
8. Competence management	31
9. Two-yearly appraisal	24
10. 180-degree feedback system	20

TABLE 8.1 Characteristics of PM
Source: Reproduced with permission from Armstrong and Baron (1998).

One core part of the PM process is undoubtedly the (annual) appraisal meeting. This is 'the system whereby an organization assigns some 'score' to indicate the level of performance of a target person or group' (DeNisi, 2000: 121). This may or may not then be linked to an employee's rewards. A second core feature is the focus on competence development (through training, coaching and feedback) and individual career planning (Fletcher, 2001; Roberts, 2001). Third, there is the important task of goal-setting: the setting of corporate, departmental, team and individual objectives (sometimes labelled 'policy deployment', a cascading of strategic objectives to a meaningful set of targets for every individual involved) (Roberts, 2001). Thus, PM involves the day-to-day management, as well as the support and development of people.

Alongside the variation in content of a PM system, according to Baron and Kreps (1999), PM can also have *different purposes,* including:

- an extensive evaluation to improve job matching;
- communication of corporate values and objectives;
- providing information for self-improvement, training and development, and career development;
- linking pay to individual and/or team performance;
- collecting information for hiring strategies;
- validating HR practices, including appraisal and rewards, retention and reductions in workforce;
- input for legal defences (e.g. when an organization is trying to fire an employee because of poor job performance).

However, how does an organization know what elements to include in a PM system in order to achieve the desired outcomes? Baron and Kreps (1999) summarize the *important and relevant aspects of different performance evaluation systems* that need to be taken into account when designing a PM system.

1 *Who or what is to be evaluated?* One can look at an individual's attitudes, behaviours or cognitive abilities, but one can also look at team performance or sub-unit outcomes.
2 *Who performs the evaluation?* Traditionally, the direct supervisor plays an important role in being the evaluator. However, more recently we have seen developments including self-evaluations, evaluations by peers and even including evaluations by customers.
3 *What is the time frame?* Traditionally, appraisals took place on an annual basis. Nowadays, we can see illustrations in practice of employee monitoring on a monthly, weekly and even daily basis.
4 *Should we be using objective or subjective evaluations?* Objective evaluations include hard data; for example, productivity and service quality outcomes, while subjective data is mainly collected using questionnaires ranking the candidate on the basis of multiple criteria; for example, with regard to the candidate's individual job performance, employee development and general attitude towards the job and colleagues.
5 *Do we apply relative or absolute performance indicators?* Relative performance indicators represent an individual's score in comparison to another person or the general average score. Absolute performance indicators focus on the real score.
6 *Should we use a forced distribution?* In a forced distribution approach, individual employees are ranked and the evaluator is forced to classify the candidates into different groups ranging from poor to high performers. Forced distribution is often introduced to create variance in scores, otherwise the organization runs the risk of ending up with 80 per cent of relatively good performers, 10 per cent of excellent performers and only 10 per cent of poor performers.
7 *How many performance indicators should be used?* The evaluation might include multiple outcome variables rather than a single one. However, using multiple performance indicators raises questions about the weights of the indicators and the technique for calculating the overall score.

PM developments over time[2]

PM has it roots in the early 1900s with special attention focused on this practice in the USA, and UK military for evaluating officers (Den Hartog et al., 2004). Furthermore, Drucker's (1954) concept of 'management by objectives', being part of a new school of thought (business administration and management), has played an important role in linking appraisal to goal-setting and PM. Bach (2000: 241) argues that 'assessment of performance has become a pervasive feature of modern life', identifying three main reasons for the growing popularity of PM in the 1980s:

1 Globalization resulted in increased competition and therefore a growing performance focus and more attention on achieving organizational goals by good people management.
2 Everybody, including HR professionals, line managers and employees, was dissatisfied with the administrative nature of the classic performance appraisals, mainly perceived as annual administrative obligations.

[2] This section was inspired by Chapter 19 in Boselie et al., in Brewster and Mayrhofer (2010).

3 The HR professionals saw in PM an instrument for showing the added value of HRM in an organization.

'assessment of performance has become a pervasive feature of modern life'
(Bach, 2000: 241)

Guest and Conway (1998) argue that PM before 1990 was focused primarily on the content and the system, with an emphasis on the direct supervisor as the evaluator (see Table 8.2). They also point out that PM before 1990 was typically top-down, being the property of the HR department and with a strong link to performance-related pay. After 1990, PM changed fundamentally to include more attention on the underlying process, a joint evaluation (employee and supervisor), 360-degree feedback instead of top-down evaluation, PM being the property of line management, and finally a strong focus on employee development instead of PRP (Guest and Conway, 1998).

In summary, in recent times there has been quite a marked shift in PM from content to process, from supervisor evaluation to joint evaluation, from top-down to 360-degree, from PRP to development, and from PM being the property of the HR department to it being owned by line management. As PM has been expanding in these new directions, what does this mean for its linkage with other aspects of the HRM system?

Before 1990	From 1990
Attention to the content and the system	Attention to the underlying process
Appraisal by direct supervisor	Joint evaluation (employee and supervisor)
Top-down evaluation	360-degree feedback
Link to pay for performance	Focus on employee development
PM is property of the HR department	PM is property of line managers

TABLE 8.2 Shifts in PM
Source: Reproduced with permission from Guest and Conway (1998).

PM and HRM

PM is often seen as a microcosm of HRM, transferring the broader debate around the added value of HRM to the PM arena (Bach, 2000; Den Hartog et al., 2004; Dewettinck, 2008). Special attention in both areas (HRM and PM) is paid to the alignment with the overall business strategy (strategic fit), the alignment of practices towards HPWSs (horizontal or internal fit), line management involvement in the enactment of the practices, soft versus hard approaches (stressing the employee developmental side versus the individual performance side), and the special attention to the search for interventions to increase organization performance. An ideal PM system of practices is actually a sort of mini-HPWS focused on goal-setting, monitoring, appraising, developing and rewarding employees in order to increase employee performance and to achieve organizational goals.

'An ideal PM system of practices is actually a sort of mini-HPWS'

However, this PM system can take many guises. Several authors emphasize the relevance of different contextual factors that affect the ideal system for an organization (Den Hartog et al., 2004; Dewettinck, 2008). These contextual factors may include industry characteristics, organization size, degree of unionization and the history of the organization. Most importantly here, they may also include potential country and cultural differences affecting PM in an organization in a specific geographical location (Boselie et al., 2010).

Stop and reflect

Discuss the relationship between PM as an HPWP and other HPWPs (selective recruitment and selection, training and development, compensation and employee participation). For example, think of PM elements of an organization that can be applied in the recruitment and selection process.

Goal-setting theory

Goal-setting theory (Locke and Latham, 1990) is a theory of motivation to explain human action in specific work situations. A **goal** is 'what an individual is trying to accomplish; it is the object or aim of an action' (Locke et al., 1981: 126). Performance goals have a motivational impact in organizations (Kreitner et al., 2002). Goals motivate the individual employee (Locke and Latham, 1990) by:

- directing one's attention;
- regulating one's effort;
- increasing one's persistence;
- encouraging the development of goal-attainment strategies or action plans.

Attention direction (or focus), effort regulation (e.g. meeting deadlines), persistence (or determination) and goal-attainment strategies and action plans have a positive impact on the task performance of an individual employee. Locke (2003: 116–21) himself summarizes the most important findings of the goal setting theory in empirical studies:[3]

1. **The more difficult the goal, the greater the achievement**. *Goal difficulty* challenges the individual employee under the assumption that the employee is committed to the goal and possesses the ability and knowledge to achieve it. 'Mission impossibles' are only achieved in action movies by actors such as Tom Cruise. In real life the (difficult) goals as part of PM should be feasible.
2. **The more specific or explicit the goal, the more precisely performance is regulated**. This finding suggests that high *goal specificity* can be achieved mainly through quantification. It is important to be as specific as possible about the goals for an employee. This way the employee can focus. The goal-setting effects are stronger for easy tasks than for complex tasks. Vague goals, such as 'do your best', should be avoided.
3. **Goals that are both specific and difficult lead to the highest performance**. This finding suggests an interaction effect between specificity and difficulty, as summarized in finding (1) and finding (2). Another way of putting it is that other combinations – (a) specific goals that are easy, (b) broad goals that are difficult and (c) broad goals that are easy – show lower performance than a combination of specific and difficult goals.

[3] A selection of the most practical empirical findings of Locke (2003) is presented here in this chapter. For an extended version of all findings, see Locke (2003), Chapter 2, 'Conceptual approaches to motivation at work', in Porter et al. (2003), pp. 116–19.

4 **Commitment to goals is most critical when goals are specific and difficult.** Locke (2003: 116) explains that when goals are easy and vague, it is not difficult to get commitment, 'because it does not require much dedication to reach easy goals, and vague goals can be easily redefined to accommodate low performance'.

5 **High commitment to goals is attained when (a) the individual is convinced that the goal is important and (b) the individual is convinced that the goal is attainable.** The front-line manager or direct supervisor can play an important role in convincing employees of the goal relevance for the individual and the organization. The other aspect of this finding reflects the notion that a goal can be extremely difficult as long as the individual employee perceives it as possible to achieve.

6 **Goal-setting is most effective when there is feedback showing progress in relation to the goal.** It helps when employees are given feedback on their performance, in particular feedback on improving their performance in the direction of the ultimate goals. This is also known as 'knowledge of score' (Locke, 2003).

7 **Goals stimulate planning.** Task or goal-relevant plans can be the result of experience or training. These plans can have a positive effect on the task performance of an individual employee as suggested in the scheme by Locke and Latham (1990).

PRP is often linked to goal-setting theory as an incentive for goal achievement. Kreitner et al. (2002: 222) argue that pay should not be linked to goal achievements unless the following aspects are satisfied:

- Performance goals are under the employees' control (the goals are manageable by the employees).
- Goals are quantitative and measurable.
- Frequent, relatively large payments are made for performance achievement.

The global financial crisis of 2008/2009 has probably shed new light on the third aspect. The performance-related pay schemes for employees in the financial sector are most likely directly negatively related to the performance of these companies. Therefore we need to be very careful with financial incentives. There are of course many other non-financial reward types available for motivating employees (see Chapter 9 on compensation for alternatives).

A practical application of the goal-setting theory is offered by Kinicki (1992, in Kreitner et al., 2002) and called SMART. SMART is an acronym for specific, measurable, attainable, results-oriented and time-bound.

SMART: goals should be ...

- *specific*: goals should be formulated in precise terms; vagueness should be avoided.
- *measurable*: goals should be measurable and a measurement device can be very helpful in doing so (see Chapter 4 on HR metrics and measurements).
- *attainable*: goals should be realistic, challenging and attainable in the perceptions of those who are submitted to it. Impossible goals should be avoided because these cause decreasing employee motivation.
- *results-oriented*: the goals should be in line with the corporate goals, with a focus on desired end results in line with the business strategy.
- *time-bound*: goals should be linked to specific target dates for completion; so-called deadlines.

Goal-setting theory contributes to the optimal design and development of a PM system in an organization. It helps to understand the underlying principles and provides yardsticks for concrete PM actions in organizations. One of these aspects is related to the role of the direct supervisor.

Stop and reflect

The image of an athlete competing to win the 100 metres is often used when explaining goal-setting theory. The athlete's goal is difficult, challenging and specific and the rewards (fame and money) are substantial.

Can you think of other images that illustrate the key characteristics of goal-setting theory? Explain and justify your choice(s).

The role of the supervisor[4]

Managers put PM into practice, and by doing so will affect employees' perception as well as their commitment, motivation and trust. Work on leadership, leader–member exchange, goal-setting and motivation, perceived supervisory and organizational support, and procedural and interactional justice may help further delineate the importance of direct supervisors and front-line managers in implementing HR practices (e.g. De Haas et al., 2000; Colquitt et al., 2001; Den Hartog and Koopman, 2001; Locke and Latham, 2002; Rhoades and Eisenberger, 2002).

> 'managers' skill and fairness in performing these tasks as well as their relationships with their different subordinates will play a key role in the success of PM.'

An HR department can develop (or buy in) sophisticated PM tools. However, whether these sophisticated PM tools contribute to organization performance depends heavily on appropriate enactment by line managers (e.g. Gratton and Truss, 2003). Their consistency, fairness and skill in using tools such as holding consultation meetings and conducting appraisal interviews will to a large degree determine whether such tools indeed generate positive effects on commitment and employee performance. The role of first-line managers in carrying out policies set by the organization is mentioned in the HRM literature (e.g. Storey, 1995); however, studies have mostly ignored this role. PM clearly and directly involves managers in the process. In an ideal situation managers set challenging yet attainable objectives, appraise performance and give feedback. They ensure possibilities for subordinates' development and stimulate a climate in which high performance is stressed. Thus, managers' skill and fairness in performing these tasks, as well as their relationships with their different subordinates, will play a key role in the success of PM.

Locke (2003: 117) summarizes relevant leadership techniques for optimal goal-setting that can be used in PM systems. According to the author, *relevant leadership techniques* include:

- providing and communicating an inspiring vision for the company or organization;
- acting as role model for the employees;
- expecting outstanding performance;
- promoting employees who embrace the vision and dismissing those who reject it;

[4] This section was inspired by an earlier study of Den Hartog et al. (2004), in *Applied Psychology: An International Review.*

- delegating responsibility for key tasks; goal setting itself can be delegated for capable, responsible employees;
- expressing (genuine) confidence in employee capabilities;
- enhancing capabilities through training;
- asking for commitment in public.

360-degree feedback systems

A popular appraisal technique for evaluating the performance of individual employees from multiple perspectives or sources is the 360-degree feedback system (see Figure 8.3). The evaluations or ratings can be collected from the direct supervisor, peers, subordinates, or a combination of these sources (Bracken, 1994). The inclusion of multiple raters supports the reliability of the measurement. The inclusion of different rater groups – managers, peers and subordinates – improves the validity of the measurement. In other words, different views and perspectives on the individual employee's performance increase the quality of the evaluation and the chance that the evaluation is correct. In some cases self-ratings and customers are part of the 360-degree feedback system.

The selection of raters is crucial and avoidance of ratees nominating 'friendly raters' is necessary (Bracken, 1994). It is also important to make the ratings anonymous if possible (Bracken, 1994). Finally, raters should be trained to use the feedback system (Bracken, 1994). A 360 degree feedback system is time-consuming because of all the different raters involved. These systems can also be very expensive, not only because of the time required from the raters, but the complexity of the data collection and data analysis as well. The support of information technology (IT) is desirable for data warehousing (data storage), data analysis on aggregated levels (e.g. team level, department level, business unit level and/or company level), and monitoring the instrument itself in terms of the application in practice (e.g. keeping track of the employee coverage and the intensity).

PM and procedural justice

The concept of perceived justice is discussed in Chapter 4, in which two types of perceived justice are discussed: procedural and distributive justice. Procedural justice deals with the fairness of the procedures used to determine outcome distributions or allocations (Colquitt et al., 2001). Procedural justice is often related to workers' perception of the supervisor, their attachment to the organization and their willingness to engage in various kinds of organizational citizenship behaviour (Paauwe and Boselie, 2007). A poor PM system is most likely to negatively affect employee outcomes through employee's perceived injustice. It is therefore important to create not only a valid and reliable PM system, but also a fair system as well. Procedural justice in the context of PM is linked to the process of evaluation and those who do the evaluation. Perceived procedural injustice by ratees (employees) can be minimized when the ratees or evaluated employees (Bracken, 1994; Locke, 2003; Noe et al., 2006):

- participate in the development of the appraisal system (involvement);
- understand the PM system, the feedback process and the evaluation criteria (awareness and understanding);
- agree with and accept the PM system (agreement and acceptance);

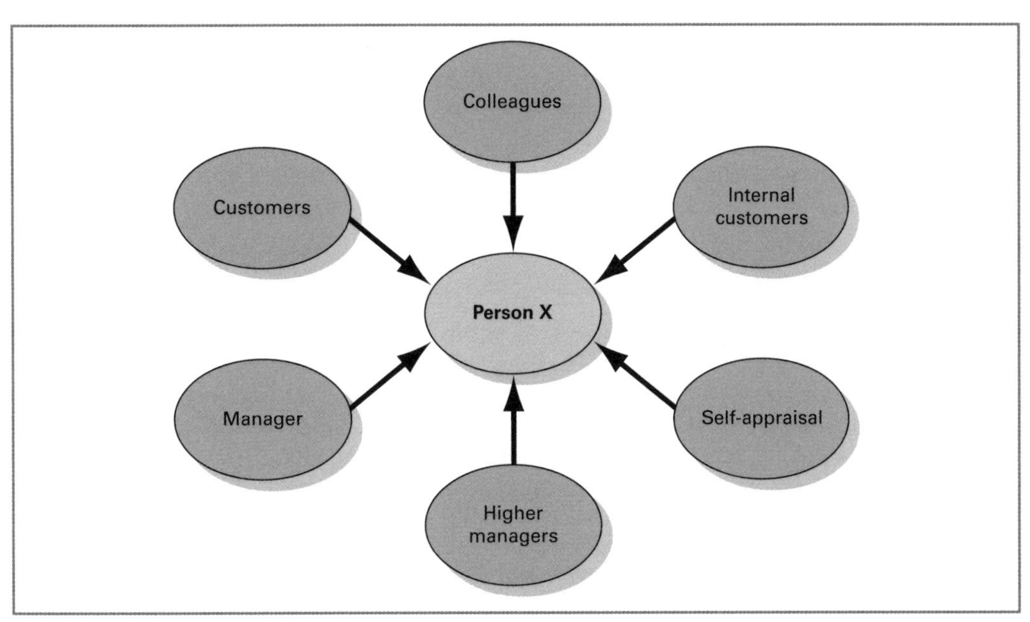

FIGURE 8.3 A 360-degree feedback system

- perceive well-trained raters (supervisor, peers and subordinates);
- perceive a constructive and development-oriented PM environment focused on rewards for good performance and development opportunities in case of low performance (constructive atmosphere and support);
- get regular feedback, not once a year (frequent evaluations);
- have the opportunity to rate their performance (self-ratings);
- get the opportunity to participate in the evaluation session.

PM and distributive justice

The other type of perceived justice – distributive justice – is also highly relevant in the context of PM. Distributive justice concerns people's perception of outcomes or rewards and the way they are allocated (Baron and Kreps, 1999: 107). This form of justice is relevant for workers' satisfaction with decisions concerning their jobs and pay. Distributive justice is relevant for PM when it comes to rewards or punishments of employees caused by the performance evaluation. Perceived distributive injustice may occur when employees who perform similarly get treated differently; for example, by the direct supervisor. This is often the case in circumstances of extra bonuses for employees based on their past performance and in circumstances of internal promotion opportunities. Poor PM systems are most likely to create perceived procedural injustice (the system is considered to be unfair) in combination with perceived distributive injustice (the rewards linked to the evaluation outcomes are considered to be unfairly distributed among the employees who are being evaluated). Perceived distributive injustice can be minimized by:

- training supervisors who are in charge of rewarding or punishing ratees;

- monitoring supervisors on their performance evaluation and the consequences for their ratees;
- rewarding supervisors for excellent PM in practice;
- creating transparency of the PM system, the process and the consequences for an individual employee and for other employees within a department.

PM and balanced approaches

Chapter 5 focuses on balanced approaches in HRM, explicitly taking into account both the employer's and the employee's interests. PM is an HPWP that may disturb the balance between the latter two interests. The performance and goal orientation of PM easily become too focused on practices (e.g. individual PRP and close monitoring by the direct supervisor) and outcomes (e.g. productivity, quality, sales and profits) that mainly serve the employer's and shareholders' interests. To restore the balance, an ideal PM system also pays attention to 'what employees want' (see Chapter 5); for example, reflected in opportunities for PD, an optimal work–life balance through flexible working arrangements, employment security through permanent contracts and fixed pay (in contrast to variable pay). HR outcomes for inclusion in the PM system that represent employee well-being and employee perspective are, for example, employee satisfaction, job stress, work intensification, employee trust, perceived justice (distributive and procedural) and commitment. See Chapter 4 for a more detailed presentation of a balanced HR scorecard and the presentation of specific HR outcomes such as perceived justice and employee commitment.

'To restore the balance an ideal PM system also pays attention to "what employees want"'

Another important feature of a balanced PM system is related to employee involvement or participation. Balanced approaches are characterized by extensive employee involvement; for example, in the design of the PM system, but also in the actual PM process. Self-appraisal as part of PM is an illustration of active employee involvement in the evaluation that potentially avoids too much top-down and one-way appraisal by the direct supervisor. The inclusion of subordinate appraisals is also a type of evaluation that restores the balance in a PM system, because in that approach line managers are not only appraised by their supervisors but also by their own employees as well. This is a system applied within Siemens.

Table 8.3 summarizes illustrations of employers' and employees' interests translated into a PM system including practices, outcomes and process features. This overview suggests that pay for performance can be a successful element of a PM system when it is 'balanced' or compensated with aspects of employment security (e.g. fixed pay) and opportunities for PD. Close monitoring by the supervisor can be part of a PM system as long as it is balanced with sufficient employee autonomy. Motivation and organizational commitment can be used as indicators or outcomes in PM, but other outcomes that represent employee well-being and employee perspective (e.g. satisfaction, job stress, commitment to the occupation and trust) should be taken into account as well from this balanced approach. Finally, process aspects of PM should also explicitly acknowledge 'what employers want' and 'what employees want'. Employee involvement appears to be an important aspect that will be discussed in more detail in Chapter 11 on employee participation in general. The balanced approach described here is highly related to the HR balanced scorecard presented in Chapter 4. HR scorecards are often an integrated part of PM.

The employers' perspective	The employees' perspective
HR practices	
Pay for performance	Fixed pay and employee development
Close monitoring by supervisor	Employee autonomy and flexible work arrangements
HR outcomes	
Employee motivation	Employee satisfaction and job stress
Organizational commitment	Occupational commitment
Organizational citizenship behaviour	Employee trust and perceived justice
Processes	
Supervisor appraisals	Self-evaluations and peer evaluations
Supervisor decision making	Employee involvement

TABLE 8.3 Balanced PM approaches

The future of PM

The growing importance of PM in both theory and practice is clear for all to see (Boselie et al., 2010). A special issue of the *European Journal of International Management* (2008) emphasizes this further. The discussions presented suggest the latest trends in PM include:

- a global tendency towards PM through culture management;
- aligning corporate goals with individual employee goals;
- using PM for talent management and leadership development (LD);
- using PM as a mechanism for distinguishing good performers from bad performers;
- linking PM and 360-degree feedback systems;
- integrating PM and IT systems;
- emphasizing self-appraisal and appraisals by peers;
- PM as a tool for general employee development purposes.

Boselie et al. (2010) present empirical data on PM from the Global HR Research Alliance case studies and the Cranet survey. These data show some interesting findings with regard to PM in contemporary organizations. First, PM is linked to or embedded in relevant areas of interest in practice such as (1) culture management, (2) talent management, (3) succession planning, (4) competence management, and (5) new technology. Second, there is an overall increase in the use of appraisal systems; in particular for clerical workers and manual workers. There is also a shift towards a 360-degree feedback system with an emphasis on self-evaluation. The appraisal system is mainly in place to determine career management, promotion and PRP; however, most emphasis is on training and development. Third, there are few differences between regions in the case studies (probably because of their multinational nature), but there are also few differences between countries in the Cranet data on appraisal systems. Perhaps this is indicative of the increasing standardization of PM practices across the globe. If we look in a little more detail, there are some contextual differences that may affect PM in different countries. The main driver of these differences between countries appears to be associated to cultural differences reflected in variance in leadership, communication and self-evaluation. In other words, the leadership styles, the nature of communication and information sharing and the role of the individual in the appraisal procedure differ between countries when looking through the lens of PM. Therefore, context matters in the optimal PM design (see Chapter 2).

The strategic relevance of PM

PM can be the bridge between the overall business goals and the specific goals of every individual employee. In this chapter it is concluded that PM represents a sort of mini high performance system in which the alignment of individual practices (e.g. monitoring, evaluation, rewards and development) strengthens the achievement of the individual employee goals and the overall business goals. Goals at the individual employee level and business goals (in particular if these are aligned) are the guidelines for employee behaviour and their orientation towards certain achievements. The strategic relevance of PM is mainly in the creation of opportunities for business awareness at all levels, focus and concrete targets, employee motivation and employee engagement.

Summary

- PA is the process of identifying, observing, measuring and developing human performance in organization.
- PM is a more sophisticated evaluation system that deals with the challenge organizations face in defining, measuring and stimulating employee performance with the ultimate goal of improving organizational performance.
- PM provides direction and stimulates employee motivation.
- PA is characterized by goal-setting, evaluation, yearly appraisal sessions, PD programmes, self-evaluation, PRP, coaching and mentorship, career management, competence management and 180 or 360-degree feedback mechanisms.
- PM has shifted from a content to a process focus, from appraisal by the direct supervisor to joint evaluation (employee and supervisor), from top-down evaluation to a 360-degree feedback, from a strong emphasis on PRP to a strong emphasis on employee development, and from PM being the property of the HR department to PM being the property of the line managers.
- Goal-setting theory examines employee job performance through setting challenging goals, communication and close monitoring.
- Goals for individual employees and groups of employees should be specific, measurable, attainable, results-oriented and time-bounded.
- The direct supervisor of an employee plays an important role in the successful enactment of PM in practice.
- A 360-degree feedback system may include evaluations from colleagues, internal customers, external customers, subordinates, the direct supervisor, higher managers and self-appraisal.
- Procedural justice deals with the fairness of the PM procedures used to determine outcome distributions or allocations.

- Distributive justice concerns people's perception of PM outcomes and rewards and the way they are allocated.
- PM systems tend to emphasize the 'hard' aspects of HRM; for example, reflected in practices such as individual PRP and close monitoring through direct supervision.
- The ideal PM system takes into account both the employer's interests and the employees' interests, reflected in balancing practices (e.g. PRP versus employee development), balancing outcomes (e.g. employee motivation versus job stress) and balancing processes (e.g. appraisal by direct supervisor versus joint appraisal).
- PM is linked to other relevant areas in practice such as: (1) culture management, (2) talent management, (3) succession planning, (4) competence management, and (5) new technology.
- There is an overall increase in the use of appraisal systems particularly for clerical and manual workers.
- The leadership styles, the nature of communication and information sharing and the role of the individual in the appraisal procedure differ between countries when looking through the lens of PM.

Glossary of key terms

A goal is what an individual is trying to accomplish; it is the object or aim of an action.
Performance appraisal (PA) is the process of identifying, observing, measuring and developing human performance in organizations.
Performance management (PM) is the strategic process of linking individual goals to organizational goals to improve individual job performance and organizational performance through goal-setting, evaluation, regular appraisal, employee development, rewards, coaching and mentorship, career management and 180 or 360-degree feedback systems.
360-degree feedback is a popular technique for evaluating the performance of individual employees from multiple perspectives or sources.

Personal development

Determine the three most important goals in your career for the next two to five years. Think of the personal actions you need to take to achieve these three goals (actions taken next week; actions taken within the next three months; and actions taken within the next year).
Determine the way you are going to measure your own progress on your goal achievement.
Discuss your personal goals, actions and evaluation approach with somebody else.

Individual task

What are your personal goals as a worker or student? Try to be as concrete and specific as possible. Try to define your personal goals according to the basic rules of goal-setting theory:

- The more difficult the goal, the greater the achievement.
- The more specific or explicit the goal, the more precisely performance is regulated.
- Goals that are both specific and difficult lead to the highest performance.
- Commitment to goals is most critical when goals are specific and difficult.
- High commitment to goals is attained when the individual is convinced that the goal is important and the individual is convinced that the goal is attainable.
- Goal setting is most effective when there is feedback showing progress in relation to the goal.
- Goals stimulate planning.

Identify potential weaknesses in your current personal goal-setting system and think of ways (and practices) to overcome these issues; for example, in terms of development, evaluation and rewards.

Team task

Discuss the advantages and disadvantages of applying 360-degree feedback systems as part of a PM system applied to:

1. unskilled workers (for example in retail);
2. highly educated knowledge workers in a high-tech environment (e.g. in the IT sector);
3. higher level managers in a multinational company.

Discuss the advantages and disadvantages in terms of the employer's interests (e.g. with regard to training costs, increased productivity and employee motivation) and in terms of the employees' interests (e.g. with regard to satisfaction, perceived justice and employee involvement).

Learning checklist

After studying this chapter, you should be able to do the following:

- Understand the role of PM in translating strategy and goals into concrete employee action.
- Outline the key characteristics of PM.
- Identify the different purposes of evaluation and PM.
- Understand the relationship between HRM and PM.
- Evaluate goal-setting theory.
- Understand the relevance of goal-setting in improving job and organizational performance.
- Recognize the role of the direct supervisor in the application of successful PM.
- Discuss performance and perceived justice (procedural and distributive).

References

Armstrong, M. and Baron, A. (1998) *Performance Management: The New Realities*. London: CIPD.

Bach, S. (2000) From performance appraisal to performance management, in S. Bach and K. Sisson (eds), *Personnel Management*, 3rd edn. Oxford: Blackwell.

Baron, J.N. and Kreps, D.M. (1999) *Strategic Human Resource Management: Frameworks for General Managers*. Danvers, MA: Wiley.

Boselie, P., Farndale, E. and Paauwe, J. (2010) Performance management, in C. Brewster and W. Mayrhofer (eds), *Handbook of Research in Comparative Human Resource Management*, Chapter 19. Cheltenham: Edward Elgar.

Bracken, D.W. (1994) Straight talk about multi-rater feedback, *Training and Development*, 48: 44–51.

Brewster, C. and Mayrhofer, W. (2010) *Handbook of Research in Comparative Human Resource Management*. Cheltenham: Edward Elgar.

Cardy, R.L. and Dobbins, G.H. (1998) Performance management, in C.L. Cooper and C. Argyris (eds), *Encyclopedia of Management*. Oxford: Blackwell.

Colquitt, J.A., Conlon, D.E., Wesson, M.J., Porter, C.O.L.H. and Ng, K.Y. (2001) Justice at the millennium: a meta-analytic review of 25 years of organizational justice research, *Journal of Applied Psychology*, 86(3): 425–45.

De Haas, M., Algera, J.A., Van Tuijl, H.F.J.M. and Meulman, J.J. (2000) Macro and micro goal setting: in search of coherence, *Applied Psychology: An International Review*, 49: 579–95.

Den Hartog, D.N. and Koopman, P.L. (2001) Leadership in organizations, in N. Anderson, D.S. Ones, H. Sinangil and C. Viswesvaran (eds), *Handbook of Industrial, Work and Organizational Psychology*, Volume 2, pp. 166–87. London: Sage.

Den Hartog, D.N., Boselie, P. and Paauwe, J. (2004) Performance management: a model and research agenda, *Applied Psychology: An International Review*, 53(4): 556–69.

DeNisi, A. (2000) Performance appraisal and performance management: a multilevel analysis, in S. Kozlowski and K.J. Klein (eds), *Multilevel Theory, Research and Methods in Organizations*. San Francisco, CA: Jossey-Bass.

Dewettinck, K. (2008) Employee performance management systems in Belgian organisations: purpose, contextual dependence and effectiveness, *European Journal of International Management*, 2(2): 192–207.

Drucker, P. (1954) *The Practice of Management*. New York: Harper & Row.

Fletcher, C. (2001) Performance appraisal and management: the developing research agenda, *Journal of Occupational and Organizational Psychology*, 73(4): 473–87.

Gratton, L. and Truss, C. (2003) The three-dimensional people strategy: putting human resource policies into action, *Academy of Management Executive*, 17: 74–86.

Greenberg, J. (1990) Organizational justice: yesterday, today, and tomorrow, *Journal of Management*, 16(2): 399–432.

Guest, D.E. and Conway, N. (1998) Appendix 4, analysis of survey data, in M. Armstrong and A. Baron, *Performance Management: The New Realities*. London: CIPD.

Kreitner, R., Kinicki, A. and Buelens, M. (2002) *Organizational Behavior*, 2nd European edn. London: McGraw-Hill.

Latham, G., Sulsky, L.M. and MacDonald, H. (2007) Performance management, in P. Boxall, J. Purcell and P.M. Wright (eds), *The Oxford Handbook of Human Resource Management*, Chapter 18. Oxford: Oxford University Press.

Locke, E.A. (2003) Motivation through conscious goal setting, in L.W. Porter, G.A. Bigley and R.M. Steers (eds), *Motivation and Work Behavior*, Chapter 2, pp. 113–25. New York: McGraw-Hill Higher Education.

Locke, E.A. and Latham, G.P. (1990) *A Theory of Goal Setting and Task Performance*. Englewood Cliffs, NJ: Prentice Hall.

Locke, E.A. and Latham, G.P. (2002) Building a practically useful theory of goal setting and task motivation, *American Psychologist*, 57: 705–17.

Locke, E.A., Shaw, K.M., Saari, L.M. and Latham, G. (1981) Goal setting and task performance: 1969–1980, *Psychological Bulletin*, 90: 125–52.

Molleman, E. and Timmerman, H. (2003) Performance management when innovation and learning become critical performance indicators, *Personnel Review*, 32(1): 93–113.

Noe, R.A., Hollenbeck, J.R., Gerhart, B. and Wright, P.M. (2006) *Human Resource Management: Gaining Competitive Advantage*, 5th edn. Boston, MA: McGraw-Hill.

Paauwe, J. (2007) HRM and performance: in search of balance. Inaugural lecture, Tilburg University, Tilburg.

Paauwe, J. and Boselie, P. (2007) HRM and societal embeddedness, in P. Boxall, J. Purcell and P.M. Wright (eds), *The Oxford Handbook of Human Resource Management*, Chapter 9, pp. 166–84. Oxford: Oxford University Press.

Porter, L.W., Bigley, G.A. and Steers, R.M. (eds) (2003) *Motivation and Work Behavior*. New York: McGraw-Hill Higher Education.

Rhoades, L. and Eisenberger, R. (2002) Perceived organizational support: a review of the literature, *Journal of Applied Psychology*, 87: 698–714.

Roberts, I. (2001) Reward and performance management, in I. Beardwell and L. Holden (eds), *Human Resource Management: A Contemporary Approach*, 3rd edn, pp. 506–58. Edinburgh: Pearson.

Storey, J. (ed.) (1995) *Human Resource Management: A Critical Text*. London: Routledge.

Further reading

Boselie, P., Farndale, E. and Paauwe, J. (2010) Performance management, in C. Brewster and W. Mayrhofer (eds), *Handbook of Research in Comparative Human Resource Management*, Chapter 19. Edward Elgar.

Den Hartog, D.N., Boselie, P. and Paauwe, J. (2004) Performance management: a model and research agenda, *Applied Psychology: An International Review*, 53(4): 556–69

DeNisi, A.S. (2000) Performance appraisal and performance management: a multilevel analysis, in S. Kozlowski and K.J. Klein (eds), *Multilevel Theory, Research and Methods in Organizations*. San Francisco, CA: Josey-Bass

European Journal of International Management (2008) Special issue on performance management.

Latham, G., Sulsky, L.M. and MacDonald, H. (2007) Performance management, in P. Boxall, J. Purcell and P.M. Wright (eds), *The Oxford Handbook of Human Resource Management*, Chapter 18. Oxford: Oxford University Press.

Varma, A., Budhwar, P.S. and DeNisi, A.S. (2008) *Performance Management Systems: A Global Perspective*, Global HRM Series. London Routledge.

CHAPTER

09 Compensation

Learning Objectives

After studying this chapter, you should be able to do the following:

- ❖ Understand the different aims of compensation
- ❖ Discuss top management compensation
- ❖ Review financial and non-financial compensation
- ❖ Identify the different forms of pay (fixed pay, variable pay, employee benefits and cafeteria plans)
- ❖ Discuss the increasing popularity of employee benefits in Europe
- ❖ Evaluate the pros and cons of performance-related pay (PRP)
- ❖ Outline equity, tournament, expectancy and agency theory in relationship to compensation

CASE STUDY: INVESTMENT BANKING AND BONUSES

Jeroen Smit (2008), in his book on the rise and fall of the Dutch bank ABN AMRO, discusses the bonuses culture within the bank's investment banking division. The traders and merger specialists within investment banking receive bonuses on their performance.

> 'Year after year they [investment bankers of ABN AMRO] ask for higher bonuses. Time and time again they explain the value of good specialists in trading, mergers and acquisitions. These specialists are only willing to work for ABN AMRO when paid 'decent' bonuses. In the Anglo-Saxon culture it is quite common that a group of investment bankers receive up to 15 percent of the deal. The bonus can go up to millions of Euros for an individual employee.'
>
> (Smit, 2008: 99)

The Dutch Board of Directors of ABN AMRO is annoyed by the bonus demands of the investment bankers. They propose an alternative reward system including more employment security and less strict performance targets. The Board's perspective is more consistent with the continental European approach, also known as the Rhineland model (see Chapter 1). Their proposal happens to be naïve. The only thing the investment bankers are really interested in are the yearly bonuses linked to their achievements.

> 'Van Tets [the managing director of the division investment banking] has little joy in the days on which the yearly bonuses are paid. One by one the investment bankers enter his room. Often they earn more than he does. Occasionally a cheque with two million Euros bonus is given back to him with the words: "I am worth much more than this." When Van Tets answers with "take it or leave it" the money is accepted with an angry face. This angriness is part of the game, because if you are happy about your bonus the boss might think you are happy with the same bonus next year.'
>
> (Smit, 2008: 100)

? Discussion questions

- Can you think of motives for paying core employees high yearly bonuses?
- Discuss the potential negative effects of *not* giving the investment bankers their high bonuses?
- Discuss the potential positive effects of giving the investment bankers their high bonuses?
- Can you think of the effects of the high bonuses for investment bankers on other employees within ABN AMRO?

Introduction

How do you think ABN AMRO employees feel when reading the introduction case, knowing that hundreds of employees lost their job as a result of a decade of bad management? Compensation in large profit organizations has become a synonym for 'greed'. Charles Dickens' character of Ebenezer Scrooge in the novel *A Christmas Carol* is a softy in comparison to the top managers of leading MNCs that went bankrupt or almost went bankrupt over the last decade because of bad management and 'greedy' behaviour (e.g. Enron, Ahold, RBS and Parmalat). Nowadays, compensation, in particular PRP, is often associated with perversity of the 'happy few' or core employees of an organization. In fact, top management pay has also affected the public organizations, for example with regard to senior civil servants and board members. An important question remains: 'Where were the HR professionals when these pay systems emerged?'

> 'Compensation in large profit organizations has become a synonym for "greed".'

What is a fair pay system? The Netherlands Bureau for Economic Policy Analysis (CPB) reports that the most common income (the median pay) before taxes in 2009 is €32 000 per year (vacation allowances and bonuses included) (www.cpb.nl/eng/). The Dutch Investors' Association (VEB) – an independent organization positioned between investors and listed organizations – reports the income of chief executive officers (CEOs) of Dutch MNCs on their website (www.bestuursvoorzitter.nl/beloningonline/). In 2007 Shell's CEO earned more than €10 million. That is more than 300 times the most common income before taxes in 2009. In other words, Shell CEO's payment in 2007 could cover the yearly expenses of more than 300 families in the Netherlands in theory. Shell's CEO fixed pay for 2007 according to the VEB was nearly €1.8 million, still 56 times the most common income as reported by CPB.

In the Dutch public sector there is also a debate on pay. It is known as the 'Balkenende Norm', referring to the Prime Minister's yearly income as a benchmark for all other rewards in the public sector. In March 2009 this norm was set at €171 000. The general idea behind this norm is that this is the maximum pay for employees in the public sector and in sectors related to the public sector including universities. In practice there are dozens of executives and specialists in the public sector who earn much more than the 'Balkenende Norm'. One could argue that €171 000 is not an extremely high income in comparison to the incomes of CEOs in the private sector.

According to the British National Statistics (www.statistics.gov.uk/), the median monthly pay for full-time employees in the UK in 2008 was £1916 before taxes (approximately £23 000 per year, comparable to €28 000 per year). The annual salary for the British Prime Minister in 2009 was £64 766 (approximately €82 000). In addition, Members of Parliament (MPs) receive allowances to cover the costs of running an office and employing staff, cost of living in London and travel expenses. The British situation with regard to the median pay of full-time employees and the Prime Minister's salary is comparable to the Dutch situation. Shell is a British-Dutch MNC and therefore the above analysis could also be applied to the British situation revealing similar outcomes.

On a yearly basis Shell's CEO earns 50 times more than the Dutch Prime Minister. Shell's CEO is responsible for an MNC employing more than 100 000 people worldwide with a revenue of nearly US$460 billion in 2008. In 2007 the Dutch Prime Minister was running a country with 16 million citizens and a gross national product (GNP) of nearly US$770 billion. In 2007 the British Prime Minister was running a country with 58 million citizens and a GNP of nearly US$2800 billion. Who do you think has more responsibilities? And does this justify the pay difference between Shell's CEO and the Dutch Prime Minister or the British Prime Minister?

Stop and reflect

Think about arguments for Shell CEO's yearly pay and the Prime Minister's yearly pay.

Compensation and pay are much more than top management rewards. Top management compensation is a small part of the total compensation system in an organization. Pay and compensation contain basic HR elements (including monthly salaries paid to employees) and possibilities for building high-performance work systems (HPWS) (e.g. through PRP) linked to the strategy of the organization. Employees expect their monthly salaries to be paid. This, however, is still no guarantee of a highly committed and motivated workforce. More advanced pay components are required for building a high performance culture, as suggested in Chapter 6 on high-performance work systems. More advanced or sophisticated compensation may include pay for performance and employee benefits. It also includes a good fit between compensation and other high-performance work practices (HPWPs) such as appraisal (internal fit). Additionally, this advanced and sophisticated compensation includes the alignment of compensation and the business strategies of an organization (strategic fit). See Chapters 2 and 6 on these notions of fit.

An organization such as the United Nations (UN) may decide to emphasize employee well-being for its workers through extensive employee benefits (e.g. health insurance for individual employees and their families) in line with the core business of the UN to make contributions to a better world for all people. The airline company easyJet may decide to install individual PRP linked to cost reductions and excellent service quality for customers aligned to its business strategy. Large MNCs such as Shell may use their compensation package to attract talent. And local governments may apply compensation systems that stress employment security in order to attract and retain employees. Different strategic considerations can shape the actual compensation in an organization. For a full understanding of the strategic components of compensation, the basics of payment are discussed first.

This chapter examines the HPWP of compensation. Different elements of compensation, including 'high wages', 'fair payment', 'pay for performance' and 'employee benefits', are considered best practices or best principles for creating organizational success (e.g. Walton, 1985; Arthur, 1994; Pfeffer, 1994). It discusses the aims of compensation, financial and non-financial compensation, the basis for pay, transactional employment contract types in relationship to pay, different forms of pay (fixed pay, variable pay, benefits and cafeteria plans), and theories for compensation. The theories can be used to structure compensation issues; for example, linked to employee motivation and expectations, hierarchical pay structures in organizations, fair payment and the management of different interests of **principals** (owners) and **agents** (managers).

Compensation systems refer to outcomes that an individual employee receives in an organization. Compensation or rewards include wages, bonuses, benefits (e.g. medical insurance and retirement plan), praise, recognition, esteem and self-competence (Barr, 1998). Compensation systems should be designed to achieve organizational objectives. Barr (p. 570) states that compensation can contribute to the organization's effectiveness in three ways:

1. the reward system can help attract the best human assets to the firm;
2. the reward system can help retain good performers; and
3. the reward system can motivate to affect performance.

In other words, compensation can contribute to *employee attraction, employee retention* and *employee motivation.*

Aims of compensation

Employees are generally paid by the employer for the effort they put into a job. The transactional component of the contract between an employee and an employer is mainly focused on compensation. Therefore, one of the main purposes of compensation is to *influence employee attitudes and behaviours*. The employer pays the employee, for example, for the number of hours the employee is performing a certain set of tasks. Teachers are paid on an hourly basis and for compensation they are willing to prepare classes, teach students and develop new courses. Another form of influencing employee attitudes and behaviours is to pay them on the basis of their performance. Salespeople are paid on the basis of the number of products sold to a customer independently of the time they require for product selling. A talented salesperson is capable of making a lot of money, while a less talented person is probably better off finding a job with an hourly wage.

A second aim of compensation *is controlling labour costs* and maintaining efficiency. In many situations a person's total wage can be contrasted with that person's job performance; for example, in terms of productivity, service and/or product quality and flexibility. This way, the organization can monitor the added value of an individual employee to some degree. Unfortunately, not all factors can easily be taken into account and therefore there are no simple input–output models for employee compensation and individual job performance. However, a rough estimation can be made of a person's job performance in comparison to that person's wages, and therefore compensation can be used for labour costs control.

A third aim of compensation is *employer branding,* as discussed in Chapter 7 on selective recruitment and selection. High wages and excellent compensation can be used to attract certain employees. Offering high wages sends a signal to potential employees; for example, signalling that the organization is taking its human assets very seriously and therefore the organization pays employees high wages. The disadvantage of offering high wages and excellent compensation is that doing so attracts employees who are mainly focused on financial rewards rather than other relevant drivers, including challenges, learning opportunities and organizational commitment. The 'Signalling: message in a bottle' section in Chapter 7 (p. 153) offers solutions for overcoming this problem using low wages in the probation period and above-average compensation after positive evaluation following the probation period.

Financial and non-financial compensation

Praising an employee for excellent performance is easy, cheap and potentially has a positive effect on the motivation of the individual. Chapter 5 highlights 'what employees want', including fun, a good social atmosphere and the recognition by the direct supervisor for achievements. Non-financial compensation is an important incentive for employees, in particular in circumstances where the organization has serious financial limitations. The nature of the business of voluntary organizations (e.g. Greenpeace) is the absence of payment to volunteers. But also public organizations can be restricted in terms of financial compensation. In those circumstances the organization is challenged to design and implement alternative compensation systems that are often non-financial oriented or cost little. Non-financial compensation might include:

- organizing a social event celebrating the successes of a team or department;
- celebrating successes with cake and coffee during a break;
- nominating and publishing excellent achievements in the organization's newsletter;
- putting the 'high performers' in the spotlight during regular meetings;
- complementing individual employees on good performance;
- providing additional training facilities for good performance;
- giving extra days off to good performers.

In practice, there is often too much focus on financial incentives and a lack of attention to alternative non-financial incentives. Offering non-financial compensation can also be part of an organization's strategy. The recent financial and global crisis of 2008/2009 shed a different light on financial PRP, in particular for financial institutions. To restore the balance in the pay systems within financial institutions, alternative non-financial pay elements can be applied emphasizing that it is not all about making money in the name of shareholders' interests. Work–life balance practices (e.g. flexible work arrangements as a reward for organizational citizenship behaviour of employees) represent an alternative non-financial incentive that aims at employee well-being (see Chapter 5, 'Achieving the right balance', on balancing employers' and employees' interests). Providing additional training facilities as a reward for excellent employee behaviour, for example, potentially increases customer satisfaction. The bank and insurance company of tomorrow do not want to be exclusively known for excellent financial pay (e.g. large guaranteed bonuses, individual PRP, profit-sharing schemes and high wages); instead, the organization requires a corporate image that reflects trust and integrity that are embedded in a balanced compensation system for employees. It would be interesting to compare salaries within financial institutions with those in, for example, retail, benchmarking top management salaries and salaries of secretaries in both sectors. This exercise is most likely to reveal an enormous gap between a sector that used to make a lot of money before the global crisis (financial institutions) and a sector that is always under pressure with very small margins on activities (retail organizations).

'it is not all about making money in the name of shareholders' interests.'

Stop and reflect

Can you think of any other non-financial compensation practices that could be applied in an organization?

Basis for pay

There are different ways to pay employees for their efforts. Most employees are paid on the basis of a set of *tasks* within a given position. The job description is a written summary of the tasks a person is expected to perform in a given job. The job description includes (Brannick and Levine, 1998):

- a job identification and the job title (e.g. account manager);
- a job overview that states the mission of the job and the products and services produced by the employee;
- the primary tasks involved in the job;
- a list of equipment, machines and tools used;
- raw materials, goods, data, or other materials used in the job;
- the processes used to transform materials into products and services;
- guidelines and controls that limit the discretion of the worker, such as supervision;
- required knowledge, skills, abilities and other characteristics;
- a description of the work context, such as working conditions;
- a statement of the qualifications required, such as a licence or a level of education.

This job description serves as a guideline for the compensation system of the individual employee. Job evaluation is a systematic process designed to aid in establishing pay differentials across jobs within a single employer (Milkovich and Newman, 1996). Hay Group is a global management consulting firm known for its expertise in job descriptions and job evaluations. One of the tools Hay Group applies for job evaluation and job description linked to compensation systems is benchmarking. This benchmarking includes comparing the existing job descriptions and job evaluations in an organization with other organizations in comparable situations (industry, country, region and size).

Another method of employee payment is based on the individual's *skills and knowledge*. The knowledge and skills of employees can be determined by the level of education, by the years of experience, through work samples, and through psychological tests. Within the university system a distinction can be made between a BA degree, an MA degree and a PhD. For example, an academic career in any university nowadays requires a PhD. A PhD is received when the candidate has successfully written and defended a thesis. The level of education is one element; the employee's experience is another relevant indicator for some jobs. Psychiatrists and psychologists, for example, experience a substantial amount of learning in terms of skills and knowledge on the job. Their diagnostic abilities are generally improved through years of experience and therefore job experience reflects an individual's potential contribution and compensation requirements. Knowledge and skills can also be tested using work samples and psychological tests (see Chapter 7 on selective recruitment and selection with regard to these selection techniques). The outcomes of these tests can be linked to the level of compensation for the individual employee.

In some situations employees are paid on the basis of their *seniority*. In many European countries employees automatically receive a yearly pay increment. The logic behind the yearly increments is the assumed increase in job experience and knowledge of the individual employee. Within a certain pay scale an individual employee can get eight to sometimes 14 increments over time depending on the job evaluation system in an organization. The pay scales and pay increments are often determined by the collective bargaining agreements (CBAs) in the branch of industry or by the company CBA. For example, a civil servant is paid on the basis of scale 10. Within this scale she has received three increments over the last three years. Therefore her compensation is determined on the basis of the job evaluation system linked to the 10.3 division. Scale 10.0 results in a monthly payment of €3000, while 10.3 is linked to a monthly payment of €3240. In other words, the yearly automatic pay increment for this civil servant is approximately €80 per month extra based on the assumed increased skills, knowledge and experience of the individual.

Finally, employees can be paid on the basis of their *status or reputation*. The transfer of football player David Beckham from Manchester United to Real Madrid in 2003 was largely paid by the German company Siemens. At that time Beckham was enormously popular in many Asian countries and Siemens was interested in the Real Madrid merchandise for the Asian market, including Beckham T-shirts with the Siemens logo on them. The transfer money included a substantial amount of compensation for David Beckham himself. Status and reputation can therefore also be a basis for compensation.

Stop and reflect

Can you think of jobs that are compensated on the basis of the status or reputation of the employee?

In the next section different contract types are summarized. The contract type affects the nature of the compensation of an employee.

Contract types

A salary is a periodic payment from an employer to an employee often linked to a contract. There are different forms of economic or transactional contract[1] between the employer and the employee:

- The *permanent contract* is a deal between the employer and the employee for an indefinite time.

[1] Next to the transactional or economic contract, the general employment contract contains psychological, sociological and legal elements (see Chapter 1).

- The *temporary contract* is a deal between the employer and the employee for a fixed time; for example, one year, one month or for one specific project.
- The *absence of a contract* is a situation in which there is no formal contract (permanent or temporary) and the employee is paid immediately after finishing the tasks, often the same day. The relationship between the employer and the employee is purely based on *trust*. Often this type of contract (or better called 'the absence of it') manifests itself in illegal working environments (e.g. illegal immigrants in restaurants or the agricultural business).
- The *full-time contract* represents a temporary or permanent contract for five days a week or 1.0 full-time equivalents (FTEs).
- The *part-time contract* represents a temporary or permanent contract for less than five days a week or less than 1.0 FTEs.

The full-time permanent contract is the most common contract type, although there is a growing emergence of part-time permanent contracts, full-time temporary contracts and part-time temporary contracts (Green, 2001; Koene and Van Riemsdijk, 2005). The increased number of part-time workers is typical for European countries, often representing dual careers and women with children being more likely to work under part-time conditions.

Organizations can make strategic choices with regard to contract types. From a short-term oriented shareholder perspective, temporary contracts might be preferable, because of apparent relatively low risks in the case of necessary downsizing. In other words, workers on a temporary contract are easily fired thus saving labour costs. The downside of this approach is the potential low commitment of these workers to the organizations with the risk of high employee turnover in the case of labour market shortages. The valuable knowledge workers presented in Chapter 7 are not likely to be attracted and retained when given only a temporary contract. In other cases temporary contracts are quite common given the nature of the work; for example, seasonal work in the agricultural businesses.

Forms of pay

Employees can generally be paid through four forms of pay: fixed pay, variable pay, employee benefits and cafeteria plans. *Fixed pay* or base pay is usually based on the number of hours an employee works for the organization. Fixed pay is also known as salary. In many European countries employee salaries are determined by CBAs. These CBAs are mostly negotiated on a yearly or two-yearly basis at branch of industry or company level. The employers' associations and trade unions are the actors in the negotiation process. In the Netherlands, for example, almost 85 per cent of all employees are covered by a CBA mainly focused on salaries and working conditions (Schilstra and Smit, 2005). Employee salaries or employee fixed pay can be different based on the branch of industry, the employee age, work experience, position and responsibilities (e.g. number of tasks). In most countries there is a legal minimum wage for employees depending on the employee age up until 23 years. The fixed pay of an employee may include:

- pension schemes partly paid by the employer and partly paid by the employee;
- taxes of up to 50 per cent depending on the country legislation;
- collective health care payment;
- unemployment contributions;
- disability contributions.

Illustration

A police officer in the Netherlands receives a monthly fixed pay of €3500. She is a detective in the Dutch police force and she works full-time (40 hours per week). The net salary of the detective is €2194 per month. The difference between these two figures is caused by taxes (approximately €1000), contributions to the collective pension scheme (around €200) and legal social security contributions including unemployment, disability and health care contributions.

(www.loonwijzer.nl)

To calculate the total salary costs for an individual employee in most continental European countries, the employer has to take into account taxes, collective social security arrangements including pension schemes and additional costs (e.g. reservations for unemployment pay). An easy rule of thumb for calculating the total monthly costs for an individual employee is to add 30 per cent to the fixed pay. The police officer in the illustration above therefore costs: 1.3 × €3500 = €4550 on a monthly basis. This rule of thumb can be used to calculate the maximum available budget for an individual employee.

Fixed pay is part of the total rewards system or compensation package that includes variable pay (e.g. bonuses and incentive pay) and employee benefits. *Variable pay* or PRP is used to incentivize employee performance and reward employees for being productive, delivering high service quality, being flexible and/or contributing to innovation. Variable pay makes an explicit linkage between the employee efforts and the employee performance. A recent Norwegian study shows that PRP is more widespread in large firms, is more prevalent in firms where workers of the main occupation have a high degree of autonomy in how to organize their work (e.g. workers) and is less common in highly unionized firms and in firms where wages are determined through centralized bargaining (Barth et al., 2008). Pay for performance is not exclusively the domain of the private sector. Marsden and French (1998), for example, review PRP systems in the UK employment services, within two NHS trust hospitals and in UK primary schools. The authors argue that many civil servants are now subject to new forms of PRP.

Empirical evidence from previous research suggests the potential positive impact of PRP on employee outcomes and organizational performance. Kalleberg and Moody (1994) find a positive relationship between rewards and different dimensions of firm performance, including product quality, product development, profits, market share, customer satisfaction and sales growth. Delaney and Huselid (1996) show a positive relationship between incentive compensation and perceived organizational performance. Lazear (1996) presents strong empirical evidence suggesting that PRP positively affects labour productivity. Banker et al. (1996) find a positive relationship between outcome-based incentives and sales, customer satisfaction and profits. McNabb and Whitfield (2003) present positive relationships between PRP through employee share ownership schemes and PRP, on the one hand, and financial performance, on the other. The empirical findings of Appelbaum et al. (2000) suggest a positive relationship between pay for performance and employee trust and organizational commitment. Finally, Dowling and Richardson (1997) show a positive relationship between PRP and employee motivation.

PRP can be applied to individual employees; for example, linked to job performance, to teams or groups of employees (team-based PRP), and the organization as a whole, for example in terms of profit-sharing schemes and company bonuses. PRP or variable pay, however, has some serious limitations that need to be taken into account:

- If the outcomes of an employee or the employees in a team are not measurable it is impossible to apply PRP (*measurement*).

- If the employee or the team members have no influence on the outcomes, for example as a result of the nature of their job (e.g. staff function, administrative function), it is difficult to design a PRP (*influence*).
- The evaluation system needs to be transparent and fair towards those involved (*transparency and fairness*).
- Too much focus on PRP potentially endangers organizational goals other than financial outcomes, such as environmental pollution issues, corporate social responsibility and compliance issues (*too narrow focus on financial success*).
- The impact of PRP practices tends to be temporary and therefore continuous renewal of PRP systems is required (*continuous renewal of PRP systems*).

The 'dark side' of PRP is the potential negative impact on employee well-being in terms of employee dissatisfaction, increased job stress in relation to achieving goals and a poor work–life balance because of the work intensification caused by goal achievement (Legge, 2005). Several academics stress the importance of employee well-being in the HR debate (Guest, 1999; Purcell, 1999; Wright and Boswell, 2002; Peccei, 2004) and some even make a plea for 'building the worker into HRM' again when focusing on human resource management (HRM) and performance (Guest, 2002). The case study on p. 189 of this chapter illustrates another serious downside of PRP: the bonuses in investment banking representing the financial greed of investment bankers before the major financial and economic crisis that started in 2008. Top management rewards and bonuses are now critically reviewed since major corporations are running the risk of bankruptcy while having top managers still getting millions in bonuses and rewards (see the Introduction to this chapter).

'The "dark side" of PRP is the potential negative impact on employee well-being'

Next to fixed pay and variable pay, there is a third component of the total reward system for employees: employee benefits. These benefits might include health benefits with regard to health care insurances (medical plan), life insurances and dental insurances, contributions to pension schemes, unemployment payments and support, paid vacation, additional vacation days, family-friendly employment policies including (paid and unpaid) parental leave and child day-care compensation, support for the computer and the Internet connection at home, a laptop, a mobile phone and a lease car. *Employee benefits* represent indirect and non-cash compensation paid to an employee. Employee benefits are often considered an additional payment to fixed pay and variable pay.

In contrast to, in particular the USA, many continental European countries' employee benefits have been institutionalized and collectively arranged (so-called legally required benefits) through labour legislation and CBAs (Paauwe, 2004). There is, however, a tendency of deregulation that causes less collective arrangements with regard to employee benefits in European countries and more leeway for organizations to apply these practices at company level as a best practice in HRM (so-called optional employee benefits).

Jones (2005) summarizes the following benefits for employees in the private industry (see Table 9.1). In the USA in 2005 the average employer in private industry spent over $7 on employee benefits and about $17 on salaries (fixed and variable pay) for every hour an employee worked. This is an indication that employee benefits constitute a substantial amount of the total reward system offered to an employee. Full-time workers, trade union members and professionals (e.g. an engineer and an accountant) are more likely than others to have access to employee benefits. Employee benefits can be applied to attract and retain certain employees or employee groups.

Insurance	Paid leave and retirement	Career-related benefits	Health promotion	Family-friendly benefits
• medical (medical care; dental care; vision care) • life and other (life; short-term disability; long-term disability; long-term care)	• holidays • vacations • jury duty leave (specific for the US context and countries with a jury system) • funeral leave • sick leave • military leave (specific for countries with a military obligation for citizens) • personal leave • family leave	• education assistance • non-production bonus (this could also be part of the variable pay) • stock options (this could also be part of the variable pay) • subsidized commuting	• employee assistance programmes (for example related to addictions) • wellness programmes • fitness centres	• child care assistance • adoption assistance • flexible workplace • employer-provided personal computer

TABLE 9.1 An overview of possible employee benefits
Source: Reproduced with permission from Jones (2005).

The *cafeteria plan* represents a combination of fixed pay, variable pay and employee benefits and offers the individual employee the opportunity to choose the nature and type of rewards (Benders et al., 2006). The cafeteria plan is also known as 'cafeteria systems' or 'individualized pay systems'. Employees can make their own choices with regard to the reward system. Some employees might prefer additional vacation days, while others prefer good health insurance. The cafeteria plan creates opportunities for tailor-made practices for individual employees. The downside of this system is the risk of losing control of the arrangements for each individual and the risk of high personnel administration costs. A supporting information technology (IT) system is therefore required.

Theories on fairness, differentiation, behaviour and agents

In the next sections several theories are discussed that can help structure compensation debates: equity theory, tournament theory, expectancy theory and agency theory. When is payment fair? How can an organization differentiate pay among employees and managers? How do rewards affect employee behaviour? And how can we restore the balance between shareholder, top management and other relevant stakeholder interests within an organization through payment systems?

What is a fair payment? Notions from equity theory and i-deals

Equity theory proposes that people's attitudes and behaviour are affected by their assessment of their work contributions (inputs) and the rewards they receive (outputs) (Greenberg, 1998). The theory was first introduced by Adams (1965) and states that employees compare the ratios of their own perceived outcomes/inputs to the corresponding ratios of other people or groups. Social comparisons may include colleagues, industry standards, or oneself at an earlier time (ibid.). Perceptions are central in the theory. In fact, reality often significantly differs from individuals' perceptions. But it is the perception that drives individual employees to experience potential overpayment inequity when individuals get more than they deserve or experience potential underpayment inequity when they perceive a lower outcome/input ratio than another's. Equitable payment is the situation in which individual employees experience their own outcome/input ratio to match that of others. Equitable payment results in pay satisfaction and avoids negative emotions; for example, in the case of underpayment inequity. Underpayment inequity can lead to less employee motivation and a lack of willingness to put extra effort into the job (organizational citizenship behaviour). Equity theory can be linked to notions of perceived distributive justice, in particular with regard to HR practices that reflect compensation (Greenberg, 1990; Baron and Kreps, 1999). The theory stresses the importance of employee perceptions of their input and output in comparison to others.

Boselie et al. (2005) argue that, in the case of compensation, the focus in theory and practice tends to be on 'high wages', while employee perceptions of the fairness of wages and compensation are often ignored (Wright and Boswell, 2002). Notions on 'high wages' are important and relevant; however, equity theory also suggests the importance of 'fair wages', particularly linked to the perceptions of employees. Employees will ask themselves if the compensation package is fair in comparison to others with similar tasks and responsibilities, to others putting similar amounts of effort into their job, and to managers. The perceived distributive justice with regard to compensation mostly affects HR outcomes positively, such as employee motivation and citizenship behaviour (see also Chapter 8 on notions of procedural and distributive justice).

Fair pay for all employees can become a crucial part of corporate strategy and human resource (HR) strategy. The starting point for a fair pay system throughout the organization is openness and transparency. The HR department (see Chapter 12) plays an essential role in the design and implementation of a pay structure that is clear, understandable and transparent for all organizational members. A strategic justification for the pay system of all organizational members (including top management) is also required for a general fair pay system. The 'mystery' surrounding top management compensation (see the Introduction to this chapter) does not support a (perceived) fair pay system by employees. It is remarkable that in times of a financial and global crisis little is known about the processes with regard to top management rewards. How can you expect employees on the shopfloor to trust their leaders, become engaged in a new corporate strategy and 'follow the leaders' when the mystique about their payment potentially covers their true motives? Communication and information are crucial instruments for supporting a fair and commonly accepted pay system.

> 'The "mystery" surrounding top management compensation does not support a (perceived) fair pay system by employees.'

Another challenging aspect about fair payment is linked to notions made by Rousseau et al. (2006) on idiosyncratic terms in the employment relationship (i-deals). I-deals refer to unique terms in an employment relationship, often not written down on paper, between a direct supervisor and an employee. These idiosyncratic elements may include special allowances (e.g. covering additional travel expenses), special job design (e.g. flexible working hours) and extra bonuses for additional individual tasks. In practice almost every worker has some kind of idiosyncratic elements in the employment relationship. To some extent these i-deals are required to establish an optimal person–environment (P–E) fit (see Chapter 7 on this). A lack of structure and rules on pay, however, might result in an out of control i-deal system negatively affecting perceived justice among employees and potentially damaging employee trust levels. To overcome this issue there needs to be some kind of balance between rules and regulations on the one hand and some flexibility towards individuals on the other hand. The HR department again plays an important role here, implementing and maintaining structures, rules and procedures, while simultaneously facilitating and supporting line managers who are confronted with individual employee demands. The cafeteria plan presented earlier in this chapter can provide solutions for overcoming idiosyncratic dilemmas presented above. The cafeteria plan allows for individual differences with regard to pay with a central responsibility for individual employees themselves. There tends to be, however, a continuous tension between the strict HR policies and the actual HRM in practice, in particular with regard to employee payment.

Stop and reflect

Can you think of ways to apply the cafeteria plan to overcome idiosyncratic problems within organizations?

How do we differentiate payment between employees and managers?

Notions from tournament theory

How much do we need to pay our employees in comparison to the front-line, middle and top managers? Lazear (1995, 1998) introduces the tournament model or relative compensation theory in order to consider appropriate increases in salaries and promotions in organizations. The author uses the metaphor of a tennis match for explaining this model. A grand slam tournament has over 100 participants, but only one of them can win the tournament in the end. Would anybody participate in the tournament if there was only one prize to win (e.g. €1 million)? The risk of participating and getting nothing is probably too high for most players. Only self-confident top players and opportunistic low-ranked tennis players are likely to participate in this event. Therefore, the tennis tournament is designed in such a way that money is given to the players every round. Lazear (1998: 225–26) summarizes key features of a tennis match that are relevant for thinking about the corporate hierarchical compensation structure:

1. Prizes are fixed in advance and are independent of absolute performance. The winner gets a fixed prize that is higher than the prize of the loser. In an organization promotion leads to better compensation.
2. A player receives the winner's prize not by being good, but by being better than the other player. This refers to the notion of relative performance or the individual performance in comparison to others. In a normal organization workers are not promoted because they are good, but because they are better than the others at their current level.
3. The level of effort with which employees pursue the promotion depends on the size of the potential increase in their wages. The difference between the compensation for the winner and the compensation for the loser increases the efforts participants are willing to invest in the game. If the compensation were equal, the theory suggests that neither player is likely to be motivated to put maximum effort into it. In an organization the best employee not only gets promotion to a higher position, but a higher salary as well. Promotion and substantial salary differences are likely to increase employees' efforts in job performance.
4. There is a limit to spread in the model. People are not likely to participate in a winner-takes-all tournament because of the high risks of ending with nothing.

Tournament theory helps us to understand hierarchical pay structures in organizations (see Figure 9.1). The model explains why managers get paid more than employees and how it is linked to efforts individuals are willing to put into their job.

The tournament approach presented here is related to notions on fair pay. Would employees be willing to work for supervisors who earns ten times more than them? Perhaps not, because the employees might perceive the deal unfair since they would get to do all the work, while the manager gets away with a salary ten times more than theirs. How many employees would be willing to get promoted to a managerial level if the salary of the manager is similar to the salary at shopfloor level? Perhaps not many employees would be willing to take this promotion, because it does involve more responsibilities and more work, while at the same time offering little additional reward. The latter situation we can find in many health care organizations where there is only limited leeway for additional salary in the case of an internal promotion. Many nurses, for example, are therefore not likely to take a managerial position.

It is a strategic challenge for organizations to design an ideal pay system for the organization that looks like the tournament model presented above. A lot of organizations in practice, however, have a pay system installed that does not meet the requirements of the (ideal) tournament. Top management's pay might be over the top, for example a hospital director earning €400 000 per year, as a result of past negotiations at a time when top management compensation was not an issue. Organizations can also be limited by their financial resources. The yearly CBAs might have increased the total labour costs of employees at the lowest levels of the organization over the last decade, limiting the leeway for pay increases in the case of internal promotion. This appears to be the case in many public sector organizations where salaries have increased while governmental financial support has not increased or in some cases diminished. These limitations have to be taken into account when discussing corporate and HR strategies about ideal pay systems in an organization. A rigorous context analysis (see Chapter 2) is required for gaining a full understanding of the unique characteristics of an organization and its historical background.

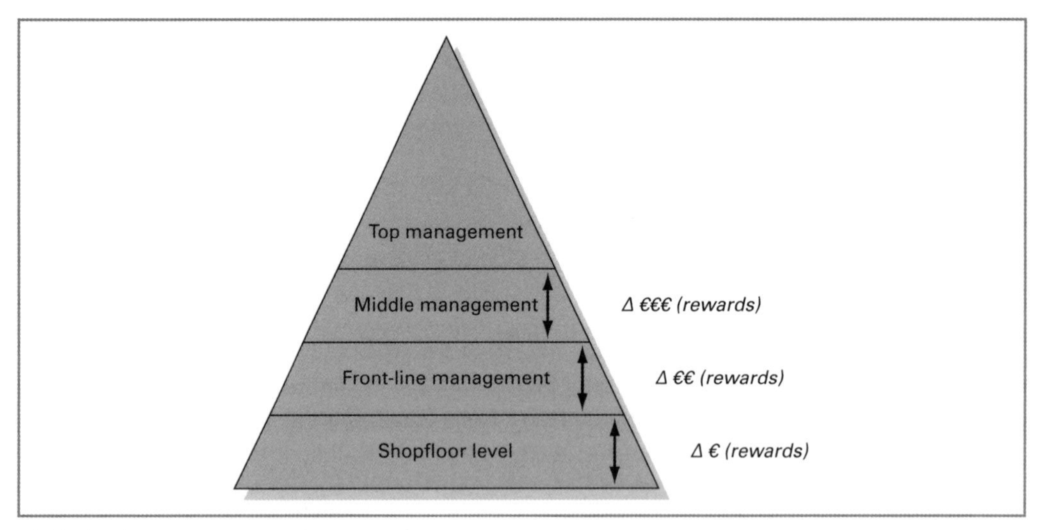

FIGURE 9.1 Tournament theory and compensation

How do rewards affect employee behaviour?

Notions from expectancy theory

Expectancy theory has its roots in psychology and focuses on the links between rewards and employee behaviours. Vroom (1964) is generally considered to be the founding father of this

! *Stop and reflect*

Think of a situation in which employees at shopfloor level are paid the same as their front-line managers. What is the potential impact of this pay system on (a) employee efforts in their jobs and (b) promotion incentives?

- Discuss the potential effects of a pay difference between the average employee (e.g. €40 000 on a yearly basis) and the CEO (e.g. €4 000 000 on a yearly basis, options and shares excluded) of an organization.
- Discuss a reasonable pay increase should an employee get promoted to front-line manager.

framework, which focuses on employee expectations with regard to their efforts, job performance and the rewards that they will receive for their efforts and performance. Expectancy perceptions represent the perceived link between effort and performance (Noe et al., 2008). The theory suggests that there is a higher level of employee motivation in cases when increased reward is given for performance. The following aspects are important for an optimal PRP scheme using expectancy theory:

- There should be a clear relationship between employee effort and employee outcomes (job performance).
- There should be a clear relationship between employee outcomes (job performance) and rewards.
- The rewards for certain employee outcomes (job performance) should matter to the actor or employee. In other words, the rewards are significant and relevant to the employee.
- The system as a whole needs to be fair towards an individual employee and towards the total workforce of an organization.

The three key concepts in expectancy theory are:

1. expectancy representing the individual employee belief 'that a particular degree of effort will be followed by a particular level of performance' (Kreitner et al., 2002: 212);
2. instrumentality representing the perceived link between employee behaviour and pay;
3. valence representing 'the positive or negative value people place on outcomes' (ibid.).

The model is actually quite clear and plausible. Reality, however, is much more complicated. In many cases there is no clear relationship between employee effort and employee outcomes. What motivates and drives employees cannot always be clearly linked to (desirable) job performance. Chapter 5 highlights the possible differences between what employers want and what employees want.

Many employers are naïve with regard to incentives and employee behaviour, believing employees generally strive for organizational success, personal financial gains and internal promotion, while in reality many employees want fun at work, a good social atmosphere and a good work–life balance (see Chapter 5). Often 'what matters to the company' (e.g. increased profits and high productivity standards) does not really matter to the employee, who is more likely to search for employment security, health and safety (working conditions) and a fair amount of pay.

Stop and reflect

Discuss expectancy theory with regard to the design of a pay for performance system for the following jobs:

- a police officer;
- a firefighter;
- a nurse in a general hospital;
- a soldier on a peace-keeping mission.

How can we restore the balance between shareholder interests, the interests of top management and other relevant stakeholders?

Notions from agency theory

When the owner of an organization (principal) hires managers (agents), agency theory (Jensen and Meckling, 1976) suggests the emergence of principal–agent problems or agency dilemmas as a result of incomplete and asymmetric information. In essence, agency theory focuses on the relationship between principals and agents and the costs related to optimally managing this relationship (agency costs). These agency costs can be defined as the sum of the principal's monitoring expenditures, the agent's bonding expenditures and the residual loss (ibid.). Various mechanisms, including compensation systems (e.g. bonuses, PRP of top managers and stock option sharing schemes) may be used to try to align the interests of the principals (e.g. market value of the firm, profits and long-term success) and the agents (e.g. reinvestment of profits in innovation and market expansion). Without these mechanisms the top managers' (agents) behaviour may fundamentally differ from the principals' interests.

The financial crisis of 2008/2009 and recent large-scale corporate scandals (e.g. Enron, Ahold and Parmalat) put agency theory back in the spotlight, in particular with regard to the PRP of top managers (agents) and firm performance. The basic idea that financial PRP serves the interests of both the agents (who will earn more money when the company is doing better) and the principals (who will receive more yearly profits and benefit from the increased market value of the firm) has failed in practice, causing banks worldwide to collapse (e.g. Lehmann Brothers) and companies to go bankrupt (e.g. Enron).

Agency theory can be extended by including not only owners (the traditional principals) and top managers (the traditional agents), but other relevant actors such as the government, society and employees as well. Society and the government can be seen as an extension of the principal agent perspective, while the employees of an organization can be seen as agents together with the managers of the organization. The main question in the contemporary principal–agent approach remains the same: What kind of mechanisms and practices (e.g. incentive systems) can be installed that serve the interests of both the principals and the agents of an organization?

There is a general need for more extensive supervision of corporate strategic decision making. The introduction of new legislation, for example the 2002 Sarbanes–Oxley Act, to control and monitor corporate actions is a reaction to a number of major corporate and accounting scandals highly affecting not only strategic decision making, but also people management as well; for example, through new internal compliance procedures. Another alternative is the explicit involvement of multiple stakeholders in the strategic decision-making process and in the supervision of the company. The German chemical giant BASF, for example, applies a model in which employee representatives (through the works councils) participate in the supervision of the company's strategies and policies (see Chapter 12 for a more detailed description). The multiple stakeholder approach applied in this book suggests the involvement of employees, trade unions, works councils, customers and government in the supervision of companies, in particular with regard to top management compensation.

Stop and reflect

Discuss the application of agency theory and incentive systems for medical specialists in a hospital. First, define the agents and the principals. Second, think of incentive systems that serve the interests of both the agents and the principals. Finally, summarize the advantages and disadvantages of applying an agency approach to medical specialists in hospitals.

One of the serious threats resulting from top management PRP is decoupling (Tosi and Gomez-Mejia, 1989). Decoupling can be defined as the top management's inclination to link their pay to performance outcomes that they can directly influence (e.g. market growth through mergers and acquisitions) and cut out pay related to performance systems that are more difficult to affect (e.g. profits). Decoupling is often not in the interest of the owners of the organization (principals) and therefore potentially damages the relationship between the principals and the agents. Tosi and Gomez-Mejia find empirical support that decoupling is more likely to occur in management-controlled firms than in owner-controlled firms.

In summary, these four theories on pay and compensation – equity theory, expectancy theory, tournament theory and agency theory – can help us in the debates on the design of an optimal reward system; for example, with regard to basic principles of PRP, pay differences between hierarchical levels, top management payment and fair payment. These principles can be applied in the strategic decision making of an organization, taking into account the very specific contextual factors of that organization (see Chapter 2) and the need for the right balance between what employers want and what employees want as described in Chapter 5.

The strategic relevance of compensation

Compensation, in particular PRP and bonuses, gets a lot of (negative) attention in both theory and practice (e.g. in the media with regard to top management rewards). Compensation was and shall always be relevant for both the employer and the employee. It is part of the transaction and the labour contract between the two parties in the shaping of the employment relationship. The recent corporate scandals and the financial crisis, however, have shown the serious downside of compensation. And it could therefore even be argued that the strategic relevance of compensation is to avoid or minimize PRP and bonuses as much as possible.

The absurd bonuses in the financial sector have seriously damaged the reputation of financial institutions. This might have had very negative effects on the feelings and attitudes (e.g. trust) of customers (citizens) and employees. Integrity and trust are two essential components in the financial sector. If these elements are undermined by wrong or false compensation systems, this potentially damages the reputation of an organization, leads to low employee motivation, causes higher risks of employee misbehaviour linked to the notion that leaders are examples for the workforce, and has negative effects on customers.

summary

- Compensation in organizations can contribute to employee attraction, retention and motivation.
- The aims of contemporary compensation systems are to influence employee attitudes and behaviour, control labour costs and create a strong employment brand.
- There are basically two types of compensation: financial (e.g. wages) and non-financial (e.g. social events).
- There are generally four different bases for pay: pay based on a set of tasks, on skills and knowledge, on seniority, and on status and reputation.
- Employee contracts can be permanent (indefinite) or temporary.
- Employee contracts can be full time and part time.
- There are four forms of pay: fixed pay, variable pay, employee benefits and cafeteria plans.
- In many continental European countries, the fixed pay of employees is determined by CBAs, including elements of employee benefits such as pension schemes, collective medical insurance, employment security and disability insurance.
- Variable pay or PRP has gained popularity in the last two decades.
- PRP has serious limitations linked to the employee outcome measurement, the employee influence on outcomes, the transparency and fairness of the system, the narrow focus on financial success and the need for continuous renewal of the incentive structures for optimal employee motivation.
- Deregulation in many continental European countries causes less collective arrangements for employees and more leeway for employee benefits as best practices at the organizational level.
- Best practices in employee benefits may include insurances, paid leave and retirement, career-related benefits, health promotion and family-friendly benefits.
- Equity theory focuses on people's attitudes and behaviours affected by their assessment of their work contributions (inputs) and the rewards they receive (outputs). The concepts of social comparison, employee perception and justice are relevant building blocks for this theoretical framework.
- Tournament theory examines pay rises and promotions in organizations. The theory helps us to understand hierarchical pay structures in organizations.
- Expectancy theory focuses on employee expectations with regard to their efforts, their job performance and the rewards that they will receive for their efforts and performance.
- Agency theory examines the relationship between principals (owners) and agents (managers), and the costs related to optimally managing this relationship with potentially different interests, incomplete information and asymmetric information.

Glossary of key terms

Agents are the managers of the organization responsible for strategic decision making.
Employee benefits represent indirect and non-cash compensation paid to an employee.
Fixed pay or base pay is the reward system based on the number of (fixed) working hours per week or per month.
Full-time contract is a contract between the employer and the employee for five days a week or 1.0 full-time equivalent (FTEs).
Part-time contract is a contract between the employer and the employee for less than five days a week or 1.0 full-time equivalent (FTEs).
Permanent contract is a deal for an indefinite time between the employer and the employee.
Principals are the owners of the organization.
Temporary contract is a deal for a fixed time between the employer and the employee.
Variable pay or PRP is the reward system based on the employee outcomes or job performance (e.g. productivity or service quality).

Personal development

This chapter focuses on different types of compensation, in particular (1) fixed pay or base pay, (2) variable pay or PRP, and (3) employee benefits (e.g. medical insurance and sick leave). Tsui et al. (1997) make a distinction between an HR system of underinvestment and an HR system of overinvestment that can also be applied specifically to compensation. Both systems present an imbalanced situation, with potential negative effects on individual employee and on the organization. An underinvestment compensation system represents a situation in which an individual employee or a group of employees gets underpaid. An overinvestment compensation system represents a situation in which an individual employee or a group of employees gets overpaid.

- Can you think of a real-life situation that presents an underinvestment compensation system?
- Can you think of a real-life situation that presents an overinvestment compensation system?
- What are the potential negative effects of an underinvestment compensation system on an individual employee and on the organization?
- What are the potential negative effects of an overinvestment compensation system on an individual employee and on the organization?
- Can you think of ways to overcome both imbalance situations?

Team task

Discuss your personal preferences with regard to the amount of fixed pay and variable pay in your current job or in a potential future job. In other words, would you be willing to get paid on the basis of your job performance (variable pay)? And what are the conditions for PRP?

Find out more about jobs where variable pay is quite common. What are the reasons for the application of variable pay in these jobs? What are the advantages and disadvantages of pay for performance in these jobs?

Learning checklist

After studying this chapter, you should be able to do the following:

- Understand the different aims of compensation.
- Discuss top management compensation.
- Review financial and non-financial compensation.
- Identify the different forms of pay (fixed pay, variable pay, employee benefits and cafeteria plans).
- Discuss the increasing popularity of employee benefits in Europe.
- Evaluate the pros and cons of PRP.
- Outline equity, tournament, expectancy and agency theory in relationship to compensation.

References

Adams, J.S. (1965) Inequity in social exchange, in L. Berkowitz (ed), *Advances in Experimental Social Psychology,* Volume 2, pp. 267–99. New York: Academic Press.

Appelbaum, E., Bailey, T., Berg, P. and Kalleberg, A.L. (2000) *Manufacturing Advantage: Why High-performance Work Systems Pay Off.* Ithaca, NY: Cornell University Press.

Arthur, J.B. (1994) Effects of human resource systems on manufactoring performance and turnover, *Academy of Management Journal*, 37(3): 670–87.

Banker, R.D., Lee, S.-Y., Potter, G. and Srinivasan (1996) Contextual analysis of performance impacts of outcome-based incentive compensation, *Academy of Management Journal*, 39(4): 920–48.

Baron, J. and Kreps, D. (1999) *Human Resource Management: A Framework for General Managers.* New York: Wiley.

Barr, S.H. (1998) Reward systems, in C.L. Cooper and C. Argyris (eds), *The Concise Blackwell Encyclopedia of Management*, p. 570. Oxford: Blackwell.

Barth, E., Bratsberg, B., Haegeland, T. and Raaum, O. (2008) Who pays for performance?, *International Journal of Manpower*, 29(1): 8–29.

Benders, J., Delsen, L. and Smits, J. (2006) Bikes versus lease cars: the adoption, design and use of cafeteria systems in the Netherlands, *International Journal of Human Resource Management*, 17(6): 1115–28.

Boselie, P., Dietz, G. and Boon, C. (2005) Commonalities and contradictions in HRM and performance research, *Human Resource Management Journal*, 15(3): 67–94.

Brannick, M.T. and Levine, E.L. (1998) Job description, in C.L. Cooper and C. Argyris (eds), *The Concise Blackwell Encyclopedia of Management*, p. 337. Oxford: Blackwell.

Delaney, J.T. and Huselid, M.A. (1996) The impact of human resource management practices on perceptions of organizational performance, *Academy of Management Journal*, 39(4): 949–69.

Dowling, B. and Richardson, R. (1997) Evaluating performance related pay for managers in the National Health Service, *International Journal of Human Resource Management*, 8(1): 348–66.

Green, F. (2001) It's been a hard day's night: the concentration and intensification of work in late twentieth-century Britain, *British Journal of Industrial Relations*, 39(1): 53–80.

Greenberg, J. (1990) Organizational justice: yesterday, today and tomorrow, *Journal of Management*, 16(2): 399–432.

Greenberg, J. (1998) Equity theory, in C.L. Cooper and C. Argyris (eds), *The Concise Blackwell Encyclopedia of Management*, pp. 201–2. Oxford: Blackwell.

Guest, D.E. (1999) Human resource management: the workers' verdict, *Human Resource Management Journal*, 9(3): 5–25.

Guest, D.E. (2002) Human resource management, corporate performance and employee well-being: building the worker into HRM, *Journal of Industrial Relations*, 44(3): 335–58.

Jensen, M. and Meckling, W. (1976) Theory of the firm: managerial behaviour, agency costs, and ownership structure, *Journal of Financial Economics*, 3: 306–60.

Jones, E. (2005) An overview of employee benefits, *Occupational Outlook Quarterly*, 202: 691–719.

Kalleberg, A.L. and Moody, J.W. (1994) Human resource management and organizational performance, *American Behavioral Scientist*, 37(7): 948–62.

Koene, B.A.S. and Van Riemsdijk, M. (2005) Managing temporary workers: work identity, diversity and operational HR choices, *Human Resource Management Journal*, 15(1): 76–92.

Kreitner, R., Kinicki, A. and Buelens, M. (2002) *Organizational Behavior*, 2nd European edn. London: McGraw-Hill.

Lazear, E.P. (1995) *Personnel Economics*. Cambridge, MA: MIT Press.

Lazear, E.P. (1996) Performance pay and productivity. NBER working paper.

Lazear, E.P. (1998) *Personnel Economics for Managers*. New York: Wiley.

Legge, K. (2005) *Human Resource Management: Rhetorics and Realities*. Basingstoke: Palgrave Macmillan.

McNabb, R. and Whitfield, K. (2003) Varying types of performance related pay and productivity. Working paper, Cardiff Business School, Cardiff.

Marsden, D. and French, S. (1998) *What a Performance: Performance Related Pay in the Public Services*. London: Centre for Economic Performance.

Milkovich, G.T. and Newman, J.M. (1996) *Compensation*, 5th edn. Homewood, IL: Richard D. Irwin.

Noe, R.A., Hollenbeck, J.R., Gerhart, B. and Wright, P.M. (2008) *Human Resource Management: Gaining a Competitive Advantage*. Boston, MA: McGraw-Hill.

Paauwe, J. (2004) *HRM and Performance: Achieving Long-term Viability*. Oxford: Oxford University Press.

Peccei, R. (2004) Human resource management and the search for the happy work place. Inaugural lecture, Erasmus Institute of Management (ERIM), Nota, Rotterdam.

Pfeffer, J. (1994) *Competitive Advantage through People*. Boston, MA: Harvard Business School Press.

Purcell, J. (1999) Best practice and best fit: chimera or cul-de-sac?, *Human Resource Management Journal*, 9(3): 26–41.

Rousseau, D.M., Ho, V.T. and Greenberg, J. (2006) I-deals: idiosyncratic terms in employment relationships, *Academy of Management Review*, 31(4): 977–94.

Schilstra, K. and Smit, E. (2005) *Voeten op de Vloer: Strategische Keuzes in Belangenbehartiging van Werknemers [Feet on the Floor: Strategic Choices in Employee Participation]*. Amsterdam: Aksant.

Smit, J. (2008) *De Prooi: Blinde trots breekt ABN AMRO*. Amsterdam: Prometheus.

Tosi, H.L. and Gomez-Mejia, L.R. (1989) The decoupling of CEO pay and performance: an agency theory perspective, *Administrative Science Quarterly*, 34: 169–89.

Tsui, A.S., Pearce, J.L., Porter, L.W. and Tripoli, A.M. (1997) Alternative approaches to the employee–organization relationship: does investment in employees pay off?, *Academy of Management Journal*, 40(5): 1089–121.

Vroom, V.H. (1964) *Work and Motivation*. New York: Wiley.

Walton, R.E. (1985) From control to commitment in the workplace, *Harvard Business Review*, March–April: 77–84.

Wright, P.M. and Boswell, W.R (2002) Desegregating HRM: a review and synthesis of micro and macro human resource management research, *Journal of Management*, 28(3): 247–76.

Further reading

Eisenhardt, K.M. (1989) Agency theory: an assessment and review, *Academy of Management Review*, 14(1): 57–74.

Gerhart, B. and Rynes, S.L. (2003) *Compensation: Theory, Evidence, and Strategic Implications*. Thousand Oaks, CA: Sage.

Guthrie, J.P. (2007) Remuneration: pay effects at work, in P. Boxall, J. Purcell and P.M. Wright (eds), *The Oxford Handbook of Human Resource Management*, Chapter 17, pp. 344–63. Oxford: Oxford University Press.

Lazear, E.P. (1998) *Personnel Economics for Managers*. New York: Wiley.

Rousseau, D.M. and Schalk, R. (eds) (2000) *Psychological Contracts in Employment: Cross-national Perspectives*. Thousand Oaks, CA: Sage.

Rynes, S.L. and Gerhart, B. (eds) (2000) *Compensation in Organizations*. San Francisco, CA: Jossey-Bass.

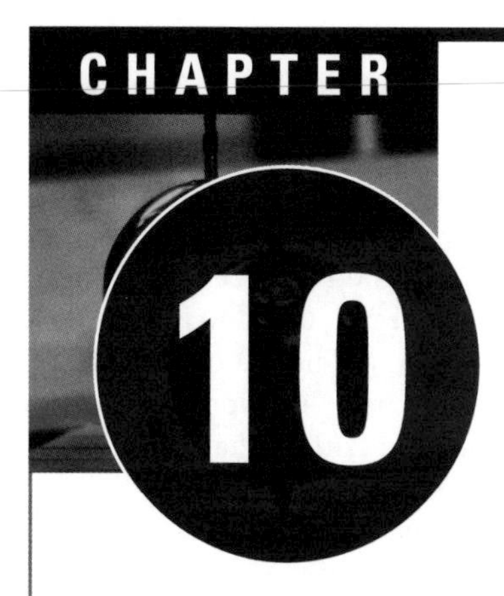

CHAPTER 10 Development

LEARNING OBJECTIVES

After studying this chapter, you should be able to do the following:

- Understand the concepts of education, training and development
- Outline notions on the employability concept
- Understand the line manager or direct supervisor as 'the subject' and 'the framer' of employee development
- Recognize the institutionalization of employee development
- Review human resource development (HRD)
- Discuss management development (MD)
- Review leadership development (LD)
- Review the concept of the learning organization
- Outline knowledge management and competence management
- Consider eLearning
- Discuss the downside of the development of the 'happy few'

CASE STUDY: IKEA

The Swedish furniture company IKEA is a leading organization in global retail, with stores in Asia, Australia, Europe, North America and the Middle East (more than 235 stores all over the world). The firm's aim is to provide functional, well-designed furniture at prices so low that as many people as possible will be able to afford them: 'to create a better everyday life for the many.' The company was founded by Ingvar Kamprad in southern Sweden in the late 1940s. He built an empire on basic principles of working hard, living frugally and making the most out of limited resources. These principles were characteristic for the region Ingvar came from. Cost-cutting in combination with maintaining high-quality standards for his products made the firm what it is today. IKEA employs more than 110 000 people worldwide, in more than 30 countries. The backbone of IKEA's business model is combining low price with good design and function. The price–quality ratio of IKEA products is generally considered to be high.

IKEA stores have always fascinated me because of the smart design of the interiors. First, customers are guided through the store on a carefully designed route that leads to individual rooms with complete kitchens and bedrooms, but all other kinds of goods can be found along the way as well. I always end up with stuff in my IKEA bag that I did not intend to buy when I entered the store; however, I give all due credit to IKEA for this. Second, most products can be collected in the warehouse when you have finished shopping. This is a very efficient method of product storage and it enables customers to walk around the store without having to carry shopping around with them.

IKEA has a strong people management system grounded on the organization's corporate culture and based on shared values. Culture management and human resource management (HRM) appear to be one and the same within the organization. The shared values include, for example, togetherness, cost-consciousness, respect, simplicity and humbleness. How many organizations promote 'humbleness' as an explicit value for employees? It all fits the IKEA way of doing business. IKEA is not famous for its high wages; however, employee involvement and employee development are applied widely and intensively. Training and development of employees within IKEA can be seen as the fuel for the organization's culture management. IKEA has an excellent training and development infrastructure, but perhaps even more important is the fact that IKEA workers are used to continuous and regular training and development.

Training and development within IKEA can be on the job (gaining shopping experience), through eLearning using games and regular training sessions. IKEA was one of the first companies to apply a continuous development approach by putting every manager on the shopfloor to experience customer service for at least one day per year.

? Discussion questions

As IKEA operates in different countries, it is confronted with different national cultures that potentially affect people management. Find out more about IKEA on the Internet. Discuss the relevance (or irrelevance) of IKEA's global corporate culture management (including shared values). What role can the corporate and local HRM departments play in the shaping of a global culture management? And what is the role of line managers in the training and development of subordinates with regard to managing the global corporate culture?

Introduction

Employee training and development is an essential part of people management in organizations. Education provides the basics and is often represented by certificates, diplomas and titles that reflect the person's capabilities. Bloisi (2007: 218) defines education as 'the behavioural process of learning that applies to the whole person rather than specific skills'. Employee development, however, is much more than formal education in school, college, university and other institutes. Learning on the job through, for example, knowledge sharing with colleagues and coaching by managers is an important aspect of employee development as well.

There is a growing awareness of the relevance and importance of the line manager in the shaping of HRM, including employee development (see Chapter 3 on actual HR practices and the role of line managers as HR enactors). In fact, managers are both (a) *subjects of employee development* (e.g. with regard to MD and LD) and (b) *framers of employee development* (e.g. with regard to talent management and employee coaching). This duality – subject and framer – is the guideline for this chapter on employee development. The role of the manager in relation to employees in employee development and the development of the manager are considered of strategic importance for the overall success of employee development in an organization. Therefore, employee development in this chapter is studied through the lense of the manager.

> 'managers are both (a) subjects of employee development and (b) framers of employee development'

The chapter starts with an overview of basic concepts, including those related to training, employability, development, knowledge, skills and abilities. Next, three relevant and important types of development are discussed: HRD, MD and LD. The line manager duality of manager as subject of development and manager as framer of development is linked to these three development approaches commonly used in organizations. Finally, general strategic learning and development themes are highlighted, including the learning organization, knowledge management, competence management, eLearning and a critical reflection on the development of the 'happy few'.

Training

Winterton (2007: 328) argues that 'the objective of **training** is to ensure that all employees have and maintain the requisite competences to perform in their roles at work.' Bloisi (2007: 218) defines training as 'the process of change used to develop specific skills, usually for a job'. The education of workers is mainly shaped by governmental institutions (schools, colleges and universities). Continuing training is the concern of the employer and the employee (Winterton, 2007).

Training usually has specific ends or learning outcomes, for example in terms of the understanding and use of new concepts. More concretely, training goals include knowledge, skills and abilities required to do the job, for example:

- training employees in negotiation and communication;
- training employees in the latest insights/knowledge within a certain profession such as medical specialists, accountants and lawyers;
- training employees to become assertive towards suppliers.

> 'HRM and training in particular can be characterized by long-term effects.'

The notion of reversed causality in the HRM and performance debate was discussed in Chapter 2. Reversed causality in HRM is in particular relevant for training. When organizations make a lot of profit, there is generally a greater willingness to invest in people. In other words, organizations that make more money spend relatively more money on employee training. In contrast, when organizations are confronted with serious losses and crisis, in most cases the training budgets are frozen.

An explanation for the upward effect (more willingness to invest in employees in times of prosperity) and downward effect (less willingness to invest in employees in times of major losses) can be found in the short-term costs and benefits orientation of many organizations. HRM and training in particular can be characterized by long-term effects.

Employability

Less than two decades ago, most European workers enjoyed excellent employment security and lifetime employment within one organization. Nowadays, employees with more than 25 years of service within one organization have become rare. The next generation of employees is often told to change jobs every four or five years in order to build a healthy career. Lifetime employment has been replaced by lifelong career, with major implications for the development of an individual. The concept of **employability** is focused on this shift and has become popular in career management. The employee development of the individual is no longer considered to be the single responsibility of the employer. According to the notions on employability, the employee is equally responsible for personal development (PD), necessary for a new form of employment security. Only those employees that are employable (e.g. flexible, capable, able, up to date and skilful) will have good career opportunities and employment security.

> 'The next generation of employees is often told to change jobs every four or five years in order to build a healthy career.'

Employability is a joint effort and interest of the employer and the employee in the continuous development of an individual that will enable an optimal use of the individual employee's qualities and capabilities (Van Der Heijden, 2002). The line manager or direct supervisor of an employee represents the employer's interests and can support individual employees in creating the joint responsibility for employability. The individual employee on the other hand can claim supervisor's support (e.g. training budget and coaching) for PD in line with increasing employability levels. Another feature of employability is the idea that employable employees who get fired (e.g. because of a necessary downsizing exercise) will find a new job much more easily than employees who are not employable because there was little or no training investment. The recent financial and global crisis of 2008/2009 shows the relevance of 'employable' workers, in particular for those organizations that have been reorganized (e.g. downsizing the workforce by 10–15 per cent) and shut down. Workers in those situations are more likely to lose their jobs and for them employability is considered highly relevant in finding new jobs elsewhere.

> 'Employability is a joint effort and interest of the employer and the employee in the continuous development of an individual'

Stop and reflect

- Can you think of the benefits of employee development for the employer?
- Can you think of the benefits of employee development for the individual employee?
- Can you think of reasons why trade unions in continental European contexts are in favour of employability?

Institutionalized employee development

Collective HR investments in workers through, for example, collective bargaining agreements (CBAs) occur in some European countries such as Germany and the Netherlands (Paauwe, 1998). In those situations employers' associations and trade unions agree on a certain percentage of the total labour costs of an organization that is compulsory for all organizations under this CBA to be spent on employee training and development. This could be, for example, a minimum of 4 per cent of the total yearly labour costs that organizations are required to invest in their employees in a given year. At a branch of industry level this type of construction has a number of positive effects on organizations and workers:

- employees are guaranteed a yearly training and development budget for PD (e.g. 4 per cent of total labour costs);
- in general, trained employees are more valuable for organizations;
- the collective system takes away potential prisoner dilemmas for individual organizations. All organizations in the sector have to invest in their people, reducing the chance that some employers do not invest in their people while still hoping to benefit from employees trained elsewhere.

The latter issue on the lack of a good collective system for training and development caused serious issues in the UK in the 1990s. Employers were not willing and able to invest in employees because they were afraid that well-trained personnel would leave their organizations after finishing their training programmes. The answer to this lack of faith in HR investment at organization level was the British government's initiative labelled 'Investors In People' (Ram, 2000). **Investors In People (IIP)** represents a standard for training and development of employees in an organization. IIP is comparable to total quality management (TQM) standards on service and product quality; however, IIP is purely focused on HR investment and the application of good employee development practices. Organizations that meet the standard receive an IIP accreditation (Hoque, 2003). It is thought that this accreditation has a positive effect on current employees, potential employees (being part of employment branding), suppliers and customers. Hoque's analysis of WERS 1998 data, including IIP information, shows mixed results. On average, training practice is better in accredited workplaces than in non-accredited workplaces. A large number of accredited workplaces, however, are failing to engage in good practice. In other words, even though these workplaces have an IIP accreditation, this is no guarantee that the training practices are good. IIP has been applied to organizations outside the UK, for example in the Netherlands (Gaspersz and Van Den Hove, 2000).

Stop and reflect

- Discuss the advantages and disadvantages of an IIP system for the UK and for your own country.
- Can you think of benefits which may result from introducing IIP in the Netherlands?

Education, training and employee development are often heavily affected by institutionalization or institutional mechanisms (DiMaggio and Powell, 1983), as discussed in Chapter 2. Normative mechanisms represent institutional mechanisms that affect the shaping of organizations through professional norms and professional networks (Paauwe and Boselie, 2003). Medical specialists are educated and trained in an institutionalized setting. The formal education entitles an individual to practise the medical profession. The professional norms of the medical profession are protected by the medical association and often specialists are required to update their knowledge and skills to maintain their 'licence' to practise their occupation. Similar principles are in place for professionals such as lawyers, accountants, pilots, nurses, police officers, firefighters and civil servants. Education, training and employee development for these professionals are highly institutionalized and often standardized to meet the general requirements of the profession's norms.

Development

This brings us to notions on employee **development**. Winterton (2007) states that a major difference between training and development is that development covers a wider range of activities with less specific goals or outcomes than training. The author argues that development is focused more on the individual than the occupation 'and is concerned with longer-term personal growth and career movement' (p. 331). Spending an academic sabbatical outside one's own university (e.g. abroad) is a nice example of employee development of scholars that potentially contributes to a long-term career in academia. The direct supervisor plays an essential role in the development of an employee, in particular with regard to:

- stimulating employee development initiatives (*motivation*);
- facilitating development through financial resources (budget) and time available for attending programmes (*facilities* and *resources*);
- knowledge and experience sharing (*knowledge* and *experience*);
- supporting the candidate during the development programme through regular feedback sessions, communication and progress monitoring (*coaching*).

Knowledge, skills and abilities

In Chapter 7, 'Selective recruitment and selection', a distinction was made between: (1) skills, (2) knowledge, and (3) abilities (or competences). This trilogy can also be applied to training and development of employees. Skills may include administration using specific computer programs, advising people, analysing data, interpreting languages, teaching and instructing others, presenting findings and new policies, and chairing meetings. Knowledge is the theoretical or practical understanding of a subject. Knowledge may include firm-specific understanding of systems, procedures and operations, but may also include a general understanding of the business and society. Ability is also known as 'capability' or 'capacity'. Abilities represent the individual employee's capacity to perform certain tasks in the future. Employee abilities or competences reflect the individual's potential contribution.

Human resource development (HRD)

The long-term learning and employee development notions are emphasized in what is known as HRD (Poell et al., 2004; Swart et al., 2005). HRD represents a discipline focused on individual and group learning in the context of work. HRD places less attention on training, but rather focuses on different types of learning, including learning on the job. Yorks (2005) summarizes some key commonalities of HRD:

- Learning is central to the notion of HRD.
- Learning manifests on multiple levels of the organization, including the individual employee level, team or group level, and organization level.
- Learning is intended to improve the learner's job performance.
- Learning serves the individual's long-term career.
- Learning can be intended and unintended.

According to Yorks, much learning and development takes place outside of the classroom:

> 'HRD practitioners organize problem- and issue-focused conferences among executives to identify various best practices; they explore in detail how these practices work in different business settings, creating communities-of-practice for the purpose of sharing experiences and learning among professionals who work in similar functions yet are often isolated from each other'.
>
> (2005: 9)

Nurses represent a group of professionals that benefit from HRD insights since learning on the job is essential for this profession (Berings et al., 2008). Sharing experiences and learning by doing helps these professionals to improve their skills, knowledge and abilities. Van Woerkom and Croon (2009) show the results of teamwork and team learning representing collective learning in workplaces. Yorks argues that

> 'the fundamental purpose of HRD is to contribute to both long-term strategic performance and more immediate performance improvement through ensuring that organizational members have access to resources for developing their capacity for performance and for making meaning of their experience in the context of the organization's strategic needs and the requirements of their jobs.'
>
> (2005: 20–21)

HRD often takes the individual employee as the starting point in theory and practice. In contrast, MD and LD generally take the employer's perspective as the starting point.

In HRD the direct supervisor is mainly 'the framer' of employee development (not so much 'the subject' of employee development), in particular with regard to shaping a learning context on the shopfloor in which employees can interact and learn from each other.

Stop and reflect

Can you think of the advantages of on-the-job learning of nurses in hospitals?

Management development (MD)

In contrast to HRD, **MD** is mainly focused on line managers or supervisors (Van Der Sluis-den Dikken and Hoeksema, 2001). The MD approaches mainly consider line managers or supervisors as 'the subjects' of development. In other words, managers are those who are educated, trained and/or developed. It is very important to note that at least part of the MD success is supposed to be reflected in line managers as successful 'framers' of employee development in relation to their subordinates.

The managers in MD programmes are usually first-line (or front-line) and middle managers. Jansen et al. (2001: 106) define MD as 'the system of personnel practices intended to ensure that an organization can rely on timely availability of qualified and motivated employees.' There has been a growing organizational awareness of the importance of good managers. Weick (1979) introduced the concept of enactment. Enactment is used to describe the way an organization (and its actors such as managers and employees) adapts and adjusts to its context (or environment) by acting on it to change it (Weick, 1979). This concept can also be applied to HRM in the sense that managers give actual meaning to HR practices during HR implementations and interventions. Wright and Nishii (2007) (see Chapter 3), label this the role of line managers in shaping the actual HR practices. There is general agreement that the majority of HR practices are handled by line managers; for example, selecting candidates, appraising subordinates, rewarding good performers and getting subordinates promoted (Den Hartog et al., 2004). If this is the case, then the development of managers is crucial for good HRM. Therefore, MD is essential for every organization as a first step towards good people management.

MD can be applied through many different practices and systems:

- Through programmes in universities (e.g. MBA programmes and executive training) (e.g. Sturges et al., 2003).
- External and internal courses on, for example, job appraisal and 'bad news' meetings.
- In-house MD programmes that are organization-specific (mainly in large organizations). Some organizations have their own (non-accredited) university (e.g. Disney University).
- Mentorships linking an experienced senior manager with a more junior manager.
- Job coaching using an external coach.
- Self-managed learning, for example through the intranet or Internet.

The Chartered Management Institute (CMI) is a British professional institution for managers with about 80000 members (www.managers.org.uk). CMI distinguishes multiple essential management skills:

- leading people (e.g. provides clear purpose and direction; inspires trust, respect and shared values);
- managing change (e.g. identifies opportunities for change and development; takes account of all stakeholder issues);
- meeting customer needs (e.g. develops effective customer relationships);
- managing information and knowledge (e.g. provides and uses appropriate information to support decision making);
- managing activities and resources (e.g. optimizes use of financial and other resources, including human resources);
- managing yourself (e.g. develops effective personal networks).

CMI provides training at different levels and provides certificates and executive diplomas for those who have attended management courses. CMI also reports data on education and training for managers.

	UK	France	Germany	Spain	Denmark	Norway	Average
HR manager	8	7	7	13	12	8	9.3
Line manager	10	7	8	13	7	7	8.8

TABLE 10.1 Amount of management training per year (days per manager)

Source: Reproduced with permission from the Chartered Management Institute (2004).

Table 10.1 shows the average amount of management training in days per year of both line managers and HR managers in several European countries. On average, both HR managers and line managers receive almost two weeks of MD training on a yearly basis within European organizations.

Country	Euros per manager on average per year
Germany	4438
Denmark	3387
Norway	2734
France	2674
Spain	1803
UK	1625

TABLE 10.2 Management development spend in Europe

Source: Reproduced with permission from the Chartered Management Institute (2004).

Table 10.2 shows the average budget expenses per manager on a yearly basis. In Germany more than twice the amount of money is spent on MD per manager (€4438) than in the UK (€1625). If people (employees) are the most important assets of an organization, then the development of those who manage these assets (managers) is crucial in creating an HR value chain that leads to excellent performance.

Stop and reflect

Think of a multinational company (MNC) that operates in both Germany and the UK. In Germany there is a general tendency to spend more money on MD per manager than in the UK. What is the impact on managers of this MNC in Germany and the UK if the MD budget for an individual manager in Germany is more than twice the MD budget for a similar individual manager in the UK?

Leadership development (LD)

Management development (MD) is mainly focused on first-line (or front-line) and middle managers, as discussed in the previous section. These managers, however, also require good management in particular leadership. A leader is much more than a manager. Bennis and Goldsmith's (1997) book builds on the notion that leaders and managers are slightly different. Throughout the book they argue that a good manager does things right and a leader does the right things. Leadership development (**LD**) is often related to leadership styles. Lewin et al. (1939), for example, were among the first to make a distinction between leadership styles, including:

- authoritarian or autocratic leadership;
- participative or democratic leadership;
- delegative or free reign.

'A good manager does things right. A leader does the right things.'

In the case of authoritarian and autocratic leadership, managers are in control mainly because management has the knowledge and skills to do the job. In contrast, in the case of delegative leadership and free reign, employees are in control mainly because of their knowledge and skills for the job. The latter situation can be found in professional organizations (e.g. hospital, university) where professionals have a certain degree of leeway to do their job based on their professional knowledge and skills. Authoritarian and autocratic leadership can be found in Tayloristic organizations (see Chapter 6).

The three leadership styles of Lewin et al. (1939) can also be recognized in the more contemporary distinction between (Bass, 1990):

- transactional leadership;
- *laissez-faire* leadership;
- transformational leadership.

The transactional leadership style is mainly focused on rewarding and punishing subordinates for job and team performance in continuous bargaining about the tasks, targets and responsibilities. Direct supervision as part of the control HR system (see Chapter 6) is often related to the transactional leadership style. *Laissez-faire* leadership represents the lack of leadership and management of people. At first this might be appealing to most employees because the boss is not supervising at all and employees can do whatever they like. The downside of this leadership style, however, is the lack of focus, vision and control of the daily work with a potentially negative impact on organizational performance. The transformational leadership style is all about listening to employees, motivating and encouraging people, being visible for employees, having a vision about the team and the organization, setting challenging goals, celebrating successes with all team members and being an example for everybody (e.g. integer, hard-working and committed). Transformational leadership represents the ideal leadership style for getting the best out of people; however, not everybody is likely to act transformationally without proper LD.

LD is crucial for improving existing leadership and for developing the next generation of leaders (executive succession). Yukl (1999) provides some issues for the further development of transformational leadership in an organization:

- develop an attractive and challenging vision of the work in close cooperation with all employees;
- create a clear link between this vision and the strategy for achieving the goals;
- make the vision concrete by translating it into concrete actions;
- express confidence (belief), decisiveness and optimism about the vision;
- realize the vision step by step and celebrate each success.

Empirical evidence suggests that many aspects of transformational leadership are strongly and universally endorsed across cultures (Den Hartog et al., 1999). In the leadership management approaches the leaders are 'the subjects' of development. Successful leadership management is considered positively related to leaders as 'the framers' of further employee development across middle managers, front-line managers and employees on the shopfloor.

LD:

- top managers and talents are 'the subjects' of development
- top managers and talents become 'the framers' of the development of managers and employees

MD:

- middle and front-line managers are 'the subjects' of development
- middle and front-line managers become 'the framers' of the development of employees

HD:

- employees on the shopfloor are 'the subjects' of development
- employees become 'the framers' of their own PD and the development of their peers

In summary, HRD, MD and LD present three different perspectives for developing people in organizations at different levels. HRD is more likely to be focused on employee development on the shopfloor level, while MD and LD mainly apply to management levels.

The learning organization

Senge (1990) is mainly responsible for the popularity of the concept of the learning organization. The **learning organization** represents the concept of organizations as dynamic systems that can change (self-changing) and have the ability to develop to achieve organizational goals. Excellent organizations have the capability to change fundamental purposes, visions and operational procedures. The high-performance work systems (HPWSs), discussed in Chapter 6, are aligned with notions on the learning organization. Employee involvement, teamwork, employee autonomy, extensive training and development, pay for performance and performance management (PM) are thought to enhance a learning spirit within an organization and more willingness to change. One of the most challenging aspects in organizational change is the human component (employees). If the employees are willing and able to change (important components of the AMO model also discussed in Chapter 6), it is more likely that organizations can learn and eventually change.

The learning organization is a slightly different representation of the high performance organization known from the HPWS approaches (see Chapter 6). Senge (ibid.) characterizes learning organizations by the shared all-embracing company philosophy, the shared vision and related goals, continuous personal learning by all organizational members, mental process models on how the organization and its context works, and team learning particularly with regard to problem-solving.

The concept of the learning organization can also be linked to another concept that gained popularity in the 1990s: organizational agility (Dyer and Shafer, 1999). Creation, adaptation and replication of knowledge are key characteristics of a learning organization aimed at single-loop learning (continuous improvements in current operations) and double-loop learning (questioning and challenging the organizational basics, including the core values and the basic business model). Agile organizations use ongoing education, training and employee development (ibid.) in order to maintain high levels of flexibility throughout the organization. See Chapter 3 for a more detailed overview of the concept of agility related to different types of flexibility.

In an ideal situation organizational members can and will share their knowledge and experiences with other organizational members in the interest of the organization. Reality is often much more complicated. Different aspects can hinder organizational members sharing knowledge and experiences, for example, because of:

- a lack of trust among organizational members;
- the geographical distance between organizational members and the absence of a digital information system for internal communication (e.g. intranet and Internet);
- the absence of a databank of all the organizational members and their expertise;
- the lack of incentives for information sharing.

Knowledge management

Knowledge management is a bundle of practices applied to the organization to identify, store, share, process and distribute insights and experiences of organizational members (Nonaka and Takeuchi, 1995). Knowledge management is often part of organizational learning programmes aimed at gaining competitive advantage through optimal use of knowledge and experience within the organization. The approach often includes both structural and cultural aspects. Structural issues include having the right infrastructure (information technology (IT)) for data collection, data storage, data analysis and data availability. Specific issues may arise in the design of the infrastructure for knowledge management; for example, who can gain access to the data (think of confidential information and privacy issues), and how can the organization avoid information overload?

Cultural aspects linked to knowledge management are the ability and willingness of organizational members to fully participate in the programme. It is more likely that knowledge management will be successful in an open culture where employees trust each other and their managers than in a closed culture characterized by mistrust of other organizational members. Knowledge management is often linked to and integrated with PM (see Chapter 8).

Concrete knowledge management practices that stimulate the sharing of knowledge and experience include:

- establishing master–apprentice relationships comparable to mentorship;
- building communities of practice similar to the ones in HRD (e.g. for nurses in hospitals);
- storytelling (transferring the organization's legacy, roots and core values);
- cross-utilizing employees, including job rotation on projects;
- mapping knowledge in a central data system, available for other organizational members;
- creating digital discussion platforms on the intranet for sharing new ideas, problems and possible solutions;
- organizing focus groups comparable to quality circles in TQM with organizational members with different backgrounds.

! *Stop and reflect*

- Can you think of concrete reasons why employees do not want to share their knowledge and experiences with other organizational members?
- Think of at least two HR practices that can help overcome the reluctance of employees to share their knowledge and experiences with other organizational members.

Competence management

Very popular frameworks in practice are the so-called competence management frameworks. **Competence management** is definitely part of strategic human resource management (SHRM) and is mostly aimed at learning and development in organizations. The CIPD (2007) reports that 60 per cent of UK organizations have a competence framework installed; on average, these competence frameworks cover almost 80 per cent of the workforce. Competences are similar to the concept of ability discussed earlier in this chapter; however, the competences in the competence management framework are often much more broadly defined and include skills and knowledge issues. Table 10.3 summarizes the most important subjects included in the competence frameworks according to the CIPD (2007) research. Communication, people management, cooperation (teamwork), service quality in relation to clients, leadership and problem-solving are the most important aspects of competence frameworks in practice.

Subjects	% of respondents
Communication skills	63
People management	59
Team skills	58
Customer service skills	54
Leadership decision-making	53
Problem-solving skills	50
Technical skills	45
Results orientation	42
Other	9

TABLE 10.3 Subjects included in competence frameworks

Source: Reproduced with permission from the Chartered Institute of Personnel and Development (2007, Figure 7, p. 20).

The CIPD (2007) report also includes information on the main purposes of the competence frameworks in practice. The results are summarized in Table 10.4. The main purpose of the frameworks in practice is related to people management (see Chapter 8), improving job and organizational performance, improving training and development, more effective recruitment (see Chapter 7) and better job design.

Fifty-two per cent of respondents have developed a competence framework in-house without external support, 33 per cent of the respondents have developed a framework in-house with support from external consultants, 8 per cent applied an external framework with the help of an external organization, and 7 per cent did it differently (CIPD, 2007). You can see that competence management frameworks are big business for external consultants. The CIPD (2007) data show that more than 40 per cent of all frameworks in practice were supported to some degree by consultants.

eLearning

The use of IT has also had a major impact on training and development. **eLearning** has become a popular instrument for both training and development of employees (Bates, 2005). The CIPD (www.cipd.co.uk) defines eLearning as the 'learning that is delivered, enabled or mediated using electronic technology for the explicit purpose of training in organizations'. Web-based learning is a popular form of eLearning. There are several advantages of web-based learning, including:

- relatively low costs when applied to a substantial number of employees (the start-up costs and development costs are high);
- flexibility for those who participate in the learning program (the program is not necessarily fixed on a specific time, date and location);

Main purpose	% of respondents
Underpins performance reviews/appraisals	57
Greater employee effectiveness	47
Greater organizational effectiveness	44
More effective training needs analysis	36
More effective career development	36
More effective recruitment	28
Greater customer satisfaction	26
Better job design	19
Other	3

TABLE 10.4 Main use of competence frameworks

Source: Reproduced with permission from the Chartered Institute of Personnel and Development (2007, Table 15, p. 20).

- opportunities for standardization of training and development in such a way that all organizational members receive the same training and development practices;
- accessibility for organizational members worldwide (the only requirements are a computer and access to the organization's intranet).

A typical example of an eLearning program is the regular compliance training, in some cases on a yearly basis, of the whole workforce. The compliance training can deal with issues such as safety procedures, confidentiality issues, employee misbehaviour, whistle-blowing procedures, and integrity and environmental pollution. In the eLearning module of the compliance training, the participants are first educated and briefed about new rules and regulations. Then they are tested and examined through concrete questions and fictitious cases. The answers are digitally collected and analysed by the HR department and/or compliance department. Employees have to pass these tests to continue working in the organization. Most companies have compliance training programs installed and more and more of these companies apply some form of eLearning to support the compliance learning process.

Shifts in career responsibilities

In the past managing careers was considered the main responsibility of the employer or organization (Schreiner, 2009). The employability notions, discussed earlier in this chapter, reflect a shift in career responsibilities from the employer to the individual employee. In other words, individual workers have become their own career facilitator. In some cases there will be a joint career responsibility (employer and employee), while there might even be situations in which the individual employee is fully self-responsible. Organizational changes in the 1980s and 1990s, mainly caused by increased complexity and more dynamics, have had significant effects on the nature of careers. Fournier (1998, in Schreiner, 2009: 14) distinguishes three major differences between traditional careers (and career development) and the new career approaches:

1. The new career is less structured, less predictive and can be characterized by radical changes. Internal promotion as part of the traditional career tracks is replaced by employee development, job enlargement and job enrichment.

2 In the traditional career models, individual employees could take a passive position absorbing career facilities offered by their employer. In the new career models, much more proactivity is expected and demanded of the employee with regard to personal career building.

3 The career boundaries (e.g. between work and non-work) have disappeared in some cases. Employee development and careers are no longer strictly bonded to a job or function. The new career perspective incorporates notions beyond regular work (the boundaryless career).

Reflections on the development of the 'happy few'

Chapter 7 includes the HR architecture framework by Lepak and Snell (2007). In this approach a distinction is made between core employees and peripheral employees. In other words, a distinction is made between those employees that matter for the (financial) success of an organization and those employees that are of relatively low (economic) value to the organization. The authors make a strong plea for HR differentiation towards different employee groups and, though plausible, it does have potentially serious negative effects on people, in particular differentiation related to the investment in people (employee development). From a distributive justice perspective, 'peripheral workers' may perceive injustice when other employees (the core employees) get extensive training and development opportunities, while their resources, facilities and opportunities are limited. Talent management is one of these popular contemporary topics in practice that has a potential negative impact on those organizational members who are not 'marked' as talents.

From a social legitimacy perspective (see Chapters 2 and 3), too much focus on HR investments in a very selective employee group potentially also has a negative impact on the organization, in particular with regard to the organization's corporate reputation (see 'Employment branding' in Chapter 7, p. 154). From a social legitimacy perspective, employers have a moral obligation to develop all workers continuously. This moral obligation is balanced by employability notions described earlier in this chapter stating that individual employees also have a moral obligation to develop themselves continuously. As suggested by Boxall and Purcell (2003) and Paauwe (2004), HRM, including employee development, covers all workforce groups, including core employees, peripheral employees and contingent workers.

The strategic relevance of development

From the employability perspective, continuous employee development is strategically relevant for both the employer and the employee. For the individual worker, part of employee development has become a substitute for lifetime employment. In essence, employee development positively affects employment security at a time when workers cannot expect to work for one boss for the rest of their career. Development creates windows of opportunity to move on to other jobs and organizations without having to fear being unemployed for too long. In reality, however, this idea may apply to knowledge workers (e.g. highly educated workers) but be slightly different for the less-skilled. Employee development is also strategically relevant as a motivator for workers, in particular for starters. It can be applied to attract and retain good workers. Development is also relevant to keep up with the latest developments; for example, with regard to technological developments and IT.

CASE STUDY: TOPDESK

ToPdesk is a medium-sized software service organization (250 employees) mainly operating in the UK, Germany, the Netherlands and Belgium. The company was founded in 1993 by two technical engineers and its headquarters are located in Delft, the Netherlands. The company claims that it is characterized by 'a curious and optimistic outlook, an interest in technology and a hunger for knowledge' (www.topdesk.com). The average age of their employees is 28 and the majority of the workforce is highly educated.

ToPdesk is a technology-driven organization with an egalitarian culture, little hierarchy and substantial employee autonomy. Teamwork and team learning is considered essential within the organization. Each individual employee receives a 'learning budget' of €2000 per year that can be used for courses and education. The employee has a lot of leeway in spending this budget on development. The only requirement is the specification of the learning goals that will be evaluated after the course or education has finished. The company offers internships and thesis projects for students interested in software and consultancy. In 2006 and 2007 ToPdesk was voted most fun employer of the Netherlands (*source*: Intermediair Magazine), with high scores on:

- work atmosphere;
- freedom in your work;
- job content;
- job satisfaction.

? Discussion questions

ToPdesk appears to be a typical ICT company from the 1990s with IT technicians who are 'crazy' about their job. The job content (technology-driven), autonomy and a good work atmosphere (informal and little hierarchy) play an important role for the employees of ToPdesk. You can image that the employees are not only highly satisfied, but committed and motivated as well. The commitment, however, might be mainly towards the occupation (e.g. being a software engineer) and the team. The first is also known as occupational commitment and the latter as team or group commitment. Organizational commitment of employees towards ToPdesk as an organization is essential and important for organizational performance.

Think of ways in which ToPdesk can stimulate organizational commitment without negatively affecting their occupational and team commitment.

Knowledge transfer among ToPdesk employees can be a powerful source for gaining competitive management. Can you think of knowledge management practices that can be applied to the organization to stimulate the sharing of knowledge and experience within ToPdesk? Keep in mind that this is a high-tech firm with an excellent IT infrastructure for the business that can also be used for internal purposes.

summary

- Education is an important part of our learning and development process often institutionalized through schools, colleges and universities.
- Employee development, however, is much more than formal education in schools, colleges, universities and other educational institutions.
- Development can have many different faces, including HRD, MD and LD.
- Line managers or direct supervisors play a crucial role in the shaping of employee development throughout the organization.
- Line managers or direct supervisors can be both 'the subject' and 'the framer' of employee development in an organization.
- Lifetime employment has been replaced by lifelong career notions.
- Employability is an approach aimed at individual employee development for the benefit of both the employee and the employer. Employability is a joint responsibility for the employee and the employer aimed at improving organizational performance and gaining a lifelong career.
- In some continental European countries, training and education related to work are heavily institutionalized and embedded in CBAs.
- IIP is a UK collective approach aimed at creating more willingness among employers to investment in their employees. IIP has also been applied in other countries.
- For some professions (e.g. medical specialists, nurses, police officers, accountants, lawyers and pilots) education, training and development are highly institutionalized and even protected by law.
- HRD is a discipline aimed at individual and group learning in the context of work, often characterized by on-the-job learning principles and notions of communities of practice.
- MD is a discipline focused on management learning. MD is considered more important from an HR perspective since line managers are seen as the enactors of good HRM in practice.
- LD is a discipline aimed at improving current leadership styles towards transformational leadership. LD also focuses on growing future leaders.
- The learning organization builds on notions of business excellence through organizational learning.
- Knowledge management is an approach for stimulating the sharing of knowledge and experience among employees in an organization aimed at gaining competitive advantage.
- Competence management is an approach aimed at improving employee abilities.
- eLearning is a specific learning device using modern technology and information communication technology (ICT) to transfer knowledge and skills.
- Exclusive development of core employees (the 'happy few') has serious potentially negative effects on fairness towards other individual employees (the peripheral workers) and on social legitimacy (corporate image).

Glossary of key terms

Competence management is a bundle of practices aimed at developing individual employees' abilities that will enhance job performance, organizational performance, individual learning, organizational learning, selective recruitment and customer satisfaction.

Development is focused on individual learning broader than the occupation and aimed at longer-term personal growth and career movement.

Education is the behavioural process of learning that applies to the whole person rather than specific skills.

eLearning is the learning that is delivered, enabled or mediated using electronic technology for the explicit purpose of training in organizations.

Employability is a joint effort and interest of the employer and the employee in the continuous development of an individual that will enable an optimal use of the individual employee's qualities and capabilities.

Human resource development (HRD) is a discipline focused on individual and group learning in the context of work.

Investors In People (IIP) represents a standard for training and development of employees in an organization.

Knowledge management is a bundle of practices applied to the organization to identify, store, share, process and distribute insights and experiences of organizational members.

Leadership development (LD) is the discipline focused on improving current leadership styles in the organization and growing future leaders.

Learning organization represents the concept of organizations as dynamic systems that can change (self-changing) and have the ability to develop to achieve organizational goals.

Management development (MD) is the system of personnel practices intended to ensure that an organization can rely on timely availability of qualified and motivated employees.

Training is the process of change used to develop specific skills, usually for a job.

Personal development

Summarize your current skills, knowledge and abilities that you think are relevant for your next job. Try to determine your strengths and weaknesses on these three concepts. And think of ways to overcome your weaknesses.

Individual task

Discuss the advantages and disadvantages of an employability approach in an organization for (1) the individual employee and (2) the employer.

You can choose an organization in practice and discuss possible managerial actions that potentially increase the employability of individual employees. Then summarize the positive and negative aspects of these actions for the individual employee and the employer. Finally, think of ways to overcome these issues.

Learning checklist

After studying this chapter, you should be able to do the following:

- Understand the concepts of education, training and development.
- Outline notions on the employability concept.
- Understand the line manager or direct supervisor as 'the subject' and 'the framer' of employee development.
- Recognize the institutionalization of employee development.
- Review HRD.
- Discuss MD.
- Review LD.
- Review the concept of the learning organization.
- Outline knowledge management and competence management.
- Consider eLearning.
- Discuss the downside of the development of the 'happy few'.

References

Bass, B.M. (1990) From transactional to transformational leadership: learning to share the vision, *Organizational Dynamics*, 18: 19–31.

Bates, A.W. (2005) *Technology, E learning and Distance Education*, 2nd edn. London: Routledge.

Bennis, W. and Goldsmith, J. (1997) *Learning to Lead: A Workbook on Becoming a Leader*. Reading, MA: Addison-Wesley.

Berings, M., Poell, R.F. and Gelissen, J. (2008) On-the-job learning in the nursing profession: developing and validating a classification of learning activities and learning themes, *Personnel Review*, 37(4): 442–59.

Bloisi, W. (2007) *An Introduction to Human Resource Management*. London: McGraw-Hill.

Boxall, P. and Purcell, J. (2003) *Strategy and Human Resource Management*. New York: Palgrave Macmillan.

Chartered Institute of Personnel and Development (2007) *Annual Survey Report 2007: Learning and Development*. London: CIPD.

Chartered Management Institute (2004) *Developing Managers: A European Perspective*. Northamptonshire: CMI.

Den Hartog, D.N., Boselie, P. and Paauwe, J. (2004) Performance management: a model and research agenda, *Applied Psychology: An International Review*, 53(4): 556–69.

Den Hartog, D.N., House, R.J., Hanges, P.J., Ruiz-Quintanilla, S.A. and Dorfmann, P.W. (1999) Culture specific and cross-culturally generalizable implicit leadership theories: are attributes of charismatic/transformational leadership universally endorsed?, *Leadership Quarterly*, 10(2): 219–56.

DiMaggio, P.J. and Powell, W.W. (1983) The iron cage revisited: institutional isomorphism and collective rationality in organizational fields, *American Sociological Review*, 48(2): 147–60.

Dyer, L. and Shafer, R. (1999) Creating organizational agility: implications for strategic human resource management, in P.M. Wright, L. Dyer, J. Boudreau and G. Milkovich (eds), *Research in Personnel and Human Resource Management,* Supplement 4. Stamford, CT and London: JAI Press.

Gaspersz, J.B.R. and Van Den Hove, N.H.L. (2000) *Investors in People: De sleutel tot het Talent in uw Organisatie* [*Investors in People: The Key to Talent in Your Organization*]. Samson: Bedrijfswetenschappen.

Heijden, B. Van Der (2002) Prerequisites to guarantee life-long employability, *Personnel Review*, 31(1): 44–61.

Hoque, K. (2003) All in all, it's just another plaque on the wall: the incidence and impact of the investors in people standard, *Journal of Management Studies*, 40(2): 543–71.

Jansen, P.G.W., Van Der Velde, M.E.G. and Mul, W. (2001) A typology of management development, *Journal of Management Development*, 20(2): 106–20.

Lepak, D.P. and Snell, S.A. (2007) Employment subsystems and the 'HR architecture', in P. Boxall, J. Purcell and P.M. Wright (eds), *The Oxford Handbook of Human Resource Management,* Chapter 11, pp. 210–30. Oxford: Oxford University Press.

Lewin, K., Lippitt, R. and White, R.K. (1939) Patterns of aggressive behavior in experimentally created social climates, *Journal of Social Psychology*, 10: 271–301.

Nonaka, I. and Takeuchi, H. (1995) *The Knowledge-creating Company: How Japanese Companies Create the Dynamics of Innovation*. Oxford: Oxford University Press.

Paauwe, J. (1998) HRM and performance: the linkage between resources and institutional context. RIBES working paper, Erasmus University, Rotterdam.

Paauwe, J. (2004) *HRM and Performance: Achieving Long-term Viability*. Oxford: Oxford University Press.

Paauwe, J. and Boselie, P. (2003) Challenging 'strategic HRM' and the relevance of the institutional setting, *Human Resource Management Journal*, 13(3): 56–70.

Poell, R.F., Van Dam, K., Berg, P.T. Van Den (2004) Organising learning in work contexts, *Applied Psychology: An International Review*, 53(4): 529–40.

Ram, M. (2000) Investors in People in small firms: case study evidence from the business services sector, *Personnel Review*, 29(1): 69–91.

Schreiner, N. (2009) *Loopbaanontwikkeling voor het Individu* [*Career Development for Individuals*]. Wassehage BV: Wassenaar.

Senge, P. (1990) *The Fifth Discipline: The Art and Practice of the Learning Organization*. New York: Doubleday.

Sluis-den Dikken, L. Van Der and Hoeksema, L.H. (2001) The palette of management development, *Journal of Management Development*, 20(2): 168–79.

Sturges, J., Simpson, R. and Altman, Y. (2003) Capitalising on learning: an exploration of the MBA as a vehicle for developing career competencies, *International Journal of Training and Development*, 7(1): 53–66.

Swart, J., Mann. C., Price, A. and Brown, S. (2005) *Human Resource Development: Strategy and Tactics*. London: Butterworth-Heinemann.

Van Woerkom, M. and Croon, M. (2009) The relationship between team learning activities and team performance, *Personnel Review*, 38(5): 560–77.

Weick, K. (1979) *The Social Psychology of Organizing*, 2nd edn. Reading, MA: Addison-Wesley.

Winterton, J. (2007) Training, development and competence, in P. Boxall, J. Purcell and P.M. Wright (eds), *The Oxford Handbook of Human Resource Management*. Oxford: Oxford University Press.

Wright, P.M. and Nishii, L.H. (2007) Strategic HRM and organizational behavior: integrating multiple levels of analysis. Working paper 26, Ithaca, NY: CAHRS at Cornell University.

Yorks, L. (2005) *Strategic Human Resource Development*. Mason, OH: Thomson South-Western.

Yukl, G. (1999) An evaluation of conceptual weaknesses in transformational and charismatic leadership theories, *Leadership Quarterly*, 10(2): 285–305.

Further reading

Mintzberg, H. (2004) *Managers not MBAs: A Hard Look at the Soft Practice of Managing and Management Development*. San Francisco, CA: Berrett-Koehler.

Noe, R.A. (2002) *Employee Training and Development*, 2nd edn. Colombus, OH: McGraw-Hill.

Swart, J., Mann. C., Price, A. and Brown, S. (2005) *Human Resource Development – Strategy and Tactics*. London: Butterworth-Heinemann.

Yorks, L. (2005) *Strategic Human Resource Development*. Mason, OH: Thomson, South-Western.

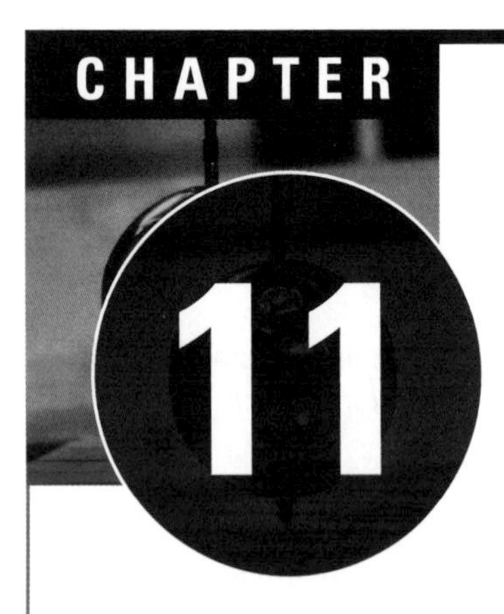

Employee Participation

Learning Objectives

After studying this chapter, you should be able to do the following:

- ❖ Outline the roots of employee participation
- ❖ Discuss employee participation from a unitarist and a pluralist perspective
- ❖ Identify the industrial democracy approach
- ❖ Recognize employee participation at different levels, including participation as a best practice at individual employee level and participation at organization, sector and national level
- ❖ Outline the escalator of employee participation
- ❖ Review works councils and employee involvement
- ❖ Discuss trade unions and employee involvement
- ❖ Outline financial participation
- ❖ Evaluate participation in relationship to other human resource (HR) practices, including teamwork, job design and decentralization

CASE STUDY: BASF

BASF is a leading German chemical organization employing nearly 100 000 people worldwide. Approximately 49 per cent of the total workforce is employed in Germany, with about one-third of all employees working in Ludwigshafen. The Ludwigshafen site is a large integrated chemical complex covering an area of 10km^2, which is also the base of BASF headquarters and all corporate functions. BASF's portfolio comprises chemicals, plastics, performance products (e.g. care chemicals for cosmetics), functional solutions (e.g. coatings), agricultural solutions and oil and gas. In 2008 the company had sales of €62.3 billion and an income of approximately €6.9 billion before taxes. BASF's strategy is built on four strategic guidelines:

1 We earn a premium on our cost of capital.

2 We help our customers to be more successful.

3 We form the best team in industry.

4 We ensure sustainable development.

BASF has formulated a vision, values and principles to achieve goals for and serve their customers, shareholders, employees and the countries in which the company operates. The organizational values include:

- personal and professional competence (with specific attention on intercultural competence);
- mutual respect and open dialogue, including social legitimacy towards society and relevant groups in society;
- integrity (complying with the laws and respecting the good business practices of countries in which BASF operates).

BASF explicitly acknowledges multiple stakeholders, including trade unions and works councils. It has a global strategy and an aligned global HR strategy; however, part of the corporate strategy is the leeway given to local operations because of, for example, national legislation. BASF promotes employee participation within the organization, in particular through works councils, and intends to export this typical continental European employee representation model to BASF operations outside Europe (e.g. China). An illustration of BASF works councils' influence is summarized below.

Employee representatives appoint members to BASF SE Supervisory Board
Ludwigshafen, Germany – March 19, 2009 – In its regular meeting on March 18 in Ludwigshafen, the BASF Europa Betriebsrat (European works council) appointed (six) employee representatives to the Supervisory Board of BASF SE.... The appointments are based on the Agreement Concerning the Involvement of Employees in BASF SE (Employee Participation Agreement) signed in relation to the transformation of BASF Aktiengesellschaft into a European Company (Societas Europaea, SE). According to this agreement, the BASF Europa Betriebsrat appoints employee representatives to the Supervisory Board on the basis of proposals from the German Group works council and the Belgian works council.

(www.basf.com)

The Supervisory Board of BASF SE comprises 12 members. BASF SE follows the principle of parity between shareholder representatives (n = 6) and employee representatives (n = 6).

? Discussion questions

- Why does BASF promote employee representation and participation through works councils?
- Can you think of the opportunities and threats in relation to the employee representatives appointing 50 per cent of the BASF SE Supervisory Board?

Introduction

The word 'participation' has its roots in the Latin word 'pars'. 'Pars' means being part of something. The Latin word 'participare' literally means 'sharing something with another person'. The sharing may involve information, but also responsibility or materialistic objects (e.g. money). Participation also requires more than one person. Another characteristic of participation is that one entity is able to share something with the other. In other words, at least one actor has the possibility of sharing something with the other actor. Employee participation is one of the key high-performance work practices (HPWPs) in human resource management (HRM) because of the underlying assumption that employees behave optimally when they are involved in decision making and when they are given responsibility and autonomy (Appelbaum et al., 2000).

Scientific management (Taylor, 1911) and Henry Ford's managerial approach to building T-Fords paid little or no attention to employee participation. In fact, these classic models suggested direct supervisor and minimization of employee involvement in work design (see Chapter 6 on high-performance work practices). Since the emergence of the Human Relations Movement (Mayo, 1933) and the revisionistic approaches (Maslow, 1943), employee participation has been given substantial attention in both theory and practice.

This chapter focuses on employee participation and the different ways of looking at participation. First, the increased attention on employee participation as a best practice in HRM has multiple causes, including the human relations focus on employee attention (Mayo, 1933) and the socio-technical systems (STS) approaches' interest in blending technical design and work design, including increased employee responsibility and delegation of tasks (Emery and Trist, 1960). McGregor's (1960) ideas on the basic need of employees to be involved and to have responsibilities in an organization, employee democracy notions on the rights of individual employees to be represented in, for example, works councils (Wigboldus et al., 2008), and total quality management (TQM) notions (Wilkinson et al., 1992) can also be linked to the HPWSs debate (see Chapter 6).

Second, employee participation is a very broad concept that also includes elements of information sharing, decentralization of responsibilities and work design, in particular job enrichment and enlargement. Third, participation manifests itself on multiple levels, including employee participation as a best practice on an individual employee level, participation at an organization level manifested in a works council and employee participation at a sector or national level through trade unions. The latter two represent institutionalized forms of employee participation that are in particular relevant in many European countries (Paauwe and Boselie, 2003). Fourth, financial participation is a specific form of employee involvement focused on the employer sharing the profits and/or the ownership of the organization with employees (Pendleton et al., 2001). Finally, employee participation can be integrated with other HR practices, in particular teamwork.

The roots of employee participation

Since the emergence of the Human Relations Movement in the 1930s (Mayo, 1933) an emphasis has been placed on good communication and information sharing. Sharing information with employees and management communication can be considered the first steps towards employee involvement in organizations. However, the nature of the relationship between manager and employee is still very much one way: from the manager to the employee. Employee participation, including sharing responsibilities with employees, employee autonomy and involvement, was stressed some two decades after the Human Relations Movement was founded, for example reflected in the work by McGregor. McGregor's (1960) Theory Y explicitly builds on notions of self-control and self-direction, with a central role for the HR practice called 'employee participation' or 'employee involvement'. He assumes that individual employees search for responsibilities and want to be involved in decision making within the organization (see Chapter 6 for a more detailed description).

The STS theory (Emery and Trist, 1960) also emphasized the need for employee participation linked to job design (job enlargement and enrichment), employee autonomy and teamwork. The

STS theory is focused on optimization of technical production environments through combining production elements with social elements. Employee participation from an STS theory perspective is required for flexibility (numerical and functional flexibility) and for solving problems on the assembly line.

The TQM movement in the 1980s and the HPWS models in the 1990s also gave employee participation a central role in the search for adding value through people (Walton, 1985). The AMO theory (Bailey, 1993) explicitly stresses the importance of employee involvement through the third dimension of the model: opportunity to participate. AMO's 'opportunity to participate' is a broad concept, including (Appelbaum et al., 2000):

- employee participation in decision making;
- employee autonomy;
- teamwork;
- employee survey research;
- regular employee/supervisor meetings.

(See Chapter 6 for an overview of scientific management, human relations, McGregor's Theory Y, STS theory, TQM, HPWSs and AMO theory.)

The approaches summarized above all consider employee participation as an HR practice that can be applied by organizations to improve organizational performance. This is a highly managerial approach to participation in line with Pfeffer's (1994) **best (HR) practice approach** to HRM. This managerial approach can be characterized by its unitary underlying assumption that what is good for an employee is good for the employer, and vice versa. The **unitarist HRM approach** is typical in an Anglo-American context (Keegan and Boselie, 2006). The European context however is often much more closely related to a pluralist approach (Brewster, 2007). The **pluralist HRM approach** takes into account different stakeholders, including trade unions and works councils that may have conflicting interests with the employer. Employee participation from a pluralist perspective is extremely important for organizations operating in a European context.

Industrial relations (IR) traditionally paid a lot of attention to the institutionalized parts of the employment relationship (Paauwe and Boselie, 2003), including the role of trade unions, collective bargaining agreements (CBAs) and labour legislation. In contrast to the dominant HRM approaches, the IR approaches focus on the differences between employees and employers (Storey, 1992; Legge, 1995), often reflected in power relationships and conflicts (e.g. strikes). The IR approaches were very popular in the 1960s and 1970s, partly because of increased attention paid to the further emancipation of the individual worker. Some scholars have labelled this the **industrial democracy perspective** (Emery and Thorsrud, 1976; Sorge, 1976; Van Zuthem, 1976; Van Dijck, 1984; Looise and Paauwe, 2001), focusing on the effect of IR shaped through labour conditions and stakeholder influence (trade unions and works councils) on the employment relationships in organizations. From this perspective employee participation is not necessarily a best practice in HRM, but an employee right. Margaret Thatcher in Great Britain, Ronald Reagan in the USA and right-wing oriented governments in multiple European countries in the 1980s caused a major shift from the pluralist IR perspective to the unitarist (managerial) HRM perspective. IR considerations, however, in particular those linked to employee participation, should be taken into account in the European context because of the huge impact of trade unions, works councils and legislation on organizations (Leisink, 1997). These factors cannot be neglected and should therefore be part of the HRM strategy of organizations operating in these institutionalized contexts. The BASF case at the start of this chapter illustrates how a continental European organization applies stakeholder management, in particular emphasizing the relevance of employee representation through works councils.

Employee participation as an HR practice (individual level)

Multiple authors stress the importance of employee participation as a best practice in HRM, including Walton (1985) who discusses 'broad employee participation', Arthur (1994) who talks about 'participation' and Pfeffer (1994) who introduces 'participation and empowerment'. Closely linked to the concept of employee participation as an HR practice are practices such as 'employee ownership' through shares and options (Pfeffer, 1994), 'self-managed teams' (ibid.) and 'decentralization' (Arthur, 1994). Employee participation at the individual employee level is also known as direct participation (Marchington and Wilkinson, 2005).

Employee participation or involvement can have many different faces. Participation might include employee involvement in decision making with regard to the recruitment and selection of a new colleague. Employee participation can also include the degree of influence/leeway employees have in a department, for example manifested at regular departmental meetings. A yearly employee survey can also be seen as a form of employee participation. In these surveys employees are, for example, asked to rate the leadership qualities of their supervisor, the intensity and quality of HR practices available (e.g. employee development and internal promotion opportunities), the information sharing and communication within the organization, the degree of cooperation within and between departments and multiple outcome variables, including employee satisfaction, commitment and trust (see Chapter 4 on HR metrics and measurement for further information on this topic).

These illustrations of employee participation highlight the different techniques that can be used to create employee participation in an organization. The illustrations also show that there are different degrees of employee participation possible in an organization. Applying a yearly employee survey does not fully involve workers in the strategic decision making of an organization. Employee membership of a selection committee for a job vacancy, however, is an example of a higher degree of employee involvement in an organization. The degree of employee participation might depend on the employee type. Knowledge workers and highly educated employees (core employees) are more likely to expect and demand involvement than unskilled workers (peripheral employees) (Lepak and Snell, 2002), although the general theory behind employee participation assumes that all employees want some degree of involvement.

In some cases, employee involvement can be a necessary condition for the success of another HR practice. Empirical research on performance appraisals (PAs), for example, suggests a positive impact of employee involvement in the design of a new performance evaluation system on employees' perception of procedural justice (Baron and Kreps, 1999; Boselie et al., 2010). In other words, employees are more likely to accept a new performance evaluation system and perceive it as fair when they are involved in the design of the system.

! *Stop and reflect*

In Chapter 7 on selective recruitment and selection, a distinction was made between three types of employee according to Baron and Kreps (1999):

1 stars;
2 guardians;
3 foot soldiers.

- Can you think of one illustration in practice of each employee type?
- What kind of employee participation do you think these employee types ideally require for optimally performing in their jobs?

The escalator of participation

Marchington and Wilkinson (2005) provide an extensive overview of employee participation and employee involvement. The HR practices at the individual employee level (direct participation) can have many different shapes from basic information sharing (e.g. through newsletters) to full control through, for example, self-managing teams. Marchington and Wilkinson present five stages of participation in their 'escalator of participation', referring to different degrees of employee involvement and direct participation in organizations (see Figure 11.1).

Information sharing is the lowest level in the escalator, representing one-way (top-down) information towards employees. The next level is *communication*, referring to more involved forms of involvement; for example, through regular briefings. During these briefings employees can pose questions and there is room for interaction between management and employees. The third level – *consultation* – incorporates elements of two-way interaction between management and employees. Employees are asked about their opinions and management may decide to make use of the suggestions made. At the *codetermination* level, employees and managers jointly make decisions. The highest level in the escalator model is *control* or *self-control*. At this level the individual employee or autonomous team are in control of decision making. The classic management models presented in Chapter 6 (in particular the 'scientific management approach') tend to build on lower levels of participation in the escalator (e.g. mainly focused on information sharing and communication), while the more recent HPWS approaches (see Chapter 6) emphasize consultation, codetermination and self-control.

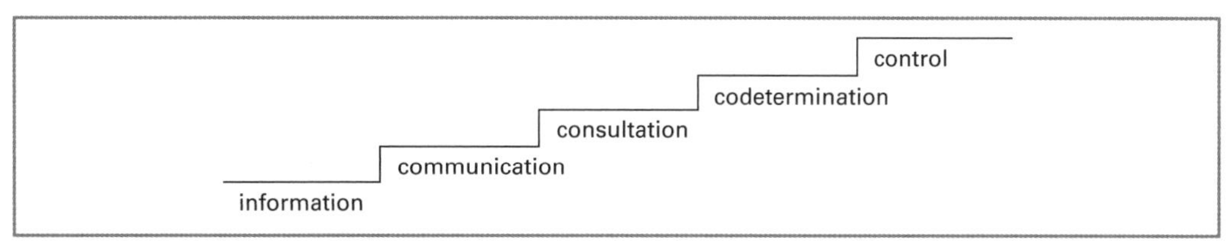

FIGURE 11.1 The escalator of participation

Source: Reproduced with permission from Marchington and Wilkinson (2005, Figure 15.1, p. 401).

Stop and reflect

A trade union experimented with extensive employee involvement and direct participation in decision making for bus drivers in a large public transportation company. The trade union got full support and cooperation from the management of the organization. The general idea behind this intervention was to involve bus drivers in day-to-day planning and decision making. In Marchington and Wilkinson's (2005) escalator of participation terms, the intervention took place at the codetermination level.

After three months the trade union was forced to end the experiment because of multiple bus driver complaints about having too many administrative tasks and meetings. They all wanted to go back to the 'old' model where they could just drive the buses.

Discuss the intentions of the trade unions for more employee involvement within this public transportation company. Think about the motives of the bus drivers in opposing the employee involvement programme after three months. Discuss possible solutions for restoring the balance between employee participation and regular work (driving buses) for the bus drivers in this illustration.

Employee participation at the organizational level

An institutionalized form of employee participation is the **works council**. The works council is an employee representation at organization level focused on all issues that affect the employment relationship within that specific organization. In some countries organizations are obliged to have a works council installed. For example, in the Netherlands all organizations with more than 50 employees need to have a works council installed. This obligation is embedded in the works council's law, which stems from 1950, and over the years Dutch works councils have gained more rights and have a stronger legal position towards employers because of the further developments of it (Looise and Drucker, 2003). The works council consists of employees that are elected by the workforce of that specific organization. Works council members are partly or in some cases full-time exempted from their regular job. In smaller organizations the exempted time might be two hours per week. In large MNCs some works council members have a full-time job working on works council's issues. The employer is usually obliged to facilitate the works council and its members with financial resources, for example when it is necessary to hire external experts and consultants, and office space. The size of the works council depends on the organization size.

The works council focuses on all issues that affect the employment relationship in the organization, including working conditions (health and safety), major organizational changes (mergers, acquisitions and reorganizations), massive layoffs (downsizing) and HR policies (payment, employee training and development, etc.). The works council meets on a regular basis with the top manager in charge of social affairs within the organization. Nowadays, it is usually the chief human resource officer (CHRO) who is in charge of representing the organization during a meeting with the works council (Boselie, 2009). The works council has several rights, including the right to advise the organization on issues that affect the employment relationship and the right to be informed about major organizational changes that affect the employment and the HRM of the organization. In most continental European countries, such as Germany and the Netherlands, the works council is considered a social partner for the HR function that should be consulted and informed on all HR issues (Looise and Drucker, 2003). Some organizations even consider works councils as strategic partners in the shaping of HRM in the organization (Boselie, 2009).

Works councils can operate at different levels of an organization depending on the legal position of the business units within it. In some large companies there is a high degree of business unit autonomy supported by legal autonomy. In those circumstances it is likely that there are multiple works councils operating within one large company:

- works councils at business unit level (e.g. linked to regions or a specific country);
- a works council at the group level of an organization (Group Works Council);
- a European Works Council (EWC) operating at European level (Wills, 2000).

The EWC is relatively new and not that common yet in organizations operating in Europe within multiple EU countries, although it is considered to have much potential for employee participation in the near future, because of the general tendency of strategic decision making in organizations at continental or global level.

The Federation of European Employers (FedEE; www.fedee.com) defines the criteria for installing a European Works Council as follows:

- An employer is required to establish an EWC if they employ at least 1000 employees within the EU member states and at least 150 employees in each of two member states.

- The 'controlling undertaking' for the purposes of the Directive shall be any body which can exercise a 'dominant influence' over another undertaking. This is automatic when more than half the share capital is owned by one body.
- Those organizations which had in place an 'agreed' mechanism for informing and consulting their entire workforce on transnational issues when the Directive took effect are excluded from compliance with the strict terms of the Directive (Article 13 Agreements).
- The EWC shall be established at a group level unless the management agrees, in writing, to establish more than one consultation procedure.

Members of a works council are often trade union members. In the case of trade union membership, the works council members are often supported by an external trade union; for example, in terms of strategic advice and training and development (negotiation skills).

What are the advantages of a works council for the individual employee?

The works council is a representation of all employees at the organization level. This way there is an infrastructure for complaints and issues that are relevant for individual employees. In case of a major crisis, for example a reorganization including a downsizing of the workforce by 10 per cent, the works council can represent the interests of the employees. Another advantage of a works council for the individual employee is the result of the institutionalization of the works councils in many European countries throughout the years. This institutionalization has resulted in a general acceptance of the works council by management as an intermediary between the employer and the employees. Empirical HR research shows that a mainland European country such as the Netherlands can be characterized by employers who are either neutral or in favour of works councils, in contrast to the UK where employers tend to be neutral or against works councils (Bruining et al., 2005). General acceptance of works councils can have a positive effect on the social atmosphere between the employer and the employees.

What are the disadvantages of a works council for the individual employee?

Employee motivation and enthusiasm for joining a works council is generally low in many organizations. This is reflected in the difficulties of finding new members and the low employee participation in the works council elections (Kaar and Smit, 2007). A works council's activities can be time-consuming. Poor representation can negatively affect the relationship between the employer and the employees. Another potential disadvantage of a works council from the position of the employee is linked to management strategy. Top management can choose to search for legitimacy and approval for a major organizational change (e.g. a merger, acquisition or downsizing) from either the works council or the trade unions.

The works council is an internal stakeholder that is sometimes more easily manipulated than the external trade unions, who often have a much stronger position and more resources for putting pressure on the organization. Top management can therefore play a game with the works council and the trade unions in order to achieve the desired organizational goals. Often the final legitimacy and approval for a major organizational change needs to come from the official trade unions (Schilstra, 1998). However, the works council involvement in an early stage can be beneficial to the organization, because the works council can act as the messenger delivering the bad news to the workforce. Works councils have to be very careful with their position and the risk of being used by top management.

! Stop and reflect

An ice cream producer has decided to close down one of its factories and transfer the ice production to another factory in a different region. The factory that is closing down employs about 100 people and has a works council installed. The management of the organization has decided to negotiate on a social plan with the (internal) works council first. If that does not work out, they will start negotiating with the (external) trade unions. The social plan is required for the 100 employees and may include a financial incentive for those who leave, and employee support in finding another job.

- Can you think of any reason why the management decided to negotiate with the (internal) works council first?
- Discuss the possible risk factors related to keeping the trade unions out.
- What actions can be expected from the trade unions if they are not involved in this process?

What are the advantages of a works council for the employer?

First, it is much easier to communicate and cooperate with a group of employees that officially represent the total workforce. Without employee representation the employer is bound to deal with all employees on an individual basis or to deal with an external stakeholder such as the trade unions. Trade unions are a form of employee representation, in particular for those employees who are trade union members. However, these stakeholders are more distant from the organization, with potentially broader agendas. In contrast, works councils represent all employees and are a form of employee representation from inside the organization. Another advantage of the works council is that this medium can be used as messenger of organizational changes to the workforce.

What are the disadvantages of a works council for the employer?

Works councils can limit the room to manoeuvre in an organization. In case of a merger or reorganization, the works council generally has rights to be informed and in some cases the legal rights to slow down organizational changes by up to six months. A good relationship between management and the works council is therefore desirable. A second disadvantage of the works council for the employer is linked to the often internal weaknesses of the works council (Kaar and Smit, 2007). This can be caused by a lack of motivation of employees to be involved and/ or a lack of training and development of works council's members. The latter potentially causes procedural problems and frustration for both the employer's representation and the works council's members.

Overall, there is empirical evidence that high-performance organizations are more likely to have a good works council installed (Hubler and Jirjahn, 2001; Addison et al., 2004). It is not fully clear what the causal relationship is:

- good works councils have a positive impact on organizational performance;
- high organizational performance has a positive impact on the quality of works councils; for example, through a higher willingness of the employer to invest in works councils through financial resources and training and development;
- it works both ways.

Employee participation at the organizational, sector and national level

Trade unions represent employees at different levels, including the organizational, branch of industry and national level. Trade union recognition can differ significantly between countries (Hoque and Bacon, 2008). In the UK, for example, trade union recognition is generally lower than most continental European countries, including Belgium, France, Germany, the Netherlands and the Scandinavian countries. The power of the trade unions is partly determined by the trade union membership. One way of measuring membership is through the **degree of unionization**, which can be calculated at organization, sector and national level. This measure represents the percentage of all workers (in an organization, in a sector or in a country) who are members of a trade union.

The European Industrial Relations Observatory On-line (part of Eurofound) presents the trade union membership figures for 2003. The degree of unionization is calculated by dividing the total number of trade union members by the number of employees as defined in national labour force surveys in a country (see Table 11.1).

%	Country
Over 90	Romania
80–89	Belgium, Denmark, Finland and Sweden
70–79	Italy and Norway
60–69	Cyprus and Malta
50–59	Luxembourg
40–49	Austria and Slovenia
30–39	Hungary, Ireland and Portugal
20–29	Bulgaria, Germany, Greece, the Netherlands, Slovakia and the UK
10–19	Estonia, Latvia, Poland and Spain

TABLE 11.1 The degree of unionization per country, 2003

Source: The European Industrial Relations Observatory On-line (www.eurofound.europa.eu).

These findings suggest major differences with regard to trade union membership in different European countries. In some countries with relatively low degrees of unionization (e.g. in the Netherlands less than 25 per cent of all workers are members of a trade union) in combination with a traditional strong position of the trade unions in national IR, it puts the relationship between the social partners (employers' associations, trade unions and the government) under pressure. Schilstra and Smit (2005), for example, report a relatively low degree of unionization (< 25 per cent) in combination with a relatively high degree of CBA coverage (> 85 per cent). CBA coverage refers to the percentage of all workers that is covered by a **CBA** at company or sector level, which is negotiated by trade unions and employers' associations. In other words, the trade unions negotiate CBAs for the majority of the workers while less than 25 per cent of them are a trade union member.

Trade unions, however, are involved in many other activities aimed at improving the position of the worker. Trade unions are often also active at a national level; for example, influencing politics and the government. In the Netherlands there is a unique approach in IR at the national level. Employers and trade unions have been represented in the Labour Foundation (Stichting van de

Arbeid) since 1945. The Labour Foundation is a national consultative body and a forum in which members (the three peak employers' associations and the three peak trade union federations in the Netherlands) discuss relevant issues in IR; for example, with regard to employment security, new CBAs, social innovation and flexibility. This foundation works closely together with the Social and Economic Council of the Netherlands (SER). The SER is also an advisory and consultative body, with representatives of the employers (one-third), the employees (trade unions) (one-third) and independent experts (one-third). The SER aims to help create social consensus on national and international socio-economic issues. The statements made by the Labour Foundation and the SER have a stabilizing effect on the IR in the Netherlands (Visser and Hemerijck, 1997). Both institutions advise all involved parties, including their own constituencies.

Stop and reflect

Discuss the advantages and disadvantages of employee participation at a national level (through employers' associations and trade unions) for organizations and individual employees.

The European Trade Union Confederation (ETUC) represents trade unions at European level. The ETUC has 82 national trade union confederations as members from 36 countries, making a total of 60 million trade union members. There is an increased relevance and importance for employee representation across borders, including the ETUC and EWCs within organizations, because of globalization and internationalization of, in particular, MNCs. The strategic decision making of these MNCs mainly takes place at a global or continental level. National bodies for employee representation are not adequate for influencing decision making that potentially affects the employees of an organization. People management issues in MNCs at a global or continental level may include offshoring operations from Western European countries to Asia or Eastern Europe, downsizing business units in multiple countries as part of a global cost-reduction strategy, mergers between large companies (e.g. the merger between the two airlines Air France and KLM), and the acquisition of companies.

Stop and reflect

A large MNC intends to close down one of its factories in France and transfer production to another factory in Hungary. The main purpose of this organizational change is to save costs, because the labour costs in Hungary are significantly lower than the costs in France. Think of the position of the French trade unions and the local French works council of this MNC. Also think about the interests of the Hungarian trade unions and the local Hungarian works council of this MNC.

- What role could the ETUC play in this situation?
- What role could the EWC of this MNC play in this context?

The financial and global crisis of 2008/2009 has had a major impact on organizations, employment and employees. Large-scale plant closures are the result; for example, in the UK:

- A Grangemouth plastics factory with the loss of 95 jobs (BBC, 4 June 2009).

- The Teesside Corus steel plant with the loss of nearly 3000 jobs (*Daily Telegraph*, 25 June 2009).

Table 11.2 presents the job losses in the UK in 2008 alone that have been caused by the financial and global crisis. In the case of downsizing, plant closures and redundancies, employers have to deal with employees, works councils and/or trade unions to negotiate the terms and conditions for these organizational changes, in particular the consequences for employees.

2008	Description	Job losses
3 October	Swiss bank UBS – plant closure	2000
14 October	Cadbury – redundancy	600
23 October	Goldman Sachs – downsizing	600
28 October	Credit Suisse – downsizing	500
8 November	Babcock Marine – downsizing	300
8 November	Corus Steel – redundancy	400
10 November	Cable & Wireless – downsizing	700
10 November	Dairy Crest – downsizing	100
11 November	Virgin Media – downsizing	2200
11 November	GlaxoSmithKline – plant closure	620
11 November	*Yellow Pages* – downsizing	1300
11 November	Housebuilder Taylor Wimpey – downsizing	1000
11 November	Technology firm Psion – downsizing	200
13 November	JCB – redundancy	398
13 November	Telecom company BT – downsizing	6000
17 November	Citigroup – downsizing	1500
17 November	Avis Group – downsizing	315
18 November	Newspaper *The Independent* – downsizing	90
19 November	SIG – downsizing	900
20 November	Rolls-Royce – downsizing	140
20 November	BAE Systems – downsizing	200
20 November	AstraZeneca – downsizing	250
28 November	Newspaper *The Independent* – downsizing	100
28 November	Aon Corporation – downsizing	700
1 December	Aston Martin – downsizing	600
1 December	Halfords – downsizing	250
1 December	HSBC – downsizing	500

2008	Description	Job losses
1 December	Credit Suisse – downsizing	650
2 December	Glasgow-based Bowie Castlebank Group – downsizing	817
3 December	GlaxoSmithKline – downsizing	200
3 December	Experian – downsizing	300
3 December	JA Magson – downsizing	200
3 December	Pinnacle Entertainment – downsizing	94
4 December	Noruma – downsizing	1000
4 December	HMRC – downsizing	3400
5 December	Deliotte – downsizing	450
8 December	British Airways – redundancy	100
8 December	Postman Pat – downsizing	50
12 December	Santander – downsizing	1900
12 December	Entertainment UK – downsizing	700
16 December	HP Bulmer – downsizing	54
17 December	National Express – downsizing	750
23 December	The Officer's Club – shutting down stores	280

TABLE 11.2 The UK in a time of global crisis: 'axing jobs'
Source: www.telegraph.co.uk.

Employee participation at different levels: institutionalized HR practices and best HR practices

In the European context, it is most likely that employee participation occurs at (1) multiple levels (individual, organizational, sector and national) and (2) in different forms, including both institutionalized practices and best practices. Institutionalized employee participation was discussed earlier in this chapter with regard to employee representation through works councils and trade unions. These stakeholders often have a legal position to negotiate with employers on CBAs and social plans in the case of a reorganization or downsizing. In many European countries an organization is obliged to consult its works council in the case of organizational changes that affect the employment relationship. Trade unions operate at organization, branch of industry and national level (e.g. the SER in the Netherlands).

Table 11.3 provides an overview of illustrations of different forms of employee participation at different levels. In Anglo-American contexts (often with a strong unitarist orientation) organizations tend to focus on employee participation as a best practice at individual employee (direct participation) and organization level, leaving the organization room to manoeuvre in the actual design of these best practices. In continental European contexts (often with a strong pluralist orientation) employee participation is highly institutionalized through works councils and trade unions at organization, branch of industry and country level.

There are a couple of notions that need to be considered. First, institutionalized employee participation may appear in combination with employee participation as a best practice (direct participation). Companies such as Shell and Unilever acknowledge the relevance and importance of both works councils and trade unions; however, these companies also apply best practices in employee participation at individual employee and organization level. Second, the concept of employee participation potentially has a positive effect on the individual employee (e.g. in terms of job satisfaction, trust and organizational commitment) and the organization (e.g. in terms of a good social atmosphere between the workers and the employer) (see Chapter 3 on HRM and performance and Chapter 4 on HR metrics and measurement), whether participation is institutionalized or applied as a best practice.

Level	Institutionalized practices	Best practices
Individual employee	Regular meetings and consultations	Selecting a new colleague Autonomy Involvement in the decision on a new appraisal system Attitude survey
Organization	Works council Company CBAs Trade union representation	Decentralization Attitude survey
Branch of industry	Sector CBAs Trade union representation	–
Country	Trade union representation Labour legislation	–

TABLE 11.3 Illustrations of employee participation at different levels

Financial participation

A very specific form of employee participation is **financial participation** (Pendleton et al., 2001). Financial participation may include employee stock ownership (Poutsma et al., 2003), profit-sharing schemes (Kruse, 1996) and employee buyouts (Wright and Bruining, 2008). The underlying idea of financial participation is that employees will be more motivated, more committed to the organization and improve their job performance when they receive ownership (e.g. through stock ownership or in the case of an employee buyout) and/or when they receive part of the yearly profits. The empirical research on financial participation, however, reports mixed results and no strong support for the positive impact of financial participation on HR outcomes and organizational performance (Kalmi et al., 2005).

The financial and the global economic crisis of 2008/2009 started a debate about the financial participation schemes of bankers and top managers of large MNCs. The bankers (in particular traders) in New York and London often received 10–15 per cent of the profits in the case of a new deal, equalling up to millions of euros every year for each individual. The questions with regard to this phenomenon are whether it will make these employees work harder because of these huge financial incentives, whether they are actually worth it and whether this is socially acceptable (social legitimacy)? Top managers of large MNCs often receive fixed pay, profit-related pay (PRP) and stock ownership; again, worth up to millions of euros each year. Does that make them work harder? Or does it make them greedier?

Links with other HR practices: the first step to horizontal fit and an HPWS

Employee participation and involvement in practice is often closely related and in some cases fully integrated with other HR practices. Participation and involvement can be applied to the other four HPWPs discussed in this book:

- selective recruitment and selection (Chapter 7);
- performance management (Chapter 8);
- compensation (Chapter 9);
- training and development (Chapter 10).

Employees can be involved in the selection and recruitment process of new colleagues; for example, during job interviews or as observers in assessment centres. The benefits of employee involvement in the recruitment and selection process are twofold:

1 Employees are taken seriously by having a say in important decisions, possibly affecting satisfaction, commitment and citizenship behaviour positively.
2 Employees cannot blame others for recruiting and selecting poor candidates since they have been part of the process as well.

Employee involvement in the design of an appraisal or PM system was discussed in Chapter 8. Empirical findings show that employee participation in the design results in higher perceived procedural justice (Locke, 2003). In other words, it pays to involve employees in the design of a new PM system. Employees will be more likely to engage positively in the new PM system because they perceive it as a fair one.

Employees can also be involved in decisions with regard to internal promotions (as part of pay for performance) and additional bonuses given to excellent job performers. One way of doing it is anonymously to avoid a negative atmosphere among colleagues. Each employee can nominate one or more candidates for an extra bonus, for example.

The human resource development (HRD) principles discussed in Chapter 10, in particular on-the-job learning, often capture elements of employee involvement and participation. Employees are partly self-responsible for their learning and are also actively involved in sharing knowledge with others.

Besides the four HPWPs discussed in this book, other HR practices can be integrated with elements of employee participation as well, for example:

- teamwork and cooperation (autonomous teams);
- job design and self-responsibility for dividing tasks;
- decentralization of decision making to individual employees or teams.

The strategic relevance of participation

Employee involvement, autonomy and participation in decision making are generally considered to be highly relevant to motivate, commit and satisfy employees. However, little attention is paid to the strategic relevance of institutionalized forms of employee participation through, for example, trade unions and works councils. This chapter highlights the possibilities of strategic alliances between the HR function (e.g. represented by the CHRO) and social partners (trade union officers and works councils). Building long-term relationships with these social partners is relevant in times of radical organizational change (e.g. mergers, acquisitions, downsizing). The works councils can act as the intermediate between top management (represented by the CHRO) and the employees. The trade unions are important to gain social legitimacy for organizational change. Ignoring the role of social partners, in particular in continental European countries, potentially results in strikes, negative media attention, reputation damage and court cases.

Summary

- Employee participation has roots in the Human Relations Movement, the revisionistic approaches, Theory Y, STS approaches, the industrial democracy perspective and TQM.
- Employee participation has received a lot of attention from both a managerial best-practice perspective and an (institutionalized) IR perspective.
- The managerial perspective considers employee involvement as a best practice for achieving employee motivation, commitment and organizational citizenship behaviour.
- The IR perspective on employee participation is mainly manifested through trade unions and works councils aimed at workers' rights to be involved.
- The unitarist approach mainly focuses on the shareholders' interests and builds on the notion that employers and employees mainly share common interests.
- The pluralist approach acknowledges different stakeholders, including social partners (trade unions and works councils), that often have different interests to the managers and/or shareholders. This often leads to conflicts that are inherent to organizing work.
- The industrial democracy perspective pays specific attention to institutionalized forms of employee participation and has a strong tradition in Europe.
- Works councils are a form of employee representation within organizations.
- Trade unions are a form of employee representation outside organizations that operate at different levels, including the organization, branch of industry and national level.
- An EWC is a form of employee representation in large MNCs that operates in multiple European countries.
- The ETUC represents trade unions at a European level.
- In many European countries some forms of employee participation (e.g. works councils) are institutionalized and required by law, while other forms of participation are not and therefore can be used by employers to create unique best practices.
- Financial participation is a specific type of employee involvement through stock ownership and profit sharing based on the assumption that sharing ownership and profits will increase employee commitment, employee motivation, organizational citizenship behaviour and job performance. The empirical results on this relationship, however, are not strong and the evidence is mixed.
- Employee participation is often embedded in other HR practices, including selective recruitment and selection, appraisal and PM systems, compensation, training and development, teamwork, job design and decentralization.

Glossary of key terms

Best (HR) practices are people management activities that are created and implemented by organizations to increase organizational performance without any institutional obligation (e.g. by law).
Collective bargaining agreement (CBA) coverage refers to the percentage of all workers who are covered by a CBA.
Degree of unionization represents the percentage of all employees who are trade union members.
Financial participation involves employee participation in organizational ownership and profits.
Industrial democracy perspective pays specific attention to and highlights the importance of the further emancipation of individual workers and their involvement in an organization.
Institutionalized HR practices are people management activities that are determined by legislation or CBAs; for example, with regard to wages, pension schemes, employment benefits, training budget and employee participation.
Pluralist HRM approach takes into account the interests of different stakeholders of an organization and builds on the notion that their interests can be conflicting.
Trade unions are a form of institutionalized employee representation at organization, branch of industry and national level mainly engaged in CBAs and relationship management with other social partners (employers and the government).
Unitarist HRM approach mainly focuses on the interests of the shareholders of an organization in combination with the assumption that employers and employees share common goals and interests.
Works councils are a form of institutionalized employee representation within organizations mainly engaged in organizational issues that affect the employment relationship.

Personal development

1 Are you a member of a trade union? If you are still a student, do you think you will become a member of a trade union? What are your criteria for membership or non-membership of a trade union?
2 Would you be willing to become a member of the works council of your (current or future) organization? Can you think of reasons for participating or not participating in your works council?

Individual task

To what extent would you like to be involved (employee involvement/employee participation) in the following practices:

(1 = very little; 2 = little; 3 = neutral; 4 = intensive; 5 = very intensive)

	Practice					
1	The design of a new training and development programme	1	2	3	4	5
2	The development of a new appraisal system	1	2	3	4	5
3	The recruitment and selection of a new colleague	1	2	3	4	5
4	The decision making on who gets an extra bonus	1	2	3	4	5
5	Decisions on internal promotions	1	2	3	4	5
6	The design of your own job (job design)	1	2	3	4	5
7	The content and design of the yearly employee survey	1	2	3	4	5
8	Discussing the outcomes of the yearly employee survey	1	2	3	4	5
9	Works council membership	1	2	3	4	5
10	Organizing social events	1	2	3	4	5

Calculate your total score by adding up the item scores (minimum score = 10; maximum score = 50).

- What are the most important practices to you in this list?
- What are the least important practices to you in this list?
- Overall, do you want to be involved to a high or low extent?
- Think of the advantages and disadvantages of your involvement.

Team task

Find out more about the main *trade unions in your country* in terms of:

- the total number of trade union members of each union;
- their main goals and philosophy (e.g. some trade unions have a Christian foundation and related values);
- the hot issues and concrete current activities.

Find out more about the main *employers' associations in your country* in terms of:

- the nature of the membership of these associations;
- their main goals and philosophy;
- the hot issues and concrete current activities.

Try to find out how the trade unions and the employers' associations are related and what the atmosphere between them is. It might be a good idea to check recent newspapers and magazines on this issue.

The overall goal of this team task is twofold:

1. getting a better understanding of the potential stakeholders of organizations in a specific country;
2. getting a better understanding of the relationship between employee representatives (trade unions) and employers' associations.

Learning checklist

After studying this chapter, you should be able to do the following:

- Outline the roots of employee participation.
- Discuss employee participation from a unitarist and a pluralist perspective.
- Identify the industrial democracy approach.
- Recognize employee participation at different levels, including participation as a best practice at individual employee level and participation at organization, sector and national level.
- Outline the escalator of employee participation.
- Review works councils and employee involvement.
- Discuss trade unions and employee involvement.
- Outline financial participation.
- Evaluate participation in relationship to other HR practices, including teamwork, job design and decentralization.

References

Addison, J.T., Schnabel, C. and Wagner, J. (2004) The course of research into the economic consequences of German works councils, *British Journal of Industrial Relations,* 42(2): 255–81.

Appelbaum, E., Bailey, T., Berg, P. and Kalleberg, A. (2000) *Manufacturing Advantage: Why High-performance Work Systems Pay Off.* Ithaca, NY: Cornell University Press.

Arthur, J.B. (1994) Effects of human resource systems on manufacturing performance and turnover, *Academy of Management Journal*, 37(3): 670–87.

Bailey, T. (1993) Organizational innovation in the apparel industry, *Industrial Relations*, 32: 30–48.

Baron, J.M. and Kreps, D.M. (1999) *Strategic Human Resources: Frameworks for General Managers*, New York: Wiley.

Boselie, P. (2009) A balanced approach to understanding the shaping of human resource management in organisations, *Management Revue*, 20(1): 90–108.

Boselie, P., Farndale, E. and Paauwe, J. (2010) Performance management, in C. Brewster and W. Mayrhofer (eds), *Handbook of Research in Comparative Human Resource Management*, Chapter 19. Cheltenham: Edward Elgar.

Brewster, C. (2007) Comparative HRM: European views and perspectives, *International Journal of Human Resource Management*, 18(5): 769–87.

Bruining, J., Boselie, P., Bacon, N. and Wright, M. (2005) Business ownership change and effects on the employment relationship: an exploratory study of buyouts in the UK and the Netherlands, *International Journal of Human Resource Management*, 16: 345–63.

Emery, F.E. and Thorsrud, E. (1976) *Democracy at Work: The Report of the Norwegian Industrial Democracy Program.* Leiden: Nijhof.

Emery, F.E. and Trist, E.L. (1960) Sociotechnical systems, in C.W. Churchman and M. Verhulst (eds), *Management Science: Models and Techniques*, Volume II. Oxford: Pergamon Press.

Hoque, K. and Bacon, N. (2008) Trade unions, union learning representatives and employer-provided training in Britain, *British Journal of Industrial Relations*, 46(4): 702–31.

Hubler, O. and Jirjahn, U. (2001) Works councils and collective bargaining in Germany: the impact on productivity and wages. IZA working paper 322.

Kalmi, P., Pendleton, A. and Poutsma, E. (2005) Financial participation and performance in Europe, *Human Resource Management Journal*, 15(4): 54–67.

Keegan, A. and Boselie, P. (2006) The lack of impact of dissensus inspired analysis on developments in the field of human resource management, *Journal of Management Studies*, 43(7): 1491–511.

Kruse, D.L. (1996) Why do firms adopt profit-sharing and employee ownership plans?, *British Journal of Industrial Relations*, 34(4): 515–38.

Legge, K. (1995) *Human Resource Management: Rhetorics and Realities*. London: Macmillan Business.

Leisink, P. (ed.) (1997) *Globalization and Labor Relations*. Cheltenham: Edward Elgar.

Lepak, D.P. and Snell, S.A. (2002) Examining the human resource architecture: the relationships among human capital, employment, and human resource configurations, *Journal of Management*, 28(4): 517–43.

Locke, E.A. (2003) Motivation through conscious goal setting, in L.W. Porter, G.A. Bigley and R.M. Steers (eds), *Motivation and Work Behavior*, Chapter 2, pp. 113–25. New York: McGraw-Hill Higher Education.

Looise, J.C. and Drucker, M. (2003) Dutch works councils in times of transition: the effects of changes in society, organizations and work on the position of works councils, *Economic and Industrial Democracy*, 24(3): 379–409.

Looise, J.C. and Paauwe, J. (2001) HR research in the Netherlands: imitation and innovation, *International Journal of Human Resource Management*, 7(12): 1203–17.

Marchington, M. and Wilkinson, A. (2005) Direct participation and involvement, in S. Bach (ed.), *Managing Human Resources: Personnel Management in Transition*, 4th edn, Chapter 15, pp. 398–423. Oxford: Blackwell.

Maslow, A.H. (1943) A theory of human motivation, *Psychological Review*, 50: 370–96.

Mayo, E. (1933) *The Human Problems of an Industrial Civilization*. New York: Macmillan.

McGregor, D. (1960) *The Human Side of Enterprise*. New York: McGraw-Hill.

Paauwe, J. and Boselie, P. (2003) Challenging 'strategic HRM' and the relevance of the institutional setting, *Human Resource Management Journal*, 13(3): 56–70.

Pendleton, A., Poutsma, E., Ommeren, J. Van and Brewster, C. (2001) *Employee Share Ownership and Profit Sharing in the European Union*. Luxembourg: Office for Official Publications of the European Commission.

Pfeffer, J. (1994) *Competitive Advantage through People*. Boston, MA: Harvard Business School Press.

Poutsma, E., Henderickx, J. and Huijgen, F. (2003) Employee participation in Europe: in search of the participative workplace, *Economic and Industrial Democracy*, 24(1): 45–76.

Schilstra, K. (1998) Industrial relations and human resource management: a network approach. Dissertation, Erasmus University Rotterdam, Thela Thesis and Tinbergen Institute.

Schilstra, K. and Smit, E. (2005) *Voeten op de vloer: Strategische Keuzes in Belangenbehartiging van Werknemers* [*Feet on the Floor: Strategic Choices in Employee Representation*]. Amsterdam: Aksant.

Sorge, A. (1976) The evolution of industrial democracy in the countries of the European community, *British Journal of Industrial Relations*, 14(3): 274–94.

Storey, J. (1992) *Developments in the Management of Human Resources*. Oxford: Blackwell.

Taylor, F.W. (1911) *Principles of Scientific Management*. New York: Harper.

van Dijck, J.J.J. (1984) *The sociotechnical systems approach to organizations*, in P.J.D. Drenth, H. Thierry, P.J. Willems and C.J. de Wolff (eds), *Handbook of Work and Organizational Psychology*. New York: Wiley.

Van Kaar, R. and Smit, E. (eds) (2007) *Vier Scenario's voor de Toekomst van de Medezeggenschap* [*Four Scenarios for the Future of Employee Participation*]. Delft: Eburon.

Visser, J. and A. Hemerijck (1997) *'A Dutch miracle': Job Growth, Welfare Reform and Corporatism in the Netherlands*. Amsterdam: Amsterdam University Press.

Walton, R.E. (1985) From control to commitment in the workplace, *Harvard Business Review*, March–April: 77–84.

Wigboldus, J.E., Looise, J.C. and Nijhof, A. (2008) Understanding the effects of works councils on organizational performance: a theoretical model and results from initial case studies from the Netherlands, *Management Revue*, 19(4): 307–23.

Wilkinson, A., Marchington, M., Goodman, J. and Ackers, P. (1992) Total quality management and employee involvement, *Human Resource Management Journal*, 2(4): 1–20.

Wills, J. (2000) Great expectations: three years in the life of a European works council, *European Journal of Industrial Relations*, 6(1): 85–107.

Wright, M. and Bruining, J. (eds) (2008) *Private Equity and Management Buy-outs*. Cheltenham: Edward Elgar.

Zuthem, H.J. Van (1976) *Arbeid en Arbeidsbeleid in de Onderneming* [*Labour and Social Policies in Organization*]. Holland: Assen.

Further reading

Boselie, P. (2009) A balanced approach to understanding the shaping of human resource management in organisations. *Management Revue*, 20(1): 90–108.

Hyman, R. and Leisink, P. (2005) Introduction: the dual evolution of Europeanization and varieties of governance, *European Journal of Industrial Relations*, 11(3): 277–86.

Kalmi, P., Pendleton, A. and Poutsma, E. (2005) Financial participation and performance in Europe. *Human Resource Management Journal*, 15(4): 54–67.

Pil, F.K. and MacDuffie, J.P. (1996) The adoption of high-involvement work practices, *Industrial Relations*, 3(35): 423–55.

Verma, A. and Kochan, T.A. (2004) *Unions in the 21st Century*. Toronto: Palgrave.

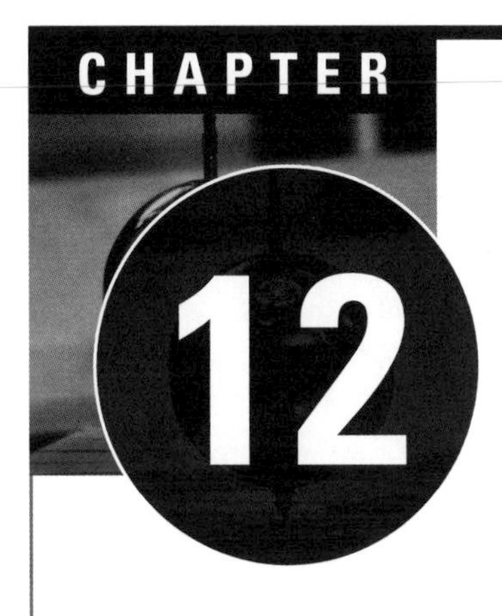

Human Resource Roles

❖ Learning Objectives

After studying this chapter, you should be able to do the following:

- ❖ Understand Legge's (1978) three ambiguities as the source for the lack of power of personnel managers in practice
- ❖ Discuss Legge's (1978) three vicious circles that block personnel managers' opportunities to overcome the human resource (HR) ambiguities
- ❖ Outline the conformist innovator and deviant innovator HR roles
- ❖ Understand the changing HR roles
- ❖ Review Storey's (1992) HR role model
- ❖ Review Ulrich's (1997) HR role model
- ❖ Evaluate the advantages and disadvantages of HR role models
- ❖ Outline the HR competence models
- ❖ Discuss the HR qualities of the contemporary and future HR professional

CASE STUDY: UNILEVER AND PEOPLELINK

Outsourcing and offshoring HRM

Unilever is a major manufacturer of food, home care and personal products including margarine, tea and Dove soap. This British-Dutch multinational company (MNC) operates in more than 100 countries and employs 170 000 people worldwide. In 2003 Unilever introduced the human resource (HR) shared services centre PeopleLink. This was Unilever's first attempt to run human resource management (HRM) as a business. The transactional and administrative components of the HR function were no longer performed by HR managers 'in the field', but embedded in the shared services centre (SSC). The introduction and operations of PeopleLink were soon considered successful with regard to cost reduction, (internal) customer satisfaction and cost effectiveness. This transition from the 'traditional' personnel management by personnel managers to the introduction of a SSC was just the first step in a new era of HR restructuring within Unilever. In 2006 the British-Dutch MNC signed a contract with Accenture to outsource and offshore all HR shared services. From that moment on mainstream HRM would be handled by a regional network of Accenture SSCs. The more strategic HR issues, for example organizational change and strategic decision making, were still tackled from within Unilever, but the basic HR practices (e.g. recruitment and selection, training and development, and compensation) were under the umbrella of Accenture. The Dutch component of Unilever, for example, would get an Accenture HR SSC located in Prague. Similar outsourcing and offshoring initiatives were developed and introduced by Unilever with regard to ICT (with Dell) and finance (with IBM).

(Bosna, 2007)

However, is the outsourcing and offshoring of PeopleLink a blessing or a nightmare for those involved?

Over one-third of all HR professionals within Unilever were about to lose their job as a result of the outsourcing and offshoring operation. For those who stayed new challenges emerged as strategic partners and change agents. It is unclear whether the line managers were happy about the HR restructuring. In the past line managers could meet face to face with HR professionals. From now on the main contacts between line management and HRM would be through a telephone line (with Prague) or through intranet communication. It is also unclear whether the employees were happy with the new situation either. For them it might also have led to a further depersonalized relationship with one of the key staff functions of the organization. An SSC and the outsourcing/offshoring of it can result in cost reduction, but what about its impact on employment relations, for example between employees and HRM or between line managers and HRM.

? Discussion questions

- What do you think of the impact of Unilever's transition to outsourcing and offshoring HRM on the HR professionals within Unilever?
- The HR professionals that stay within Unilever after the outsourcing and offshoring of PeopleLink will operate more as strategic partners and change agents. What is the impact of this organizational change on the position of these HR professionals within Unilever?
- What are the potential negative effects of this organizational change on the (internal) customers of Unilever (employees and line managers)?

Introduction

HRM is an area of expertise within organizations comparable to other disciplines such as finance, marketing and accounting. After more than two decades of debates about the position of HRM, we can conclude that 'human resource management is on the table' in most organizations (Ulrich and Brockbank, 2005). Employee retention in times of labour market shortages as a result of an ageing population, in particular in Western countries, talent management for the most valuable employees of an organization, leadership development (LD) and succession planning, and performance management (PM) in order to create long-term success are just a few examples of HRM themes that dominate the top management's agenda of many contemporary organizations. The majority of chief executive officers (CEOs) of leading organizations are most likely to state that their employees are the most valuable assets of the organization. Implicitly, this indicates the relevance and importance of good people management in order to select, retain, motivate, reward and develop the human capital pool (the workforce) of an organization. In other words, there is an important role for HRM in achieving organizational goals.

'Human resource management is on the table.'

The question remains: Who is responsible for the HRM in an organization? The answer to this question is rather complicated. Ulrich and Brockbank (2005), for example, argue that:

- When asked who is responsible for finance in an organization, the respondents are more likely to answer that it is the responsibility of the chief financial officer (CFO) and the financial department of an organization.
- When asked who is responsible for marketing in an organization, the respondents are most likely to answer it is the responsibility of the chief marketing officer (CMO) and the marketing department.
- But when asked who is responsible for HRM in an organization, the respondents are more likely to answer that it is everybody's responsibility in an organization, including line managers, top management, the chief human resource officer (CHRO) and the HRM department.

Although there is general agreement about HRM being an area of expertise required in an organization comparable to finance and marketing, it is more difficult to determine the HR responsibilities, and therefore the position of the HR department in an organization (Legge, 1978; Guest and King, 2004). This is a topic of ongoing debate among HR scholars and HR practitioners versus non-HR practitioners. The HR department and its professionals are often *'the victim'* of strategic decision making in organizations, implying that HR is involved after the initial strategic decision making. Therefore, the HR department and the HR professionals are limited to tactical interventions with little or no influence on the strategic decision making right from the start. Ulrich and Brockbank (2005) refer to this issue as *'human resource management is not at the table'*.

This chapter starts with an historical overview of the HR function. The analysis of Legge (1978) is used to show the ambiguities that characterize the HR profession. Guest and King (2004) showed that much of Legge's (1978) analyses and conclusions are still relevant in practice. The overview results in a summary of the most important developments in HR roles and HR competences for personnel managers necessary to attain or maintain a strong position in an organization.

'Human resource management is not at the table.'

HR ambiguities

The **personnel function** represents the HR responsibilities and tasks that are bundled in an HR department and performed by HR professionals. It is important to note that the personnel function is part of the HRM of an organization, although the latter represents a much broader concept, including the role of line managers, top management, works councils and employees.

Legge's (1978) study focuses on the personnel function, in particular on the analysis of the challenges personnel managers are confronted with in practice. The nature of the HRM creates three HR ambiguities for personnel managers in practice. According to Legge, these **three ambiguities** are the source for the lack of power of personnel managers in practice. First, there is a substantial overlap between personnel management as a set of activities for all managers and personnel management as a specialist function. Many HR practices, including appraisal and promotion, are enacted by the direct supervisor (line manager) of an employee, and not by the personnel manager. The personnel manager however is often the specialist in these HR practices, causing a potential tension and ambiguity between who is in charge of the practice (often the line manager) and who is an expert on the practice (the personnel manager).

The second ambiguity reflects the difficulty of defining success in personnel management, determining who or what was responsible for success or failure and identifying the unique contribution of the personnel function. Legge's second ambiguity is related to the first one. The personnel managers are often unable to celebrate HR successes because multiple actors, in particular front-line managers, are involved in the successful implementation of HR practices. HR successes are easily claimed by others and HR failures are easily blamed on the personnel managers and their department.

The third ambiguity represents Legge's notion that personnel managers are part of management, while having a 'special' relationship with and responsibility for the workers. This ambiguity reflects the potential tension between the employer's and the employees' interests and the possible mediating role of personnel managers. For example, when there is a serious conflict between a supervisor and a subordinate, the personnel manager often takes the role of mediator.

To overcome these three ambiguities, Legge argues that personnel managers need *power* and *authority*. This is however easier said than done. The capital society, with its dominant profit motive, created *three vicious circles* that block personnel managers' opportunities to overcome the three ambiguities (ibid.). First, the lack of power and centrality of decision making results in non-involvement of the personnel department and its professionals in the business strategy. To put it differently, HRM is not at the table; it is a victim of decision making. The second vicious circle represents the phenomenon that personnel managers are uncertain about their success criteria, and therefore uncertain of their priorities. The result is the absence of strategic focus within the personnel department and in the heads of personnel managers. The lack of priorities can negatively affect customer satisfaction (e.g. from front-line managers) with HR outcomes. The third circle in Legge's analysis shows the personnel department's inability to authorize collective bargaining agreements (CBAs). At the time of Legge's study, apparently most organizations still had personnel departments that were not authorized to make decisions about aspects of CBAs; for example, with regard to wages, employee benefits, pension schemes and health care insurance for employees. The authorization on HR issues often had to come from the CEOs themselves.

To overcome these ambiguities and vicious circles, personnel managers can choose two roles (Legge, 1978): (1) the conformist innovator role or (2) the deviant innovator role.

The **conformist innovator** role acts in line with the business and mainly emphasizes the economic value of employees. The conformist innovator speaks the (business) language of the CEO, CFO and other disciplines such as marketing. The success of some HR directors in recent years might be the result of their conformist innovator role; for example, reflected in their ability to downsize and reorganize the organization (Wright and Snell, 2005). Overall, the conformist innovator identifies with managerial values and criteria such as cost–benefit analysis. This innovator personnel management role might include knowledge and skills in human capital valuation (HR measurement), quantitative analysis (statistics), finance, accounting and computer systems.

The **deviant innovator** puts forward long-term issues related to people management and highlights the continuous search for balancing economic interests and human aspects (Legge, 1978), for example embedded in employee well-being and corporate reputation. Deviant innovators identify with different but not necessarily conflicting sets of values and take a powerful independent professional stance *vis-à-vis* managerial clients. They are much more critical of decision making in searching for a balance between the employer and the employee, and a balance between short- and long-term effects. Deviant innovators attempt to change the 'means–ends relationship', they are not afraid to discuss a different set of criteria for decision making and are open to alternative perspectives.

Legge's distinction between conformist and deviant innovators is a theoretical one, interesting for discussing the role and position of personnel managers, but difficult to apply in practice. Therefore, Legge (in Guest and King, 2004: 404) highlights a third option:

> 'Without the power that derives from external sources, many personnel managers will find it difficult to operate as deviant innovators while conformist innovation is unlikely to result in significant change. The core of Legge's argument is therefore that personnel managers need to become problem-solvers.'

The problem-solver role presented by Legge is less ambitious than the conformist and deviant innovator roles, but perhaps more realistic. The problem-solver in HRM represents a personnel manager who is capable of delivering the basic HR practices to HR customers (e.g. employees and line managers). According to this ideal role, personnel managers need basic skills and knowledge of personnel planning, recruitment and selection practices, socialization of newcomers, training and development, performance appraisal (PA), compensation and benefits, teamwork, employee involvement, employee participation, job rotation programmes, job enlargement and job enrichment and managing employee absence. The idea behind the relevance of this role is that solving problems of customers such as line managers and employees will gain credibility and strengthen the reputation of personnel managers. Credibility and a good reputation are most likely to positively affect the position and power of the personnel function within an organization.

Guest and King's (2004) analysis of the original framework of Legge (1978) shows that most ambiguities and vicious circles are still relevant in contemporary organizations.

Stop and reflect

Legge's (1978) third vicious circle – the personnel department's inability to authorize CBAs – is partly solved in many organizations. Nowadays, the CHRO of a large organization is in charge of the CBAs with social partners (trade unions and works councils). Think of reasons why and how the CHRO is capable of strengthening the value of the personnel function to the organization through CBAs.

Changing roles and expectations for the HR manager[1]

The readjustment and recalibration of the HR function and the different roles of HR professionals has been going on for some time. A review of the literature throws up many frameworks for considering the evolution and development in HR tasks, skills and roles. Some are merely a listing of things that HR specialists do, while others are more encompassing, considering the HRM pattern from a more ideal type perspective (Tyson and Fell, 1986; Ulrich, 1997). Tyson (1987) provides a good start for an overview of the changing roles and, struck by the increased

[1] This section was inspired by an earlier study of Boselie and Paauwe (2005), published in *Personnel Review*.

fragmentation of the personnel function, which he describes as its 'Balkanization', distinguishes three Weberian ideal types or models:

1. *The clerk of works model*: personnel management is an administrative support activity with no involvement in business planning. All authority is vested in line managers. The principal activities for these personnel staff are recruitment, record-keeping and welfare.
2. *The contract manager model*: this approach is concerned with confronting unions with a regulatory system as part of a comprehensive policy network. Acting on behalf of line managers, the personnel department staff are the experts on trade union agreements, fixing day-to-day issues with the unions and responding in a reactive way to problems.
3. *The architect model*: in this model personnel executives seek to create and build the organisation as a whole. This creative vision of personnel contributes to the success of the business through explicit policies, which seek to influence the corporate plan, with an integrated system of controls between personnel and line managers. The personnel function is represented within the dominant coalition in the organization.

Schuler (1990) increasingly discerns a shift from a specialist staff function to the HR manager as business manager and part of the management team. He claims that the following roles became more prominent in the 1990s: business person, shaper of change, consultant to the organization, strategy formulator and implementer, talent manager, assets manager and cost controller.

Caroll (1991) also envisages a shift in HR roles as a consequence of the more pronounced links to business needs and a greater requirement to contribute to organizational effectiveness. In addition to the traditional roles of policy formulator and provider of personnel services, Caroll expects certain roles to take on greater importance:

1. *Delegator*: this role enables line managers to serve as primary implementers of HRM systems.
2. *Technical expert*: this function encompasses a number of highly specific HR-related skills in, for example, areas such as remuneration and management development (MD).
3. *Innovator*: as innovators, HR managers recommend new approaches in solving HRM-related problems, such as productivity and a sudden increase in absenteeism due to illness.

Storey (1992), intensively involved in the HR characteristics debate in the UK in both the 1980s and 1990s, develops the following typology based on: (1) action orientation (interventionary versus non-interventionary) and (2) strategic versus tactical choices/considerations (see Figure 12.1).

These two dimensions lead to the following four different HR roles:

1. *Advisors* act as internal consultants. They are in tune with recent developments, but leave the actual running to line and general management colleagues.
2. *Handmaidens* are primarily customer-oriented in the services they offer, based on a rather subservient, attendant relationship with line management.
3. *Regulators* are more interventionary. They formulate, promulgate and monitor observance of employment rules. These rules range from personnel procedure manuals to joint agreements with trade unions.
4. *Changemakers* are seeking to put relationships with employees on a new footing, one that is in line with the 'needs of the business'.

Finally, I refer to the typology developed by Ulrich (1997), who also uses two dimensions (people versus process and strategic versus operational) in order to highlight the following roles by which the HR managers can contribute to added value (see Figure 12.2):

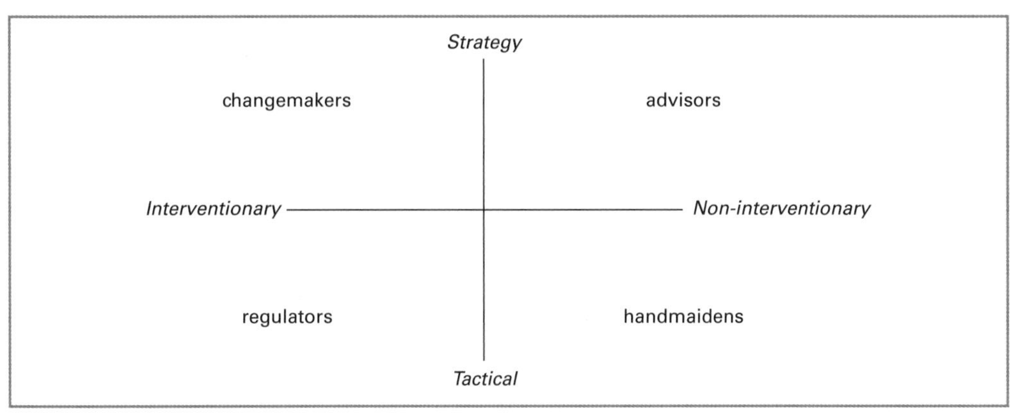

FIGURE 12.1 HR role model (1992)
Source: Reproduced with permission from Storey (1992).

1 *Administrative expert role*: in this role the HR professional designs and delivers efficient HR processes for staffing, training, appraising, rewarding, promoting and otherwise managing the flow of employees through the organization. The deliverable from this role is administrative efficiency.
2 *Employee champion role*: the employee contribution role for HR professionals encompasses their involvement in the day-to-day problems, concerns and needs of employees. The deliverables aimed at are increased employee commitment and competence.
3 *Change agent role*: this role focuses on managing transformation and change. The deliverable is aimed at developing a capacity for change. HR managers help employees to let go of the old culture and adapt to a new culture.
4 *Strategic partner role*: the strategic HR role focuses on aligning HR strategies and practices with business strategy. The deliverable is strategy execution. HR practices help accomplish business objectives.

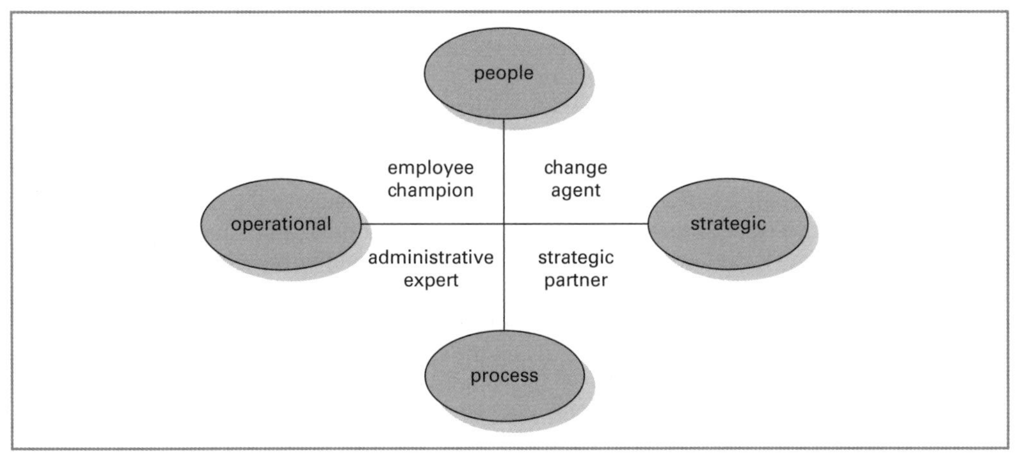

FIGURE 12.2 HR role model (1997)
Source: Reproduced with permission from Ulrich (1997).

The Ulrich (1997) model is by far the most widely used HR role model. It is also one of the few academic HR models that is used in practice on a large scale worldwide. The four roles provide a clear yardstick for developing HR profiles and roles in the business. The model can also be used as a tool for self-reflection of the individual personnel manager or for the positioning of the HR department as a whole within the organization.

Stop and reflect

Imagine yourself being a newcomer in HRM. This is your first job in HRM.

- What kind of role from the Ulrich (1997) model do you see yourself in?
- What do you think is expected from you in that role? For example, what kinds of deliverables are expected from your customers?

(*Note:* Choose one HR role: employee champion, strategic partner, change agent or administrative expert.)

A critical reflection on the HR role models

What is the relevance and significance of the different typologies, as put forward during the 1980s and 1990s, for today's practice? Authors such as Schuler (1990), Caroll (1991) and Tyson (1987) all discern a shift towards a more strategic, business-like approach and a more intensive relationship with line and top management. This is fully in line with the writings on (strategic) HRM as encountered during that same period (Boselie et al., 2005).

However, the balance seems to be restored by the typology of Storey (1992), which is more empirically based than the aforementioned typologies. In his overview, we still encounter the 'handmaidens' and 'regulators', both of which are more reminiscent of the traditional personnel management role, which apparently happened to be still quite common in practice. Based on more recent empirical data (both survey-based and interviews), Caldwell (2003) re-examines the relevance of the typology as put forward by Storey (1992). His conclusion is that the regulator role appears to have declined and the advisor role has become more strongly entrenched. The service provider role (a renaming of Storey's (1992) original 'handmaiden' role in order to avoid any overly negative meaning; see Caldwell, 2003) has been remodelled to deliver the administrative infrastructure of HR more effectively.

Finally, the change agent role has grown in significance along with the ascendancy of HRM (Caldwell, 2003). Caldwell claims that using typologies such as the one of Storey (1992) or Ulrich (1997) potentially incorporates intrinsic weaknesses, because the generic roles within these frameworks do not capture the increasingly complex and multifaceted nature of personnel and HR roles. Based on his empirical research (especially the qualitative part), he is indeed able to establish a range of role ambiguities and conflicts. Making use of a 2 × 2 matrix has, on the one hand, the charm of simplicity and expressiveness but, on the other, generates the problem of oversimplification by disguising the complexity of empirical reality. We can avoid this by making use of 'competences', as is the case in the human resource competence survey (HRCS), which not only focuses on the USA (Ulrich, 1997) or the UK (Storey, 1992; Caldwell, 2003) but is truly global in nature, at least since its latest two versions (2005 and 2007).

A 2 × 2 matrix generates four different roles based on a distinction between just two dimensions. Ulrich's (1997) model, for example, is based on the dimensions of people–process and strategic–operational. The application of a competence approach (in contrast to a 2 × 2 matrix approach) creates opportunities for incorporating multiple dimensions (or competences) that do justice to the complexity and the dynamics in practice (Caldwell, 2008).

The HRCS[2]

The HRCS has been an ongoing research project since the late 1980s. Major blocks of data were gathered and analysed in 1988, 1992 and 1997 in the USA (Brockbank et al., 2002). In the first two rounds, three competence categories were uncovered: business knowledge, HR functional capability and change management. In 1997 two additional categories were added: culture management and personal credibility. In 2002 the HRCS Michigan research team and its associated partners around the globe performed research in four continents: North America, Latin America, Asia and Europe. In the 2002 survey, out of a range of 78 items and 15 distilled competences, five domain factors emerged as making a difference in terms of performance:

1. *Strategic contribution*: high-performing organizations have HR professionals involved in the business at a strategic level. These HR professionals manage culture, facilitate fast change, are involved in strategic decision making and create market-driven connectivity.
2. *Personal credibility*: HR professionals must be credible to both their HR counterparts and the business line managers whom they serve. They need to promise and deliver results and establish a reliable track record. In addition, HR professionals must have effective written and verbal communication skills.
3. *HR delivery*: HR professionals deliver both traditional and operational HR activities to their business in four major categories. First, designing development programmes and challenging work experiences, offering career planning services and facilitating internal communication processes. These efforts include both individual development as well as organization-wide development. Second, structure and HR measurement, involving restructuring the organization, measuring impact of HR practices and managing global implications of HR practices. Third, attracting, promoting, retaining and outplacing appropriate people. Finally, PM in terms of designing performance-based measurements and reward systems.
4. *Business knowledge*: to become key players in the organization, HR professionals must understand the business and industry of the organization they serve. Key areas of knowledge include applied understanding of the integrated value chain (how the firm horizontally integrates) and the firm's value proposition (how the firm creates wealth). Labour, representing institutional constraints such as labour legislation, is the third factor constituting the domain of business knowledge.
5. *HR technology*: HR professionals need to be able to leverage technology for HR practices and use e-HR/web-based channels to deliver value to their customers.

Boselie and Paauwe (2005) performed an analysis on the European dataset of the HRCS 2002 dataset. They find empirical evidence for a positive relationship between (1) HR delivery and the position of the personnel function and (2) personal credibility and the position of the personnel function. The respondents in the analysis include both HR professionals and line managers. These findings suggest a potential positive impact on the reputation and power position of a personnel manager's competence to (a) deliver HRM to customers and (b) build and maintain credibility from customers (Boselie and Paauwe, 2005). HR delivery represents the competence to meet the customer's expectations with regard to the functional areas of HRM, including

[2] This section was inspired by an earlier study by Boselie and Paauwe (2005), published in *Personnel Review*.

recruitment, selection, development, compensation and promotion. Personal credibility is created by building effective relationships with customers (e.g. line managers), providing results and excellent communication to all stakeholders involved. The personal credibility competence domain asks for a proactive attitude from personnel managers who are willing to 'manage by walking around'. The other striking finding in the empirical analysis of Boselie and Paauwe (2005) is the positive relationship between the competence domain of strategic contribution of a personnel manager and the financial competitiveness of an organization. In other words, the results suggest a potential positive effect of the personnel manager's strategic contribution, in terms of managing culture management, supporting decision making, enabling fast organizational change and creating market-driven connectivity, on the competitive position of the organization.

Boselie and Paauwe (2005) suggest the possibility of a hierarchy in the three competence domains. In order to add value to an organization, the personnel manager should first gain personal credibility and HR delivery. This is closely related to what Legge (1978) calls the problem-solving role in personnel management. Ulrich's (1997) administrative expert role shows similarities with these two competence domains as well. The underlying idea is that the HR basics should be sufficient, otherwise the personnel manager will not be taken seriously in other areas or on other subject matters. Personnel managers who score highly on personal credibility and HR delivery can achieve the next level of adding value (strategic contribution) through culture management, fast change, supporting strategic decision making and market-driven connectivity.

> Personal credibility + HR delivery → strong position of the personnel manager → strategic contribution → financial competitiveness of the organization

Only a few personnel managers are in the position of strategically contributing to the competitiveness of the organization (Hope-Hailey et al., 2005). It is therefore important to first start focusing on the personal credibility and delivery domain.

The new HR competence model

The HRCS 2007 covered approximately 10 000 respondents in six regions around the world (Ulrich et al., 2007). The new HR competence model covers six HR competence domains:

1. the credible activist;
2. the operational executor;
3. the business ally;
4. the talent manager and organizational designer;
5. the culture and change steward;
6. the strategic architect.

The model by Ulrich et al. (2007) incorporates multi-level notions and distinguishes a people versus a business orientation. There are three levels in the model linked to the six domains. The credible activist focuses on individual relationships. The operational executor and the business ally are linked to systems and processes at a team, group or business unit level. Finally, the talent manager and organizational designer, the culture and change steward and the strategy architect are mainly at the organization and strategy level, aimed at creating organizational capabilities.

The *credible activist* is a *credible* and *active* HR professional (Ulrich et al., 2007). Credibility is represented by being respected, admired and listened to. The notion of active represents offering a point of view, taking a position and challenging assumptions. Challenging assumptions is an HR quality, which is also part of Legge's (1978) deviant innovator, though her role is more critical towards the dominating managerial paradigm.

The *operational architect* executes the operational aspects of managing people and organizations. The key aspects of this domain are *drafting, adapting* and *implementing* HR policies. The importance of HRM implementation for organizational success is also put forward by Becker and Huselid (2006). Technology plays an important role in this domain. The operational architect answers basic HR needs through technology, shared services, outsourcing and offshoring. Knowledge and skills of HRM and information technology (IT) are crucial for this domain.

The *business ally knows the social context* or setting in which their business operates, *knows how the business makes money* (the value chain of the business) *and has a good understanding of the different parts of the business,* including finance, marketing and engineering (Ulrich et al., 2007). HR professionals are business allies when:

- they know who their customers are and what these customers are doing with regard to HRM;
- they know the social partners (e.g. trade unions and works councils), society (norms and values) and the legislation in a given country or region;
- they have business knowledge of other disciplines.

The *talent manager and organizational designer* is an expert in *attracting and retaining talent* and *masters organization design focused on how a company embeds capability* into the organization's structure, processes and policies. Talent management is one of the key areas in contemporary organizations, mainly as a result of serious labour market shortages in many Western countries, caused by baby-boomers who will be retiring in the next five to ten years. Another reason for talent management's popularity is the tendency in both theory and practice to focus on the core employees of an organization because of added-value considerations (Lepak and Snell, 2002). Organizational design refers to choosing structures and associated managerial processes to enable an organization to operate effectively. Organizational design and HRM is about choices with regard to the degree of cooperation within an organization; for example, through teams, the degree of employee involvement in decision making, job autonomy, decentralization or centralization, the degree of job enlargement and the degree of job enrichment among employees.

The *culture and change steward* is the helper of culture management in an organization (Ulrich et al., 2007). The culture steward *nurtures the organization's culture,* for example through socialization and training of new employees. The change steward *helps to shape a new culture,* for example through coaching line managers, translating the new culture into HR practices and making culture real and visible to employees. This domain explicitly acknowledges the crucial role of line managers in enacting HR practices, but also acknowledges their role in managing the culture of an organization in relation to their employees (Wright and Nishii, 2007).

The *strategic architect has a vision* on how the organization can create sustained competitive advantage through human resources (Ulrich et al., 2007). The HR professional needs to recognize trends and their impact on the organization's business. These trends may include labour market shortages, new legislation (e.g. European Union (EU) legislation), technological developments (e.g. IT and the Internet) and new markets (e.g. China). The strategic architect is capable of translating these trends into concrete HR policies and HR practices putting customers first.

The Ulrich et al. (2007) model represents the fifth round of HR research since 1987. The model highlights six HR competence domains for future HR professionals (see Figure 12.3). The model could be interpreted as a combination of Ulrich's (1997) HR role model and the Ulrich and Brockbank (2005) HR competence model, emphasizing both underlying HR competences and different HR roles required for running the HR business in an organization. The talent manager and organizational designer domain is relatively new.

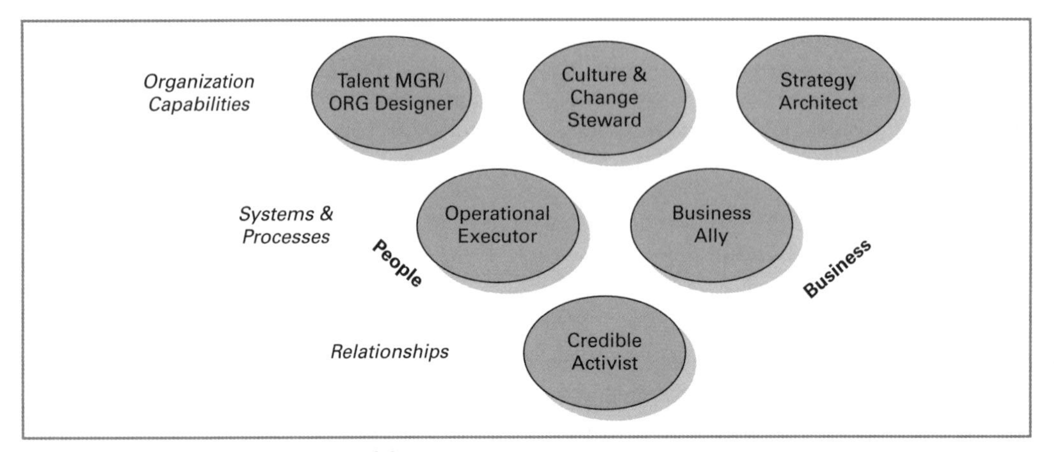

FIGURE 12.3 The new HR competence model
Source: Reproduced with permission from Ulrich et al. (2007).

Evidence-based HRM

Huselid et al. (1997) studied the impact of HRM capabilities of HR professionals on the HR function's effectiveness in 293 US companies. Their results suggest that professional HRM capabilities – including capabilities linked to change management, leadership, creating added value, sharing and communicating vision, line management support, entrepreneurship and risk-taking, broad knowledge of HR tools and instruments, knowledge of the key competitors, service quality focus, international experience and flexibility/adaptability, speaking multiple languages and knowledge of ICT – have a positive effect on the overall effectiveness of the HR department. This HRM effectiveness is positively related to labour productivity and financial performance of the organization (Huselid et al., 1997).

Biemans (1999) presents an empirical study using both survey and interview data on the perceptions of the HR department and its HR professionals. The author collected perception data in the Netherlands from employees, line managers and HR professionals. The results suggest significant and systematic perception differences between the three respondent groups. HR professionals are more positive about themselves and the HR department than line managers and employees. Line managers are primarily interested in HR reliability with regard to administrative issues (e.g. salary administration) and to HR delivery of the basic personnel tools, including recruitment and selection, training and development, compensation and appraisal. HR professionals run the risk of being too focused on HR strategy and policies. The distinction between intended HR practices (policies), actual HR practices (implemented practices) and perceived HR practices made by Wright and Nishii (2007) (see Chapter 3) is an extension of Biemans' (1999) empirical findings.

> Intended practices (HR professionals) → actual practices (line managers) → perceived practices (employees)

Wright et al. (2001) studied line managers' and HR managers' perceptions of HR effectiveness in US organizations. Again, these results suggest that HR professionals are much more positive about themselves than others are of them. Line managers appear to be much more critical and demanding. Line management expects support and facilities from the HR department and HR professionals in order to run their daily business. Line managers are less interested in long-term strategies and policies involving a strategic role for the HR function. Their concerns are much more short- and middle-term focused, closely linked to the actual business of the organization. It is a serious challenge for HR professionals to blend the long-term HR issues (e.g. developing strategies for the labour market shortage in the next five to ten years) with the short-term HR problems of line managers that need to be solved on a daily basis.

The Society for Human Resource Management (2002) is the largest professional association for HR managers in the world, with over 200000 members. It is based in the USA, with members from all over the world. Another large personnel management association is the British Chartered Institute of Personnel and Development (CIPD), with over 120000 members and the UK as its home base. See Farndale and Brewster (2005) for a global overview of the personnel management associations. The Society for Human Resource Management did a study among US HR practitioners, scholars and students on the most important knowledge, skills and abilities for HR professionals in 2002. The findings suggest the significance and importance of the following HR qualities:

- interpersonal communication skills;
- knowledge of labour law;
- knowledge of business ethics;
- writing and communication skills;
- leadership skills and abilities;
- management skills and abilities;
- presentation skills;
- writing a business plan;
- change management skills and abilities;
- strategic management knowledge;
- knowledge of business law;
- advisory skills;
- negotiation skills.

The Society for Human Resource Management (2002) stresses the relevance and importance of personal credibility (Ulrich and Brockbank, 2005) through good communication, advisory and negotiation skills in combination with leadership and management abilities. However, knowledge of labour law, business law, business ethics and strategic management is also required for the HR professional.

Farndale and Paauwe (2007) studied the HR roles in six multinational companies (MNCs) in Europe (ABB, EDF, IKEA, Procter & Gamble, Siemens and Unilever). Their rich dataset is built on 65 interviews with HR managers, line managers and senior executives as part of the Global Human Resource Research Alliance (GHRRA). The GHRRA is a global research project on the HR function sponsored by the Japanese Sanyo Corporation. The research partners of the GHRRA are the University of Cambridge (Judge Institute of Management), Cornell University, INSEAD and Erasmus University Rotterdam/Tilburg University (Paauwe, 2007). The empirical findings presented by Farndale and Paauwe (2007) suggest HR centralization within three companies and HR decentralization within the other three. The centralization–decentralization of the HR function is a strategic choice in all six MNOs, with major implications for the HR professionals. In the centralized companies the HR roles of the personnel managers at a corporate level are mainly focused on becoming and maintaining the role of 'champion of processes', while their role at a corporate level in the three decentralized companies is much more focused on being an 'effective political influencer' and a 'network leader' (Farndale and Paauwe, 2007). These empirical findings suggest the interrelationship between required HR roles and the organizational structure (centralized versus decentralized) within organizations. Another way of putting it is 'context matters', with regard also to ideal HR roles and competences.

Overall, these empirical findings suggest the following HR qualities required from contemporary and future personnel managers (Boselie, 2007):

- HR professionals need excellent administration skills in line with the administrative expert role of Ulrich (1997).
- The HR professional is capable of delivering the traditional personnel management tools such as HR planning, recruitment and selection, training and development, appraisal and compensation in line with Ulrich and Brockbank's (2005) HR delivery domain.
- Basic knowledge of labour law, business law and strategic management is required in line with the SHRM (2002) results.
- The ideal personnel manager possesses excellent communication, negotiation and advisory skills, as suggested by the SHRM (2002) findings.
- The HR professional has up-to-date knowledge of management, strategy, leadership and organizational change models with a critical attitude towards management fads and fashions.
- Critical self-reflection and the ability to listen to what the customer (line manager, senior management and/or employee) wants is a necessary quality for all personnel managers to avoid an overoptimistic view of the HR function (Buyens and De Vos, 2001).

If personnel managers are experts in HR administration, capable of delivering the basic HR instruments, with basic knowledge of the law and the business and with the right interpersonal skills, and not afraid to critically assess their own position, this might be the first step to becoming a business partner in an organization through (Boselie, 2007):

- effective relationship management building social networks with key partners, customers and relevant stakeholders, including works councils and trade union representatives;
- taking charge of organizational change projects in line with Ulrich's (1997) change agent role;
- transparency, clear personal goals, monitoring and evaluating goals, and regular presentation of key performance indicators (KPIs);
- management and leadership skills and abilities to lead other personnel managers and facilitate senior management in strategic decision making.

However, the findings of Farndale and Paauwe (2007) suggest the relevance of context. There appears to be no universalistic set of best practices in HR knowledge, skills and abilities (see Chapter 2 on strategic human resource management and context). The above lists of desirable HR qualities are mainly best principles for personnel managers. The further refinement of these best principles is heavily dependent on the organizational context.

HR roles in different contexts

The majority of the HR role models discussed in this chapter were developed in the USA or the UK. In Chapter 2 it was argued that these contexts tend to be less institutionalized than most continental European countries. In a context with low degrees of institutionalization (e.g. little labour legislation and the absence of trade unions), HR managers have more leeway for strategic choice and organizational change. Therefore, it is more likely that change agent roles and strategic partner roles in HRM are likely to occur in those circumstances in contrast to organizations operating in highly institutionalized environments. Downsizing and outsourcing, for example, are generally less restricted in the US context in comparison to countries such as Austria, Belgium, France, Germany, Italy, the Netherlands and Sweden.

In highly institutionalized countries, characterized by extensive labour legislation and substantial influence of social partners (e.g. trade unions and works councils), HR roles mainly include:

- the administration and translation of (new) legislation into HR practices (e.g. with regard to compensation determined by CBAs);
- the regulation of HRM in an organization according to the laws, protocols and procedures, an HR role comparable to Storey's (1992) regulator;
- the management of stakeholders, including trade unions, works councils, governmental officials and other relevant groups.

Organizational change in Europe, for example a merger or an acquisition, often implies intensive stakeholder management with a key role for the CHRO. This is not only a social legitimacy issue characteristic of the majority of continental European countries, but it is also embedded in national and EU legislation as well. In other words, openness towards social partners is part of societal norms and values in many European countries (e.g. a general acceptance of trade unions by all actors involved), but it is also part of the legislation. Trade unions and works councils have legal rights to be involved in organizational change processes. These two notions are often neglected or ignored by large multinationals, in particular by those MNCs that do not have roots in Europe.

The BASF case in Chapter 11 (p. 232) and the ING Group case in Chapter 13 (p. 275) highlight two characteristic European MNCs that explicitly acknowledge the impact of different institutional contexts on HRM. These two companies tend to be much more sensitive towards stakeholders, in particular trade unions and works councils, than MNCs from the USA. The HR professionals in these organizations are socialized and trained to work with these social partners as strategic partners.

From this point of view, Ulrich's (1997) strategic partner role in practice is not solely aimed at satisfying the needs and wants of top management, but is also aimed at creating a long-term relationship with social partners. The benefits of a good long-term relationship with trade unions and works councils emerge in times of organizational crisis and necessary organizational changes. A good social relationship between HR professionals and social partners is most likely to positively affect negotiations in times of crisis.

The HR roles in practice often tend to be too focused on 'what employers want' (see Chapter 5). Wright and Snell's (2005) comment on the risk of getting too many successful 'downsizers' (e.g. HR professionals representing 'hard' HRM views) at the top of the organization emphasizes the importance of a balanced approach in HR roles. The knowledge, skills and competences needed to 'get rid of people' is just one aspect of professional HRM. Even the US model by Ulrich (1997) incorporates the 'employee champion' role, acknowledging the employee perspective as an essential part of HR professionalism.

Balanced approaches and HR roles

In practice the position of the HR professional is often weak. In the case of a strong position, it is most likely that the HR professional is a problem-solver and/or conformist innovator. In other words, HR professionals are taken seriously because they solve day-to-day problems of the line managers and/or support top management according to economic goals.

The (critical) deviant innovator is very hard to find, while this HR role is crucial for organizations. Would the financial crisis of 2008/2009 have been so dramatic if HR professionals had had a stronger position and leeway for taking a deviant innovator role, in particular with regard to performance-related pay (PRP) systems and top management rewards? The deviant innovator role in HRM does not make an HR professional popular in practice, but the recent global crisis has shown that a much more critical and transparent approach is required to avoid the dramatic events that occurred in the financial sector.

HRM can be characterized by ambiguities, dualities, tensions, paradoxes and different interests (Boselie et al., 2009). HR professionals are expected to cope with these issues, often acting as a moderator or mediator in conflicts; for example, between managers and subordinates or between the organization and social partners. Often there is no one-way solution and the HR professional's competences with regard to negotiation, communication, persistence and patience are essential in these difficult situations. Top management and line managers, on the other hand, should become aware of the relevance of the deviant innovator HR role in serving both the employer's and the employees' interests (see Chapter 5).

To restore the balance in practice, HR professionals need qualities that satisfy the interests of both parties (see Table 12.1).

The employer's perspective	The employees' perspective
Economic value	Moral values
Conformist innovator	Deviant innovator
Change maker and advisor	Regulator
Strategic partner and change agent	Employee champion

TABLE 12.1 Balanced HR roles

Note: HR competences for managing dualities: communication, advisory, negotiation, persistence, critical attitude, patience and sensitivity to ambiguities.

Glossary of key terms

Administrative expert role represents the HR role focused on cost-effective design and delivery of the functional areas of HRM.

Change agent role focuses on managing organizational change.

Conformist innovator role represents the HR business role mainly emphasizing the economic value of employees.

Deviant innovator role emphasizes the long-term perspective and the necessary balance between the economic value and the human side of organizing.

Employee champion role concentrates on blending employees' needs with organizational goals.

Personnel function is defined as the HR responsibilities and tasks that are bundled in an HR department and performed by HR professionals.

Strategic partner role involves the alignment of the HR strategy with the overall business strategy in the process of strategic decision making of an organization.

Three HR ambiguities reflect the dualities and paradoxes in HRM.

summary

- HRM is now on the (executive) table, but not always at the (executive) table.
- The personnel function can be characterized by three ambiguities that cause a potential lack of power for personnel managers.
- Three vicious circles block personnel managers' opportunities to overcome the three ambiguities.
- To overcome the three ambiguities and vicious circles, personnel managers can choose the conformist innovator role or the deviant innovator role.
- There was a shift in HR roles in the 1980s and 1990s from an administrative emphasis to a strategy and change focus.
- Storey (1992) presented four different HR roles (advisors, handmaidens, regulators and change makers) that reflect the shifts in HR roles in the 1980s.
- Ulrich (1997) presented another HR role model, including the administrative expert, the employee champion, the change agent and the strategic partner. His model is probably one of the most widely used HR approaches in both theory and practice.
- The late 1990s showed another shift from HR role models towards HR competence approaches.
- The new HR competence model covers six HR competence domains: the credible activist, the operational executor, the business ally, the talent manager and organizational designer, the culture and change steward, and the strategic architect.
- HR roles in organizations are affected by context, in particular the institutional context.
- HR roles in practice can be characterized by working with ambiguities, dualities, tensions, paradoxes and different interests.

★ *Personal development*

- What kind of training and development would help you to improve your role as strategic partner?
- What kind of training and development would help you to improve your role as change agent?
- What kind of training and development would help you to improve your role as employee champion?
- What kind of training and development would help you to improve your role as administrative expert?

Individual task

***HR role assessment survey*: adapted version of Ulrich's model (1997) by Jaap Paauwe and Paul Boselie**

There are 20 statements in this individual task. For each statement you have to make a choice between two alternatives. Choose the alternative that applies best to you and your organization. You need to focus on the current situation and *not* the desired or intended situation. There are no wrong answers. Do not take too much time making the choices. The exercise will take you five minutes.

1 *HR helps the organization to*:
- take care of employees' personal needs (c)
- adapt to change (d)

2 *HR participates in*:
- the process of defining business strategies (a)
- improving employee commitment (c)

3 *HR develops processes and programmes to*:
- link HR strategies to accomplish business strategy (a)
- help the organization transform itself (d)

4 *HR makes sure that*:
- HR processes are efficiently administered (b)
- HR policies and programmes respond to the personal needs of employees (c)

5 *HR is an active participant in*:
- business planning (a)
- designing and delivering HR processes (b)

6 *HR works to*:
- monitor administrative processes (b)
- reshape behaviour for organizational change (d)

7 *HR spends time on*:
- strategic issues (a)
- supporting new behaviours for keeping the firm competitive (d)

8 *HR effectiveness is measured by its ability to*:
- help make strategy happen (a)
- efficiently deliver HR processes (b)

9 *HR is seen as*:
- an administrative expert (b)
- a change agent (d)

10 *HR helps the organization*:
- accomplish business goals (a)
- improve operating efficiency (b)

11 *HR participates in*:
- delivering HR processes (b)
- shaping cultural change for renewal and transformation (d)

12 *HR makes sure that*:
- HR strategies are aligned with business strategy (a)
- HR processes and programmes increase the organization's ability to change (d)

13 *HR effectiveness is measured by its ability to*:
- help employees meet personal needs (c)
- help an organization anticipate and adapt to future issues (d)

14 *HR is seen as*:
- a business partner (a)
- a champion for employees (c)

15 *HR's credibility comes from*:
- helping employees meet their personal needs (c)
- making change happen (d)

16 *HR spends time on*:
- operational issues (b)
- listening and responding to employees (c)

17 *HR is an active participant in*:
- listening and responding to employees (c)
- organization renewal, change or transformation (d)

18 *HR works to*:
- align HR strategies and business strategy (a)
- offer assistance to help employees meet family and personal needs (c)

19 *HR develops processes and programmes to*:
- efficiently process documents and transactions (b)
- take care of employee personal needs (c)

20 *HR's credibility comes from*:
- helping to fulfil strategic goals (a)
- increasing productivity (b)

When you have finished filling in the 20 statements, you can calculate the total score using the codes (a, b, c or d) at the end of each statement that you have picked. For example, when you picked 'HR's credibility comes from ... increasing productivity' (statement 20) you have one 'b' score.

Calculate the total scores of all 20 statements.

What are your total 'a', 'b', 'c' and 'd' scores?

What does your overall HR profile look like?

Do you recognize yourself in the overall profile?

Sum score 'a' represents the strategic partner role

Sum score 'b' represents the administrative expert role

Sum score 'c' represents the employee champion role

Sum score 'd' represents the change agent role

Ulrich's (1997) HR roles	Minimum score	Maximum score	Your sum score
Strategic partner	0	10	
Administrative expert	0	10	
Employee champion	0	10	
Change agent	0	10	

Team task

Collect between 10–20 advertisements in newspapers and on the Internet for vacancies in HR-related jobs (e.g. personnel manager, HR development specialist, recruiter, HR manager and compensation expert).

- Analyse the requirements for these vacancies using the Ulrich (1997) model with the four HR roles.
- Put the specific requirements in the four quadrants of Ulrich's model and compare the vacancies.
- Discuss the implications of this analysis for the potential candidate and for the organization.
- What lessons can be learned from it for applicants?
- What can organizations learn from it?

Learning checklist

After studying this chapter, you should be able to do the following:

- Understand Legge's (1978) three ambiguities as the source for the lack of power of personnel managers in practice.
- Discuss Legge's (1978) three vicious circles that block personnel managers' opportunities to overcome the HR ambiguities.
- Outline the conformist innovator and deviant innovator HR roles.
- Understand the changing HR roles.
- Review Storey's (1992) HR role model.
- Review Ulrich's (1997) HR role model.
- Evaluate the advantages and disadvantages of the HR role models.
- Outline the HR competence models.
- Discuss the HR qualities of the contemporary and future HR professional.

References

Becker, B.A. and Huselid, M.A. (2006) Strategic human resources management: where do we go from here?, *Journal of Management*, 32(b): 898–925.

Biemans, P.J. (1999) *Professionalisering van de Personeelsfunctie: een Empirisch Onderzoek bij Twintig Organisaties [Professionalization of the HR function: An Empirical Study within Twenty Organizations]*. Delft: Eburon.

Boselie, P. (2007) HR professional as business partner?, *Tijdschrift voor HRM*, 3: 34–51.

Boselie, P. and Paauwe, J. (2005) Human resource function competencies in European companies, *Personnel Review*, 34(5): 550–66.

Boselie, P., Brewster, C. and Paauwe, J. (2009) In search for balance: managing the dualities of HRM – an overview of the issues, *Personnel Review*, Special Issue, 38(5): 461–71.

Boselie, P., Dietz, G. and Boon, C. (2005) Commonalities and contradictions in HRM performance research, *Human Resource Management Journal*, 15(3): 67–94.

Bosma, M. (2007) Cases Unilever en Philips centraal tijdens debat Hay Group Vision Society: Zijn we al zo ver met off-shoring? [Cases Unilever and Philips put forward during Hay Group Vision Society debate. What has been achieved in off-shoring?], *Management Executive*, July–August: 58–9.

Brockbank, W., Sioli, A. and Ulrich, D. (2002) So we are at the table! Now what? Working paper, University of Michigan Business School, Ann Arbor, MI, available online at: www.webuser.bus.umich.edu/Programs/hrcs/res_NowWhat.htm.

Buyens, D. and Vos, A. De (2001) Perceptions of the value of the HR function, *Human Resource Management Journal*, 11(3): 70–89.

Caldwell, R. (2003) The changing roles of personnel managers: old ambiguities, new uncertainties, *Journal of Management Studies*, 40(4): 983–1004.

Caldwell, R. (2008) HR business partner competency models: re-contextualising effectiveness, *Human Resource Management Journal*, 18(3): 275–94.

Caroll, S.J. (1991) The new HRM roles, responsibilities, and structures, in R.S. Schuler (ed.), *Managing Human Resources in the Information Age*, pp. 204–26. Washington, DC: Bureau of National Affairs.

Farndale, E. and Brewster, C. (2005) In search of legitimacy: personnel management associations worldwide, *Human Resource Management Journal*, 15(3): 33–48.

Farndale, E. and Paauwe, J. (2007) Uncovering competitive and institutional drivers of HM practices in multinational corporations, *Human Resource Management Journal*, 17(4): 355–75.

Guest, D.E. and King, Z. (2004) Power, innovation and problem-solving: the personnel manager's three steps to heaven?, *Journal of Management Studies*, 41(3): 401–23.

Hope-Hailey, V., Farndale, E. and Truss, C. (2005) The HR department's role in organisational performance, *Human Resource Management Journal*, 15(3): 49–66.

Huselid, M.A., Jackson, S.E. and Schuler, R.S. (1997) Technical and strategic human resource management effectiveness as determinants of firm performance, *Academy of Management Journal*, 40(1): 171–88.

Legge, K. (1978) *Power, Innovation, and Problem-solving in Personnel Management*. New York: McGraw-Hill.

Lepak, D.P. and Snell, S.A. (2002) Examining the human resource architecture: the relationships among human capital, employment, and human resource configurations, *Journal of Management*, 28(4): 517–43.

Paauwe, J. (2007) HRM and performance: in search of balance. Inaugural lecture, Tilberg University, Tilburg.
Schuler, R.S. (1990) Repositioning the human resource function: transformation or demise?, *Academy of Management Executive*, 4(3): 49–59.
Society for Human Resource Management (2002) *Society for Human Resource Management, Research Report on HR Professionalization*, available online at www.shrm.org/foundation/.
Storey, J. (1992) *Developments in the Management of Human Resources*. Oxford: Blackwell.
Tyson, S. (1987) The management of the personnel function, *Journal of Management Studies*, 24(5): 523–32.
Tyson, S. and Fell, A. (1986) *Evaluating the Personnel Function*. London: Hutchinson.
Ulrich, D. (1997) *Human Resource Champions*. Boston, MA: Harvard Business School Press.
Ulrich, D. and Brockbank, W. (2005) *The HR Value Proposition*. Boston, MA: Harvard Business School Press.
Ulrich, D., Brockbank, W., Johnson, D. and Younger, J. (2007) Human resource competencies: responding to increased expectations, *Employment Relations Today*, 34(3): 1–12.
Wright, P.M. and Nishii, L.H. (2007) Strategic HRM and organizational behavior: integrating multiple levels of analysis. Working paper 07–03. CAHRS at Cornell University, Ithaca, NY.
Wright, P.M. and Snell, S.A. (2005) Partner or guardian? HR's challenge in balancing value and values, *Human Resource Management*, 44(2): 177–82.
Wright, P.M., McMahan, G., Snell, S.A. and Gerhart, B. (2001) Comparing line and HR executives' perceptions of HR effectiveness: services, roles and contributions, *Human Resource Management*, 2: 111–23.

Further reading

Caldwell, R. (2003) The changing roles of personnel managers: old ambiguities, new uncertainties, *Journal of Management Studies*, 40(4): 983–1004.
Farndale, E. and Brewster, C. (2005) In search of legitimacy: personnel management associations worldwide, *Human Resource Management Journal*, 15(3): 33–48.
Gratton, L. and Truss, C. (2003) The three-dimensional people strategy: putting human resource policies into action, *Academy of Management Executive*, 17: 74–86.
Guest, D.E. and King, Z. (2004) Power, innovation and problem-solving: the personnel manager's three steps to heaven?, *Journal of Management Studies*, 41(3): 401–23.
Paauwe, J. (2004) Changing HR roles: towards a real balanced HRM scorecard, in J. Paauwe (ed.), *Human Resource Management and Performance: Unique Approaches for Achieving Long Term Viability*, Chapter 9. Oxford: Oxford University Press.
Ulrich, D. (1997) *Human Resource Champions*. Boston, MA: Harvard Business School Press.

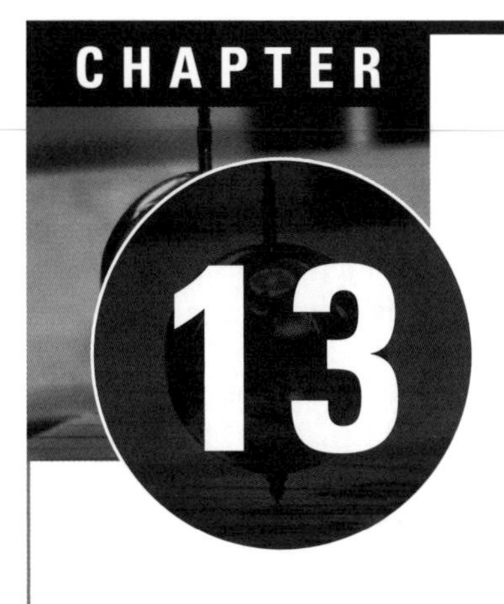

International Human Resource Management

Learning Objectives

After studying this chapter, you should be able to do the following:

- Outline globalization and internationalization
- Evaluate the universalist and the contextual paradigm in International HRM (IHRM)
- Identify multiple levels in IHRM
- Understand cross-cultural and institutional differences between countries and regions
- Consider global HR strategies and local HR strategies
- Examine convergence and divergence issues in human resource management (HRM)
- Outline expatriate management and culture shock
- Review the potential impact of knowledge transfer within multinational companies (MNCs) on performance
- Review outsourcing, offshoring and IHRM issues

CASE STUDY: ING GROUP

The ING Group is an international financial services organization with headquarters in the Netherlands (The ING House in Amsterdam). This MNC was founded in the early 1990s through a merger between banking and insurance. ING is a global financial services organization of Dutch origin, its roots going back more than 150 years. The core business of the MNC comprises retail banking (including insurance and asset management services), wholesale banking, retirement services, direct banking, life insurance, property and casualty insurance. It operates in more than 50 countries and its banking, insurance and asset management services employ over 120 000 employees worldwide. Based on market capitalization, this MNC is one of the 20 largest financial institutions worldwide.

The merger between Nationale-Nederlanden insurance and the NMB Postbank Group in 1991 marks the foundation of ING and the start of further internationalization of the organization. This merger is unique because of the nature of the two businesses (insurance and banking) that were integrated into one new organization. The founding of ING as one organization began in 1990 when the legal restrictions on mergers between insurers and banks were lifted in the Netherlands. The insurance organization had over 25 000 employees and the bank organization about 23 000 employees at the time of the merger. The merger involved an integration of two organizations with authentic cultures and businesses (insurance versus banking). Growth and expansion have been key characteristics of the ING Group over the last 15 years.

Globalization resulted in further internationalization of the ING Group. Within a decade the MNC was transformed from a mainly local operating financial services organization into an international organization. To give you an idea of this shift towards expansion and internationalization: less than 25 per cent of all employees now work in the Netherlands compared to over 70 per cent in the 1980s.

The net income of the ING Group was €7.7 billion in 2006 and €9.2 billion in 2007. The financial crisis hit the MNC hard, like most other financial services worldwide, resulting in a net income loss of €729 million in 2008.

The chief human resource officer (CHRO) of the ING Group directly reports to the chief executive officer (CEO) of ING. One of the main challenges for the CHRO is the further integration of the HR policies throughout the business lines worldwide. For many MNCs, it is a big challenge to globally manage human resources. MNCs such as ING that operate in multiple countries are confronted with different national cultures and different institutional arrangements that affect HRM. In some countries (e.g. Belgium, Germany and the Netherlands) strict collective bargaining agreements (CBAs) heavily determine compensation and benefits, while in other countries (e.g. the UK and the USA) an organization has much more leeway in relation to payment. Cultural differences, for example with regard to hierarchy and power distance, can also affect HRM. In Japan, for example, employees take hierarchical differences between them and their supervisors for granted. In the Netherlands, however, there is little power distance between supervisors and subordinates. These cultural differences can also have an effect on other HR practices, including communication, employee development, performance appraisal (PA), internal promotion and teamwork.

? Discussion questions

Discuss the challenges for the CHRO of the ING Group and team for integrating HR policies and practices worldwide.

- What are the advantages and disadvantages of one global HR strategy and policy?
- Can you think of HR practices that are more likely to be applied similarly within ING worldwide?

Introduction

Emphasizing the relevance of globalization for organizations has become a cliché. The globalization trend started in the 1970s and created increased global competition. Chapter 6 discusses the impact of globalization, in particular the total quality management (TQM) movement in Asia, on US and European companies, affecting not only the businesses but the people management as well. According to Legge (1995), this trend created the introduction of HRM in both theory and practice.

Globalization is the transition from local or regional activities to global ones. These activities can include markets, products, services, information sharing, communication and many other aspects. Mass media and the emergence of the Internet, for example, resulted in instant global news from professionals, but more importantly from citizens as well. Digital platforms such as YouTube have made the world a lot smaller and even made it possible to get access to information from the other side of the world, often for free. Some of these developments have made an impact on existing businesses, for example:

- the development of digital photography and new possibilities for data transmission;
- the development of new methods of global communication (e.g. YouTube, MSN and Skype);
- the Internet as a marketplace for buying and selling products and services.

Globalization has affected large companies (MNCs, international governmental organizations (IGOs)[1] and non-governmental organizations (NGOs)[2]) and small and medium enterprises (SMEs). Cheap labour transfer, for example from Poland to the UK, has affected several industries such as construction. Markets have opened (e.g. China) and production facilities are being transferred to cheaper countries (offshoring).

Many mainly larger organizations have decided to expand their international activities. This phenomenon is called **internationalization**. The ING Group case study illustrates the internationalization of the organization in less than a decade from 70 per cent of the employees working in the home country in the 1980s to less than 25 per cent in 2009.

Defining IHRM

In Chapter 1 **IHRM** is defined as 'HRM in MNCs and HRM across borders' (Brewster, 2004). IHRM is focused on, for example, the transferability of HR practices across business units in different countries and the management of expatriates (employees who are sent abroad for a longer time period). IHRM is often closely related to micro HRM (MHRM) and strategic HRM (SHRM), as discussed in Chapter 1. An organization, for example, might consider applying a specific best practice in HRM (e.g. a specific 360-degree feedback system as part of employee appraisal) to all its business units worldwide. The HRM considerations and insights are put in an international perspective that is studied through IHRM. The strategic decision making in HRM of MNCs is often continental (e.g. the European continent or the South American continent) or global. This almost automatically relates IHRM to HRM issues.

Brewster et al. (2000) make a distinction between two paradigms: (1) the universalist and (2) the contextual. They argue that the **universalist paradigm** assumes the existence of best practices in HRM that can be applied by multinational companies successfully worldwide:

> 'careful and extensive systems for recruitment, selection and training; formal systems for sharing information with the individuals who work in the organization; clear job design; local level participation procedures; monitoring of attitudes; PAs; properly functioning grievance procedures; and promotion and compensation schemes that provide for the recognition and financial rewarding of high performing members of the workforce.'
>
> (Brewster et al., 2000: 11)

[1] The United Nations (UN) and affiliated organizations (e.g. United Nations Educational, Scientific, and Cultural Organization (UNESCO)) and United Nations International Children's Emergency Fund (UNICEF) are illustrations of international governmental organizations.

[2] The Red Cross and Medicins Sans Frontieres are illustrations of NGOs.

In Europe, in particular, the **contextual paradigm** is more widespread (Brewster et al., 2000), building on the notion that there might be some general best principles in HRM (Boxall and Purcell, 2008), but the organizational context ultimately determines the nature of the specific HR practice. An illustration of the contextual paradigm in an IHRM perspective is the typical recruitment and selection of employees in much of southern Europe through the network of family and friends (Brewster et al., 2000). Employee participation, as discussed in Chapter 11, can have different shapes as well, including employee involvement on the shopfloor as a high-performance work practice (HPWP) in the US context versus institutionalized employee participation through works councils in the German context. The contextual paradigm often also includes a broader stakeholder perspective, including social partners (trade unions and works councils). This distinction between the universal paradigm and the contextual paradigm in IHRM is closely related to the SHRM distinction between the 'best-practice' school and the 'best-fit' school discussed in Chapter 2 (Delery and Doty, 1996).

Stop and reflect

Can you think of typical HR practices in your country comparable to the *cunha* (family and friends recruitment) in Portugal (Brewster et al., 2000) or the employee participation through works councils in Germany and the Netherlands?

You can use Pfeffer's (1994) list of best practices, discussed in Chapter 2, as a guideline.

Multiple levels

IHRM is manifested at different levels, including individual employee level issues (e.g. related to expatriate management), site level issues (business unit), organization level issues in the case of multiple sites in a country and across countries, national level issues (e.g. related to labour legislation and CBAs), regional or continental level issues (e.g. Africa, Asia, Europe, Middle East, North America and South America), and international level issues (e.g. the UN operating on a global scale).

The ING Group, for example, applies global and local HRM at different levels, including:

- a yearly global employee engagement survey (universalist at the individual employee level);
- a company CBA for all employees in the Netherlands (contextual at the national level);
- a global HR strategy aimed at creating a high-performance culture (universal HR strategy at the international level).

The differences between countries, regions and continents can be based on cultural and institutional variations (e.g. European Union (EU) legislation).

HRM and cross-cultural differences

Hofstede's (1980) work on international cultural differences related to work is probably one of the most famous studies on **cross-cultural differences**. He was also one of the first to classify countries through so-called cultural maps. A cultural map presents the differences and similarities of countries on different dimensions; for example, Hofstede's (1980) dimensions:

1 individualism (the degree to which individuals look out for themselves first and the organization and society next);
2 masculinity (e.g. aggressiveness and assertiveness);
3 power distance (the degree to which individuals accept unequal distribution of power; for example, with regard to their supervisor);
4 uncertainty avoidance (the way individuals accept and deal with uncertain situations and their willingness to make decisions in uncertain situations).

Table 13.1 presents some of Hofstede's (1980) findings with regard to European countries. Most countries show relatively high scores on individualism except for Austria, Finland, Greece and Spain. The Netherlands and the UK reveal very high scores on this dimension, reflecting potential key cultural characteristics of the workforce in these two countries. The other three dimensions show a more mixed pattern across the countries. There are serious criticisms of Hofstede's dimensions (e.g. McSweeney, 2002; Gerhart and Fang, 2005) and their potential application to policies and practices in organizations. The findings, however, show differences between countries that seem plausible with regard to some HR practices. Portugal's low score on individualism, for example, potentially explains part of the typical recruitment and selection using networks of family and friends discussed earlier. O'Connell (1998: 140) states that 'the idea of a cultural map is not the source of all answers, but it is a valuable tool for use by international organizations'.

Country	Individual	Masculinity	Power distance	Uncertainty avoidance
Austria	Medium	High	Low	High
Belgium	High	Medium	Medium	High
Denmark	High	Low	Low	Low
Finland	Medium	Low	Low	Medium
France	High	Medium	High	High
Germany	High	High	Medium	High
Greece	Medium	Medium	Medium	High
Ireland	High	High	Low	Medium
Italy	High	High	Medium	High
Netherlands	High	Low	Medium	Medium
Norway	High	Low	Low	Medium
Portugal	Low	Low	Medium	High
Spain	Medium	Medium	Medium	High
Sweden	High	Low	Low	Low
Switzerland	High	High	Low	Medium
United Kingdom	High	High	Medium	Medium

TABLE 13.1 Cultural maps in Europe: illustrations
Source: www.clearlycultural.com.

HRM and institutional differences

An alternative approach for the possible impact of **institutional differences** between, for example, countries is based on institutional notions (Gooderham et al., 1999; Paauwe and Boselie, 2003; Brookes et al., 2005; Brewster et al., 2008). In Chapter 2 specific attention was paid to the impact of institutional mechanisms on organizations and people management issues. A further distinction was made between the general environment (e.g. labour legislation in a specific country or within the EU) and the population environment often related to the branch of industry. It is clear to see that there are significant differences between countries and regions/continents that affect MNCs and their HRM, in particular IHRM. Compensation and benefits represent an HR area that is heavily affected by the general environment of an organization. In the USA there is much more leeway with regard to compensation and benefits than in more institutionalized countries such as Belgium, Germany, the Netherlands and Sweden. In contrast, recruitment and selection legislation, in particular with regard to discrimination issues on age, race and gender, are much more extensive in the USA than in most continental European countries. Employee participation and employee development tend to be much more institutionalized in Europe (e.g. through works councils) than in the USA; however, there are always exceptions. Compliance training of all employees, for example through a yearly eLearning program, is much more regulated in the USA than in many European countries, where the same organization can apply a less extensive compliance training programme every three or four years.

The population environment can also be different across countries and regions. The chemical industry (e.g. BASF) and the pharmaceutical industry (e.g. AstraZeneca) have created regulations and procedures on health and safety embedded in EU legislation. This EU legislation for the specific branch of industry is often significantly different from US legislation, with major implications for working conditions and the employment relationship of workers of an MNC in different parts of the world. It makes IHRM and IHRM strategies challenging and difficult to implement.

Global and local HR strategies

This brings us to corporate HR strategies and notions on global differentiation within an MNC (Farndale and Paauwe, 2007). An organization or international organization can roughly decide to apply one **global HR strategy** or use a differentiated model with maximum leeway for local HR strategies. The **local HR strategy** option can be based on cultural and/or institutional notions mentioned before. To some extent organizations have no choice in applying local HR policies, for example with regard to compensation, simply because national legislation differences affect the HRM of organizations operating in different countries.

Farndale and Paauwe (2007) present empirical findings on the HR function and roles in large MNCs operating in Europe. The empirical data were collected through a case study method using interview data, archival data, annual reports and internal policy reports. A company such as ABB (engineering and electrical engineering) applies a global HR strategy with the main locus of power at corporate HR level. The HR approach is highly centralized and the managerial leeway towards HRM at subsidiary level is small (Farndale and Paauwe, 2007). In contrast, EDF (power generation and distribution, mainly in France) and IKEA (retail) apply local HR strategies in a decentralized approach with the main locus of power at the subsidiary HR level. According to the authors, the leeway for the subsidiaries of both organizations with regard to HRM is considerable. They distinguish a third category of organizations, including Unilever, Siemens and Procter & Gamble, that apply HR strategies with elements of a global HR strategy and leeway for local HR strategies.

It is important to acknowledge notions of strategic choice (see Chapter 2) for HR decision making. In other words, although it is likely that cultural and institutional aspects affect and perhaps restrict HR strategies of organizations operating in different countries, the same organizations have some room to manoeuvre and choices with regard to applying a global HR strategy versus a local HR strategy.

Convergence and divergence issues in HRM

An important debate linked to global and local HR strategies of MNCs focuses on convergence or divergence in HRM across countries (Sparrow et al., 1994; Rowley and Benson, 2002). The universalistic views with the key assumption of best practices in HRM mainly propose further convergence in HRM worldwide, mainly as a result of globalization and internationalization. In other words, MNCs transfer best practices in HRM (e.g. related to compensation and employee involvement) to other countries as part of a dominant global HR strategy. The transfer of certain HR principles from the home country of the MNC to other countries is most likely; however, this does not automatically imply a convergence of HRM worldwide (Rowley and Benson, 2002).

BASF's HR initiative to transfer employee participation through works councils from Germany to other BASF subsidiaries all over the world is a good example of the transfer of HR principles that are typically embedded in its culture and institutions. A US chemical organization operating in the same markets as the German BASF is not likely to transfer BASF's employee participation approach. Instead, the US MNCs might choose a different employee involvement model based on the US high-performance work systems (HPWSs) model, as discussed in Chapter 6. Brewster et al. (2008) find evidence for similarity and dissimilarity in HR practices among MNCs. Apparently there are some global HR practices, for example related to performance-related pay (PRP) (see Chapter 9). There is also sufficient diversity in HR practices, partly caused by cross-cultural and institutional differences.

Expatriates

The management of employees that are transferred abroad (expatriates) has received much attention within IHRM (Brewster and Scullion, 1997; Dowling et al., 2004; Caligiuri and Colakoglu, 2007; Haslberger and Brewster, 2008; Harvey and Moeller, 2009). **Expatriates** are employees who temporarily or permanently work in a different country than their home country. Sending employees to subsidiaries in other countries creates internal mobility and knowledge transfer within an MNC across countries. In some organizations becoming an expatriate for a certain time period is a necessary condition for further internal promotion opportunities. Expatriates are often given a specific assignment that requires them to move their entire household to a foreign location. The transfer usually has major implications for expatriates and their families.

Expatriates and their families are most likely to be confronted with cultural differences between their home countries and the new countries of residence. Cross-cultural adjustment is one of the most challenging issues for expatriates and their families. One important element of adjustment is to become a member of social networks for all involved in the transfer (expatriates and families). As soon as expatriates arrive in the new country, they will become absorbed by business obligations related to getting to know everybody at work and getting started in the new job (e.g. office space, computer access and identity cards). The family is also challenged by all kinds of new experiences, ranging from finding out where the supermarkets are, where the schools are located and how to get in touch with a doctor. The first couple of weeks and months often result in serious culture shocks for expatriates and their families. These culture shocks are often inevitable and part of the adjustment process.

Graphic Arts Centre Publishing provides a wonderful series of books on culture shock for many countries[3] in the world that are highly recommended reading for expatriates (www.gacpc.com/titles). The starting point of this book series is that everybody will experience some kind of culture shock when going abroad for a significant amount of time and partly this shock is inevitable. Good preparation is required (1) for the culture shock that is most likely to occur and (2) as a practical guideline with regard to the customs and habits of the new country.

Expatriate support systems (ESSs) help expatriates in the preparation of the transfer. The ESS often incorporate the training and development of multicultural skills among employees. Blanco (1998: 208) states that, 'the most effective ESS is that which allows employees to become open-minded, to learn how to adapt to a new environment, and even to enjoy cultural transition as a valuable learning experience.' In general, too little attention is paid to the preparation of employees' spouses and children travelling with them (Black and Stephens, 1989; Shay and Tracey, 1997). According to Blanco (1998), an ESS may include the following:

- educational programmes to develop employees' multicultural skills;
- a mentorship in the foreign country to help employees during the first period abroad;
- short travel programmes to the country of destination prior to the assignment as a form of preparation and getting to know the new environment;
- information sharing and communication about schools, churches, recreational activities, native meals, transportation systems, driver's licence and health care.

In the case of expatriate management, specific attention should be paid to:

- expatriate compensation approaches;
- expatriate allowances: cost of living and housing;
- expatriate health and benefits plans;
- expatriate insurance and emergency plans;
- expatriate taxation management;
- family and cross-cultural support: education system for children (e.g. international schools) and language skills training.

There is a growing awareness among organizations that perspectives of expatriates and spouses may include dual-career opportunities (Riusala and Suutari, 2000). Dual-career couples' career considerations can play an important role in the motivation of employees to go abroad. DSM is a Dutch chemical organisation that has proved successful in cooperating with other organizations (e.g. the Dutch Ministry of Foreign Affairs) for dual-career couples. Further cooperation between MNCs on dual-career couples increases the likelihood of expatriate success.

Finally, most expatriates are confronted with another culture shock when they go back to their country of origin. It is therefore important that MNCs also have programmes for returning expatriates to minimize the risks of decreased employee motivation, lack of organizational commitment and employee turnover.

[3] Books on culture shock exist for the following countries: Argentina, Australia, Austria, Britain, Chile, China, Cuba, Germany, Hungary, India, Indonesia, Iran, Israel, Japan, Laos, Mexico, Norway, South Africa, Taiwan, Thailand and Vietnam.

Stop and reflect

Discuss the opportunities and threats of sending an employee abroad as an expatriate from the employer's perspective and from the employee's perspective.

- Can you think of HR interventions that potentially overcome at least some of the threats?

Knowledge transfer in a global arena

In times of increased globalization and international competition, MNCs continuously aim for performance improvements through, for example, technological innovation and alternative production systems (e.g. lean production). Another area for potential performance improvements is of course related to the human factor in companies in terms of both human capital (knowledge, skills and abilities of employees) and social capital (social networks between relevant actors in the organization).

Sharing knowledge and experiences between employees on a global scale is a powerful instrument for increasing the MNC's global performance (Bonache and Brewster, 2001; Minbaeva et al., 2003). An illustration of knowledge transfer within a global consultancy organization is shown below:

> The consultancy organization operates in multiple industries (including automotive and assembly, chemicals, financial services, public sector, retail and telecommunications), covering different functional areas (including information technology (IT), corporate finance, marketing and sales, operations, management and organization, HRM and strategy), and in most countries worldwide. Consultant A is invited by a Belgian financial services company to provide support on developing and implementing a new HR strategy aimed at creating a high-performance culture. This Belgian organization operates worldwide and the consultancy organization has recently provided other services to different subsidiaries of this organization worldwide. Consultant A now has the opportunity to access its intranet in search of colleagues who were involved in past projects for the Belgian financial services company. The intranet provides short summaries of all the past projects, reports and names of employees who were involved. Consultant A can benefit from these past experiences in at least two ways; first, by downloading information on the organization from past projects, and second, by inviting colleagues to join the project team.

The illustration above shows the potential gains of knowledge transfer in an MNC. There are, however, some necessary conditions for this type of knowledge transfer across boarders, including:

- the existence of an information and communication network (intranet and/or Internet);
- access to the network for employees;
- employee knowledge and skills to operate the knowledge information system (often training and development is required first);
- the willingness of employees to share knowledge and experiences with others as part of a corporate culture in which knowledge sharing is essential and common;
- cross-cultural awareness of all employees and good communication among employees who are able to deal with different norms and values of colleagues in other countries.

Outsourcing and offshoring

Outsourcing and offshoring business activities are popular concepts for MNCs, for example with regard to IT outsourcing (Barthelemy, 2001). **Outsourcing** is basically subcontracting business activities to external companies. Key drivers for outsourcing activities are cost reduction and a renewed strategic focus on core businesses. **Offshoring** is the relocation of business activities to other countries or regions mainly for cost-reduction purposes (e.g. cheap labour costs in other countries). Typical offshoring activities are related to call centres (e.g. in India for the USA and the UK markets mainly because of the English language skills of Indian workers), manufacturing (e.g. from European plants to Chinese plants), and supporting processes (e.g. administration in former Eastern European countries for Western European countries).

Offshoring and outsourcing are often combined (Doh, 2005). **Offshore outsourcing** implies an outsourcing of business activities to an external company in another country. The Unilever case study in Chapter 12 illustrates the offshore outsourcing of the HR function of Unilever from the Netherlands to Prague under the umbrella of the consultancy firm called Accenture. Outsourcing, offshoring and offshore outsourcing usually have major implications for employees and therefore require specific HRM to manage these organizational changes.

In 2007 the Organization for Economic Co-operation and Development (OECD) published a report on the impact of offshoring on employment worldwide. The main conclusions of this report include the following:

- The primary motivation for the offshoring of the production of goods and services is to cut costs.
- Skilled jobs are no longer safe from being sent offshore.
- Offshoring is no longer limited to traditional (manufacturing) industries but is increasingly spreading to knowledge and technology-intensive industries.
- China and India are two emerging economies that absorb many offshoring activities from Western countries.
- All industries are affected by offshoring but industrial sectors that have downsized their workforce the most are not the ones that have engaged in offshoring the most.
- Offshoring by European companies is responsible for less than 5 per cent of total job losses in Europe, far behind bankruptcies, shut-downs and organizational restructuring.

! ***Stop and reflect***

Search the newspapers for a recent case of offshoring and study its impact on the employment relationship (e.g. in terms of potential job losses) and the impact on the corporate image of the organization.

- Can you think of communication strategies that minimize reputation damage in that offshoring example?

The things they do not teach you in school

What do you do as a manager or a personnel officer when a colleague is killed or seriously injured in the line of duty? The World Food Programme (WFP; www.wfp.org) is the UN front-line agency in the fight against global hunger: 'In emergencies, we get food to where it is needed, saving the lives of victims of war, civil conflict and natural disasters. After the cause of an emergency has passed, we use food to help communities rebuild their shattered lives.'

The WFP operates in more than 80 countries and employs 12 000 people worldwide. Every day WFP workers risk their lives bringing food to the poor and every year WFP workers die in the line of duty:

> *'WFP National Officer killed in Southern Somalia'*
>
> The Executive Director of WFP expressed shock and sadness today at the killing of one of the agency's staff members in southern Somalia. Details surrounding the death of Somali national Abdulkadir Diad Mohamed, who joined WFP as an administration and finance assistant in June, are still being gathered. However, all indications are that Mr. Mohammed was abducted by unidentified armed men and killed after trying to escape. 'I am shocked by this senseless and barbaric attack on one of our staff,' said WFP Executive Director, Josette Sheeran. 'Our thoughts and prayers are with his family, friends and colleagues.'
>
> (www.wfp.org, 18 August 2008)

The tragic loss of a colleague can of course also occur in private companies as a result of an accident during operations. Deaths and injuries in an international context, in particular in the context of dangerous job assignments, introduce real challenges for the management and HRM of the organization. Peace-keeping missions in Iraq and Afghanistan have recently shown the number of casualties among soldiers who were sent to these countries. Preparing both employees and the family back home, supporting all actors (including family back home) during missions abroad and emergency programmes in case of accidents are crucial elements of international HRM in these organizations.

HRM risks related to expatriates are as follows:

- natural disasters (e.g. earthquake, tsunami, flooding, hurricane and pestilence) – *the 2005 bird flu epidemic in China* and *the global swine influenza outbreak in 2009*;
- political instability (e.g. coup) – *the 2009 coup in Madagascar*;
- war – *the war in Sudan (Africa)*;
- acts of terrorism (e.g. bomb attack) – *the hotel attacks in Mumbai (India) in November 2008* and *the hotel attacks in Jakarta (Indonesia) in July 2009*;
- kidnapping (e.g. kidnapping in combination with ransom demands) – *the recent attacks of Somali pirates on oil tankers*;
- traffic accidents (e.g. serious injuries or death of an employee).

! Stop and reflect

Think about possible HR policies and practices for managing employees abroad (expatriates and local employees) in the case of:

- a natural disaster;
- political instability in the country of the business operations;
- war in the region of the business operations;
- acts of terrorism;
- kidnapping;
- traffic accidents.

CASE STUDY: UNITED NATIONS

The UN is an IGO focused on international law, international security, economic development, social progress, human rights and world peace. The UN was founded in 1945 and currently has over 190 member states. The organization employs more than 14 000 people worldwide. Integrity is one of the core values of the UN and includes probity, impartiality, fairness, honesty and truthfulness in all matters affecting employees' work and status. It is clearly stated that 'staff members shall exhibit respect for all cultures' (www.jobs.un.org). The UN headquarters are located In New York with important UN Offices in Geneva and Vienna. The UN recruits and selects people from all over the world making it one of the most international organizations worldwide. Bringing together different nationalities with different languages and customs is a major challenging task for the UN with a crucial responsibility for the HR function, for example, with regard to recruitment and selection, employee development, compensation and benefits and employee appraisals. The political environment adds another dimension to the organization in which diplomacy among people is essential. Most UN employees can speak multiple languages and are highly educated, often the best in their profession. More recently the UN has been under a lot of pressure partly because of efficiency notions and partly because of global emergencies (e.g. regional conflicts and earthquakes).

? Discussion questions

Language skills (reading, writing and presenting) are crucial for UN employees in combination with communication skills linked to diplomacy notions. Discuss the advantages and disadvantages of (1) a global HR development strategy versus (2) a local HR development strategy towards UN personnel.

The UN reports 1500 applicants on average for every vacancy within the organization. The organization therefore applies eRecruitment practices using filters for prescreening candidates. This way the HR department is not overloaded with administrative tasks, for example related to rejecting applicants who do not meet the required selection criteria. Find out more about the electronic recruitment system of the UN on their website.

summary

- Globalization has a major impact on organizations and employees.
- Globalization basically is the transition from local or regional activities to global activities.
- Organizational expansion across borders with regard to business activities, products, services and markets is called internationalization.
- IHRM is people management across country borders; for example, focused on the transferability of HR practices across business units in different countries and the management of expatriates.
- IHRM is often closely related to SHRM and MHRM issues.
- The universalist paradigm in IHRM builds on the assumption that best practices in HRM exist and that these can be applied in all contexts.
- The contextual paradigm in IHRM builds on the assumption that HR practices always require some form of adjustment to the context to be successful.

- The universalist paradigm in IHRM is closely related to the 'best-practice' proposition in SHRM and the contextual paradigm in IHRM is closely related to the 'best-fit' practices proposition in SHRM.
- International HRM is manifested at different levels of analysis including the individual employee level, the site level, the organization level, the national level, the regional or continental level and the international or global level.
- HRM in MNCs is affected by cross-cultural differences between countries and regions.
- HRM in MNCs is affected by institutional differences between countries and regions.
- Organizations operating in different countries may apply a global universal HR strategy or adapt their HR strategies to local circumstances (local HR strategy). In practice, organizations often combine a global HR strategy with local HR strategies mainly as a result of national legislation and stakeholder differences at country level.
- The convergence–divergence debate in IHRM is focused on the issue of organizations becoming more homogeneous worldwide with regard to their HRM.
- There is evidence for both convergence and divergence tendencies in HRM.
- Expatriate management is focused on the people management of those transferred abroad (expatriates) for a longer time period, often with a specific job assignment.
- Most expatriates, their spouses and children are confronted with a culture shock when transferred to another country. Culture shocks are often inevitable and part of the adjustment process.
- Good preparation, for example through expatriate and family training, can reduce the impact of a culture shock and smooth the transition process.
- Knowledge transfer, in particular across borders, has become a key issue in MNCs to achieve excellent performance.
- Outsourcing, offshoring and offshore outsourcing are popular practices for organizations operating in different countries or regions.
- Offshore outsourcing implies an outsourcing of business activities to an external company in another country.
- Internationalization may include serious risks for people employed in other countries. These risks not only potentially affect the employees, but their families and the reputation of the organization as well.

Glossary of key terms

Contextual paradigm assumes that there might be some general best principles in HRM, but the organizational context in the end determines the nature of the specific HR practice.

Cross-cultural differences are the differences between countries based on norms, values, rituals and habits of its citizens.

Expatriates are employees that temporarily or permanently work in a different country than their home country.

Global HR strategy is one corporate people management strategy applied to all units of an MNC across the world.

Globalization is the transition from local or regional activities to global activities.
Institutional differences are the differences between countries based on legislation, procedures and stakeholders (e.g. trade unions).
International HRM (IHRM) is the people management (or HRM) in MNCs and HRM across borders.
Internationalization is the expansion of business activities, products, services and markets of an organization to other countries.
Local HR strategy is a people management strategy within an MNC adapted to national or regional contextual factors.
Offshore outsourcing is the subcontracting and relocation of business activities to external companies in other countries or regions.
Offshoring is the relocation of business activities to other countries or regions.
Outsourcing is subcontracting business activities to external companies.
Universalist paradigm assumes the existence of best practices in HRM that can be applied by organizations successfully worldwide.

★ ***Personal development***

- Determine your personal human capital value based on your level of education, job experience, skills (e.g. language skills) and abilities (competences).
- How do you think you compare with workers from China and India?
- What are your strengths and weaknesses?
- What are their strengths and weaknesses?
- In Thomas Friedman's (2005) best-selling book *The World is Flat*, he argues that the majority of highly educated workers in Western countries in Europe and the USA will be threatened by equally highly educated workers from China and India. Think of ways in which you can remain an attractive and valuable employee to an organization.

 ***Individual task***

Find out more about the international career opportunities within one of the following organizations:

- Shell (www.shell.com)
- United Nations (www.un.org)
- Medicins Sans Frontiers (www.msf.org)

Shell is a private company, the UN an IGO and Medicins Sans Frontiers an NGO. Private companies, IGOs and NGOs operate in developing countries, for example on the African continent.

Think of the challenges for the transition of employees (expatriates) from Western countries to these developing countries and the role for the HR function in it; for example, in terms of recruitment and selection, training and development, compensation and information sharing.

Learning checklist

After studying this chapter, you should be able to do the following:

- Outline globalization and internationalization.
- Evaluate the universalist and the contextual paradigm in HRM.
- Identify multiple levels in IHRM.
- Understand cross-cultural and institutional differences between countries and regions.
- Consider global HR strategies and local HR strategies.
- Examine convergence and divergence issues in HRM.
- Outline expatriate management and culture shock.
- Review the potential impact of knowledge transfer within MNCs on performance.
- Review outsourcing, offshoring and HRM issues.

References

Barthelemy, J. (2001) The hidden costs of IT outsourcing, *MIT Sloan Management Review*, 42(3): 60–69.

Black, J.S. and Stephens, G.K. (1989) The influence of the spouse on American expatriate adjustment and intent to stay in Pacific rim overseas assignments, *Journal of Management*, 15(4): 529–44.

Blanco, R.I. (1998) Expatriate support system, in C.L. Cooper and C. Argyris (eds), *The Concise Blackwell Encyclopedia of Management*, p. 208. Oxford: Blackwell.

Bonache, J. and Brewster, C. (2001) Knowledge transfer and the management of expatriation, *Thunderbird International Business Review*, 43(1): 145–68.

Boxall, P. and Purcell, J. (2008) *Strategy and Human Resource Management*, 2nd edn. New York: Palgrave Macmillan.

Brewster, C. (2004) European perspectives on human resource management, *Human Resource Management Review*, 14(4): 365–82.

Brewster, C. and Scullion, H. (1997) A review and agenda for expatriate HRM, *Human Resource Management Journal*, 7(3): 32–41.

Brewster, C., Mayrhofer, W. and Morley, I. (2000) *New Challenges for European Human Resource Management*. London: Macmillan.

Brewster, C., Wood, G. and Brookes, M. (2008) Similarity, isomorphism or duality: recent survey evidence on the HRM policies of multinational corporations, *British Journal of Management*, 19(4): 320–42.

Brookes, M., Brewster, C. and Wood, G. (2005) Social relations, firms and societies: a study of institutional embeddedness, *International Sociology*, 20(4): 403–26.

Caligiuri, P.M. and Colakoglu, S. (2007) A strategic contingency approach to expatriate assignment management, *Human Resource Management Journal*, 17(4): 393–410.

Delery, J.E. and Doty, D.H. (1996) Modes of theorizing in strategic human resource management: tests of universalistic, contingency, and configurational performance predictions, *Academy of Management Journal*, 39(4): 802–35.

Doh, J.P. (2005) Offshore outsourcing: implications for international business and strategic management theory and practice, *Journal of Management Studies*, 42(3): 695–704.

Dowling, P.J., Welch, D.E. and Schuler, R.S. (2004) *International Human Resource Management: Managing People in a Multinational Context*. London: Thomson Learning.

Farndale, E. and Paauwe, J. (2007) Uncovering competitive and institutional drivers of HRM practices in multinational corporations, *Human Resource Management Journal*, 17(4): 355–75.

Friedman, T. (2005) *The World is Flat: A Brief History of the Twenty-first Century*. New York: Farrar, Straus & Giroux.

Gerhart, B. and Fang, M. (2005) National culture and human resource management: assumptions and evidence, *International Journal of Human Resource Management*, 16(6): 971–86.

Gooderham, P., Nordhaug, O. and Ringdal, K. (1999) Institutional and rational determinants of organizational practices: human resource management in European firms, *Administrative Science Quarterly*, 44: 507–31.

Harvey, M. and Moeller, M. (2009) Expatriate managers: a historical review, *International Journal of Management Reviews*, 11(3): 275–96.

Haslberger, A. and Brewster, C. (2008) The expatriate family: an international perspective, *Journal of Managerial Psychology*, 23(3): 324–46.

Hofstede, G. (1980) *Culture's Consequences: International Differences in Work-related Values*. Beverly Hills, CA: Sage.

Legge, K. (1995) *Human Resource Management, Rhetorics and Realities*, London: Macmillan Business.

McSweeney, B. (2002) Hofstede's model of national cultural differences and their consequences: a triumph of faith – a failure of analysis, *Human Relations*, 55: 89–118.

Minbaeva, D., Pedersen, T., Bjorkman, I., Fey, C.F. and Park, H.J. (2003) MNC knowledge transfer, subsidiary absorptive capacity, and HRM, *Journal of International Business Studies*, 34: 586–99.

O'Connell, J. (1998) Cultural maps, in C.L. Cooper and C. Argyris (eds), *The Concise Blackwell Encyclopedia of Management*, p. 140. Oxford: Blackwell.

OECD (2007) *Offshoring and Employment: Trends and Impacts*. Paris: OECD.

Paauwe, J. and Boselie, P. (2003) Challenging 'strategic HRM' and the relevance of the institutional setting, *Human Resource Management Journal*, 13(3): 56–70.

Pfeffer, J. (1994) *Competitive Advantage through People*. Boston, MA: Harvard Business School Press.

Pfeffer, J. (1998) *The Human Equation: Building Profits by Putting People First*. Boston, MA: Harvard Business School Press.

Riusala, K. and Suutari, V. (2000) Expatriation and careers: perspectives of expatriates and spouses, *Career Development International*, 5(2): 81–90.

Rowley, C. and Benson, J. (2002) Convergence and divergence in Asian human resource management, *California Management Review*, 44(2): 90–109.

Shay, J. and Tracey, J.B. (1997) Expatriate managers, *Cornell Hotel and Restaurant Administration Quarterly*, 38(1): 30–35.

Sparrow, P., Schuler, R. and Jackson, S. (1994) Convergence or divergence: human resource practices for competitive advantage worldwide, *International Journal of Human Resource Management*, 5(2): 267–99.

Further reading

Brewster, C. (2007) Comparative HRM: European views and perspectives, *International Journal of Human Resource Management*, 18(5): 769–87.

Brewster, C. Sparrow, P. and Dickmann, M. (eds) (2008) *International Human Resource Management: Contemporary Issues in Europe*, 2nd edn. London: Routledge.

De Cieri, H., Fenwick, M. and Hutchings, K. (2005) The challenge of international human resource management: balancing the duality of strategy and practice, *International Journal of Human Resource Management*, 16: 584–98.

Doh, J.P. (2005) Offshore outsourcing: implications for international business and strategic management theory and practice, *Journal of Management Studies*, 42(3): 695–704.

Dowling P.J., Festing, M. and Engle, A.D. (2008) *International Human Resource Management: Managing People in a Multinational Context*, 5th edn. London: Cengage Learning.

Evans, P., Pucik, V. and Barsoux, J.-L. (2002) *The Global Challenge: Frameworks for International Human Resource Management*. Boston, MA: McGraw-Hill.

Harzing, A.-W. and Ruysseveldt, J. van (eds) (2004) *International Human Resource Management*, 2nd edn. London: Sage.

Stahl, G. and Bjorkman, I. (eds) (2006) *Handbook of Research in International Human Resource Management*. Cheltenham: Edward Elgar.

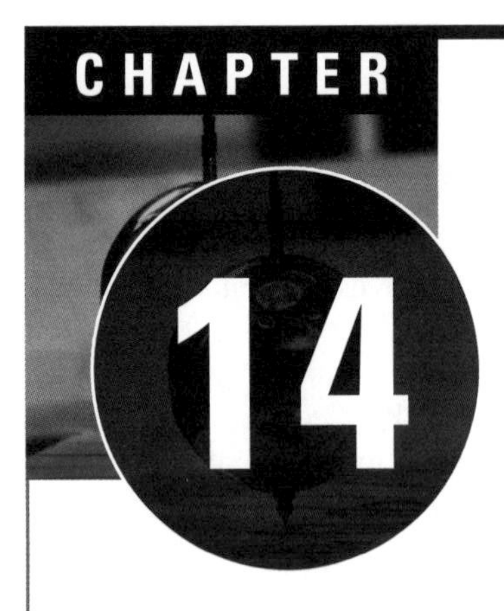

Human Resource Transformation

Learning Objectives

After studying this chapter, you should be able to do the following:

- Outline the multi-actor perspective in human resource management (HRM)
- Outline the broad societal view in HRM
- Outline the multi-level perspective in HRM
- Discuss the issue of 'best principles' with regard to the 'best-practice school' and the 'best-fit school' in HRM
- Understand the strategic-fit dilemma in HRM and provide possible solutions for theory and practice
- Consider the deterministic nature of the configuration of and the leeway for strategic choices with regard to HRM
- Review the reversed approach for creating a human resource (HR) value chain
- Recognize that HRM is not always the source of corporate success and failure
- Discuss the multidimensional performance construct in HRM
- Outline the concepts of harmony, conflict and coalition with regard to the employee–employer relationship and their interests
- Evaluate high-performance work systems (HPWSs) in different organizations of a population
- Identify possible mini-bundles of high-performance work practices (HPWPs)
- Recognize the institutionalization of compensation and employee participation in many European countries
- Evaluate the critical role of the front-line manager or supervisor in the shaping of actual HR practices
- Understand that administrative excellence is the first necessary step in becoming an HR professional
- Examine global and local HR strategies of organizations
- Review the potential of HRM in transformation processes

Introduction

Many books on management and HRM end with one or more chapters on 'contemporary issues', 'future challenges' and overviews of all the topics that are highly relevant in the field but could not be discussed in the book. I have to admit that this option had crossed my mind when writing this book. The final chapter could have been focused in depth on areas of HRM that deserve serious attention; for example, the management of diversity (e.g. Tung, 2008; Brandl et al., 2008), the implementation strategy and strategy-as-practice approaches (e.g. Becker and Huselid, 2006; Regner, 2008), strategic balance approaches in HRM (e.g. Boselie, 2009), HRM and knowledge creation (e.g. Collins and Smith, 2006), HRM and private equity (e.g. Bacon et al., 2008) and talent management (e.g. Lewis and Heckman, 2006). But that would probably leave the reader in a confused state of mind. More importantly, such an approach in this chapter runs the risk of looking forward too much (e.g. to the next book or area of interest) without looking back at the key lessons learned from this book. I decided to apply a different approach in this final chapter focused on an overall reflection of the other chapters. Hopefully, this will give the reader further food for thought and help students with the preparation for their exams. The goal of this chapter is to discuss some of the more general HR issues that have emerged in the other chapters, put these issues in perspective through linking them to insights from the different chapters, and finally illustrate them with mini cases.

> 'Dynamics and complexity are key characteristics in organizational life.'

I began the preparation of this book in 2006, long before the global financial crisis in 2008 and the global economic crisis in 2009. Some of the cases in it (e.g. the Dutch ABN AMRO) were highly affected by the crises. I do not think, however, that this is relevant for gaining a better understanding of strategic human resource management (SHRM). Dynamics and complexity are key characteristics in organizational life. Long after the 2008 global financial crisis and the 2009 economic global crisis, other economic and societal developments will affect organizations and people management – HRM – in these organizations. The global financial crisis that began in early 2009 among financial institutions resulted in a global economic crisis affecting countries and most industries (e.g. car manufacturing). Other serious global challenges and threats – global warming, the crisis for raw materials, the oil crisis and the ageing workforce – disappeared or were perceived as less relevant and important. It is, however, my serious belief that these threats have *not* gone and the problems related to these have *not* yet been solved. These issues will be back on the agenda and will most likely be more serious and less predictable in combination with other threats (e.g. increases in energy prices as a result of shortages of oil in combination with increasing labour costs caused by labour market shortages). Good people management and HRM will be crucial in solving some of these threats (e.g. global warming, the crisis for raw materials, the oil crisis and the ageing workforce) that affect organizations.

> 'Good people management and HRM will be crucial in solving some of these threats (e.g. global warming, the crisis for raw materials, the oil crisis and the ageing workforce) that affect organizations.'

The application of lists of **best practices** in HRM is most unlikely to contribute to solving the next generation's organizational challenges. This book on HRM hopefully sheds light on the underlying HR principles that can be applied instead of ostensible concrete best practices in HRM. Selective recruitment and selection (see Chapter 7), for example, is much more than applying GMA tests in combination with structured interviews for getting the best candidate for the job. Successful recruitment and selection depends on many different factors, ranging from the nature of the job to the personal interests of the candidate. The point I want to make is that strategic decision-makers can make choices about actual HR practices, there is no one best way and the organizational context (including a crisis or not) will have an impact on the right HR practice.

> 'The application of lists of best practices in HRM is most unlikely to contribute to solving the next generation's organizational challenges.'

Reflections

Chapter 1 began with an overview of the foundation of the general approach labelled 'the multi-dimensional strategic HR model'. The key characteristics of this model are:

1. *a multi-actor perspective,* including multiple stakeholders such as employees, managers, HR professionals, works councils, trade unions, top managers, shareholders, financiers and government;
2. *a broad societal view* with an emphasis on different institutional contexts represented at the level of branches of industry, regions and countries;
3. *a multi-level perspective,* including the individual employee perspective and the strategic organizational perspective.

The definition of HRM in this book incorporates the multi-actor, multi-level and broad societal view: HRM involves management decisions related to policies and practices that together shape the employment relationship and are aimed at achieving individual, organizational and societal goals.

For a full understanding of the HR discipline a distinction is made between **micro HRM (MHRM)**, **strategic HRM (SHRM)** and **international HRM (IHRM)** (Boxall et al., 2007). In Chapter 5 the potential tensions and conflicts of interests between the individual employee level, which is the main focus of MHRM (or organizational behaviour (OB) and organizational health psychology), and the organization level, which is the main focus of SHRM, are discussed. Later on in the book the conclusion is reached that MHRM and SHRM are often interrelated and the more recent debates on the future of HR research emphasize the need for bridging individual employee level research and organization level strategic approaches (Bowen and Ostroff, 2004). In Chapter 13 on IHRM, the reader can detect the often strong overlap between IHRM and SHRM, for example on the selection and training of expatriates, but also with regard to strategic outsourcing–offshoring decisions. MHRM, SHRM and IHRM are actually three different lenses for studying the employment relationship.

! *Stop and reflect*

Danone is a French food products company with a strong global reputation and market position in fresh dairy products. The firm employs 80 000 people worldwide and is known for brands such as Evian (mineral water), Danone (yoghurt), Actimel (food) and Royal Numico (baby food).

- Find out more about Danone's core values, for example by visiting their website.
- Determine the different relevant actors of Danone using the multi-actor perspective in this book.
- Find out more about Danone's approach towards society.

Chapter 2 is devoted to HRM and context. Strategic decision making that results in an optimal alignment (fit) between HRM and context can be called SHRM. The chapter highlights both the internal organizational context and the external organizational context. Different mechanisms (institutional and market mechanisms) and different stakeholders (e.g. trade unions and line managers) shape the organizational context and affect HRM. There is not one way of defining what is 'optimal' with regard to the alignment between HRM and context. This issue is further explored in Chapter 3 on human resource management and performance. The *best-practice school* advocates a universalistic perspective in which a given list of HR practices will increase organizational success no matter what the organizational context looks like. In contrast to this school is the *best-fit school*, which builds on the notion that HRM is more effective when it is aligned with its internal and external context. The question remains, who is right and who is wrong. The truth is probably somewhere in the middle. The concept of *best principles* is most likely to capture the essential 'true' elements of both the 'best-practice' and 'best-fit' schools. In general, it is plausible to assume that there are some best principles in HRM, for example highlighted in the AMO model in Chapter 6. Employee development opportunities, employee involvement and participation, high and fair compensation and teamwork are just a few examples of 'best principles' in HRM. Pfeffer's (1994) best-practice list, discussed in Chapter 6, could also be interpreted as a 'best-principle' list. The success of applying these principles highly depends on the alignment or fit with the organization's context. Boxall and Purcell (2003: 68–70) locate these best principles on what they call the 'underpinning layer' representing 'generic HR processes and general principles of labour management'. On the 'surface layer' Boxall and Purcell distinguish HR policies and practices that are heavily influenced by the organizational, sectoral and societal context.

Strategic or vertical fit refers to that part of the **best-fit** school that assumes a necessary alignment between the overall business strategy and the HR strategy. Strategic fit and its true nature is one of the key HR issues in both theory and practice. Chapter 2 highlights different views and levels of strategic fit. The ultimate strategic fit between the business strategy and the HR strategy is what Golden and Ramanujam (1985) call the integrative linkage, representing full alignment often with a crucial position and role for the chief human resource officer (CHRO), who not only has a seat at the executive table, but also a substantial role in strategic decision making. Chapter 12 on HR roles and competences, however, sheds a different light on the position of most HR professionals in practice. In many organizations HRM is not at the table and the HR professionals are still 'victims of change', meaning they are getting involved after the decisions have been taken, forced into taking tactical and operational roles in dealing with the consequences of organizational change. And if there is a linkage between the business strategy and the HR strategy in an organization, it is most likely to be a one-way linkage (business strategy first) or a limited two-way linkage with a clear dominance of the business strategy. The consequence of this type of alignment between the overall business strategy and the HR strategy is that HRM is designed mainly as a result of the business strategy. In contemporary organizations this creates an interesting dilemma: a lot of organizations do not have a clear business strategy because of the complexity and dynamics in the markets and other factors (e.g. ownership issues), and as a result it is difficult to determine the HR strategy for the years to come (Boselie and Koene, forthcoming). An organization under threat of a private equity buyout (new ownership through external funding), for example, is confronted with uncertainty about its future activities, causing uncertainty about future HR strategy and policies; for example, HR investments in employee development to stimulate the new corporate strategy focused on research and development or HR downsizing to cut costs as part of the strategy of the new owners who want to make short-term profit. So what if we *abandon the search for a necessary fit between the overall business strategy and the HR strategy*?

> 'In many organizations HRM is not at the table and the HR professionals are still "victims of change"'

It seems to be much more important that employees learn how to deal with continuous change making them adaptable (agile) to whatever new business strategy emerges. Chapter 2 in Paauwe's (2004) book is titled 'HRM and strategy: Does it matter?' and this is exactly what the debate is all about. To overcome this issue, at least partly in both theory and practice, the dynamic capability approaches can be of help (Teece et al., 1998). The implications of dynamic capability approaches in HRM would be a transition in HR focus from the search for strategic alignment between business strategy and HR strategy to the design and implementation of HR strategies and policies that increase (1) the employees' individual capabilities (or competences) to cope with change and (2) the organizational capabilities through, for example, flexible HR practices and an HR infrastructure (e.g. training and development within IKEA, as presented in Chapter 10). On a tactical and operational level, the HR function, as discussed in Chapter 12 on HR roles, can continue to deal with the consequences of changes in the business strategy, but on a strategic level the HR function no longer chases strategic-fit ghosts; instead, the HR professionals focus on creating employee and organizational capabilities.

MINI CASE STUDY: AIR FRANCE-KLM

Air France-KLM is a French-Dutch airline company and the largest in the world in terms of total operating revenues and in the top five of airline companies in terms of passenger fleet size. The French Air France and the Dutch KLM (Royal Dutch Airlines) merged in 2004, creating a global giant with more than 100000 employees worldwide. In the past these types of merger often caused radical changes in the corporate strategy, core values and culture of the new organization. Air France-KLM decided to do it differently, not putting too much focus on creating one new corporate culture. The airline industry is highly competitive and organizations cannot afford to spend too much time on internal affairs such as a merger and creating one new organizational culture.

- Find out more about Air France-KLM.
- Find out more about the corporate strategy of this organization.
- Think of ways in which the HR function can contribute to the success of a merger, such as the one between Air France and KLM, without desperately searching for strategic alignment.

Chapter 2 highlights another important concept that is often neglected or simply forgotten in HR debates: the **configuration of an organization**. The most important elements of an organization's configuration include the history of the organization, the organizational culture, the technology and systems used, the ownership structure and the people employed (workforce). *The configuration is deterministic* from an institutional point of view. In other words, to some extent the strategic HR choices of an organization are determined by its roots, culture, technology, ownership structure and workforce. All these elements are not easily changed overnight and some of these elements (e.g. culture) may take years or decades to change. The strategic choice literature, however, suggests that *given these constraints there is always leeway for unique strategic choices in HRM*. From a resource-based view (RBV) (see Chapter 3), this potentially creates opportunities for unique people management approaches that cannot be copied by competitors.

MINI CASE STUDY: ANONYMOUS

Family-owned organizations represent a substantial number of organizations in most countries. Most family-owned organizations are small or medium sized, ranging from bakeries to local pubs; however, some have grown very large, for example Enterprise car rentals in the USA (65 000 employees).

- Think of the advantages and disadvantages of a large family-owned company for HR policies and practices with regard to the different stakeholders involved.

Chapter 3 focuses on the potential added value of HRM to success. This chapter raises several issues. First, there is *no general consensus on what success is*. From a narrow shareholder perspective, success can be defined in terms of profitability and market value, while from a broader stakeholder perspective including employees and external stakeholders (e.g. trade unions, government and society), success can also include long-term employment, high wages and decreased environmental pollution. The definition of success is therefore at least partly determined by the organization's mission, vision, strategy and goals; however, the organization is always constrained by legislation, societal norms and values, customer opinions and other factors that set the scene. These issues are discussed in more detail in Chapter 2 on HRM in an institutional context and in Chapter 5 with regard to balanced approaches. Organizations that break the rules and neglect public opinion for the sake of achieving financial success are most likely to fail in the long term, for example because of reputation damage that affects the recruitment of new employees (see Chapter 7 on recruitment and selection with regard to employment branding issues). Second, the debate often starts with HRM notions, for example on how important it is to develop employees. In Chapter 2 a strong plea is made for *a reversed approach for creating an HR value chain,* starting with the general individual employee, organizational and societal goals of an organizations defined as the **ultimate business goals**. These ultimate business goals can be translated into critical HR goals and so on. Step by step this reversed approach will get the practitioner closer to the actual HR interventions or practices that are required to achieve the overall goals.

'there is no general consensus on what success is'

MINI CASE STUDY: FESTINA

Festina is a Spanish watch manufacturer with Swiss origins, famous for the sponsorship of the Festina cycling team. In 1998 the Festina cycling team was caught in a doping scandal during the Tour de France, creating huge negative publicity. More than 200 bottles of EPO and other doping products were found in the team car. This type of scandal potentially damages the reputation of sponsors such as Festina. And corporate reputation is crucial in relation to customers and (potential) employees. Reputation is closely related to the crucial HR goal labelled 'social legitimacy'.

- Discuss the potential negative effects of the Festina scandal on the organization with regard to customers and employees.
- Discuss the relationship between social legitimacy and corporate reputation.

Another important lesson learned in Chapter 3 is based on the notion that *HRM is not always the source of success or failure of organizations*. There are many other internal and external factors that determine organizational success. We should always keep in mind that other internal sources than human resources can be powerful factors for sustained competitive advantage, for example:

- a unique geographical location of the organization (e.g. Europe Container Terminals in the Rotterdam harbour);
- a unique global network of offices and factories (e.g. the US Caterpillar company right after the Second World War);
- substantial financial resources or buffers from the past.

'HRM is not always the source of success or failure of organizations.'

In other cases organizational failure might have little or nothing to do with its workers or its HRM. The emergence of the digital camera, for example, caused the end of mass production of the old-fashioned camera films. This technological innovation resulted in the closure of factories and unemployment of those working in the traditional factories, for example at Fuji film. In 2009 it was announced that Kodak would stop manufacturing the famous Kodachrome camera after seven decades of success because of the digital revolution. Simon and Garfunkel's song 'Kodachrome' will now truly become a relic from the past:

Kodachrome, they give us those nice bright colours

They give us the greens of summers

Makes you think all the world's a sunny day, oh yeah

I got a Nikon camera, I love to take a photograph

So mama don't take my kodachrome away

Chapter 4 discusses HRM and metrics. The chapter is heavily influenced by balanced scorecard (BSC) notions and builds on ideas related to potential tensions between different outcome types. Excellent financial performance in terms of sales and profits can similarly cause work intensification and negatively affect other employee well-being measurements.

The question remains, how to determine when an organization is successful or not. A popular way of comparing organizations – 'ranking the stars' – is through benchmarking. Benchmarking refers to the technique of comparing (content and process) outcomes of different organizations with the purpose of, for example, ranking all the organizations, learning the best practices from other organizations or finding out how well one's own organization is doing in comparison to other organizations.

The balanced HR model in Chapter 4 and the balanced approaches in Chapter 5 suggest that *a multidimensional performance construct* is required to measure an organization's performance. In other words, comparing organizations makes sense when multiple outcome measures are taken into account, including employee-oriented HR outcomes such as satisfaction and trust and employer-oriented organizational/financial outcomes such as quality, productivity, sales and profits.

MINI CASE STUDY: MAERSK

Maersk is a Danish transportation and energy company employing more than 110 000 people worldwide. The company is famous for its container ships. The ship called *Emma Maersk*, for example, is almost 400 metres long and capable of carrying 15 000 containers. The shipping industry is characterized by multiple risks, including the loading and unloading of containers (a delicate balancing act), heavy storms at sea and piracy. In April 2009 one of its ships (*Maersk Alabama*) was hijacked by pirates near the Somali coast. The success of Maersk can be measured through its revenues and profits (financial outcomes).

- Can you think of employee-oriented outcomes that represent the success or failure of Maersk?
- Think of concrete HR outcomes that take into account Maersk's specific context.

The potential different interests and needs of employees and employers are discussed in Chapter 5 using insights from critical HR studies, OB and organizational health psychology. The chapter ends with an overview of a **balanced approach** at organizational and individual level. Overall, mainstream HRM is too consensus-oriented and is built on the assumption that employees and employers mostly share common interests in harmony. In contrast, some of the critical approaches, including the critical HR studies, OB approaches and approaches from organizational health psychology, are perhaps too negative towards HRM's aims and too focused on the conflicting interests of employees and employers. In some cases employees' interests and employers' interests are the same (*harmony*); in other cases their interests are opposite (*conflict*); but in many cases their relationship can be characterized by cooperation in an attempt to achieve own and joint interests (*coalition*).

> 'Overall, mainstream HRM is too consensus-oriented and is built on the assumption that employees and employers mostly share common interests in harmony.'

Stop and reflect

In Chapter 11 the role and position of works councils and trade unions are discussed in the context of institutionalized employee participation in many European countries. In Chapter 12 the different HR roles are summarized and highlighted in relation to adding value to an organization, including the HR role of 'strategic partner'. Discuss the possible roles of works councils and trade unions as 'strategic partners' for the HR function (e.g. for the CHRO of an organization). These roles can be highly relevant during major organizational changes (e.g. an acquisition, a merger, a reorganization, outsourcing and offshoring). Think about works councils and trade unions in their roles as 'strategic partners' from three perspectives:

- a harmony relationship with the employer/organization;
- a conflict relationship with the employer/organization;
- a coalition relationship with the employer/organization.

HPWSs are a special type of HR system, as discussed in Chapter 6. The basic idea behind HPWSs is (1) that specific HPWPs (e.g. performance-related pay (PRP) and selective recruitment and selection) can be bundled, and (2) that the **internal fit** of these bundles contributes to excellent organizational performance. The chapter starts with an historical overview showing that the notion of systems of practices is not entirely new; however, the general ideas about these systems have evolved over time, starting with scientific management systems and evolving into contemporary notions on HPWSs (Boxall and Macky, 2009). The aim of these systems is the creation of a high-performance culture through good people management. The building blocks of the HPWSs are closely related to the 'best principles' discussed earlier in this chapter constituting, for example, selectivity in recruitment and selection, extensive training and development, high and fair wages, teamwork, PM, internal promotion opportunities and employee participation/ employee involvement. Not every organization will be capable of applying an HPWS; actually, it is most likely that 80 per cent of the organizations in a population (or sector) do not have an HPWS installed. The majority of organizations in a given industry are struggling with the HR basics (e.g. administration and translation of new legislation to their own HR policies). *The upper 10 or 20 per cent of an industry are the HR leaders that operate in the 'HPWS domain'.*

> 'Not every organization will be capable of applying an HPWS; actually, it is most likely that 80 per cent of the organizations in a population (or sector) do not have an HPWS installed.'

What about the other 80–90 per cent of the organizations in a population? Should these organizations ignore HPWS notions or is there an alternative? Chapter 6 ends with the idea of *mini-bundles*. The majority of HPWSs literature is built on linking multiple HR practices. The alternative for the 80–90 per cent of non-HR leaders in a population is the application of two to three interrelated HPWPs, creating mini-bundles, for example:

- *selective recruitment and selection* (through assessment centres, intelligence tests and structured interviews focused on person–organization fit (P–O fit) and person–job fit (P–J fit)) × *employee training and development* (through skills training, socialization programmes and mentorships);
- *individual PRP* (based on productivity and service quality) × *PM* (with clear goals, development opportunities and monitoring).

In practice these mini-bundles of HPWPs or 'best principles' in HRM can positively affect employee outcomes such as motivation, commitment, satisfaction, retention and citizenship behaviour.

Stop and reflect

Think about the lessons learned from the notion of mini-bundles in HRM for local small and medium enterprises (SMLs) (e.g. the local bakery, supermarket or car dealer).

Chapters 7, 8, 9, 10 and 11 focus on five main HPWPs commonly used in both theory and practice:

- selective recruitment and selection (Chapter 7);
- performance management (Chapter 8);
- compensation (Chapter 9);
- employee development (Chapter 10);
- employee participation (Chapter 11).

At least two of these HPWPs are heavily influenced by institutional mechanisms, in particular legislation and social partners (e.g. works councils and trade unions): compensation and employee participation. Compensation in most European countries is affected by national legislation, European Union (EU) legislation and collective bargaining agreements (CBAs). Employee involvement is also institutionalized at different levels, including the organization level (works councils), the branch of industry level (trade unions) and in some cases the national level, for example illustrated by the Social Economic Council in the Netherlands (see Chapter 11). Institutionalized or not, I would argue that the overall effect of these 'best principles' is most likely to be positive with regard to employee outcomes and organizational performance. In summary, the underlying mechanisms and frameworks with respect to compensation and employee participation are different between, for example, the USA and continental Europe, while the outcomes of the application of the principles can be quite similar. Other HPWPs – selective recruitment and selection, employee development and PM – are affected by institutional mechanisms, but to a much lesser degree than the other two. Legislation on recruitment (e.g. discrimination laws and procedures) can be very different between the USA and Europe; however, the basic recruitment techniques discussed in Chapter 7 remain the same.

MINI CASE STUDY: GENERAL MOTORS AND OPEL

General Motors (GM) is a large US car manufacturer (approximately 250 000 employees in 2008) with subsidiaries all over the world, including Opel in Germany. The global economic crisis of 2009 seriously affected GM. Part of the corporate failure involves the dramatic decline of SUV (sports utility vehicles) sales. Opel is the main brand name of GM in Europe. In the UK, Opel is known as Vauxhall Motors. GM's global crisis and financial shortages in 2009 appeared to affect subsidiary Opel as well, potentially causing downsizing and cost-reduction plans affecting employment in the German Opel factories. The industrial relations (IR) in Germany are very different from the US context, in particular with regard to national legislation on payment and the role of trade unions.

- Discuss the potential role of trade unions in Germany in the context of GM's intentions to downsize its Opel subsidiary in Germany.

Another highly relevant theme in these five HPWP chapters is the *role of the front-line manager or supervisor* in the shaping of HRM. This is what Wright and Nishii (2007) call the 'actual HR practices' (in contrast to intended HR practices and perceived HR practices). The front-line manager is usually involved in the recruitment and selection of new workers, plays an important role in the appraisal of subordinates (PM), at least partly determines payment (e.g. bonuses and promotion), often decides on employee training and development programmes, and influences the degree of employee involvement in daily decision making (Renwick, 2003). Having a bad relationship with your boss is still the number one reason why employees leave an organization. Part of the manager–employee relationship is determined by the shaping of HRM in relation to the individual employee. The crucial role of the front-line manager in the shaping of HRM is underlined by only a few studies (e.g. Purcell et al., 2003; Den Hartog et al., 2004; Purcell and Hutchinson, 2007; Wright and Nishii, 2007). Throughout the book the relevance of the line manager is highlighted; for example, in the HR value chain presented in Chapter 3 and in Chapter 8 on PM. HRM is often nothing more than paper when line management is not significantly involved in the implementation of HR practices.

Chapter 12 on HR roles and Chapter 13 on HRM focus on specific HR areas. The HR roles and competences overview shows the complexity of HR tasks and operations in practice.

The starting point for HR professionalization, however, is *administrative excellence* through problem-solving, accuracy, reliability, technical HR expertise and HR delivery. When asked, most undergraduate students in HRM want to become a 'strategic partner' or a 'change agent'. In practice, it is most likely that new HR employees will start in a shared service centre in an administrative HR role.

'most undergraduate students in HRM want to become a strategic partner or change agent'

Chapter 13 puts MHRM and SHRM issues in an international perspective. The 'best-practice'–'best-fit' debate in this context is labelled 'universalist paradigm versus the contextual paradigm'. Cross-cultural and institutional differences between countries and continents affect HRM, in particular for MNCs that have to decide on applying a **global HR strategy** or a **local HR strategy**. In practice *a combination of both is most likely*:

- global HR strategy elements because of the company's corporate strategy and core values;
- local strategy elements because of national legislation, local trade unions and other specific IRs linked to the context.

HR transformation

Organizational change is inevitable for most contemporary organizations, including mergers, acquisitions, reorganizations, outsourcing and offshoring activities, cultural changes and downsizing. Organizational change directly affects business processes and those who operate these processes (Paauwe, 2004): employees. Good people management or HRM is therefore a potential key to successful organizational change. Three groups of actors play a crucial role in creating successful HRM:

- top management (leaders);
- front-line managers or supervisors;
- HR professionals.

The chief executive officer (CEO) plays an essential role in organizational change, in particular with regard to demonstrating the organization's vision, mission and strategy. Visibility (e.g. through top manager performances for the workforce), devotion to planned changes, confidence (belief), decisiveness and optimism are important aspects in initiating change. CHROs can play an important role in coaching CEOs on their communication skills by role-playing situations with employees.

HR professionals have multiple roles (see Chapter 12), including spotting new trends and potential threats (e.g. labour market shortages as a result of an ageing workforce), designing new HR policies and practices (e.g. with regard to talent management), coaching top management and facilitating line managers in the enactment process. HR monitoring (see Chapter 4) is an essential part of the HR function for keeping track of the progress of organizational change.

Line managers are the enactors of HRM. In the HR value chain and in times of organizational change, they represent the hinge between policies (HR design) and employee perceptions:

Intended HR practices → actual HR practices → **perceived HR practices**

Organizational support and facilities can and should be provided to line managers by HR professionals.

summary

- This book proposes a multi-actor perspective in HRM in combination with a broad societal view and a multi-level perspective.
- This proposition implies the acknowledgement of multiple stakeholders, including employees, customers, shareholders, managers, trade unions, works councils and the government.
- This proposition also implies the incorporation of individual, organizational and societal goals reflected in a multidimensional performance definition.
- This proposition automatically involves studying the employment relationship at different levels of analysis, including the individual employee level, team or group level, business unit level, organization level, sectoral level and national level.
- Best principles in HRM represent universalistic people management factors that increase performance.
- In the case of growing complexity and increased dynamics of the external and internal organizational context, it might be advisable to abandon the search for a necessary fit between the overall business strategy and the HR strategy.
- The configuration of an organization is highly deterministic for the shaping of HRM; however, these apparent constraints always create leeway for unique approaches in HRM.
- There is no general consensus on what organizational success is; however, there are general principles that represent organizational success or failure.
- A reversed approach to creating an HR value chain is a powerful way to link ultimate business goals to actual HR interventions.
- HRM is not always the source of success or failure of organizations.
- Employee representatives (e.g. works councils and trade unions) and employers can benefit from a coalition model in relation to the employment relationship.
- The upper 10–20 per cent of an organization are the HR leaders that operate in the HPWSs domain.
- The other 80–90 per cent of the organizations in a given industry can benefit from HPWS insights through the application and implementation of mini-bundles of HPWPs.
- Some HPWPs, in particular compensation and employee participation, are greatly affected by institutional arrangements and mechanisms in most European countries.
- The front-line manager plays a crucial role in the shaping of HRM in organizations.
- Administrative excellence is a necessary condition for the HR function in adding value to the organization.
- HRM can play an important role in organizational change processes with a key role for top managers, line managers and HR professionals.

Glossary of key terms

Balanced approach is an approach that blends the insights from an economic perspective with the insights from an institutional perspective in order to create a balanced and sustainable position for the organization.

Best-fit proposition states that specific HR practices are not universally applicable and successful when used, but can only be successful in the case of a fit between HRM and the context.

Best-practice proposition states that specific HR practices are universally applicable and successful when used.

Configuration of an organization is the cultural administrative heritage of an organization.

Global human resource (HR) strategy is a corporate people management strategy applied to all units of an MNC across the world.

High-performance work practices (HPWPs) are a special type of HR practice that enable employees' abilities, create the optimal incentive structure for employees and/or create opportunities to participate in decision making.

High-performance work systems (HPWSs) are a bundle of consistent and coherent HPWPs that potentially create employee discretionary effort.

Internal fit is the alignment between individual HR practices.

International human resource management (IHRM) is the sub-field of HRM aimed at studying the shaping of the employment relationship in an international context, with special attention to HRM for expatriates, HRM in large MNCs and HRM in international governmental organizations (IGOs).

Local human resource (HR) strategy is a people management strategy within an MNC adapted to national or regional contextual factors.

Micro human resource management (MHRM) is the sub-field of HRM aimed at studying the shaping of the employment relationship at the individual employee level.

Strategic or vertical fit is the alignment between the business and the HR strategy.

Strategic human resource management (SHRM) is the sub-field of HRM aimed at studying the shaping of the employment relationship taking into account the internal and external organization context.

Ultimate business goals are organizational targets in relation to relevant stakeholders for (1) creating and maintaining viability with adequate returns and (2) creating sustained competitive advantage.

Individual task

Preparation for your exam

- Summarize the key concepts of all the chapters in this book.
- Think of at least one exam question for every chapter using the key concepts. A typical exam question starts by asking for knowledge (e.g. 'what is an HPWS?'). The second part of the question might include asking for an illustration (e.g. 'can you give an example of an HPWS in practice?'). Finally, a typical exam question ends with testing your insights (e.g. 'explain how an HPWS can cause negative employee outcomes').
- Lecturers often combine different concepts in their exam; for example, linking the selective recruitment and selection HPWP to IHRM notions on expatriate management. Think of possible combinations of the key concepts in this book and link these to possible exam questions.

Learning checklist

After studying this chapter, you should be able to do the following:

- Outline the multi-actor perspective in HRM.
- Outline the broad societal view in HRM.
- Outline the multi-level perspective in HRM.
- Discuss the issue of 'best principles' with regard to the 'best-practices' school and the 'best-fit' school in HRM.
- Understand the strategic-fit dilemma in HRM and provide possible solutions for theory and practice.
- Consider the deterministic nature of the configuration and the leeway for strategic choices with regard to HRM.
- Review the reversed approach for creating an HR value chain.
- Recognize that HRM is not always the source of corporate success and failure.
- Discuss the multidimensional performance construct in HRM.
- Outline the concepts of harmony, conflict and coalition with regard to the employee–employer relationship and their interests.
- Evaluate HPWSs in different organizations of a population.
- Identify possible mini-bundles of HPWPs.
- Recognize the institutionalization of compensation and employee participation in many European countries.
- Evaluate the critical role of the front-line manager or supervisor in the shaping of actual HR practices.
- Understand that administrative excellence is the first necessary step to becoming an HR professional.
- Examine global and local HR strategies of organizations.
- Review the potential of HRM in transformation processes.

References

Bacon, N., Wright, M., Demina, N., Bruining, H. and Boselie, P. (2008) The effects of private equity and buy-outs on HRM in the UK and the Netherlands, *Human Relations*, 61(10): 1399–433.

Becker, B.A. and Huselid, M.A. (2006) Strategic human resources management: where do we go from here?, *Journal of Management*, 32(6): 898–925.

Boselie, P. (2009) A balanced approach to understanding the shaping of human resource management in organizations, *Management Revue*, 20(1): 1–20.

Boselie, P. and Koene, B.A.S. (forthcoming) Human resource management and private equity: 'Barbarians at the gate! HR's wake up call?', *Human Relations*.

Bowen, D.E. and Ostroff, C. (2004) Understanding HRM–firm performance linkages: the role of the 'strength' of the HRM system, *Academy of Management Review*, 29(2): 203–21.

Boxall, P. and Macky, K. (2009) Research and theory on high-performance work systems: progressing the high-involvement stream, *Human Resource Management Journal*, 19(1): 2–23.

Boxall, P. and Purcell, J. (2003) *Strategy and Human Resource Management*. New York: Palgrave Macmillan.

Boxall, P., Purcell, J. and Wright, P.M. (2007) Human resource management: scope, analysis, and significance, in P. Boxall, J. Purcell and P.M. Wright, P.M. (eds), *The Oxford Handbook of Human Resource Management,* Chapter 1, pp. 1–16. Oxford: Oxford University Press.

Brandl, J., Mayrhofer, W. and Reichel, A. (2008) The influence of social policy practices and gender egalitarianism on strategic integration of female HR directors, *International Journal of Human Resource Management*, 19(11): 2113–131.

Collins, C.J. and Smith, K.G. (2006) Knowledge exchange and combination: the role of human resource practices in the performance of high technology firms, *Academy of Management Journal*, 49: 544–60.

Den Hartog, D.N., Boselie, P. and Paauwe, J. (2004) Performance management: a model and research agenda, *Applied Psychology: An International Review*, 53(4): 556–69.

Golden, K.A. and Ramanujam, V. (1985) Between a dream and a nightmare: on the integration of the human resource management and strategic planning processes, *Human Resource Management*, 24: 429–52.

Lewis, R.E. and Heckman, R.J. (2006) Talent management: a critical review, *Human Resource Management Review*, 16(2): 139–54.

Paauwe, J. (2004) *HRM and Performance: Achieving Long-term Viability*. Oxford: Oxford University Press.

Pfeffer, J. (1994) *Competitive Advantage through People*. Boston, MA: Harvard Business School Press.

Purcell, J. and Hutchinson, S. (2007) Front-line managers as agents in the HRM–performance causal chain: theory, analysis and evidence, *Human Resource Management Journal*, 17(1): 3–20.

Purcell, J., Kinnie, N., Hutchinson, S., Rayton, B. and Swart, J. (2003) *Understanding the Pay and Performance Link: Unlocking the Black Box*. London: CIPD.

Regner, P. (2008) Strategy-as-practice and dynamic capabilities: steps towards a dynamic view of strategy, *Human Relations*, 61(4): 565–88.

Renwick, D. (2003) Line management involvement in HRM: an inside view, *Employee Relations*, 25(3): 501–23.

Teece, D.J., Pisano, G. and Shuen, A. (1998) Dynamic capabilities and strategic management, *Strategic Management Journal*, 18(7): 509–33.

Tung, R.S. (2008) The cross-cultural research imperative: the need to balance cross-national and intra-national diversity, *Journal of International Business Studies*, 39(1): 41–6.

Wright, P.M. and Nishii, L.H. (2007) Strategic HRM and organizational behavior: integrating multiple levels of analysis. Working paper 26, CAHRS at Cornell University, Ithaca, NY.

Index

D

E

F

G

H

T

U

V

W

Y